Persian Gulf States
country studies

Federal Research Division
Library of Congress
Edited by
Helen Chapin Metz
Research Completed
January 1993

On the cover: Symbol of the Gulf Cooperation Council, to
which Bahrain, Kuwait, Oman, Qatar, Saudi Arabia, and
the United Arab Emirates belong

Third Edition, First Printing, 1994.

Library of Congress Cataloging-in-Publication Data

Persian Gulf States : country studies / Federal Research Division,
    Library of Congress ; edited by Helen Chapin Metz. — 3rd ed.
        p.   cm. — (Area handbook series, ISSN 1057–5294)
    (DA Pam ; 550–185)
    "Supersedes the 1984 edition of Persian Gulf States : country
    studies, edited by Richard F. Nyrop"—T.p. verso.
    "Research completed January 1993."
    Includes bibliographical references (pp. 417–433) and index.
    ISBN 0–8444–0793–3
    1. Persian Gulf States. I. Metz, Helen Chapin, 1928– . II.
Library of Congress. Federal Research Division. III. Series.
IV. Series: DA Pam ; 550–185.
DS247.A13P47   1994   93–46476
953.6–dc20   CIP

Headquarters, Department of the Army
DA Pam 550–185

Bernan
Lanham, Maryland
December 1994

Foreword

This volume is one in a continuing series of books prepared by the Federal Research Division of the Library of Congress under the Country Studies/Area Handbook Program sponsored by the Department of the Army. The last two pages of this book list the other published studies.

Most books in the series deal with a particular foreign country, describing and analyzing its political, economic, social, and national security systems and institutions, and examining the interrelationships of those systems and the ways they are shaped by cultural factors. Each study is written by a multidisciplinary team of social scientists. The authors seek to provide a basic understanding of the observed society, striving for a dynamic rather than a static portrayal. Particular attention is devoted to the people who make up the society, their origins, dominant beliefs and values, their common interests and the issues on which they are divided, the nature and extent of their involvement with national institutions, and their attitudes toward each other and toward their social system and political order.

The books represent the analysis of the authors and should not be construed as an expression of an official United States government position, policy, or decision. The authors have sought to adhere to accepted standards of scholarly objectivity. Corrections, additions, and suggestions for changes from readers will be welcomed for use in future editions.

Louis R. Mortimer
Chief
Federal Research Division
Library of Congress
Washington, DC 20540–5220

Acknowledgments

The authors wish to acknowledge the contributions of the writers of the 1984 edition of *Persian Gulf States: Country Studies*, edited by Richard F. Nyrop. Their work provided general background for the present volume.

The authors are grateful to individuals in various government agencies and private institutions who gave of their time, research materials, and expertise in the production of this book. These individuals included Ralph K. Benesch, who oversees the Country Studies/Area Handbook Program for the Department of the Army. The authors also wish to thank members of the Federal Research Division staff who contributed directly to the preparation of the manuscript. These people included Sandra W. Meditz, who reviewed all graphic and textual material and served as liaison with the sponsoring agency; Marilyn L. Majeska, who supervised editing; Andrea T. Merrill, who managed book production; Ramón Miró, who assisted with bibliographic research and other aspects; Barbara Edgerton and Izella Watson, who did the word processing; and Stephen C. Cranton and David P. Cabitto, who prepared the camera-ready copy. Also involved in preparing the text were Sheila L. Ross, who edited the chapters and performed the prepublication editorial review, and Joan C. Cook, who compiled the Index. Special thanks are due Eric Hooglund, who kindly served as reader for the book as a whole.

Graphics were prepared by David P. Cabitto. Tim Merrill prepared map drafts, and David P. Cabitto and the firm of Greenhorne and O'Mara prepared the final versions. Special thanks are owed to Marty Ittner, who prepared the illustrations on the title page of each chapter, and to Wayne Horne, who did the cover art.

Finally, the authors acknowledge the generosity of individuals and public and private agencies, especially the embassies of the countries concerned, who allowed their photographs to be used in this study.

Contents

Chapter 7. Regional and National Security Considerations

Jean R. Tartter

List of Figures

Introduction

THE COUNTRIES OF THE PERSIAN GULF covered in this volume—Bahrain, Kuwait, Oman, Qatar, and the United Arab Emirates—have assumed added prominence as a result of Operation Desert Shield in 1990 and the Persian Gulf War in 1991. These states share certain characteristics while simultaneously differing from one another in various respects. Islam has played a major role in each of the Persian Gulf states, although Kuwait and Bahrain reflect a greater secular influence than the other three. Moreover, the puritanical Wahhabi (see Glossary) Sunni (see Glossary) sect prevails in Qatar; Bahrain has a majority population of Shia (see Glossary), a denomination of the faith that constitutes a minority in Islam as a whole; and the people of Oman represent primarily a minor sect within Shia Islam, the Ibadi.

The beduin heritage also exerts a significant influence in all of the Persian Gulf states. In the latter half of the twentieth century, however, a sense of national identity increasingly has superseded tribal allegiance. The ruling families in the Persian Gulf states represent shaykhs (see Glossary) of tribes that originally settled particular areas; however, governmental institutions steadily have taken over spheres that previously fell under the purview of tribal councils.

Historically, Britain exercised a protectorate at least briefly over each of the Persian Gulf states. This connection has resulted in the presence of governmental institutions established by Britain as well as strong commercial and military ties with it. Military matériel and training in the late 1980s and early 1990s, however, were being provided by other countries in addition to Britain.

Because of the extensive coastlines of the Persian Gulf states, trade, fishing, shipbuilding, and, in the past, pearling have represented substantial sources of income. In the early 1990s, trade and, to a lesser extent, fishing, continued to contribute major amounts to the gross domestic product (GDP—see Glossary) of these states.

Of the five states, Oman has the least coastal area on the Persian Gulf because its access to that waterway occurs only at the western tip of the Musandam Peninsula, separated from the remainder of Oman by the United Arab Emirates (UAE).

Partly as a result of this limited contact with the gulf and partly because of the mountains that cut off the interior from the coast, Oman has the most distinctive culture of the five states.

In general, the gulf has served as a major facilitator of trade and culture. The ancient civilization of Dilmun, for example, in present-day Bahrain existed as early as the fourth millennium B.C.

The Persian Gulf, however, also constitutes a ready channel for foreign conquerors. In addition to Britain, over the centuries the gulf states have known such rulers as the Greeks, Parthians, Sassanians, Iranians, and Portuguese. When England's influence first came to the area in 1622, the Safavid shah of Iran sought England's aid in driving the Portuguese out of the gulf.

Britain did not play a major role, however, until the early nineteenth century. At that time, attacks on British shipping by the Al Qasimi of the present-day UAE became so serious that Britain asked the assistance of the ruler of Oman in ending the attacks. In consequence, Britain in 1820 initiated treaties or truces with the various rulers of the area, giving rise to the term *Trucial Coast.*

The boundaries of the Persian Gulf states were considered relatively unimportant until the discovery of oil in Bahrain in 1932 caused other gulf countries to define their geographic limits. Britain's 1968 announcement that in 1971 it would abandon its protectorate commitments east of the Suez Canal accelerated the independence of the states. Oman had maintained its independence in principle since 1650. Kuwait, with the most advanced institutions—primarily because of its oil wealth—had declared its independence in 1961. Bahrain, Qatar, and the UAE followed suit in 1971. In the face of the Iranian Revolution of 1979, all of the Persian Gulf states experienced fears for their security. These apprehensions led to their formation, together with Saudi Arabia, of the Gulf Cooperation Council (GCC) in May 1981.

Of all the gulf states, Kuwait clearly has the greatest security concerns. By early 1994, Kuwait largely had succeeded in rebuilding its damaged infrastructure and oil industry facilities ravaged by Iraq in the course of its August 2, 1990, invasion and subsequent scorched-earth policy concerning Kuwait's oil wells. By June 1993, Kuwait had increased its oil production to such an extent that it refused the Organization of the Petroleum Exporting Countries (OPEC) quota of 1.8 million barrels per

States: Bahrain, Kuwait, Oman, Qatar, and the
nirates, 1993

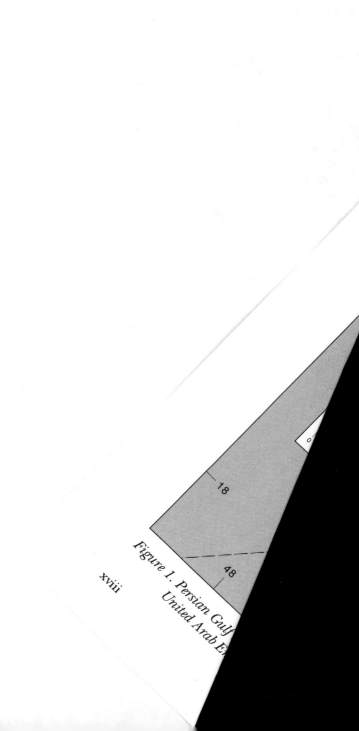

Figure 1. Persian Gulf
United Arab E...

48

18

Chapter bibliographies appear at the end of the book; brief comments on some of the more valuable sources for further reading appear at the conclusion of each chapter. Measurements are given in the metric system; a conversion table is provided to assist those who are unfamiliar with the metric system (see table 1, Appendix). The Glossary provides brief definitions of terms that may be unfamiliar to the general reader, such as the use of amir/amirate, shaykh/shaykhdom, and Al/al.

The transliteration of Arabic words and phrases posed a particular problem. For many of the words—such as Muhammad, Muslim, Quran, and shaykh—the authors followed a modified version of the system adopted by the United States Board on Geographic Names and the Permanent Committee on Geographic Names for British Official Use, known as the BGN/PCGN system; the modification entails the omission of all diacritical markings and hyphens. In numerous instances, however, the names of persons or places are so well known by another spelling that to have used the BGN/PCGN system might have created confusion. The reader will find Mecca rather than Makkah, Oman rather then Uman, and Doha rather than Ad Dawhah. In addition, although the five governments officially reject the use of the term *Persian Gulf*—as do other Arab governments—and refer to that body of water as the Arabian Gulf, the authors followed the practice of the United States Board on Geographic Names by using Persian Gulf or gulf.

The body of the text reflects information available as of January 1993. Certain other portions of the text, however, have been updated. The Introduction discusses significant events that have occurred since the completion of research; the Country Profiles include updated information as available; and the Bib___ ___lists recently published sources thought to be par___ ___er.

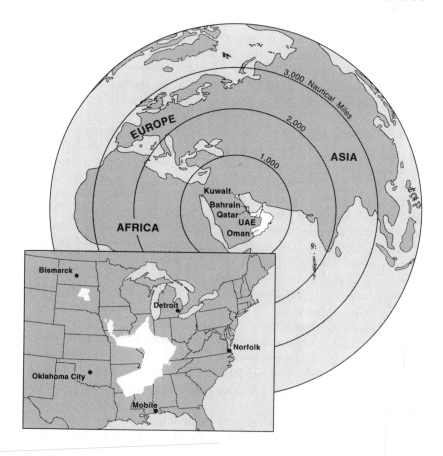

This edition of *Persian Gulf States: Country Studies* replaces the previous edition, published in 1984. Like its predecessor, the present book attempts to treat in a compact and ⬛⬛⬛⬛⬛ manner the dominant historical, socia⬛⬛⬛⬛⬛⬛⬛⬛⬛⬛d national security aspects of the ⬛⬛ Persian Gulf covered in this⬛⬛ Qatar, and the United Ara⬛⬛ included scholarly book⬛⬛ reports and documents⬛⬛ nizations; and foreign⬛⬛ cals. Available econo⬛⬛ complete or may b⬛⬛

day (bpd—see Glossary); instead, it demanded parity with the UAE at 2.2 million bpd, which OPEC refused.

The war and the occupation left significant scars on the Kuwaiti population. The war caused the departure of more than half the population, including two-thirds of the foreigners, many of them Palestinians and other Arabs. In the postwar period, most citizens returned, but the government apparently decided not to allow foreigners to exceed 50 percent of the population, and the number of Palestinians permitted to return dropped sharply.

The war also did away with most of the financial reserves from foreign investments that Kuwait had prudently accumulated in its Reserve Fund for Future Generations. War costs were estimated at a minimum of US$20 billion, a reconstruction figure less than originally feared. Economic progress in 1993, however, was such that a projected current account surplus of US$3.2 billion was predicted, together with GDP growth of 11.5 percent in 1994. Kuwait's willingness to implement World Bank (see Glossary) recommendations concerning the strengthening of its economy appeared questionable, however. The bank recommended that Kuwait eliminate subsidies, encourage government workers to move to the private sector to reduce serious government overstaffing, liberalize business regulations to promote private-sector growth, and privatize a number of state assets. Various of the recommendations would affect significantly members of the ruling family, many of whom engage in the business sector.

Kuwait's life is connected intimately with the Al Sabah, who have ruled Kuwait since 1756; the rule has alternated between the Jabir and Salim branches, descendants of two sons of the ruler Mubarak the Great. In 1963 the ruler took the first step of any gulf state to create a popular assembly. The narrow electorate and the ruler's right to dissolve the assembly have limited the influence of the legislature, and the assembly has been dissolved twice, in each case for a number of years. In October 1992, the National Assembly was reconstituted. However, only 15 percent of the Kuwaiti population was able to vote. Freedom of the press, which had been suspended in 1976, was restored in early 1992. Despite the existence of several liberal opposition movements and some Islamist (also seen as fundamentalist) pressures, the postwar government represents little change, and the ruling family continues to hold all major ministerial posts.

Apart from development of its oil industry, which dominates its economy despite attempts at diversification, Kuwait's main concern continues to be the threat from Iraq to its national security. In late 1993, incidents continued to occur along the Kuwait-Iraq border, and Iraqi media persisted in referring to Kuwait as the "nineteenth province" of Iraq. As of late 1993, Iraq was believed to hold more than 800 Kuwaiti prisoners of war.

Kuwait has taken several steps to counter the ongoing menace of Iraq. Although Kuwait sought help from its GCC allies when Iraq invaded, it recognized that the GCC states lacked the military strength to provide effective assistance. Kuwait's postwar army was reportedly down to about 8,000 from a prewar total of about 16,000 personnel. Kuwait therefore determined to build up and indigenize its own armed forces. Accordingly, a new military conscription law was enacted in December 1992. Furthermore, to upgrade matériel, a postwar 1992 decree authorized the expenditure of US$11.7 billion on military equipment over twelve years. Immediate orders included 218 M–1A2 United States main battle tanks, forty F/A–18 United States Hornet fighter aircraft, five United States Patriot missile fire units with missiles, 200 British Warrior armored personnel carriers, and miscellaneous French matériel. Kuwait also contracted in January 1993 with the United States Hughes Aircraft Company for an early warning system. In 1993, however, the National Assembly demonstrated its intent to review arms contracts and, if feasible, to reduce expenditures, in particular by eliminating commission payments to members of the royal family.

Other major steps included the signing of a security agreement and a Foreign Military Sales agreement with the United States in 1991, defense agreements with Britain and France in 1992—followed by additional matériel purchases in 1993—and an agreement with Russia in 1993. These agreements, as well as participation in the GCC, involve joint training exercises, thus strengthening the capabilities of the Kuwaiti armed forces. In line with its closer relations with the West, Kuwait took immediate action against perpetrators of the alleged Iraqi-inspired assassination attempt on former United States president George H.W. Bush during his attendance at Kuwait's April 1993 celebration of its liberation. In a further defense measure, with private donations, Kuwait in 1993 began construction of a defensive wall along its 240-kilometer border with Iraq.

With regard to regional relations, Kuwait in 1993 made conciliatory gestures toward some of the Arab countries that supported Iraq's invasion of Kuwait. Statements by Minister of Foreign Affairs Sabah al Ahmad Al Sabah in late June 1993 and by Crown Prince and Prime Minister Saad al Abd Allah Al Sabah in late October 1993 set forth conditions for such states to mend relations with Kuwait. The conditions covered support of United Nations (UN) resolutions condemning Iraqi aggression and pressure on Iraq to comply with UN resolutions, particularly those concerning border demarcation and release of prisoners. These statements, which did not name countries or organizations concerned, appear directed primarily at Tunisia and Yemen and to a lesser degree at the Palestine Liberation Organization. Relations with Jordan, however, continued to be chilly, and Kuwait's relations with Qatar cooled over the latter's rapprochement with Jordan in August and its restoration of diplomatic links with Iraq.

Bahrain, the only island state of the five Persian Gulf states, came under the rule of the Al Khalifa (originally members of the Bani Utub, an Arabian tribe) in 1783 after 180 years of Iranian control. Prior to 1971, Iran intermittently reasserted its claim to Bahrain, two-thirds of whose inhabitants are Shia Muslims although the ruling family is Sunni Muslim. Because of sectarian tensions, the Iranian Revolution of 1979 and its aftermath had an unsettling effect on the population; the government believed that a number of Shia plots during the 1980s received clandestine support from Iran. In 1992 the island's predominantly urban population (85 percent) consisted of 34 percent foreigners, who accounted for 55 percent of the labor force. The exploitation of oil and natural gas—Bahrain was the first of the five Persian Gulf states in which oil was discovered—is the island's main industry, together with the processing of aluminum, provision of drydock facilities for ships, and operation of offshore banking units.

The Al Khalifa control the government of Bahrain and held eight of eighteen ministerial posts in early 1994. A brief experiment in limited democracy occurred with the December 1972 elections for a Constituent Assembly. The resulting constitution that took effect in December 1973 provided for an advisory legislative body, the National Assembly, voted for by male citizens. The ruler dissolved the assembly in August 1975. The new Consultative Council, which began debating labor matters in January 1993, is believed to have had an impact on the provisions of the new Labor Law enacted in September 1993.

Bahrain's historical concern over the threat from Iran as well as its domestic unrest prompted it to join the GCC at the organization's founding in 1981. Even within the GCC, however, from time to time Bahrain has had tense relations with Qatar over their mutual claim to the island of Hawar and the adjacent islands located between the two countries; this dispute was under review by the International Court of Justice at The Hague in early 1994. Bahrain traditionally has had good relations with the West, particularly Britain and the United States. Bahrain's cordial association with the United States is reflected in its serving as homeport for the commander, Middle East Force, since 1949 and as the site of a United States naval support unit since 1972. In October 1991, following participation in the 1991 Persian Gulf War, Bahrain signed a defense cooperation agreement with the United States.

Bahrain's relationship with Qatar is long-standing. After the Al Khalifa conquered Bahrain in 1783 from their base in Qatar, Bahrain became the Al Khalifa seat. Subsequently, tribal elements remaining in Qatar sought to assert their autonomy from the Al Khalifa. Thus, in the early nineteenth century, Qatar was the scene of several conflicts involving the Al Khalifa and their rivals, the Al Thani, as well as various outsiders, including Iranians, Omanis, Wahhabis, and Ottomans. When the British East India Company in 1820 signed the General Treaty of Peace with the shaykhs of the area designed to end piracy, the treaty considered Qatar a dependency of Bahrain. Not until the signing of a treaty with Britain by Abd Allah ibn Qasim Al Thani in 1916 did Qatar enter into the trucial system as an "independent" protectorate. Britain's 1971 withdrawal from the Persian Gulf led to Qatar's full independence in that year.

In preparation for independence, Qatar enacted a provisional constitution in 1970 that created an Advisory Council, partly elected. Twenty members are selected by the ruler from nominees voted on in each of the ten electoral districts; fifteen members are appointed directly by the ruler. In January 1992, fifty leading Qataris petitioned the ruler for an elected council "with legislative powers" and "a permanent constitution capable of guaranteeing democracy and determining political, social, and economic structures"; as of early 1994, no action had been taken on these requests. Governmental control has clearly remained in Al Thani hands; in January 1994, ten of the eighteen members of the Council of Ministers belonged to the family.

Exploitation of the oil discovered in Qatar in 1939 was delayed until after World War II. The petroleum industry has grown steadily, and in 1991 the North Field natural gas project was inaugurated; the North Field, a 6,000-square-kilometer offshore field considered to be the world's largest, extends slightly into Iranian territorial waters. The Qatari government, however, has sought to encourage diversification and investment in such industries as steel, fertilizers, and petrochemicals. The work force is predominantly foreign; in 1992 Qataris were estimated to represent only 20 percent of the approximately 484,000 total population.

In part because most Qataris belong to the Wahhabi sect that originated in the Arabian Peninsula, Qatar historically has enjoyed close relations with Saudi Arabia, with which it settled its 1992 border dispute in 1993. Although Qatar supported Iraq in the Iran-Iraq War of 1980–88, it subsequently improved its relations with Iran, undoubtedly in part because of its shared gas field. As a GCC member, Qatar sent forces against Iraq in the 1991 Persian Gulf War but continued to maintain a diplomatic link with Iraq. Qatar's relations with the United States improved following Operation Desert Storm, and the two countries signed a defense cooperation agreement in June 1992 that includes a provision for the pre-positioning of supplies.

The UAE represents an independent state created by the joining together in the winter of 1971–72 of the seven former Trucial Coast states of Abu Dhabi, Ajman, Al Fujayrah, Dubayy, Ras al Khaymah, Sharjah, and Umm al Qaywayn. In early 1993, UAE citizens constituted about 12 percent of the total population of nearly 2 million. Oil is the major source of income for the federation, but it is found in a significant amount only in Abu Dhabi and to a lesser extent in Dubayy, Ras al Khaymah, and Sharjah. In principle, each amirate is required to contribute to the federation's budget (according to the provisional constitution, each state's natural resources and wealth are its own), but in practice only Abu Dhabi and, to a lesser degree, Dubayy have financed the federation. The resulting disagreement over budget contributions as well as over the integration of defense measures and forces led to the recurring renewal at five-year intervals of the 1971 provisional constitution, rather than the intended adoption of a permanent constitution. In fact, the separation of powers is nominal; UAE organs consist of the Supreme Council of the Union (SCU) composed of the rulers of the seven amirates (Abu Dhabi and Dubayy have a veto right on proposed measures), the Council of Ministers, and the presidency. The chairman of the SCU is the president of the UAE. In addition, there is an advisory Federal National Council (FNC) of forty members appointed by the rulers of the amirates, based on proportional representation; members serve two-year terms. Following a one-year delay in naming members, the FNC met with UAE citizens in January 1993, after which it held several sessions. FNC actions included a call for private firms to employ more UAE citizens and the establishment of a federal housing loan program for UAE nationals.

Like other gulf states, the UAE has security concerns, of which one is its dispute with Iran over the islands of Abu Musa, Tunb al Kubra (Greater Tumb), and Tunb as Sughra (Lesser Tumb). This dispute flared anew in early 1992, after lying dormant for twenty years, when Iran took actions on Abu Musa that violated a shared sovereignty agreement. The UAE was concerned that Iran intended to extend its control over the entire island. However, in November 1992 the two countries agreed to abide by the provisions of the 1971 memorandum. The UAE would prefer a final resolution of this dispute and has expressed a willingness to have its sovereignty claims arbitrated by the International Court of Justice or the United Nations.

Militarily, the UAE participated in the 1991 Persian Gulf War and contributed personnel to the UN peacekeeping force in Somalia in 1992. The UAE's experience in the Persian Gulf War led it to consider itself inadequately prepared in terms of matériel; consequently, in February 1993 it ordered Leclerc main battle tanks and other equipment from France.

Oman is the only one of the Persian Gulf states whose ruler bears the title of *sultan* instead of *shaykh*. Until 1970 the ruler was known as the sultan of Muscat (the coastal area) and Oman (the rugged interior imamate), reflecting the diverse parts of the country. To Ibadi Muslims, the political ruler is also the imam (see Glossary); the title *sultan*, taken from Ottoman usage, indicates a Muslim ruling sovereign combining religious and political connotations.

The present sultan, Qabus ibn Said Al Said, began his rule in 1970 and immediately started emphasizing economic development and modernization. Such an emphasis was essential because Oman's oil, first produced commercially in 1967, had a relatively limited production span; 1992 estimates projected seventeen more years of output at the 1992 production rate. National development plans, therefore, have focused on reducing the dependence on oil and on confronting problems occasioned by the dramatic rural-to-urban population shift, the accompanying social transformation, and the large number of foreign workers, all in the interests of promoting stability. Oman never has had a census, but in 1992, for planning purposes, the government estimated the population at 2 million persons (the actual figure may be closer to 1.5 million), of whom about 350,000 were foreigners. The latter constituted approximately 60 percent of the labor force.

Oman faces a number of problems. The government must attempt to provide adequate housing and utilities, especially water; stimulate agriculture to increase food production; and discourage urban migration. Specific development goals include establishing new industries and industrial estates; training indigenous personnel; developing minerals other than oil; encouraging agriculture, fishing, and tourism; increasing privatization of state-controlled enterprises; and diminishing regional imbalances, particularly in the Dhofar region.

On coming to power, Qabus ibn Said confronted the rebellion in the Dhofar region, which had begun in 1964. To counter the revolt, he concentrated on establishing development projects in this neglected area of the country and on improving the transportation and communications infrastructure. With the assistance of Iran, Jordan, and several gulf states, he also took military action to repress the rebellion. The sultan was aided in these efforts by the fact that the bureaucracy and major posts were largely in the hands of ruling family members. Leading government posts continued to be in the hands of ruling family members into the 1990s. For example, in early 1994 the sultan also served as prime minister, minister of defense, minister of finance, minister of foreign affairs, and chairman of the central bank. Other members of the ruling family served as deputy prime minister for legal affairs, deputy prime minister for security and defense, and minister of national heritage and culture. Still other ruling family members served as special advisers and as governors of the capital and of the Dhofar region. Close cooperation occurs between the ruling family and the merchants; tribal shaykhs now play a lesser role. Following the example of other gulf states, in 1991

Qabus ibn Said created the Consultative Council, which has representatives from the forty-one *wilayat*, or governorates, but no government officials, in contrast to the State Consultative Council, established in 1981, which the new council replaced.

In the area of foreign relations, Oman has been closely aligned with Britain and the United States; it first signed a military accord with the latter in 1980. This "facilities access" agreement was most recently renewed in 1990. In the region, Oman has sought to play an independent, nonconfrontational role. In late October 1992, Oman ended a twenty-five-year border dispute with Yemen by signing a border demarcation agreement; it also concluded a border agreement with Saudi Arabia in March 1990 as a result of which Oman began demarcating the boundary between the two countries. Moreover, Oman has acted as mediator between the United States and Iran and between Britain and Iran. Meanwhile, Oman has been increasing its arms purchases and building up its armed forces.

Oman's purchase of military matériel is consonant with the general pattern of Persian Gulf states, which have been spending heavily on military equipment since at least the early 1980s, primarily to compensate for their limited manpower. In most instances, women are not included in the armed forces. Lacking domestic arms production capability, the gulf states mainly need aircraft, air defense missile systems, early warning systems, and small missile attack craft, as well as main battle tanks and armored personnel carriers. The gulf countries recognize the potential threats they face, particularly from Iraq and possibly from Iran. In addition, they have experienced the need to counter domestic insurgencies, protect their ruling families and oil installations, and possibly use military force in pursuing claims to disputed territory. A partial solution to their defense needs lay in the formation of the GCC in 1981.

The Persian Gulf War brought with it, however, the realization that the GCC was inadequate to provide the gulf states with the defense they required. As a result, most of the states sought defense agreements with the United States, Britain, France, and Russia, more or less in that order. Concurrently, the gulf countries have endeavored to improve the caliber and training of their armed forces and the interoperability of military equipment through joint military exercises both within the GCC framework and with Western powers. The United States has sought to complement GCC collective security efforts and has stated that it does not intend to station forces permanently in the region.

At a November 1993 meeting, GCC defense ministers made plans to expand the Saudi-based Peninsula Shield force, a rapid deployment force, to 25,000. The force is to have units from each GCC state, a unified command, and a rotating chairmanship. The ministers also agreed to spend up to US$5 billion to purchase three or four more AWACS aircraft to supplement the five the Saudi air force already has and to create a headquarters in Saudi Arabia for GCC defense purposes. The UAE reportedly considered the proposed force increase insufficient; furthermore, Oman sought a force of 100,000 members.

In addition to these efforts, directed at the military aspects of national security, declining oil revenues for many of the states and internal sectarian divisions also have led the gulf countries to institute domestic efforts to strengthen their national security. Such efforts entail measures to increase the role of citizens in an advisory governmental capacity, to allow greater freedom of the press, to promote economic development through diversification and incentives for foreign investment, and to develop infrastructure projects that will increase the standard of living for more sectors of the population, thereby eliminating sources of discord. The ruling families hope that such steps will promote stability, counter the possible appeal of radical Islam, and ultimately strengthen the position of the ruling families by constituting some form of limited constitutional monarchy.

January 26, 1994   Helen Chapin Metz

Chapter 1. Historical Setting

Sharjah Mosque, built in the 1980s in traditional style

of the gulf coast and the people of the Tigris and Euphrates valley developed increasingly complex societies and beliefs.

The people of the gulf coast differed from those of the interior of the Arabian Peninsula. Many of the people in the interior were organized in tribes and pursued nomadic lifestyles. When the desert provided insufficient food for their flocks, the tribes pushed into the date groves or farmlands of the settled towns. Centers on the gulf coast were subject to such nomadic incursions, as were the people of Mesopotamia. As a result, after the second millennium B.C. the gulf began to take on an increasingly Arab character. Some Arab tribes from the interior left their flocks and took over the date groves that ringed the region's oases, while others took up sailing and began to take part in the trade and piracy that were the region's economic mainstays. These nomadic incursions periodically changed the ethnic balance and leadership of the gulf coast.

Meanwhile, trade flourished in the second millennium B.C., as reflected in the wealth of Dilmun. In about 1800 B.C., however, both the quality and the amount of goods that passed through Dilmun declined, and many scholars attribute this to a corresponding decline in the Mesopotamian markets. Concurrently, an alternate trade route arose that linked India to the Mediterranean Sea via the Arabian Sea, then through the Gulf of Aden, thence into the Red Sea where the pharaohs had built a shallow canal that linked the Red Sea to the Nile. This new route gave access not only to Mediterranean ports but also, through the Mediterranean ports, to the West as well.

One of the ways that rulers directed goods toward their own country was to control transit points on the trade routes. Oman was significant to rulers in Mesopotamia because it provided a source of raw materials as well as a transshipment point for goods from the East. Although a valuable prize, Oman's large navy gave it influence over other parts of the gulf. When Mesopotamia was strong, its rulers sought to take over Oman. When Oman was strong, its rulers pushed up through the gulf and into Mesopotamia. One of the basic conflicts in gulf history has been the struggle of indigenous peoples against outside powers that have sought to control the gulf because of its strategic importance.

Competition between Red Sea and Persian Gulf trade routes was complicated by the rise of new land routes around 1000 B.C. Technological advances in the second and first millennia B.C. made land routes increasingly viable for moving goods.

The domestication of the camel and the development of a saddle enabling the animal to carry large loads allowed merchants to send goods across Arabia as well. As a result, inland centers developed at the end of the first millennium B.C. to service the increasing caravan traffic. These overland trade routes helped to arabize the gulf by bringing the nomads of the interior into closer contact with peoples on the coast.

The Gulf in the Ancient World

Archaeological evidence suggests that Dilmun returned to prosperity after the Assyrian Empire stabilized the Tigris-Euphrates area at the end of the second millennium B.C. A powerful ruler in Mesopotamia meant a prosperous gulf. Ashurbanipal, the Assyrian king who ruled in the seventh century B.C., was particularly strong. He extended Assyrian influence as far as Egypt and controlled an empire that stretched from North Africa to the Persian Gulf. The Egyptians, however, regained control of their country about a half-century after they lost it.

A series of other conquests of varying lengths followed. In 325 B.C., Alexander the Great sent a fleet from India to follow the eastern, or Persian, coast of the gulf up to the mouth of the Tigris and Euphrates rivers and sent other ships to explore the Arab side of the waterway. The temporary Greek presence in the area increased Western interest in the gulf during the next two centuries. Alexander's successors, however, did not control the area long enough to make the gulf a part of the Greek world. By about 250 B.C., the Greeks lost all territory east of Syria to the Parthians, a Persian dynasty in the East. The Parthians brought the gulf under Persian control and extended their influence as far as Oman.

The Parthian conquests demarcated the distinction between the Greek world of the Mediterranean Sea and the Persian Empire in the East. The Greeks, and the Romans after them, depended on the Red Sea route, whereas the Parthians depended on the Persian Gulf route. Because they wanted to keep the merchants who plied those routes under their control, the Parthians established garrisons as far south as Oman.

In the third century A.D., the Sassanians, another Persian dynasty, succeeded the Parthians and held the area until the rise of Islam four centuries later. Under Sassanian rule, Persian control over the gulf reached its height. Oman was no longer a threat, and the Sassanians were strong enough to establish agricultural colonies and to engage some of the nomadic tribes in the interior as a border guard to protect their western flank from the Romans.

This agricultural and military contact gave people in the gulf greater exposure to Persian culture, as reflected in certain irrigation techniques still used in Oman. The gulf continued to be a crossroads, however, and its people learned about Persian beliefs, such as Zoroastrianism, as well as about Semitic and Mediterranean ideas.

Judaism and Christianity arrived in the gulf from a number of directions: from Jewish and Christian tribes in the Arabian desert; from Ethiopian Christians to the south; and from Mesopotamia, where Jewish and Christian communities flourished under Sassanian rule. Whereas Zoroastrianism seems to have been confined to Persian colonists, Christianity and Judaism were adopted by some Arabs. The popularity of these religions paled, however, when compared with the enthusiasm with which the Arabs greeted Islam.

Early Development of Islam

Islam is a system of religious beliefs and an all-encompassing way of life. Muslims believe that God (Allah) revealed to the Prophet Muhammad the rules governing society and the proper conduct of society's members. It is incumbent on the individual, therefore, to live in a manner prescribed by the revealed law and incumbent on the community to build the perfect human society on earth according to holy injunctions. Islam recognizes no distinctions between the religious institution and the state. The distinction between religious and secular law is a recent development that in part reflects the more pronounced role of the state in society and Western economic and cultural penetration. The impact of religion on daily life in Muslim countries is extensive.

The area that constitutes the present-day Persian Gulf states was on the immediate periphery of the rise of Islam. In A.D. 610, Muhammad, a merchant from the Hashimite branch of the ruling Quraysh tribe in the Arabian town of Mecca, began to preach the first of a series of revelations that Muslims believe was granted him by God through the angel Gabriel. A fervent monotheist, Muhammad denounced the polytheism of his fellow Meccans. Because the town's economy was based in part on a thriving pilgrimage trade to the shrine called the Kaaba and to numerous other pagan religious sites in the area, his censure earned him the enmity of the town's leaders. In 622 he and a group of followers accepted an invitation to settle in the town of Yathrib, later known as Medina (the city), after it became the center of Muhammad's activities. The move, or hijra (see Glossary), sometimes seen as the hegira, marks the beginning of the Islamic era and of Islam as a force in history; the Islamic calendar begins in 622. In Medina, Muhammad continued to preach, and he eventually defeated his detractors in battle. He consolidated the temporal and the spiritual leadership in his person before his death in 632. After Muhammad's death, his followers compiled those of his words regarded as coming directly from God into the Quran, the holy scripture of Islam. Others of his sayings, recalled by those who had known him, became the hadith (see Glossary). The precedent of Muhammad's deeds is called the sunna. Together they form a comprehensive guide to the spiritual, ethical, and social life of an orthodox Sunni Muslim.

The major duties of Muslims are found in the five pillars of Islam, which set forth the acts necessary to demonstrate and reinforce the faith. These are the recitation of the *shahada* ("There is no god but God [Allah], and Muhammad is his prophet"), daily prayer (*salat*), almsgiving (*zakat*), fasting (*sawm*), and pilgrimage (hajj). The believer is to pray in a prescribed manner after purification through ritual ablutions each day at dawn, midday, midafternoon, sunset, and nightfall. Prescribed genuflections and prostrations accompany the prayers, which the worshiper recites while facing toward Mecca. Whenever possible, men pray in congregation at the mosque with an imam (see Glossary), and on Fridays they are required to do so. The Friday noon prayers provide the occasion for weekly sermons by religious leaders. Women also may attend public worship at the mosque, where they are segregated from the men, although most frequently women pray at home. A special functionary, the muezzin, intones a call to prayer to the entire community at the appropriate hour.

The ninth month of the Muslim calendar is Ramadan, a period of obligatory fasting in commemoration of Muhammad's receipt of God's revelation. Throughout the month, all but the sick and the weak, pregnant or lactating women, soldiers on duty, travelers on necessary journeys, and young children are enjoined from eating, drinking, or smoking during the daylight hours. Those adults excused are obliged to endure an equivalent fast at their earliest opportunity. A festive meal breaks the daily fast and inaugurates a night of feasting and celebration. The pious well-to-do usually do little or no work during this period, and some businesses close for all or part of the day. Because the lunar year is about ten days shorter than the solar year, Ramadan rotates through the seasons. A considerable test of discipline at any time of the year, a fast that falls in summer imposes severe hardship on those who must do physical work.

All Muslims, at least once in their lifetime and if circumstances permit, should make the hajj to Mecca to participate in special rites held there during the twelfth month of the lunar calendar. Muhammad instituted this requirement, modifying pre-Islamic custom, to emphasize sites associated with God and Abraham (Ibrahim), founder of monotheism and father of the Arabs through his son, Ismail.

The lesser pillars of the faith, which all Muslims share, are jihad, or the permanent struggle for the triumph of the word of God on earth, and the requirement to do good works and to avoid all evil thoughts, words, and deeds. In addition, Muslims agree on certain basic principles of faith based on the teachings of the Prophet Muhammad: there is one God, who is a unitary divine being in contrast to the trinitarian belief of Christians; Muhammad, the last of a line of prophets beginning with Abraham and including Moses and Jesus, was chosen by God to present God's message to humanity; and there is a general resurrection on the last, or judgment, day.

During his lifetime, Muhammad held both spiritual and temporal leadership of the Muslim community. Religious and secular law merged, and all Muslims traditionally have been subject to the sharia, or religious law. A comprehensive legal system, the sharia developed gradually through the early centuries of Islam, primarily through the accretion of interpretations and precedents set by various judges and scholars. During the tenth century, legal opinion began to be codified into authoritative schools of interpretation.

After Muhammad's death, the leaders of the Muslim community consensually chose Abu Bakr, the Prophet's father-in-law and one of his earliest followers, to succeed him. At that time, some persons favored Ali ibn Abu Talib, Muhammad's cousin and the husband of his daughter, Fatima, but Ali and his supporters (the Shiat Ali, or Party of Ali) eventually recognized the community's choice. The next two caliphs (successors)—Umar, who succeeded in 634, and Uthman, who took power in 644—enjoyed the recognition of the entire community. When

Ali finally succeeded to the caliphate in 656, Muawiyah, governor of Syria, rebelled in the name of his murdered kinsman, Uthman. After the ensuing civil war, Ali moved his capital to Iraq, where he was murdered shortly thereafter.

Ali's death ended the last of the so-called four orthodox caliphs and the period in which the entire community of Islam recognized a single leader. Muawiyah proclaimed himself caliph from Damascus. The Shiat Ali refused to recognize him or his line, the Umayyad caliphs, and withdrew in the great schism of Islam to establish the dissident sect, known as the Shia, who supported the claims of Ali's line to the caliphate based on descent from the Prophet. The larger faction, the Sunnis, adhered to the position that the caliph must be elected, and over the centuries they have represented themselves as the orthodox branch.

Sunni Islam

Although originally political in nature, the differences between Sunni and Shia interpretations rapidly took on theological overtones. In principle, a Sunni approaches God directly: there is no clerical hierarchy. Some duly appointed religious figures, such as imams, however, exert considerable social and political power. Imams usually are men of importance in their communities, but they need not have any formal training. Committees of socially prominent worshipers usually are responsible for managing major mosque-owned lands. In most Arab countries, the administration of *awqaf* (religious endowments) has come under the influence of the state. Qadis (judges) and imams are appointed by the government.

The Muslim year has two major religious festivals: Id al Adha, a sacrificial festival held on the tenth day of Dhu al Hijjah, the twelfth, or pilgrimage, month; and Id al Fitr, the festival of breaking the fast, which celebrates the end of Ramadan on the first day of Shawwal, the tenth month. To Sunnis these are the most important festivals of the year. Each lasts three or four days, during which time people put on their best clothes and visit, congratulate, and bestow gifts on each other. In addition, cemeteries are visited. Id al Fitr is celebrated more festively because it marks the end of Ramadan. Celebrations also take place, although less extensively, on the Prophet's birthday, which falls on the twelfth day of Rabi al Awwal, the third month.

With regard to legal matters, Sunni Islam has four orthodox schools that give different weight in legal opinions to prescriptions in the Quran, to the hadith, to the consensus of legal scholars, to analogy (to similar situations at the time of the Prophet), and to reason or opinion. Named for their founders, the earliest Muslim legal schools were those of Abd Allah Malik ibn Anas (ca. 715–95) and An Numan ibn Thabit Abu Hanifa (ca. 700–67). The Maliki school was centered in Medina, and the lawbook of Malik ibn Anas is the earliest surviving Muslim legal text, containing a systematic consensus of Medina legal opinions. The Hanafi school in Iraq stressed individual opinion in making legal decisions. Muhammad ibn Idris ash Shafii (767–820), a member of the tribe of Quraysh and a distant relative of the Prophet, studied under Malik ibn Anas in Medina. He followed a somewhat eclectic legal path, laying down the rules for analogy that were later adopted by other legal schools. The last of the four major Sunni legal schools, that of Ahmad ibn Muhammad ibn Hanbal (780–855), was centered in Baghdad. The Hanbali school, which became prominent in Arabia as a result of Wahhabi (see Glossary) influence, gave great emphasis to the hadith as a source of Muslim law but rejected innovations and rationalistic explanations of the Quran and the traditions (see Wahhabi Islam and the Gulf, this ch.).

Shia Islam

Shia Muslims hold the fundamental beliefs of other Muslims (see Sunni Islam, this ch.). In addition to these tenets, however, the largest of the Shia denominations believe in the imamate, a distinctive institution. Whereas Sunni Muslims view the caliph as a temporal leader only and consider an imam to be a prayer leader, Shia Muslims known as Twelve Imam Shia hold a hereditary view of Muslim leadership. They believe the Prophet Muhammad designated Ali to be his successor as Imam (when uppercase, Imam refers to the Shia descendant of the House of Ali), exercising both spiritual and temporal leadership. Only those who have *walayat* (spiritual guidance) are free from error and sin and have been chosen by God through the Prophet. Each Imam in turn designated his successor—through twelve Imams—each holding the same powers.

The imamate began with Ali, who is also accepted by Sunni Muslims as the fourth of the "rightly guided caliphs" to succeed the Prophet. Twelve Imam Shia revere Ali as the First Imam, and his descendants, beginning with his sons Hasan and

Husayn, continue the line of the Imams until the twelfth. Shia point to the close lifetime association of the Prophet with Ali. When Ali was six years old, he was invited by the Prophet to live with him, and Shia believe Ali was the first person to make the declaration of faith in Islam. Ali also slept in the Prophet's bed on the night of the hijra, when it was feared that the house would be attacked by unbelievers and the Prophet stabbed to death. He fought in all the battles the Prophet did, except one, and the Prophet chose him to be the husband of one of his favorite daughters, Fatima.

Among Shia, the term *imam* traditionally has been used only for Ali and his eleven descendants. None of the twelve Imams, with the exception of Ali, ever ruled an Islamic government. During their lifetimes, their followers hoped that they would assume the rulership of the Islamic community, a rule that was believed to have been wrongfully usurped. Because Sunni caliphs were cognizant of this hope, Imams generally were persecuted under the Umayyad and Abbasid dynasties. Therefore, the Imams tried to be as unobtrusive as possible and to live as far as was reasonable from the successive capitals of the Islamic empire.

During the eighth century, Caliph Al Mamun, son of and successor to Harun ar Rashid, was favorably disposed toward the descendants of Ali and their followers. He invited Imam Reza, the Eighth Imam (765–816), to come from Medina to his court at Marv (Mary in present-day Turkmenistan). While Reza was residing at Marv, Al Mamun designated him as his successor in an apparent effort to avoid conflict among Muslims. Reza's sister, Fatima, journeyed from Medina to be with her brother but took ill and died at Qom, in present-day Iran. A major shrine developed around her tomb, and over the centuries Qom has become a major Shia pilgrimage site and theological center.

Al Mamun took Reza on his military campaign to retake Baghdad from political rivals. On this trip, Reza died unexpectedly in Khorasan. Reza was the only Imam to reside in, or die in, what is now Iran. A major shrine, and eventually the city of Mashhad, grew up around his tomb, which is the major pilgrimage center in Iran. Several theological schools are located in Mashhad, associated with the shrine of the Eighth Imam.

Reza's sudden death was a shock to his followers, many of whom believed that Al Mamun, out of jealousy for Reza's increasing popularity, had the Imam poisoned. Al Mamun's suspected treachery against Imam Reza and his family tended to reinforce a feeling already prevalent among his followers that Sunni rulers were untrustworthy.

The Twelfth Imam is believed to have been only five years old when he became Imam in 874 on the death of his father. Because his followers feared he might be assassinated, the Twelfth Imam was hidden from public view and was seen only by a few of his closest deputies. Sunnis claim that he never existed, or that he died while still a child. Shia believe that the Twelfth Imam never died, but disappeared. Since then, the greater occultation of the Twelfth Imam has been in force, which will last until God commands the Twelfth Imam to manifest himself on earth again as the mahdi, or messiah. Shia believe that during the occultation of the Twelfth Imam, he is spiritually present—some believe that he is materially present as well—and he is besought to reappear in various invocations and prayers. His name is mentioned in wedding invitations, and his birthday is one of the most jubilant of all Shia religious observances.

The Twelve Imam Shia doctrine of the imamate was not fully elaborated until the tenth century. Other dogmas developed still later. A characteristic of Shia Islam is the continual exposition and reinterpretation of doctrine.

A significant practice of Shia Islam is that of visiting the shrines of Imams in Iraq and in Iran. In Iraq, these include the tomb of Imam Ali in An Najaf and that of his son, Imam Husayn, in Karbala, because both are considered major Shia martyrs. Before the Iran-Iraq War (1980–88), tens of thousands made the visits each year. Other principal pilgrimage sites in Iraq are the tombs of the Seventh Imam and the Ninth Imam at Kazimayn near Baghdad. In Iran, pilgrimage sites include the tomb of the Eighth Imam in Mashhad and that of his sister in Qom. Such pilgrimages originated in part from the difficulty and the expense of making the hajj to Mecca in the early days.

In commemoration of the martyrdom of Husayn, killed near Karbala in 680 during a battle with troops supporting the Umayyad caliph, processions are held in the Shia towns and villages of southern Iraq on the tenth day of Muharram (Ashura), the anniversary of his death. Ritual mourning (*taaziya*) is performed by groups of five to twenty men each. Contributions are solicited in the community to pay transportation for a local group to go to Karbala for *taaziya* celebrations forty days after

Ashura. There is great rivalry among groups for the best performance of the *taaziya* passion plays.

Shia practice differs from Sunni practice concerning divorce and inheritance in that it is more favorable to women. The reason for this reputedly is the high esteem in which Fatima, the wife of Ali and the daughter of the Prophet, was held.

Shia Islam has developed several sects. The most important of these is the Twelver, or Ithna-Ashari, sect, which predominates in the Shia world generally. Not all Shia became Twelvers, however. In the eighth century, a dispute arose over who should lead the Shia community after the death of the Sixth Imam, Jaafar ibn Muhammad (also known as Jaafar as Sadiq). The group that eventually became the Twelvers followed the teaching of Musa al Kazim; another group followed the teachings of Musa's brother, Ismail, and were called Ismailis. Ismailis are also referred to as Seveners because they broke off from the Shia community over a disagreement concerning the Seventh Imam. Ismailis do not believe that any of their Imams have disappeared from the world in order to return later. Rather, they have followed a continuous line of leaders represented in early 1993 by Karim al Husayni Agha Khan IV, an active figure in international humanitarian efforts. The Twelver Shia and the Ismailis also have their own legal schools.

Another group, the Kharijites, arose from events surrounding the assassination of Uthman, the third caliph, and the transfer of authority to the fourth caliph, Ali. In the war between Ali and Muawiyah, part of Ali's army objected to arbitration of the dispute. They left Ali's camp, causing other Muslims to refer to them as "kharijites" (the ones who leave). The term *Kharijites* also became a designation for Muslims who refused to compromise with those who differed from them. Their actions caused the Sunni community to consider them assassins.

In the eighth century, some Kharijites began to moderate their position. Leaders arose who suppressed the fanatical political element in Kharijite belief and discouraged their followers from taking up arms against other Islamic leaders. Kharijite leaders emphasized instead the special benefits that Kharijites might receive from living in a small community that held high standards for personal conduct and spiritual values. One of these religious leaders, or imams, was Abd Allah ibn Ibad, whose followers founded communities in parts of Africa and southern Arabia. Some of Abd Allah's followers, known as Ibadis, became the leaders in Oman.

The Spread of Islam

The early Islamic polity was intensely expansionist, fueled both by fervor for the faith and by economic and social factors. After gaining control of Arabia and the Persian Gulf region, conquering armies swept out of the peninsula, spreading Islam. By the end of the eighth century, Islamic armies had reached far into North Africa and eastward and northward into Asia.

Traditional accounts of the conversion of tribes in the gulf are probably more legend than history. Stories about the Bani Abd al Qais tribe that controlled the eastern coast of Arabia as well as Bahrain when the tribe converted to Islam indicate that its members were traders having close contacts with Christian communities in Mesopotamia. Such contacts may have introduced the tribe to the ideal of one God and so prepared it to accept the Prophet's message.

The Arabs of Oman also figure prominently among the early converts to Islam. According to tradition, the Prophet sent one of his military leaders to Oman to convert not only the Arab inhabitants, some of whom were Christian, but also the Iranian garrison, which was Zoroastrian. The Arabs accepted Islam, but the Iranians did not. It was partly the zeal of the newly converted Arabs that inspired them to expel the Iranians from Oman.

Although Muhammad had enjoined the Muslim community to convert the infidel, he had also recognized the special status of the "people of the book," Jews and Christians, whose scriptures he considered revelations of God's word and which contributed in some measure to Islam. By accepting the status of *dhimmis* (tolerated subject people), Jews and Christians could live in their own communities, practice their own religious laws, and be exempt from military service. However, they were obliged to refrain from proselytizing among Muslims, to recognize Muslim authority, and to pay additional taxes. In addition, they were denied certain political rights.

The Gulf in the Middle Ages

In the Islamic period, the prosperity of the gulf continued to be linked to markets in Mesopotamia. Accordingly, after 750

17

the gulf prospered because Baghdad became the seat of the caliph and the main center of Islamic civilization. Islam brought great prosperity to Iraq during this period, thus increasing the demand for foreign goods. As a result, gulf merchants roamed farther and farther afield. By the year 1000, they were traveling regularly to China and beyond, and their trading efforts were instrumental in spreading Islam, first to India and then to Indonesia and Malaya.

The Islam they spread, however, was often sectarian. Eastern Arabia was a center for both Kharijites and Shia; in the Middle Ages, the Ismaili Shia faith constituted a particularly powerful force in the gulf. Ismailis originated in Iraq, but many moved to the gulf in the ninth century to escape the Sunni authorities. Whereas the imam was central to the Ismaili tradition, the group also recognized what they referred to as "missionaries" (*dua*; sing., *dai*), figures who spoke for the imam and played major political roles. One of these missionaries was Hamdan Qarmat, who sent a group from Iraq to Bahrain in the ninth century to establish an Ismaili community. From their base in Bahrain, Qarmat's followers, who became known as Qarmatians, sent emissaries throughout the Muslim world.

The Qarmatians are known for their attacks on their opponents, including raids on Baghdad and the sack of Mecca and Medina in 930. For much of the tenth century, the Ismailis of Bahrain were the most powerful force in the Persian Gulf and the Middle East. They controlled the coast of Oman and collected tribute from the caliph in Baghdad as well as from a rival Ismaili imam in Cairo, whom they did not recognize.

By the eleventh century, Ismaili power had waned. The Qarmatians succumbed to the same forces that had earlier threatened centers on the gulf coast—the ambitions of strong leaders in Mesopotamia or Iran and the incursion of tribes from the interior. In 985 armies of the Buyids, an Iranian dynasty, drove the Ismailis out of Iraq, and in 988 Arab tribes drove the Ismailis out of Al Ahsa, an oasis they controlled in eastern Arabia. Thereafter, Ismaili presence in the gulf faded, and in the twentieth century the sect virtually disappeared.

Ibadis figured less prominently than the Shia in the spread of Islam. A stable community, the Ibadi sect's large following in Oman has helped to distinguish Oman from its gulf neighbors. Ibadis originated in Iraq, but in the early eighth century, when the caliph's representative began to suppress the Ibadis, many left the area. Their leader at the time, Jabir ibn Zayd, had come to Iraq from Oman, so he returned there. Jabir ibn Zayd's presence in Oman strengthened the existing Ibadi communities; in less than a century, the sect took over the country from the Sunni garrison that ruled it in the caliph's name. Their leader, Al Julanda ibn Masud, became the Ibadi imam of Oman.

In the Ibadi tradition, imams are elected by a council of religious scholars, who select the leader that can best defend the community militarily and rule it according to religious principles. Whereas Sunnis and Shia traditionally have focused on a single leader, referred to as caliph or imam, Ibadis permit regions to have their own imams. For instance, there have been concurrent Ibadi imams in Iraq, Oman, and North Africa.

Because of the strong sense of community among Ibadis, which resembles tribal feelings of community, they have predominated in the interior of Oman and to a lesser degree along the coast. In 752, for example, a new line of Sunni caliphs in Baghdad conquered Oman and killed the Ibadi imam, Al Julanda. Other Ibadi imams arose and reestablished the tradition in the interior, but extending their rule to the coastal trading cities met opposition. The inland empires of Iran and Iraq depended on customs duties from East-West trade, much of which passed by Oman. Accordingly, the caliph and his successors could not allow the regional coastal cities out of their control.

As a result, Oman acquired a dual nature. Ibadi leaders usually controlled the mountainous interior while, for the most part, foreign powers controlled the coast. People in the coastal cities often have been foreigners or have had considerable contact with foreigners because of trade. Coastal Omanis have profited from their involvement with outsiders, whereas Omanis in the interior have tended to reject the foreign presence as an intrusion into the small, tightly knit Ibadi community. Ibadi Islam thus has preserved some of the hostility toward outsiders that was a hallmark of the early Kharijites.

While the imam concerned himself with the interior, the Omani coast remained under the control of Iranian rulers. The Buyids in the late tenth century eventually extended their influence down the gulf as far as Oman. In the 1220s and 1230s, another group, the Zangids—based in Mosul, Iraq— sent troops to the Omani coast; around 1500 the Safavids, an Iranian dynasty, pushed into the gulf as well. The Safavids followed the Twelve Imam Shia tradition, which they had taken over from the Arabs, and imposed Shia beliefs on those under their rule.

Oman's geographic location gave it access not only to the Red Sea trade but also to ships skirting the coast of Africa. By the end of the fifteenth century, however, an Iranian ruler, the shaykh (see Glossary) of Hormuz, profited most from this trade. The shaykh controlled the Iranian port that lay directly across the gulf from Oman, and he collected customs duties in the busy Omani ports of Qalhat and Muscat. Ibadi imams continued to rule in the interior, but until Europeans entered the region in the sixteenth century, Ibadi rulers were unable to reclaim the coastal cities from the Iranians.

The Age of Colonialism

During the Middle Ages, Muslim countries of the Middle East controlled East-West trade. However, control changed in the fifteenth century. The Portuguese, who were building ships with deep hulls that remained stable in high seas, were thereby able to make longer voyages. They pushed farther and farther down the west coast of Africa until they found their way around the southern tip of the continent and made contact with Muslim cities on the other side. In East Africa, the Portuguese enlisted Arab navigators there to take them across to India, where they eventually set themselves up in Calicut on the Malabar Coast.

Once in India, the Portuguese used their superior ships to transport goods around Africa instead of using the Red Sea route, thus eliminating the middlemen in Egypt. The Portuguese then extended their control to the local trade that crossed the Arabian Sea, capturing coastal cities in Oman and Iran and setting up forts and customs houses on both coasts to collect duty. The Portuguese allowed local rulers to remain in control but collected tribute from them in exchange for that privilege, thus increasing Portuguese revenues.

The ruler most affected by the rise of Portuguese power was the Safavid shah of Iran, Abbas I (1587–1629). During the time the shaykh of Hormuz possessed effective control over gulf ports, he continued to pay lip service and tribute to the Safavid shah. When the Portuguese arrived, they forced the shaykh to pay tribute to them. The shah could do little because Iran was too weak to challenge the Portuguese. For that the shah required another European power; he therefore invited the

Ar Rustaq fort, Oman, restored by Omani Ministry of National Heritage and Culture
Building a dhow in Sur, Oman's ancient port; ship construction is a major enterprise of Persian Gulf states.
Courtesy Embassy of the Sultanate of Oman, Washington

21

English and the Dutch to drive the Portuguese out of the gulf, in return for half the revenues from Iranian ports.

Both countries responded to the shah's offer, but it was England that proved the most helpful. In 1622 the English, along with some of the shah's forces, attacked Hormuz and drove the Portuguese out of their trading center there. Initially, the Dutch cooperated with the English, but the two European powers eventually became rivals for access to the Iranian market. The English won and by the beginning of the nineteenth century had become the major power in the gulf.

Struggles between Iranians and Europeans contributed to a power vacuum along the coast of Oman. The English attacks on the Portuguese coincided with the rise of the Yarubid line of Ibadi imams in the interior of Oman. The Yarubids took advantage of Portuguese preoccupation with naval battles on the Iranian side of the gulf and conquered the coastal cities of Oman around 1650. The imams moved into the old Portuguese stronghold of Muscat and so brought the Omani coast and interior under unified Ibadi control for the first time in almost 1,000 years.

A battle over imamate succession in the early eighteenth century, however, weakened Yarubid rule. Between the 1730s and the 1750s, the various parties began to solicit support from outside powers. The Yarubid family eventually called in an Iranian army, which reestablished Iranian influence on the Omani coast. This time the Iranian hold on Oman was short-lived. In 1742 the Al Said, an Ibadi family from one of the coastal cities, convinced the local population to help it expel the Iranians; this put the leader, Ahmad ibn Said Al Said, in control of the Omani coast. His success sufficiently impressed the Ibadi leaders that they made him imam several years later.

The title of imam gave Ahmad ibn Said control over all of Oman, and under him and his successors the country prospered for more than a century. The Omanis extended their influence into the interior and into part of the present-day United Arab Emirates (UAE), consisting of the states of Abu Dhabi, Ajman, Al Fujayrah, Dubayy, Ras al Khaymah, Sharjah, and Umm al Qaywayn. They also collected tribute from as far away as present-day Bahrain and Iraq. The Omanis conquered the Dhofar region, which is part of present-day Oman but was not historically part of the region of Oman.

Oman also strengthened its hold on the Muslim cities of East Africa. These cities had been established by Omani traders in the tenth and eleventh centuries, but their connection to Oman had grown somewhat tenuous. At the beginning of the nineteenth century, however, the Al Said reasserted Omani authority in the area. Said ibn Sultan (1806–56) encouraged Omanis to settle in Zanzibar, an island off the African coast that had retained strong connections with Oman, and, from Zanzibar, he sent expeditions to take over several cities on the mainland (see Historical Patterns of Governance, ch. 6).

Although Ahmad ibn Said had succeeded in uniting Oman under an Ibadi imamate, the religious nature of his family's authority did not last long. His son, Said ibn Ahmad Al Said, was elected to the imamate after him, but no other family member won the official approval of the religious establishment. As a result, the Al Said called themselves *sultans,* a secular title having none of the religious associations of imam. They further distanced themselves from Ibadi traditions by moving their capital from Ar Rustaq, a traditional Ibadi center in the interior, to the trading center of Muscat. As a result of the move, the dichotomy between coast and interior that had traditionally split Oman was reinstituted.

The relationship between coast and interior was becoming a major feature within the gulf. In the eighteenth century, tribes from the interior increasingly began to move and settle into the coastal centers. Although the economy on the Arab side of the gulf did not match past prosperity, coastal conditions remained better than those in central Arabia. Limited agriculture existed, and the gulf waters were the site of rich oyster beds for harvesting pearls. The area's easy access to India, a major market for pearls, made the pearling industry particularly lucrative, and this drew the attention of tribes in the interior. The tribal migrations that occurred around 1800 put in place the tribes and clans that in 1993 controlled Kuwait, Bahrain, Qatar, and the UAE.

The Bani Utub moved from central Arabia into the northern gulf in the early 1800s, and one of its families, the Al Sabah, established itself as leaders of present-day Kuwait; another family, the Al Khalifa, established itself in present-day Bahrain. In the early 1800s, a number of other tribes were living along the gulf. Thus, Al Sabah and Al Khalifa control meant that these families ruled loosely over other tribes. Before taking Bahrain, the Al Khalifa first had established a settlement across the water on the peninsula that is present-day Qatar. Although the Al Khalifa were successful in taking Bahrain, they were unable to hold Qatar. They lost the peninsula to the Al Thani, the leading family from another tribe that, like the Bani Utub, had recently moved into the area.

The exact origins of the Al Thani are unknown, but they were already in Qatar when the Al Khalifa came. The origins of the Bani Yas tribe and the Al Qasimi family that rule in the present-day UAE are somewhat clearer. The Bani Yas originated in central Arabia and probably established themselves on the coast at Abu Dhabi around 1700; they later extended their influence to Dubayy. Historical evidence indicates that the Al Qasimi lived along the gulf during the pre-Islamic period and engaged in trade, pearling, and piracy.

Wahhabi Islam and the Gulf

The eighteenth and nineteenth centuries were a turbulent time for Arabia in general and for the gulf in particular. To the southeast, the Al Said of Oman were extending their influence northward, and from Iraq the Ottoman Turks were extending their influence southward. From the east, both the Iranians and the British were becoming increasingly involved in Arab affairs.

The most significant development in the region, however, was the Wahhabi movement. The name *Wahhabi* derived from Muhammad ibn Abd al Wahhab, who died in 1792. He grew up in an oasis town in central Arabia where he studied Hanbali law, usually considered the strictest of Islamic legal schools, with his grandfather. While still a young man, he left home and continued his studies in Medina and then in Iraq and Iran.

When he returned from Iran to Arabia in the late 1730s, he attacked as idolatry many of the customs followed by tribes in the area who venerated rocks and trees. He extended his criticism to practices of the Twelve Imam Shia, such as veneration of the tombs of holy men. He focused on the central Muslim principle that there is only one God and that this God does not share his divinity with anyone. From this principle, his students began to refer to themselves as *muwahhidun* (sing., *muwahhid*), or "unitarians." Their detractors referred to them as "Wahhabis."

Muhammad ibn Abd al Wahhab considered himself a reformer and looked for a political figure to give his ideas a wider audience. He found this person in Muhammad ibn Saud, the amir (see Glossary) of Ad Diriyah, a small town near Riyadh. In 1744 the two swore a traditional Muslim pledge in which they promised to work together to establish a new state (which later became present-day Saudi Arabia) based on Islamic principles. The limited but successful military campaigns of Muhammad ibn Saud caused Arabs from all over the peninsula to feel the impact of Wahhabi ideas.

The Wahhabis became known for a fanaticism similar to that of the early Kharijites. This fanaticism helped to intensify conflicts in the gulf. Whereas tribes from the interior had always raided settled communities along the coast, the Wahhabi faith provided them with a justification for continuing these incursions to spread true Islam. Accordingly, in the nineteenth century Wahhabi tribes, under the leadership of the Al Saud, moved at various times against Kuwait, Bahrain, and Oman. In Oman, the Wahhabi faith created internal dissension as well as an external menace because it proved popular with some of the Ibadi tribes in the Omani interior.

Wahhabi thought has had a special impact on the history of Qatar. Muhammad ibn Abd al Wahhab's ideas proved popular among many of the peninsula tribes, including the Al Thani, before the Al Khalifa attempted to take over the area from Bahrain at the beginning of the nineteenth century. As a result, Wahhabi beliefs motivated Al Thani efforts to resist the attempt of the Al Khalifa, who rejected Wahhabism, to gain control of the peninsula. In the early 1990s, Wahhabism distinguished Qatar religiously from its neighbors.

Wahhabi fervor was also significant in the history of the present-day UAE. The Al Qasimi tribes that had controlled the area since the eighteenth century adapted Wahhabi ideas and transferred the movement's religious enthusiasm to the piracy in which they had traditionally engaged. Whereas Wahhabi thought opposed all that was not orthodox in Islam, it particularly opposed non-Muslim elements such as the increasing European presence in the Persian Gulf.

Treaties with the British

The increased European presence resulted in large part from commercial competition between Al Qasimi merchants and British merchants for the lucrative trade between India and the Persian Gulf in the early nineteenth century. British merchants enlisted the British navy to assist them by launching attacks on Al Qasimi strongholds in the present-day UAE as early as 1809. The navy did not succeed in controlling the situation until 1819. In that year, the British sent a fleet from India that destroyed Ras al Khaymah, an Al Qasimi port at the eastern end of the gulf. From Ras al Khaymah, the British fleet destroyed Al Qasimi ships along both sides of the gulf.

The British had no desire to take over the desolate areas along the gulf; they only wished to control the trading cities. The British decided to leave most tribal leaders in power and concluded a series of treaties with them.

As a result of these truces, the Arab side of the gulf came to be known as the "Trucial Coast." This area had previously been under the nominal control of the sultan in Oman, although the Trucial Coast tribes were not part of the Ibadi imamate. The area has also been referred to as "Trucial Oman" to distinguish it from the part of Oman under the sultan that was not bound by treaty obligation.

In 1820 the British seemed primarily interested in controlling the Al Qasimi, whose main centers were Ras al Khaymah, Ajman, and Sharjah, which were all small ports along the southeastern gulf coast. The original treaties, however, also involved Dubayy and Bahrain, which were entrepôts. The inclusion of these ports brought two other extended families, the Bani Yas and the Al Khalifa, into the trucial system.

During the next 100 years, the British signed a series of treaties having wide-ranging provisions with other tribes in the gulf. As a result, by the end of World War I, leaders from Oman to Iraq had essentially yielded control of their foreign relations to Britain. Abu Dhabi entered into arrangements similar to those of Dubayy and Bahrain in 1835, Kuwait in 1899, and Qatar in 1916. The treaty whose terms convey the most representative sense of the relationship between Britain and the gulf states was the Exclusive Agreement of 1882. This text specified that the signatory gulf states (members of the present-day UAE) could not make any international agreements or host any foreign agent without British consent.

Because of these concessions, gulf leaders accepted the need for Britain to protect them from their more powerful neighbors. The main threat came from the Al Saud in central Arabia. Although the Ottomans had defeated the first Wahhabi empire of the Al Saud around 1820, the family rose up again about thirty years later; it threatened not only the Al Qasimi, who by this time had largely abandoned Wahhabi Islam, but also the Al Khalifa in Bahrain and the Ibadi sultan in Oman. In the early 1900s, the Al Saud also threatened Qatar despite its

Boys playing on cannon at Az Zubarah fort, Qatar Courtesy Anthony Toth

Restored ancient fort at Az Zubarah, Qatar; similar forts exist in most Persian Gulf states. Courtesy Anthony Toth

Wahhabi rulers. Only with British assistance could the Al Thani and other area rulers retain their authority.

The Al Saud were not the only threat. Despite its treaty agreement with Britain, Bahrain on several occasions had claimed Qatar because of the Al Khalifa involvement on the peninsula. The Omanis and Iranians had also claimed Bahrain because both have held the island at various times. Furthermore, the Ottomans claimed Bahrain occasionally and tried throughout the latter part of the nineteenth century to establish their authority in Kuwait and Qatar.

The British wished to maintain security on the route from Europe to India so that merchants could safely send goods between India and the gulf. Britain also sought to exclude the influence in the area of other powers, such as the Ottoman Empire and France.

East-West trade through the Persian Gulf dried up in the nineteenth century after the opening of the Suez Canal, which provided an all-water route to the Mediterranean Sea. Gulf merchants continued to earn substantial income from the slave trade, but international pressure, mostly from Britain, forced them to abandon this by 1900. Thereafter, the region continued to profit from the gulf pearl beds, but this industry declined in the 1930s as a result of the world depression, which reduced demand, and as a result of the Japanese development of a cheaper way to "breed" pearls, or make cultured pearls.

Oman, which was technically cut off from the gulf after it lost the Musandam Peninsula, which fell under British influence between 1853 and 1914, fared little better during the late nineteenth century. The fifth sultan in the Al Said line, Said ibn Sultan, ruled for almost the entire first half of the nineteenth century, increasing Omani influence and revenue tremendously. The resulting prosperity, however, was short-lived. The Omani fleet could not compete with the more technologically advanced European ships; thus the sultan gradually lost much of the income he had earned from customs duties on the Indian trade. At the same time, the increasing pressure to restrict the slave trade eliminated much of the revenue the Omanis had earned from East Africa.

The final blow to Oman's economic and political viability came after the death of Said ibn Sultan. When the Al Said could not agree on a successor, the British acted. They divided the Al Said holdings and gave Oman proper to one of the claimants to the throne and awarded Omani possessions in

East Africa to another. Thus, after 1856 there were two Al Said rulers. The one in Muscat, with a weakened merchant fleet and no East African revenues, was left with little support. Because of the different centers of power, the country became popularly known as Muscat and Oman.

The sultan's financial weakness contributed to his difficulty in maintaining his hold on the interior. The devout Ibadi population of the interior had long resented the more secular orientation of the coastal centers. As the sultan grew weaker, groups in the interior raised revolts against him on several occasions. Only with British help could the sultan remain in control, and his growing dependence on outsiders caused his relations with the Ibadi population to deteriorate. Whereas other gulf rulers used the British to protect them from their more powerful neighbors, the sultan needed the British to protect him from his subjects.

Discovery of Oil

At the end of World War I, the Arab states of the gulf were weak, with faltering economies and with local rulers who maintained their autonomy only with British assistance. The rulers controlled mainly the small port cities and some of the hinterland. The sultan in Oman claimed a somewhat larger area, but resistance to his rule made it difficult for him to exert his authority much beyond Muscat.

The discovery of oil in the region changed all this. Oil was first discovered in Iran, and by 1911 a British concern, the Anglo-Persian Oil Company (APOC), was producing oil in Iran. The British found oil in Iraq after World War I. In 1932 Standard Oil Company of California (Socal) discovered oil in commercial quantities in Bahrain. Socal then obtained a concession in Saudi Arabia in 1933 and discovered oil in commercial quantities in 1938.

A flurry of oil exploration activity occurred in the gulf in the 1930s with the United States and Britain competing with one another for oil concessions. One reason for the increased activity was that in 1932 the new Iranian government of Reza Shah Pahlavi revoked APOC's concession. Although the shah and the British later agreed on new terms, the threat of losing Iranian oil convinced the British in particular that they must find other sources. The small states of the Persian Gulf were a natural place to look. Geological conditions were similar to those in Iran, and, because of treaties signed between 1820 and

1916, the British had substantial influence and could restrict foreign access.

Oil exploration did not mean immediate wealth for Arab rulers of the area. Although the oil companies struck large deposits of oil in Bahrain almost immediately, it took longer in other countries to locate finds of commercial size. Oman, for instance, was unable to export oil until 1967. World War II delayed development of whatever fields had been discovered in the 1930s; so it was not until the 1950s that countries still technically dependent on Britain for their security began to earn large incomes. The oil fields in Kuwait were developed the most quickly, and by 1953 that nation had become the largest oil producer in the gulf. Considerably smaller fields in Qatar came onstream in commercial quantities in the 1950s, and Abu Dhabi began to export offshore oil in 1962. Dubayy began to profit from offshore oil deposits in the late 1960s.

Until the 1970s, foreign companies owned and managed the gulf oil industry. In most cases, European- and United States-based concerns formed subsidiaries to work in specific countries, and these subsidiaries paid fees to the local rulers, first for the right to explore for oil and later for the right to export the oil. When the first arrangements were made, local rulers had a weak bargaining position because they had few other sources of income and were eager to get revenues from the oil companies as fast as possible. Moreover, in 1930 no one knew the size of gulf oil reserves.

As production increased and the extent of oil deposits became known, indigenous rulers improved their terms. In the 1950s, rulers routinely demanded an equal share of oil company profits in addition to a royalty fee. By the 1970s, most of the gulf countries, which by then were independent of British control, bought major shares in the subsidiary companies that worked within their borders. By the early 1990s, many of these subsidiaries had become completely state-owned concerns. They continued to employ Western experts at the highest decision-making levels, but the local government had ultimate responsibility and profits.

Independence

With the exception of Saudi Arabia and Iraq, the Arab coast of the gulf is ruled by ten families: in Kuwait the Al Sabah; in Bahrain the Al Khalifa; in Qatar the Al Thani; in the present-day UAE the Al Nuhayyan in Abu Dhabi, the Al Nuaimi in

Ajman, the Al Sharqi in Al Fujayrah, the Al Maktum in Dubayy, the Al Qasimi in Ras al Khaymah and Sharjah, and the Al Mualla in Umm al Qaywayn; and the Al Said in present-day Oman. These families owe their positions to tribal leadership. It was on this traditional basis that the British had negotiated treaties with their leaders in the nineteenth century and the early twentieth century.

A major provision of these treaties was the recognition of sovereignty. The British were concerned that rulers of the weaker gulf families would yield some of their territory under pressure from more powerful groups, such as the Al Saud or the Ottomans. Accordingly, the treaties signed between 1820 and 1916 recognized the sovereignty of these rulers within certain borders and specified that these borders could not be changed without British consent. Such arrangements helped to put tribal alliances into more concrete terms of landownership. This meant that the Al Nuhayyan of Abu Dhabi, for example, not only commanded the respect of tribes in the hinterland but also owned, as it were, the land that those tribes used—in this case, about 72,000 square kilometers of Arabia.

Controlling, or owning, land became more important with the discovery of oil. When oil companies came to explore for oil, they looked for the "owner" of the land; in accordance with British treaties, they went to the area's leading families and agreed to pay fees to the heads of these families. As oil revenues increased, the leaders became rich. Although the leaders spent much of their new wealth on themselves, they also distributed it in the area they controlled according to traditional methods, which initially consisted mostly of largesse: gifts for friends, and food for whomever needed it. As time passed, the form of largesse became more sophisticated and included, for example, the construction of schools, hospitals, and roads to connect principal cities to towns in the interior.

Oil revenues did not change traditional tribal ideas about leadership. New money, however, increased the influence of area leaders by giving them more resources to distribute. Because of oil exploration, tribal boundaries became clearer, and areas were defined more precisely. Distinctions among tribes also became more evident. A new sense of identity appeared in gulf shaykhdoms and aroused a growing expectation that they should rule themselves. To do this, shaykhs had to cut themselves off from British control and protection.

By the early 1960s, this was something to which the British had little objection. India and Pakistan won their independence in 1947, meaning that Britain no longer had to worry about protecting the western flank of the subcontinent. Britain was also burdened by the tremendous sacrifices it made during World War II and could not be as globally involved as it had been before the war. Therefore, Britain yielded many of its strategic responsibilities to the United States in the postwar period or gave them up entirely. However, the British were bound to the gulf by treaties and so remained in the region, but it was clear by the 1960s that they sought to leave the gulf.

Kuwait was the first state to terminate the agreement connecting it with Britain. Oil production in Kuwait had developed more quickly than in neighboring states; as a result, Kuwaitis were better prepared for independence. They declared independence in 1961 but ran into immediate trouble when Iraq claimed their territory. The Iraqis argued that the British had recognized Ottoman sovereignty over Kuwait before World War I and, because the Ottomans had claimed to rule Kuwait from what was then the province of Iraq, the territory should belong to Iraq.

The British immediately sent troops to Kuwait to deter any Iraqi invasion. British and Kuwaiti positions were supported by the newly formed League of Arab States (Arab League), which recognized the new state and sent troops to Kuwait. The Arab League move left the Iraqis isolated. Accordingly, when a new Iraqi government came to power in 1963, one of its first steps was to give up its claim and recognize the independence of Kuwait.

The experience of Kuwait may have increased the anxiety of other gulf leaders about declaring their independence. Even into the 1970s, Iran and Saudi Arabia continued to make claims on territory in Bahrain and the UAE, although by the end of 1971 those states were independent, and nothing came of the claims. Gulf leaders also faced uncertainty about the form their states should take. Should they all, with the exception of Oman, whose situation was different in that its treaty relationship with Britain did not guarantee its borders as did treaties of the other gulf states, band together in the largest entity possible? Or should they break up into nine separate states, the smallest of which had little territory, few people, and no oil?

British action forced gulf leaders to decide. Because of domestic financial concerns, Britain decided in the late 1960s to eliminate its military commitments east of Suez. As a result, the gulf shaykhs held a number of meetings to discuss independence. Initially, leaders considered a state that would include all nine shaykhdoms; Qatar had even drawn up a constitution to this effect.

Various obstacles existed, however, to the creation of a "superstate." The ruler of Bahrain especially and to a lesser degree the ruler of Qatar were not satisfied with the political and economic status that their countries would enjoy in such an arrangement. They wished to have a preeminent position and therefore decided that independence would be preferable to federation. Accordingly, Bahrain declared its independence on August 15, 1971, and Qatar followed suit on September 3, 1971.

With regard to the other gulf shaykhdoms, their political options were limited. The only one with significant oil revenues was Abu Dhabi; Dubayy had only just begun to receive income from its oil. The five southern shaykhdoms—Ajman, Al Fujayrah, Ras al Khaymah, Sharjah, and Umm al Qaywayh—had at the time no mineral resources to provide revenues. Therefore, realistically, their only choice was to join in a federation in which they would be strengthened by the collective resources of their neighbors. Abu Dhabi and Dubayy considered such a federation advantageous to themselves because of their small size and limited population.

Thus, in 1971 soon after Qatar became independent, the remaining shaykhs, with the exception of the Al Qasimi in Ras al Khaymah, took the preliminary constitution that Qatar had originally drawn up for a nine-member confederation and adapted it to a six-member body. On December 2, 1971, one day after the British officially withdrew, these six shaykhdoms declared themselves a sovereign state.

Ras al Khaymah originally refused to join the confederation. The Al Qasimi, who ruled the area, claimed a number of islands and oil fields within the gulf to which Iran laid claim as well. In the negotiations to form the UAE, the Al Qasimi sought support for their claims from Arab states on the peninsula as well as from some Western powers. When their efforts proved unsuccessful, the Al Qasimi pulled out of the negotiations. They quickly realized, however, that they could not exist on their own and joined the union in February 1972.

Oman, which traditionally regarded itself as an independent state, had not contemplated joining the federation. Oman had experienced considerable British involvement in its affairs since the latter half of the nineteenth century. By taking over Zanzibar and other areas of East Africa formerly controlled by Oman, Britain had destroyed much of Oman's trade. The trade loss created resentment on the part of the Omanis, which grew in the twentieth century when the ruler granted oil concessions to British companies. The increasing British presence caused tensions that resulted in charges of foreign interference in Omani affairs. Many Omanis blamed the Al Said sultan for allowing foreign influence, which they considered detrimental to the religious and cultural life of the sultanate.

In 1958 the sultan withdrew to his palace in the coastal city of Salalah in Dhofar, the southern region that the Al Said had annexed in the nineteenth century, but took little interest in maintaining stability in the country. While keeping his military relationship with the British, he restricted Oman's contacts with the rest of the world, discouraged development, and prohibited political reform.

In the end, the Al Said control over a united Oman survived, but Said ibn Taimur did not. Although the sultan had partially reestablished his authority in the Omani interior, he was unable to handle the increasing complexity of domestic politics. By the 1960s, Omani affairs had become international issues. Western oil companies sought to work in the interior of the country, and foreign governments, such as the Marxist state of the People's Democratic Republic of Yemen, were sending arms to the rebels in Dhofar.

The Al Said hold over the region remained problematic, however, and in 1964 a rebellion arose, this time in Dhofar. The Dhofar rebellion, which was not brought under control until late 1975, obliged the sultan to seek foreign military assistance; therefore, British forces, particularly the air force, resumed activity in the country. The rebels pointed to British involvement as an indication of the sultan's illegitimacy and brought their case to the United Nations (UN), which eventually censured Britain for its continuing involvement in Oman.

Said ibn Taimur's policies frustrated many, not only in Oman but also in Britain, whose citizens were heavily involved in the sultan's military and intelligence apparatus. By 1970 these elements decided they could bear with the situation no longer; a coalition of Omani military and civilian forces, as well as British forces, attacked the palace and forced Said ibn Taimur to abdicate. They replaced him with his son, Qabus ibn Said Al Said, who had played no role in Said ibn Taimur's government. The sultan had actually locked his son in the palace for fear that Qabus ibn Said, who had been educated in Britain, would challenge his archconservative policies.

On his release, Qabus ibn Said consolidated the sultanate's hold over the interior and then solicited regional rather than British help to put down the rebellion in Dhofar. Other Arab leaders, as well as the shah of Iran, sent troops to Oman in response to Qabus ibn Said's requests; with the help of this coalition, by late 1975 the sultan ended the Dhofar rebellion.

Qabus ibn Said was not an Ibadi imam as the first rulers in his line had been, but in 1970 this was less important than it had been in earlier times. Only about 60 percent of Oman's population was Ibadi, concentrated in the northern mountains. Furthermore, the Dhofar region had a relatively short history of association with the rest of Oman.

Developments since Independence

Since the early 1970s, increased oil production and regional instability have dominated events in the Persian Gulf. Revenues from the oil industry grew dramatically after oil producers raised their prices unilaterally in 1973; as a result, funds available to gulf rulers increased. Governments began massive development projects that brought rapid material and social change. As of 1993, the turmoil that these changes caused had not yet stabilized. Those states that had benefited longest from oil money, such as Kuwait and Bahrain, made the greatest progress in adjusting to the new oil wealth. Oman—which has used its oil reserves only since the early 1970s and which had suffered under the repressive policies of Said ibn Taimur—saw substantially less progress.

The Iranian Revolution of 1979 challenged gulf stability. Many gulf leaders agreed with some of the social goals of the revolution and its efforts to tie Iran more firmly to its Islamic roots. But Iran's desire to spread the movement beyond its borders clearly threatened gulf leaders. Furthermore, several gulf states have significant Shia or Iranian minorities (Bahrain has a Shia majority although the ruling family is Sunni), and gulf rulers feared that Iran would use ethnic or sectarian loyalties to stir up such minorities.

As of 1993, however, Shia of the gulf had not responded enthusiastically to the Iranian call. Kuwait and Bahrain, which have the largest Shia populations, experienced some limited pro-Iranian demonstrations in 1979.

Iran was perhaps more threatening to gulf stability because of its strong anti-Western stance in world and regional politics. The new Iranian position stood in stark contrast to the gulf amirs' long history of involvement with the British and the close ties to the West that the oil industry entailed. Thus, the Iranian political worldview was one to which rulers in the gulf states could not subscribe.

In 1980 the outbreak of the Iran-Iraq War made the Iranian threat more concrete. The gulf states supported Iraq both in the Arab League, beginning in 1980, and through loans, beginning in 1981. The tanker war began in 1984 with Iraqi air attacks on neutral ships carrying oil and other goods from Iran. Iran, in turn, responded with mine laying and attacks on merchant shipping, causing added concern among the states of the region.

In 1981, partly as a result of such concerns, Bahrain, Kuwait, Oman, Qatar, Saudi Arabia, and the UAE formed the Gulf Cooperation Council (GCC) (see Collective Security under the Gulf Cooperation Council, ch. 7). The goal of the GCC has been to provide for regional defense and to coordinate policy on trade and economic issues. Although the GCC has taken steps to increase the military capabilities of various members, the region has remained dependent to a great extent on the protection of the Western powers. For instance, when the Iran-Iraq War made the gulf unsafe for oil tankers in 1987–88, it was ships from Europe and the United States that protected shipping and cleared the area of mines.

Whereas broader, regional alliances in the gulf have changed dramatically since the 1970s, individual political systems have remained relatively unchanged. All the gulf countries grant ultimate power to a single family, whose leading member rules as amir, but they also provide for an advisory body whose members are drawn from outside the royal family. Kuwait and Bahrain have gone beyond this and have set up separate parliaments with limited power to draft legislation. However, the Al Sabah and the Al Khalifa have sometimes dissolved these bodies; thus, it remains uncertain whether parliaments will become a permanent feature of gulf politics.

The ruling families' hold on power has been challenged at various times. More problematic is the manner in which the gulf states have distributed individual citizenship. Since the 1930s, the population has increased dramatically because of the oil boom, but the number of citizens has not increased correspondingly. Most of the gulf states place restrictions on citizenship, requiring that an individual trace his or her roots in the country to before 1930. Accordingly, the millions of people that have poured into the region since the 1940s have only partial legal status and lack political rights in the countries in which they reside. Although they may have lived there for two generations, they can be asked to leave at any time.

Tribal Nature of Gulf Society

The gulf states have not granted citizenship freely for two reasons: first, they are reluctant to share wealth with recent arrivals; second, the tribal nature of gulf society does not admit new members easily. A tribe usually traces its lineage to a particular eponymous ancestor. The standard Arabic reference to tribe is *bani fulan,* or "the sons [*bani*] of so-and-so." The Bani al Murrah in Saudi Arabia, for example, trace their line back to a figure named Murrah, who lived some time before the Prophet.

Over a period of 1,500 years, the sons of Murrah, or any other ancient figure, have tended to become numerous, making further distinctions necessary. Accordingly, tribes are divided into clans and then into households (*fukhud;* sing., *fakhd*). Households include groups of single families. Together this extended group of families calls itself a tribe. Each tribe has certain characteristics, such as different speech, dress, and customs. But since the 1950s, speech has become less of a distinguishing factor because of the fluidity of gulf society.

The name of a tribe may also reflect some past event. For example, the name *Utub*—the tribe to which the Al Sabah of Kuwait and the Al Khalifa of Bahrain belong—comes from the Arabic word for wander (*atab*). In 1744 the tribe "wandered" out of the desert and into the gulf area and became the Utub.

Two of the most important tribal groups in Arabia are the Qahtan and the Adnan, whose roots stem from the belief that tribes in the north of the peninsula were descended from Adnan, one of Ismail's sons, and that tribes in the south were descended from Qahtan, one of Noah's sons. People in the gulf often attribute the structure of tribal alliances to this north-south distinction, and many still classify their tribes as Adnani or Qahtani.

Historically, the tribal nature of society has occasioned petty warfare in the gulf. Arab tribes have attacked each other since before the Islamic era, but tribal customs have prevented these attacks from turning into random violence. Clans, however, have defected from their tribe and made alliances with other tribes, and tribes have sometimes banded together to form a more powerful group.

Moreover, although some tribes may trace their lineage to some heroic figure, the real identity of the tribe lies in the people that currently compose it. In the tribe, an individual bases his or her sense of self-esteem on the honor of the tribe as a whole.

In Arabia it was impossible to survive in the desert alone, and so families banded together to find water and move their flocks to new grazing lands. Once they established the necessary resources through collective effort, they guarded them jealously and refused to share them with outsiders. It therefore became necessary to set up boundaries between members of the group or between the tribe and outsiders. The tribe worked to restrict membership in order to preserve its sense of solidarity. As a result, birth into the right family tended to be the only way to become a member of a tribe. Marriage sometimes extended the tribal line beyond blood lines, but, in general, people tended to marry within the tribe and only went outside to establish alliances with other tribes.

The emphasis on the group precluded the rise of a strong leader. Accordingly, tribal leadership is often described as "the first among equals," suggesting a collective leadership in which one among a number of leaders is recognized as the most authoritative. This principal leader must continue to consult with his lesser colleagues and so rules by consensus.

An extension of this pattern of leadership is the concept of leading families within the tribe. Although tribalism tends to discourage inherited authority, traditions of leadership are nevertheless passed down, and tribes expect that certain families will furnish them with leaders generation after generation. This pattern occurred when tribes that were previously nomadic settled down in oases or coastal areas. It then became more likely that certain families would accumulate wealth, whether in food or in goods, and with this wealth would increase their authority. In this way, the individual families that in the 1990s controlled the gulf states established themselves around 1800. Relations with the British and the discovery of oil continued that process.

The existence of these ruling families is perhaps the most obvious manifestation of Arab tribalism in gulf society in 1993. Another manifestation is the collective manner in which these families rule. In most of these states, the position of amir is not passed from father to son but rotates among different parallel patrilineal lines. This makes the appointment of the next amir an open issue and something on which the entire family must agree. The family also participates in the various consultative bodies that exist to advise the leader. Such bodies, which include figures outside the ruling family, help to institutionalize the first among equals system in these states.

The way that government officials are appointed reflects the importance of tribal connections. Members of the ruling family are accommodated first, followed by families and tribes with whom the rulers have been traditionally allied. In Bahrain, for example, the ruling Al Khalifa have given the major positions in the bureaucracy to Sunni Arabs from tribes that helped them rule the island in the nineteenth century. The Al Khalifa have given lesser positions to Shia Arabs from merchant families with whom they engaged in the pearl industry but with whom they had no tribal alliances.

Tribal cohesiveness is also reflected in the efforts of the gulf states to restrict citizenship. The gulf has always been relatively cosmopolitan, and its port cities have included Arab Shia from Iraq, freed slaves from Africa, Indian pearl traders, and Iranian merchants, in addition to tribal Sunni Arabs. (In 1939, for example, before the oil boom started, 39 percent of Qatar's population was non-Arab.) The dominant Arab tribes have accommodated many of these groups, and those who arrived in the region before 1930 became full citizens of the gulf states, albeit without the connections of tribal Arabs. The tremendous influx since 1940 has caused the naturally restrictive nature of tribal society to reassert itself to prevent a further dilution of tribal identities.

Modern Arab politics, however, often speaks of a single Arab nation in which all Arabs might be citizens. This has led to the notion that Arabs should have rights in the gulf states simply because of their ethnicity. The continuing exodus of millions of Palestinian Arabs since 1948, and their subsequent residence throughout the Arab world, has added urgency to the demand that individual Arab states define their qualifications for citizenship. Many Arabs argue that Palestinians in particular, but other Arabs as well, should be accepted as citizens in the gulf. Gulf leaders have understandably opposed this for fear that nontribal Arabs would challenge traditional ruling institutions. Although people from all over the world may come to the gulf to work, sovereignty and citizenship are closely guarded by the predominantly tribal population that has its roots in the Arabian Peninsula. In this way, the Persian Gulf coast has preserved its ties with the Arab interior that form the essence of its identity.

*   *   *

The literature on Bahrain, Kuwait, Oman, Qatar, and the UAE may be divided into two groups: books on Oman and books on the rest of the gulf states. Calvin Allen has a relatively brief study of the modern history of Oman entitled *Oman: The Modernization of the Sultanate.* John C. Wilkinson has written a number of scholarly studies on Oman, including his recent work, *The Imamate Tradition of Oman.* This is an excellent and detailed study of most aspects of Omani history.

For the rest of the gulf, a number of brief studies exist, of which the most recent is *The Arab Gulf and the Arab World,* a collection of articles on various aspects of modern gulf life edited by B.R. Pridham; it contains little on the history of the region. For more historical background, the reader may consult an older but more substantial collection edited by Alvin Cottrell entitled *The Persian Gulf States.* Further history can be found in Donald Hawley's *The Trucial States.*

Of books on particular countries or issues, among the best are Fuad Khuri's *Tribe and State in Bahrain,* which considers the social, religious, and ethnic divisions of the island nation; Fred H. Lawson's *Bahrain: The Modernization of Autocracy*; and Jill Crystal's *Oil and Politics in the Gulf* and *Kuwait: The Transformation of an Oil State.* A recent brief work on the UAE by Malcolm C. Peck, *The United Arab Emirates,* is very good. Abdulrasool al-Mossa's study, *Immigrant Labor in Kuwait,* provides a description of the situation of foreign workers in the gulf. Religious disturbances in the gulf are discussed in relevant chapters of Robin Wright's *Sacred Rage.* (For further information and complete citations, see Bibliography.)

Chapter 2. Kuwait

Crest of the State of Kuwait

Country

Formal Name: State of Kuwait.

Short Form: Kuwait.

Term for Citizens: Kuwaiti(s); adjectival form, Kuwaiti.

Capital: Kuwait (city of Kuwait frequently used to distinguish it from country).

Date of Independence: June 19, 1961.

Geography

Size: About 17,818 square kilometers.

Topography: Almost entirely flat desert.

Climate: Hot, dry, desert climate; sandstorms in June and July; some rain, mainly in spring.

Boundaries: Mostly defined; United Nations post-Persian Gulf War 1992 boundary settlement accepted by Kuwait but rejected by Iraq.

Society

Population: March 1992 estimate 1,175,000, of whom 53 percent Kuwaiti; a decline from preinvasion population of 2,155,000 (mid-1990 estimate), of whom 27 percent Kuwaiti.

Education: Free from preschool through university and compulsory to age fourteen. Adult literacy rate 74 percent in 1990.

Health: National comprehensive health care system extensive and continuing to expand and improve. Life expectancy in 1990 seventy-two years for males and seventy-six for females.

NOTE—The Country Profile contains updated information as available.

Ethnic Groups: Majority of population Arab. Noncitizen population shifted from predominantly Arab to predominantly Asian in 1980s. After 1990–91 Iraqi occupation, exodus of about 370,000 of the 400,000 Palestinians.

Religion: Most Kuwaitis are Sunni Muslims. About 20 percent of citizens are Shia Muslims. Most foreigners are also Muslims, the majority Sunni.

Economy

Gross Domestic Product (GDP): In 1990 United Nations Development Programme estimated US$15,984 per capita GDP.

Oil Industry: Provided 41 percent of GDP and 87 percent of government revenues in 1989, 58 percent of government revenues in 1990, and 11 percent of government revenues in 1991, showing effects of Persian Gulf War. Crude oil production in 1992 (after oil well restoration during year) about 41 million barrels, compared with about 387 million barrels in 1985.

Industry: About 14 percent of GDP in 1989. Largest industries petrochemicals and building materials.

Agriculture: Little farming—mostly vegetables and fruits. Most food imported. Some fishing.

Exports: US$11.5 billion in 1989; mostly crude oil and refined products. Asia and Western Europe main markets.

Imports: US$6.3 billion in 1989—largely such finished products as appliances and vehicles from industrialized nations, particularly Japan, United States, and Western Europe.

Currency and Exchange Rate: Kuwaiti dinar. On March 1, 1994, exchange rate US$1 = KD3.55.

Fiscal Year: July 1 to June 30.

Transportation and Telecommunications

Transportation: In 1993 more than 3,900 kilometers of roads, of which 3,000 kilometers paved. Three major ports: Ash Shuaybah, Ash Shuwaykh, and Mina al Ahmadi. Airlines use

Kuwait International Airport.

Telecommunications: Prior to Persian Gulf War, excellent telecommunications system; all telecommunications severely damaged during Iraqi occupation and being restored.

Government and Politics

Government: 1962 constitution specifies "hereditary amirate" and fixes succession among male "descendants of the late Mubarak Al Sabah." Ruler in 1994 was Jabir al Ahmad al Jabir Al Sabah, who became amir in 1977. Sixty-member (fifty elected, ten appointed) National Assembly created in 1963, suspended from 1976 to 1980 and again in 1986; replaced in 1990 with partially elected National Council. National Assembly reconstituted by October 1992 elections. Opposition and independent candidates—including some nineteen Islamists—won thirty to thirty-five seats.

Politics: Al Sabah family dominates political events, but several prominent merchant families also powerful. Opposition, independent, and Islamist elements becoming stronger in early 1990s. Political parties illegal.

Foreign Relations: As result of Iraqi invasion of August 2, 1990, and 1991 Persian Gulf War, Kuwait's relations with the West and Gulf Cooperation Council (GCC) states, particularly Saudi Arabia, strengthened to prevent future Iraqi incursion. In addition to GCC, Kuwait belong to more than twenty international organizations, including United Nations, League of Arab States, Nonaligned Movement, Organization of the Islamic Conference, and Organization of the Petroleum Exporting Countries.

National Security

Armed Forces: In mid-1993, according to *The Military Balance, 1993–94*, personnel strength 13,700, including 1,000 central staff: army, 9,000; navy, 1,200 (including coast guard); and air force, 2,500. Matériel of all services largely destroyed or captured in Persian Gulf War; being renewed by large-scale foreign arms purchases.

KUWAIT CAPTURED THE WORLD'S ATTENTION on August 2, 1990, when Iraqi forces invaded and occupied the country, catalyzing a series of events that culminated in military intervention and ultimate victory by United States-led coalition forces in February 1991. In 1993 it appeared that the invasion and its aftermath would have a lasting effect on the people, the economy, and the politics of Kuwait. Once a small gulf shaykh-dom known locally as a center for pearl diving and boat construction, Kuwait came to international prominence in the post-World War II era largely because of its enormous oil revenues. Yet its history as an autonomous political entity is much older, dating back to the eighteenth century. At that time, the town of Kuwait was settled by migrants from central Arabia who arrived at what was then a lightly populated fishing village under the suzerainty of the Bani Khalid tribe of Arabia. Members of one family, the Al Sabah, have ruled Kuwait from that time.

Since 1977 Kuwait has been ruled by Shaykh Jabir al Ahmad al Jabir Al Sabah and his designated successor, Shaykh Saad al Abd Allah as Salim Al Sabah, the prime minister and crown prince. In the postwar period, these men have supported, with some ambivalence, the strengthening of popular participation in decision making as provided for in the constitution.

Geography

Kuwait is located at the far northwestern corner of the Persian Gulf, known locally as the Arabian Gulf (see fig. 3). It is a small state of about 17,818 square kilometers, a little smaller than the state of New Jersey. At its most distant points, it is about 200 kilometers north to south and 170 kilometers east to west.

Shaped roughly like a triangle, Kuwait borders the gulf to the east, with 195 kilometers of coast. Kuwait includes within its territory nine gulf islands, two of which, Bubiyan (the largest) and Warbah, are largely uninhabited but strategically important. The island of Faylakah, at the mouth of Kuwait Bay, is densely inhabited. It is believed to be the outermost point of the ancient civilization of Dilmun, which was centered in what is present-day Bahrain. Faylakah is the site of an ancient Greek

47

temple built by the forces of Alexander the Great. Kuwait's most prominent geographic feature is Kuwait Bay, which indents the shoreline for about forty kilometers, providing natural protection for the port of Kuwait and accounting for nearly one-half the state's shoreline.

To the south and west, Kuwait shares a long border of 250 kilometers with Saudi Arabia. The boundary between Kuwait and Saudi Arabia was set by the Treaty of Al Uqayr in 1922, which also established the Kuwait-Saudi Arabia Neutral Zone of 5,700 square kilometers. In 1966 Kuwait and Saudi Arabia agreed to divide the Neutral Zone; the partitioning agreement making each country responsible for administration in its portion was signed in December 1969. The resources in the area, since then known as the Divided Zone, are not affected by the agreement, and the oil from onshore and offshore fields continues to be shared equally between the two countries.

The third side of the triangle is the 240 kilometers of historically contested border to the north and west that Kuwait shares with Iraq. Although the Iraqi government, which had first asserted a claim to rule Kuwait in 1938, recognized the borders with Kuwait in 1963 (based on agreements made earlier in the century), it continued to press Kuwait for control over Bubiyan and Warbah islands through the 1960s and 1970s. In August 1990, Iraq invaded Kuwait and, shortly thereafter, formally incorporated the entire country into Iraq. Under United Nations (UN) Security Council Resolution 687, after the restoration of Kuwaiti sovereignty in 1991, a UN commission undertook formal demarcation of the borders on the basis of those agreed to in 1963. The boundary was demarcated in 1992, but Iraq refuses to accept the commission's findings.

Kuwait has a desert climate, hot and dry. Rainfall varies from seventy-five to 150 millimeters a year across the country; actual rainfall has ranged from twenty-five millimeters a year to as much as 325 millimeters. In summer, average daily high temperatures range from 42°C to 46°C; the highest recorded temperature is 51.5°C. The summers are relentlessly long, punctuated mainly by dramatic dust storms in June and July when northwesterly winds cover the cities in sand. In late summer, which is more humid, there are occasional sharp, brief thunderstorms. By November summer is over, and cooler winter weather sets in, dropping temperatures to as low as 3°C at night; daytime temperature is in the upper 20s°C range. Frost

rarely occurs; rain is more common and falls mostly in the spring.

The land was formed in a recent geologic era. In the south, limestone rises in a long, north-oriented dome that lies beneath the surface. It is within and below this formation that the principal oil fields, Kuwait's most important natural resource, are located. In the west and north, layers of sand, gravel, silt, and clay overlie the limestone to a depth of more than 210 meters. The upper portions of these beds are part of a mass of sediment deposited by a great wadi whose most recent channel was the Wadi al Batin, the broad shallow valley forming the western boundary of the country. On the western side of the Ar Rawdatayn geological formation, a freshwater aquifer was discovered in 1960 and became Kuwait's principal water source. The supply is insufficient to support extensive irrigation, but it is tapped to supplement the distilled water supply that fills most of the country's needs. The only other exploited aquifer lies in the permeable zone in the top of the limestone of the Ash Shuaybah field south and east of the city of Kuwait. Unlike water from the Ar Rawdatayn aquifer, water from the Ash Shuaybah aquifer is brackish. Millions of liters a day of this water are pumped for commercial and household purposes.

The bulk of the Kuwaiti population lives in the coastal capital of the city of Kuwait. Smaller populations inhabit the nearby city of Al Jahrah, smaller desert and coastal towns, and, prior to the Persian Gulf War, some of the several nearby gulf islands, notably Faylakah.

Society

Population

In the summer of 1990, Kuwait had an estimated population of 2,155,000. The most dramatic division in this preinvasion population was that between the national population of Kuwaiti citizens and the larger population, more than 70 percent of the total population, of foreign workers (see table 2, Appendix).

The percentage of foreigners in the population grew steadily after World War II, following the rise in oil revenues and the consequent government development programs with their sudden need for substantial labor. The labor market came to consist increasingly of foreigners for a number of reasons. The most important factor was the small size of the indigenous population and, in the early years, their low level of education. As oil revenues and government investment in education produced a generation of highly educated Kuwaitis, they began to replace foreigners at the highest levels of employment, but even this highly educated population was small. The low participation rates of women in the work force also contributed to the reliance on foreign workers. Restrictions on female dress and behavior in public and consequently on labor force participation are not as strong as they are elsewhere in the gulf, notably in Saudi Arabia. Customary norms, however, coupled with higher family incomes, which reduce the need to employ more family members and lessen the incentive for individuals to undertake the more unpleasant sorts of work, combine to promote a lower labor force participation rate in the national population.

The importance of foreign workers to the economy in the post-World War II period is difficult to exaggerate. Most of these foreigners were male. Most were employed by the state. Most were in Kuwait for relatively short periods (40 percent used to stay less than five years); Arabs used to stay somewhat longer than non-Arabs. Historically, Arabs constituted the bulk of the non-Kuwaiti population. In addition to a large number of Palestinian workers, estimated at 400,000 in 1990, there were numerous Egyptians, Iraqis, Syrians, and Lebanese. A smaller but significant and growing number of workers came from Asia. In the early 1980s, the composition of the work force shifted, and by 1985 slightly more than one-half the foreign workers (52 percent) were Asian and less than one-half (46 percent) were Arab. Africans, Europeans, and United States citizens constitute the remainder. The government favors Asian workers because of their lower labor costs, and, because they are unable to speak Arabic or lay a claim to oil revenues on the basis of Arab nationalism, Asian workers are more apt to return home in a few years, thus raising fewer social and political issues.

The foreign population does not enjoy the economic and political rights of the national population. Not being citizens, they can neither vote nor run for seats in the National Assembly. They are not allowed to own real property. They cannot form their own unions; although they can join Kuwaiti unions, they are prohibited from voting or running for union offices. Acquiring Kuwaiti citizenship is very difficult, and the number of naturalized citizens remains low.

Traditional dhow, characteristic of Persian Gulf fishing and trading
Courtesy Aramco World

The large number of foreigners creates social tensions between foreigners and the indigenous population. Foreign workers, particularly those who have worked many years in Kuwait, resent the discrimination against them. Citizens often view foreign workers with suspicion, if not hostility. Even before the Persian Gulf War, public debate often focused on a perceived compromise between Kuwait's economic needs and its security needs.

Although the most important social division in the country is between citizens and foreigners, the indigenous population is internally divided along a number of lines as well. The first is sectarian. The majority of Kuwaiti nationals are Sunni (see Glossary) Muslims; the minority are Shia (see Glossary). Figures have never been published on the number of Shia, but estimates in the 1980s ranged from 15 to 25 percent of the national population. Shia are a diverse group. Some are Arab, many the descendants of immigrants from Ash Sharqiyah (Eastern Province) in Saudi Arabia or from Bahrain. Others come from Arab families who moved from the Arabian side of the gulf to Iran, stayed awhile, and then returned. Others are of Iranian origin, who often speak Farsi as well as Arabic at home and sometimes maintain business or family ties with Iranians across the gulf. After the Iranian Revolution of 1979 and the subsequent Iran-Iraq War of 1980–88, this Shia community experienced a renewed sense of sectarian identification. The identification resulted from sympathy with their revolutionary coreligionists in Iran and from increasing government and social discrimination. During the 1980s, the tension between Sunnis and Shia, which had erupted occasionally in the past, became somewhat sharper.

Kuwaitis are also divided to a certain extent along class lines. Although the national population is generally well off because of the state's generous employment policies regarding nationals and its extensive social services, important divisions nonetheless exist between the country's economic elite and the rest of the population. The wealthiest Kuwaitis are members either of the ruling family or of what was once a powerful and still distinct merchant class. Many of these are descendants of the Bani Utub, the original central Arabian tribe that settled Kuwait in the eighteenth century. The most important and wealthiest of the Bani Utub are members of the Al Sabah, the ruling family of Kuwait. The economic elite is largely Sunni. However, some Shia families and individual Shia are also wealthy.

Despite these internal divisions, the national population is also characterized by a strong sense of national identity. There are no important ethnic divisions: the national population is overwhelmingly Arab. The major sectarian divisions are subsumed in the larger shared Islamic identity. Unlike many of its neighbors, Kuwait is not a twentieth-century colonial fabrication. It has been an autonomous political and social unit since the eighteenth century. In the intervening years, a strong sense of local identity has arisen. This national sense was deeply reinforced by the Iraqi occupation.

Education

In 1993 Kuwait's population was highly educated, both in comparison to other states in the region and in comparison to its pre-oil education levels. The impressive education system was brought about by a conscious government decision, made possible by revenues from oil that began in the 1950s, to invest heavily in human resources.

Although the pre-oil education system was modest by 1993 standards, it was still impressive, given the limited finances at the time. In the early 1900s, education consisted largely of Quran schools, offering basic literacy training in the context of religious instruction. This system provided some formal schooling for nearly all boys and some girls. Wealthy families often sent sons abroad for further education. In the first decades of the twentieth century, merchants anxious for more extensive training for their sons opened a few private schools, notably the Mubarakiyyah School in 1911 and the Ahmadiyyah School in 1921. In the 1930s, merchants established the Education Council and expanded the system to include four new primary schools, including one for girls. The government soon took over this growing system and, with new oil revenues after World War II, rapidly expanded the system. In 1956 the government laid down the basis of the education system that still existed in 1993: kindergarten and primary, middle, and secondary schools. A 1965 law, largely enforced, made education compulsory until the age of fourteen. A small system of private schools also developed. Public education, including preschool and higher education, was from the beginning free for all nationals. The government absorbs not only the costs of schools but also those of books, uniforms, meals, transportation, and incidental expenses. In preinvasion Kuwait, the majority of the students in the education system were non-Kuwaitis (see table 3, Appendix).

The apex of the public education system is Kuwait University, which the government established in 1966. More than half the students at Kuwait University are women, in part because families are more likely to send boys abroad for study. The government also subsidizes hundreds of students in university study abroad, many in the United States.

As a result of these efforts, the school population and the literacy rate increased steadily. By the mid-1980s, literacy and education rates were high. Although only 55 percent of the citizen population was literate in 1975, by 1985 that percentage had increased to 73.6 percent (84 percent for males and 63.1 percent for females). In 1990 the overall literacy rate was 74 percent. The total number of teachers increased from just under 3,000 at independence in 1961 to more than 28,000 in academic year 1988–89; the number of schools increased from 140 to 642 during the same period (see table 4, Appendix).

The education system has its problems, however. For example, it relies heavily on foreign teachers. In the late 1950s, almost 90 percent were non-Kuwaitis. Despite a long-standing government effort to indigenize education, the system continues to rely heavily on foreigners. The system also often fails to train graduates in fields that correspond to Kuwait's most pressing labor needs. Especially in higher education, the system produces many graduates with training in liberal arts and few with training in vocational subjects.

Health and Welfare

The health care system and health conditions also improved dramatically in the years after oil revenues brought wealth to the country. Kuwait's first attempts to introduce a modern health care system date back to the first years of the twentieth century when the ruler, Shaykh Mubarak Al Sabah the Great, invited doctors from the Arabian Mission of the Dutch Reformed Church in the United States to establish a clinic. By 1911 the group had organized a hospital for men and in 1919 a small hospital for women. In 1934 the thirty-four-bed Olcott Memorial Hospital opened. Between 1909 and 1946, Kuwait experienced gradual, albeit limited, improvement in health conditions. General mortality stood between twenty and twenty-five per 1,000 population and infant mortality between 100 and 125 per 1,000 live births. After the government began receiving oil revenues, it expanded the health care system, beginning with the opening of the Amiri Hospital in 1949. The Kuwait Oil Company (KOC) also opened some small health facilities. By 1950 general mortality had fallen to between seventeen and twenty-three per 1,000 population and infant mortality to between eighty and 100 per 1,000 live births.

In the 1950s, the government introduced a comprehensive health care system offering free services to the entire population. Free health care was so extensive that it even included veterinary medicine. Expenditures on health ranked third in the national budget, after public works and education. As with education, the system relied heavily on foreigners. Most of the physicians were foreigners, particularly Egyptians. Critics charged the designers of the system with paying undue attention to acquiring the most modern and expensive medical equipment, without regard to the country's health priorities, and favoring treatment over prevention. Nonetheless, improvements in available health care and in public health were dramatic (see table 5, Appendix). The number of doctors grew from 362 in 1962 to 2,641 in 1988. The doctor-to-patient ratio improved from one to 1,200 to one to 600. Infant and child mortality rates dropped dramatically; in 1990 the infant mortality rate was fifteen per 1,000 live births. Life expectancy increased ten years in the postindependence years, putting Kuwait at a level comparable to most industrialized countries. In 1990 life expectancy for males was seventy-two years and for females seventy-six years.

In addition to a comprehensive system of health care, the government provides residents with one of the world's most encompassing social service systems. Not only does it indirectly support the national population through guaranteed state employment and subsidized services (such as water and electricity), but it also supports those most in need through direct subsidies. These include the disabled, the elderly, the unemployed, students and their families, the widowed, the unmarried, and even the families of prisoners.

By 1990 Kuwait had an extensive welfare program, exceeded perhaps by no other country. Citizens receive free medical services from highly trained practitioners in modern facilities; free education through the university level; subsidized food, housing, utilities, and transportation; and various other benefits. For all this, they pay no taxes: the system is supported by oil revenues from outside the country. On the eve of the Iraqi invasion, the United Nations Development Programme placed Kuwait at the top of its annual human development index with a life expectancy of 73.4 years, an adult literacy rate of 73 percent, and a real per capita gross domestic product (GDP—see Glossary) of US$15,984. The benefits of the welfare system, however, are unevenly distributed among the population. Noncitizens in particular benefit much less, and many, especially those from Arab states and those who have worked many years in Kuwait, resent their disadvantaged position.

Economy

In the eighteenth and nineteenth centuries, Kuwait's economy was based on trade. The city of Kuwait rivaled Basra in Iraq as an entrepôt for trade between India and parts of the Middle East. Kuwait became a conduit for commerce from the gulf to Asia, Africa, and Europe. It was Kuwait's fine natural harbor that first attracted the Bani Utub settlers, and they made much of this maritime advantage. In the nineteenth and early twentieth centuries, the economy relied primarily on pearl diving, and merchants and sailors harvested the gulf's natural pearl banks, which were among the richest in the world. In the first decades of the twentieth century, Kuwait had about 700 boats, employing approximately 15,000 men. When the pearl-diving season (mid-May to mid-September) ended, Kuwaiti merchants used their ships for long-distance trade. From this trade, a shipbuilding industry developed, and Kuwaiti craft became known throughout coastal Arabia for their quality. Fishing was also a small but important industry. The tradition of seafaring and trade gave Kuwait a thriving merchant class and an outward orientation that remained important into the 1990s.

Although prosperous by regional standards, Kuwait's economy offered only a meager existence to most of the population, especially those outside the ruling families and the merchant families. Even this meager existence began to suffer with the decline of pearling. That industry, the basis of Kuwait's economy, came to a sudden end in the 1920s with the development of the process of making cultured pearls in Japan and then the Great Depression. Fortuitously, the pearl industry declined just as a new source of revenue was emerging. In 1938 oil was discovered in Kuwait. Once oil exports began in the immediate post-World War II years, economic development became nearly continuous.

Oil Industry

For centuries, oil seepages in the desert had indicated oil below the surface. This oil came to the attention of European and United States developers. In 1911 the Anglo-Persian Oil Company (APOC), which was developing oil fields in Iran, requested permission to negotiate a concession from Kuwait. The British government refused the request (as it was entitled to do so under an 1899 treaty that granted Britain substantial control of Kuwait's foreign policy), but two years later the British government commissioned a geological survey of the area. In 1913 the British government signed an agreement with Kuwait's Shaykh Mubarak the Great in which he promised to grant concessions only to companies approved by the British government, clarifying and reaffirming the agreement of 1899. World War I interrupted another effort to negotiate a concession. By this time, the British government had purchased 51 percent ownership in APOC as part of an effort to ensure oil supplies for the Royal Navy.

After World War I, interest in oil grew. APOC continued attempts to obtain a Kuwait concession. Meanwhile, in the 1920s, Gulf Oil of the United States began to seek concessions in the gulf to overcome its lack of crude oil sources. British treaties with most rulers in the gulf, including Kuwait, made it difficult for non-British companies to gain access, although the United States government pressured the British to provide equal treatment to United States oil firms. In 1932 Gulf Oil and APOC formed a joint company to negotiate a concession in Kuwait, and this effort received British government approval. In 1934 Kuwait's ruler, Shaykh Ahmad al Jabir Al Sabah, signed a concession agreement with the Kuwait Oil Company (KOC), the firm jointly owned by APOC and Gulf Oil.

KOC began surveying in 1935. Drilling started in 1936 on the north shore of Kuwait Bay, but no oil was found. The second attempt, in the desert, struck a gusher in 1938 in an area that subsequently was called the Al Burqan field, one of the largest and most productive fields in the world (see fig. 4). World War II slowed the development of the industry, but at the end of the war, pipelines and other facilities were completed that could handle 30,000 barrels per day (bpd—see Glossary) of crude oil. Commercial export of crude oil began in June 1946. Production amounted to 5.9 million barrels in 1946 and 16.2 million barrels in 1947. KOC subsequently discovered seven additional oil fields, and production continued to increase until it peaked in 1972. (In 1954 KOC's parent company, APOC, was renamed British Petroleum—BP.)

In the years after World War II, other companies received smaller concessions, in particular for offshore oil, but KOC, which the government nationalized in 1976 (retroactively to 1975), retained the lion's share. Subsequent concessions contained progressively better terms for Kuwait, partly because of the entrance of small oil companies anxious to acquire crude oil sources and partly because of the activities and exchanges of information among oil-producing states. Payments were substantially higher, the length of concessions was shorter, schedules for relinquishing underdeveloped areas were established, and opportunities for Kuwaiti participation in the companies were increased.

The American Independent Oil Company (Aminoil) was the successful bidder for Kuwait's rights in the Neutral Zone, receiving in June 1948 a sixty-year concession for exploration and production. Aminoil, which was owned by a number of small United States oil companies, had a joint operation with the Getty Oil Company, which held the Saudi rights in the Neutral Zone. The Arabian American Oil Company (Aramco, the main developer of Saudi Arabia's oil fields) reportedly viewed the terms given Kuwait by Aminoil as unfavorable and relinquished its concession in the Neutral Zone, which Getty won. Aminoil started exploratory drilling in 1949 but did not strike

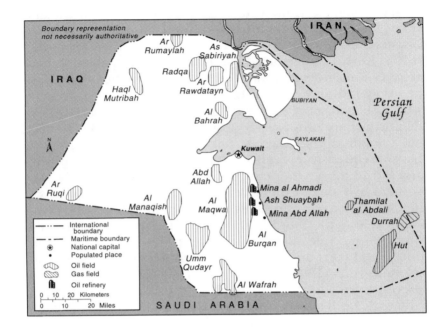

Figure 4. Kuwait: Oil Fields, Gas Fields, and Refineries, 1993

oil until 1953. Production began in 1954. Production from the Neutral Zone was shared between the two countries, and Aminoil paid royalties and taxes to Kuwait, whereas Getty paid royalties and taxes to Saudi Arabia. The zone was partitioned in 1969, but the partitioning did not affect the concession arrangements.

A group of Japanese companies formed the Arabian Oil Company (AOC), which obtained concessions from both Saudi Arabia (1957) and Kuwait (1958) for exploration and production in the offshore area of the zone. AOC started drilling in 1959, and production of crude oil began in 1961. Production was shared between Kuwait and Saudi Arabia. Some AOC production was from the northern tip of Saudi Arabia's As Saffaniyah field, the world's largest offshore field. Saudi Arabia and Kuwait each purchased 10 percent ownership of AOC soon after its formation.

From the beginning of the development of the oil industry, Kuwait's leaders had wanted to participate actively in oil policy and company management. BP and Gulf Oil rejected the demands of the amir (see Glossary) for a Kuwaiti on the KOC board of directors, but the Kuwaiti government obtained some participation in the AOC concession agreement, although it was more symbolic than real.

Frozen out of oil operations by the major oil companies, Kuwait started to develop its own proficiency in the oil industry. The Kuwait National Petroleum Company (KNPC) was formed in 1960 with the expressed intention of becoming an integrated oil company. Its founding charter allowed it to engage in almost any activity concerning oil at home or abroad. It began with 60 percent government ownership; the remaining shares were held by private Kuwaiti investors. The government bought out private investors in 1975.

KNPC started operations on a small scale, in part because of Kuwait's acute shortage of skilled workers. It bought out KOC's local oil distribution facilities and became the sole supplier of oil in Kuwait. It participated in foreign refinery operations and established subsidiaries and facilities abroad for marketing oil products. Departments for exploration and other aspects of field operations were established within KNPC to work with foreign companies in the concession area that KNPC had received from the government.

Using foreign expertise and equipment, KNPC built a modern refinery to use gas in the Al Burqan field, which would otherwise have been flared, in a hydrogenation process to convert crude oil into products and to produce sulfur as a useful by-product. Kuwait's crude is heavy and contains considerable sulfur, so the design of the refinery was excellently fitted to the local circumstances to turn out a product superior to that of a regular refinery. The refinery at Ash Shuaybah was completed in 1968, but technical problems initially caused an unprofitable mix of products. Between cost overruns during construction and a poor range of products, KNPC lost money until the problems were corrected. Nonetheless, KNPC provided useful training for Kuwaitis in upper levels of oil company management.

As oil revenues began to mount, officials increasingly favored investing a larger part of the funds in downstream (see Glossary) and upstream (see Glossary) oil operations. The petrochemical industry offered fewer obstacles to industrial development than most other industries. It needed relatively few workers, large capital investments, and substantial oil and gas sources—requirements that fit the country's circumstances well. Yet despite the apparent advantages, the government moved slowly, perhaps for good reason. In 1963 the Petrochemicals Industries Company (PIC) was formed, with 80 percent state ownership. It began with modest facilities but acquired additional plants over the years through purchase of other companies and construction of new facilities. In 1976 the government bought out private investors, and PIC became wholly government owned. PIC's chemical complexes were the country's largest manufacturing plants. A key ingredient was a gas-gathering system to use the gases produced in association with crude oil. Until the late 1970s, a considerable part of the gases had been flared. In addition to the gas-gathering system, the government expanded its investment in oil-refining capacity and petrochemical facilities.

Kuwait's goal of real participation in and control over its oil industry was achieved in 1976 when the government bought KOC, including the refinery and other installations. BP and Gulf Oil continued to provide technical services and personnel in return for access to oil supplies and service fees. In 1976 Kuwait concluded negotiations to purchase 60 percent of its one-half share of AOC's offshore operations. Negotiations for 60 percent of Aminoil foundered over the value of assets. In 1977 Kuwait nationalized the firm, paying compensation on the basis of an official estimate of the value of assets. Aminoil became the Kuwait Wafrah Oil Company. In 1978 operations of the Al Wafrah field passed to KOC, and KNPC took over the former Aminoil refinery and shipping terminal at Mina Abd Allah.

As oil revenues rose in the 1970s, the Kuwaiti government continued its upstream and downstream expansion, establishing the Kuwait Petroleum Corporation (KPC) as a semiautonomous state organization in January 1980 to rationalize the organizational structure of its oil industry. KPC became the country's national integrated oil company, with KOC, KNPC, PIC, the Kuwait Oil Tanker Company, and the Kuwait Foreign Petroleum Exploration Company among its more important wholly owned subsidiaries. KOC remained primarily responsible for domestic exploration and production of oil and gas, and KNPC was mainly the refining subsidiary. KPC also entered into joint ventures with and purchased shares in foreign companies involved in various aspects of the oil business. In 1981 KPC bought the Santa Fe International Corporation, a United States drilling and energy engineering firm. Other KPC activities abroad included part ownership in refineries and petrochemical plants, exploration and drilling in foreign concession

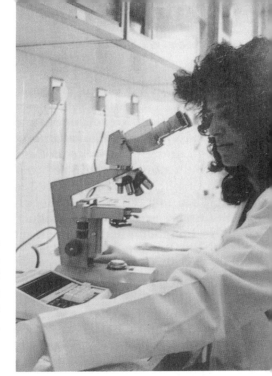

*Laboratory technician
at the Kuwait Foundation
for the Advancement
of Sciences
Courtesy Embassy
of Kuwait, Washington*

areas, and purchase of retail outlets for petroleum products. By the late 1980s, Kuwait was producing 20,000 bpd in overseas holdings, primarily in the United States and in the North Sea. It was exporting 614,000 bpd as refined products. Initially, Kuwait sold this oil primarily to Japan and Pakistan, but beginning in the late 1980s, it also sold through a large West European retail network it purchased, selling oil under the logo Q8.

Oil production levels fluctuated in the period after World War II (see table 6, Appendix). At first, production of crude oil rose rapidly, peaking at nearly 1.1 billion barrels in 1970 before falling to more modest levels. Until 1972 much of the expansion resulted from increasing crude oil production. For the rest of the 1970s, oil production was substantially lower, but higher revenues per barrel financed continued economic growth.

With regard to prices, Kuwaiti officials followed moderate policies between conflicting objectives. Initially, Kuwait actively supported the Organization of the Petroleum Exporting Countries (OPEC), which at times required oil production levels below that necessary to cover government expenditures. Kuwait, for example, reduced oil production and exports during the Arab oil embargo associated with the October 1973 War. The Kuwaiti government believed that oil in the ground was worth more to future generations than holding such paper claims as securities and corporate shares that were subject to price inflation, exchange-rate risks, and sequestration. In 1973 the Kuwaiti government set an oil production limit of 3 million bpd under pressure from the National Assembly. In 1976 the production ceiling was reduced to 2 million bpd. In the 1980s, a surplus of oil relative to demand began to emerge on the world market, and oil prices fell dramatically. As surplus oil supplies grew, Kuwait's production ceiling was further reduced to 1.5 million bpd, although actual production was appreciably lower. But as oil prices fell, and with it revenues, Kuwait increasingly resisted OPEC's efforts to limit its production. In 1986 Kuwait reluctantly agreed to an OPEC limit of 1.25 million bpd (not counting, however, output of the Divided Zone that, during this period, was earmarked as aid for Iraq). In 1989 it refused an OPEC level of just under 1.1 million bpd. In early 1990, Kuwait produced nearly 2 million bpd, a factor that the Iraqi government cited in its decision to invade Kuwait in August.

In the 1950s and 1960s, Kuwait economically had been little more than an oil well: oil was the source of most of its revenues, and the bulk of its exports were oil, mostly crude oil. But in the 1970s, officials increased refining capacity, and by the 1980s, refined products gained in value relative to crude oil exports. By the 1980s, Kuwait controlled its hydrocarbon resources and had created an international oil company, KPC, that was among the world's largest corporations. Through its subsidiaries, KPC was involved in all aspects of the oil industry and in many countries of the world. This was a remarkable achievement in view of the fact that only twenty-five years had passed since Kuwait entered the oil industry.

Diversification

Industrial development in Kuwait has always faced formidable obstacles. Kuwait, so rich in oil, is poor in most other resources, which limits the manufacturing industries that can be established. No metallic minerals and few suitable nonmetallic minerals are locally available. Most raw materials for the early industries—for example, cement—had to be imported. The limited supply of fresh water is another constraint. In a country without streams and with few underground sources, water is crucial to industrial development. The pre-oil system, where local sailing boats carried water from Iraq

*Waterfront project that extends along twenty-one kilometers
of the Kuwaiti coast
Courtesy Embassy of Kuwait, Washington*

to Kuwait, could not meet manufacturing needs. The small size of the domestic market restricts production for local consumption to small-scale operations. The open economy, which was maintained before and after the discovery of oil, provided little protection from foreign competition. The small Kuwaiti labor force, possessing limited skills, is another constraint. After the discovery of oil, labor costs escalated, and in a few years wages in Kuwait were higher than those in almost any other area of the Middle East, further hindering industrial development. Also, the commercial tradition in the country predisposes most entrepreneurs to invest in trade rather than manufacturing. As a result of these obstacles, industry, excluding oil-related industry, expanded very slowly.

The discovery of oil created a demand for new industries, initially satisfied by the oil company itself. Oil operations particularly needed water, electricity, and refined petroleum products, and these were the first modern industries created in the state. The government took over production of water and electricity, expanding the systems and subsidizing their use. Air conditioning provided the largest demand, with peak summer loads more than five times minimum winter loads, creating substantial idle capacity for about six months of the year. The need for larger and more regular supplies of water, no matter how costly, compelled KOC to install the first desalination plant. In 1953 the government installed the first unit, which had a capacity of 3.8 million liters per day. Subsequently, the government claimed that it had developed the most advanced continuously operating desalination facilities in the world.

Although oil spurred the first industries in Kuwait, after the initial push, oil did not generate much in the way of new industries locally. As a result of the many obstacles that industry faced and in light of the massive oil revenues, the government began to play a major role in all industrial development. The government undertook some efforts at diversification in the 1950s, but the first major push for industrialization occurred with the establishment of the Ash Shuaybah Industrial Zone in 1964. The zone comprised electricity and water distillation plants, expanded port facilities, metalworks, and plants manufacturing chlorine, asphalt, cement, pilings, and prefabricated housing. The government provided such necessary facilities as roads, gas, electricity, water, sewerage, port facilities, communications, and rented or leased industrial sites at nominal rates. Most of the larger industrial facilities were located in the zone.

Other small manufacturing establishments were located in the populated parts of the country.

The government provided a range of incentives to private manufacturers, who were predominantly local; 51 percent Kuwaiti ownership was required of all businesses. In addition to infrastructural support, financial aid included equity capital and loans. In 1974 the government created the Investment Bank of Kuwait to provide medium- and long-term industrial financing at low interest rates. The government also gave local industry preference in government purchases, protection from imports in some cases, and exemption from customs duties and taxes. In the 1970s, the government's Industrial Development Committee and the Industrial Bank of Kuwait established a number of incentives for private-sector participation, such as technical aid and preferential guaranteed markets in state industry. Nonetheless, industry in Kuwait never enjoyed the same level of state support that it did in other gulf states. The government, having made a conscious decision to invest its revenues overseas and locally in such human resources as education and health care, gave only minimal support, by the standards of other oil-producing countries, to non-oil manufacturing.

Agriculture and Fishing

Agriculture has also seen minimal development. Kuwait's desert climate sustains little vegetation. Kuwait has no rivers, only a few wadis that fill with winter and spring rain. Scant rainfall, little irrigation water, and poor soils have always limited farming in Kuwait. Before the discovery of oil, several occupations contributed to the economy—nomads moving livestock to the sparse forage in the desert, pearling, and fishing—but none of these occupations provided much beyond subsistence. Once the government began receiving oil revenues, the contribution of other sectors to national income was reduced still further (see table 7, Appendix). Economic growth and welfare measures since World War II drew workers away from historical pursuits and lessened the role of agriculture. In the late 1980s, fewer than 10,000 people were employed in agriculture. The government invested some money in developing hydroponics to increase vegetable production. Kuwait's most important crops in 1989 were tomatoes (40,000 tons), dried onions (25,000 tons), melons (7,000 tons), dates (1,000 tons), and smaller amounts of cucumbers and eggplants. Some of these crops are grown hydroponically. Although Kuwait manages to export some vegetables, its agricultural potential remains limited.

Fishing provides a minor but important economic contribution. Much of the fishing for the local market was historically from small boats, including many native dhows. Large-scale commercial fishing is mostly confined to the United Fisheries of Kuwait, which operates a fleet of vessels as far afield as the Indian Ocean, the Red Sea, and the Atlantic Ocean. United Fisheries is a large, international firm that processes and exports part of its catch, particularly frozen shrimp. However, in the 1970s overfishing in the gulf by many states considerably reduced catches of fish and shrimp. In 1989 Kuwait had a catch of approximately 4,700 tons of fish and 3,000 tons of shrimp and prawns. In the late 1980s, war and environmental damage, including oil spills, also reduced the attractiveness of the gulf fishing industry.

Transportation and Telecommunications

Kuwait has a modern, well-maintained transportation system. The entire system suffered extensive damage in the Persian Gulf War, but by 1993 repairs had brought most facilities back to their prewar condition. The highway system comprised more than 3,900 kilometers of roads in 1993. About 3,000 kilometers are paved, and the rest are gravel or graded earth. Expressways extend south and west from the city of Kuwait to neighboring cities. Paved highways link Kuwait with Iraq to the north and Saudi Arabia to the west and south. Despite the excellent network of roads in populated areas, traffic congestion is a growing problem. Plans to build a causeway across Kuwait Bay were delayed by the Iraqi invasion in 1990.

Three ports handle all commercial shipping and petroleum exports. The principal port for nonpetroleum products in 1993 was Ash Shuwaykh, several kilometers west of the downtown section of the city of Kuwait. Built in 1960, Ash Shuwaykh is one of the busiest ports in the Middle East, with twenty-one deepwater berths. In 1988 more than 1,100 vessels carried 3.7 million tons of cargo through Ash Shuwaykh. Ash Shuaybah was built in 1967, fifty kilometers south of the city of Kuwait, to develop the Ash Shuaybah Industrial Zone. By 1988, however, it rivaled Ash Shuwaykh in size and traffic with twenty berths and 3.5 million tons of cargo transported. Mina al Ahmadi, just north of Ash Shuaybah, handles most of Kuwait's petroleum exports. Twelve offshore berths can load more than 2 million bpd of oil and can accommodate the largest oil tankers.

Kuwait International Airport, sixteen kilometers south of the city of Kuwait, handles all international flights. The latest expansion to the airport, a new terminal, was completed in 1979. Kuwait Airways, the national carrier, has regularly scheduled service to more than twenty-four cities worldwide.

Like its transportation system, Kuwait's modern telecommunications system was heavily damaged during the Iraqi occupation. The government has made strides at reconstruction, but in 1993 work remained to restore the system to its prewar level of excellence. In 1989 there were 285,000 telephones, or fourteen telephones per 100 inhabitants. High-capacity coaxial cables and radio-relay systems linked Kuwait with its neighbors. In 1993, however, the coaxial cable to Iraq was still inoperable. Before the war, the country had four ground satellite stations working with the International Telecommunications Satellite Organization (Intelsat) and the Arab Satellite Communication Organization (Arabsat) system. All four stations were destroyed in the war, however, and smaller mobile satellite ground stations currently handle international telephone calls, data transmission, and live television broadcasts. The city of Kuwait has three AM radio stations, three FM radio stations, three television transmitters, and a powerful shortwave transmitter for international service.

Banking and Finance

Before independence in 1961, foreign monies, largely the Indian rupee in the period between 1930 and 1960, circulated in Kuwait. At independence the Kuwaiti dinar was introduced, and a currency board was established to issue dinar notes and to maintain reserves. In 1959 the Central Bank of Kuwait was created and took over the functions of the currency board and the regulation of the banking system.

The first bank in Kuwait was established in 1941 by British investors. Subsequent laws prohibited foreign banks from conducting business in the country. When the British bank's concession ended in 1971, the government bought 51 percent ownership. In 1952 another bank, the National Bank of Kuwait, the largest commercial bank, was founded. The establishment of several other banks, all under Kuwaiti ownership, followed. Some specialized financial institutions also emerged: the Credit and Savings Bank, established in 1965 by the government to channel funds into domestic projects in industry, agriculture, and housing; the Industrial Bank of Kuwait, established in 1974 to fill the gap in medium- and long-term industrial financing; and the private Real Estate Bank of Kuwait. By the 1980s, Kuwait's banks were among the region's largest and most active financial institutions. Then came the Suq al Manakh stock market crash in 1982.

The large revenues of the 1970s left many private individuals with substantial funds at their disposal. These funds prompted a speculation boom in the official stock market in the mid-1970s that culminated in a small crash in 1977. The government's response to this crash was to bail out the affected investors and to introduce stricter regulations. This response unintentionally contributed to the far larger stock market crash of the 1980s by driving the least risk-averse speculators into the technically illegal alternate market, the Suq al Manakh. The Suq al Manakh had emerged next to the official stock market, which was dominated by several older wealthy families who traded, largely among themselves, in very large blocks of stock. The Suq al Manakh soon became the market for the new investor and, in the end, for many old investors as well.

Share dealings using postdated checks created a huge unregulated expansion of credit. The crash of the unofficial stock market finally came in 1982, when a dealer presented a postdated check for payment and it bounced. A house of cards collapsed. Official investigation revealed that total outstanding checks amounted to the equivalent of US$94 billion from about 6,000 investors. Kuwait's financial sector was badly shaken by the crash, as was the entire economy. The crash prompted a recession that rippled through society as individual families were disrupted by the investment risks of particular members made on family credit. The debts from the crash left all but one bank in Kuwait technically insolvent, held up only by support from the Central Bank. Only the National Bank of Kuwait, the largest commercial bank, survived the crisis intact. In the end, the government stepped in, devising a complicated set of policies, embodied in the Difficult Credit Facilities Resettlement Program. The implementation of the program was still incomplete in 1990 when the Iraqi invasion changed the entire financial picture (see Economic Reconstruction, this ch.).

Foreign Investment

From the very beginning, government officials were keenly aware that oil was a depletable asset, that the country had few other resources, and that preparations had to be made for the day when there would be no more oil. As soon as the government began to receive oil revenues, officials spent less than the treasury received, leaving a surplus in the state's general reserve to be invested. Because of limited domestic investment opportunities, most investments were made abroad. World Bank (see Glossary) economists estimate that about 25 percent of revenues were placed in foreign assets during the 1950s, although the Kuwaiti government's published data have always been vague about reserves as well as about some other economic variables.

In the 1950s and 1960s, Kuwait began investing overseas in property and businesses in Britain. In 1952 Kuwait established an office in London, staffed with experienced British investment counselors who guided the government's placement of funds. In the same year, Kuwait created investment relations with a large New York bank. Because of the vastly expanded oil revenues of the 1970s, Kuwait's overseas investment program grew tremendously. In 1976 the government established the Reserve Fund for Future Generations, into which it placed an initial US$7 billion. It resolved to invest 10 percent of its revenues annually in the reserve fund. Money from the fund, along with other government revenues, was invested in overseas property and industry. In the 1970s, most of these funds were invested in the United States and in Western Europe: in German firms (such as Hoechst and Daimler-Benz, in each of which Kuwait owned 25 percent), in property, and in most of the United States Fortune Five Hundred firms. In the 1980s, Kuwait began diversifying its overseas investments, placing more investments in Japanese firms. By the late 1980s, Kuwait was earning more from these overseas investments than it was from the direct sale of oil: in 1987 foreign investments generated US$6.3 billion, oil US$5.4 billion. The *Financial Times* of London estimated Kuwait's overseas investments in early 1990 at more than US$100 billion, most of it in the Reserve Fund for Future Generations.

The Iraqi invasion proved the importance of these investment revenues. With oil revenues suspended, the government and population in exile relied exclusively on investment revenues, including sales of investments for sustenance, for their share of ongoing coalition expenses and for postwar reconstruction and repair of the vital oil industry.

Foreign Aid and Trade

Foreign trade has always dominated Kuwait's economy. Before the discovery of oil, merchants developed large transshipment and reexport businesses that, along with the sale of pearls to foreign dealers, yielded a substantial part of the population's income. The discovery of large quantities of oil provided a new and increasingly important export because Kuwait needed only small amounts of oil products domestically. Nonetheless, even after the discovery of oil, Kuwait's merchants continued to develop transshipment and reexport businesses with neighboring countries. During the Iran-Iraq War, goods for Iraq passed through Kuwaiti ports. Oil, however, overwhelmingly dominated Kuwait's exports (see table 8, Appendix).

Kuwait's significant foreign-exchange earnings from oil exports and investment income largely removed any constraints on imports in the pre-invasion period. Almost any commodity could be imported, and most import duties were modest. Imports for Kuwait's high-income economy were mainly finished products because of the small domestic manufacturing sector (see table 9, Appendix). These imports came predominantly from Asian countries, followed by those from European countries. Imports of all kinds came primarily from Japan and the United States. After the Persian Gulf War, imports from the United States increased dramatically (see table 10, Appendix). Huge oil revenues, paid in foreign currencies, freed Kuwait for the most part from balance of payments worries (see table 11, Appendix). The government accumulated surplus funds that were invested abroad. A large part of these reserve investments abroad, however, were cashed in during the Iraqi occupation and the liberation period that followed in order to pay the expenses of Kuwait and the allied coalition.

Historically, Kuwait also invested part of its revenues in foreign aid, primarily to Arab states. This foreign aid increased substantially as oil revenues rose in the 1970s. It took many forms, such as loans, joint financing, equity participation, and direct grants, particularly in support of Arab causes. In the 1960s, the government began placing funds in the Kuwait Fund for Arab Economic Development (KFAED), established in 1961. The best known of Kuwait's investment organizations and one that was used as a model by other oil exporters, KFAED functioned as both an investment and an aid agency, providing loans for specific projects, often on concessionary terms. KFAED's charter was changed in 1974, when capitalization was increased to KD1 billion (for value of the Kuwaiti dinar—see Glossary), and the fund began expanding its provision of funds to developing countries worldwide. Most KFAED aid went to development projects, especially in agriculture, to provide basic services such as electricity, water, and transportation and to develop human resources through education and health care. A large amount of aid went directly from the government to other states. In per capita terms, Kuwait's aid program was one of the most generous in the world. In the early 1980s, when oil prices were high, nearly 4 percent of Kuwait's gross national product (GNP—see Glossary) went to the aid program. But in the late 1980s, the levels of aid declined along with declining revenues. After the Iran-Iraq War started, in 1980, Kuwait increasingly directed its aid toward Iraq. During the 1980s, Kuwait lent Iraq an estimated US$13 billion. Kuwait's foreign aid slowed considerably after the Iraqi invasion in August 1990 and is expected to remain limited as Kuwait deals with the costs of reconstruction.

Political System

Ruling Family

The modern political history of Kuwait began in the early eighteenth century when a number of families of the Bani Utub section of the Anaizah tribe migrated from central Arabia, settling eventually in Kuwait. Once in Kuwait, they established a self-governing political unit. The date of 1756 is conventionally chosen as the year when the settlers decided to select as their leader Sabah, an Al Sabah shaykh (see Glossary), who was succeeded by his son Abd Allah, in turn succeeded by his son Jabir. All subsequent rulers historically have come from the Al Sabah line, chosen by family council, in consultation with the leading merchant families who, along with the tribal elite, exercise some restriction over the shaykhs' political autonomy.

The shaykh's primary task was to represent his community in foreign policy, negotiating with Ottoman Turkey and with neighboring tribes. The one major and unsuccessful challenge to this system of rule occurred in the 1760s when the Al Khalifa family disagreed with the Al Sabah and in consequence left Kuwait for Qatar, and then Bahrain, where the Al Khalifa continue to rule. Despite the rift, the two settlements maintained good relations, including close trade ties.

In the nineteenth century, members of the Al Sabah oversaw the growing trade and pearling settlement in Kuwait. The rulers also developed a cordial relationship with Britain, beginning with the first contacts with the British East India Company in 1775. As members of a small, vulnerable settlement, Kuwait's rulers attempted to maintain a polite but distant relationship with all the local powers, notably the British, the Wahhabis (see Glossary) of Arabia, and the Ottomans. It was only under Abd Allah Al Sabah II, who ruled from 1866 to 1892, that Kuwait began to edge away from this policy of neutrality. Abd Allah developed close ties with the Ottomans, even taking the Ottoman title, albeit largely as a formality, of provincial governor (*qaimaqam*) in 1871. In practical terms, Kuwait's domestic politics remained unchanged because the Ottoman government did not interfere in the selection of rulers and laws. In any event, this tilt was completely reversed when, following the four-year rule of Muhammad Al Sabah, Mubarak Al Sabah the Great ruled from 1896 to 1915.

Kuwait came into the British sphere of influence at the end of the nineteenth century when Mubarak sought British support against Ottoman forces. The Ottomans were backing allies of Mubarak's brothers, Kuwait's previous rulers, whom Mubarak had killed on taking power in 1896. Uneasy about Ottoman intentions, Mubarak reversed his predecessors' pro-Ottoman policy and approached Britain, seeking a more formal alliance. Britain, concerned with growing European interests and notably with an Ottoman concession to Germany for construction of a Berlin-to-Baghdad railroad—with a proposed spur line to Kuwait—agreed. Britain signed a treaty with Kuwait in 1899 that promised Mubarak British support and, in return, gave Britain control of Kuwait's foreign policy. This treaty governed relations between the two states until Kuwait's independence in 1961. It granted Britain tremendous influence, most notably in foreign and economic policy.

After Mubarak's death, Kuwait was ruled by two of his sons, Jabir Al Sabah (1915–17) and Salim Al Sabah (1917–21) (see fig. 5). Thereafter, with one exception, only descendants of Mubarak through these two sons would rule Kuwait, thus forming a major cleavage within the ruling family. After Salim's death in 1921, Kuwait was ruled for nearly three decades by Ahmad al Jabir Al Sabah. Ahmad al Jabir's rule witnessed a serious effort to constrain ruling family power. In 1938 a rebellion, known locally as the Majlis Movement, developed. New issues arose. Kuwait was in the midst of a serious recession as a result of the general decline of the pearling industry, the Great Depression, and a trade dispute with Saudi Arabia that prompted a Saudi embargo. Simultaneously, the recently signed oil concession with KOC promised better times ahead if the resulting income were not monopolized by the ruling family. To prevent that from happening, the leading merchants began petitioning the ruler for a series of reforms. In June the merchants took their protest a step further, holding elections for a legislative assembly to implement the desired reforms using these new revenues. The Legislative Assembly ruled for six months until finally abolished by the ruler and his tribal backers. The assembly, however, came to be viewed as Kuwait's first prodemocracy movement. Its popularity gave the idea of formal representation a place in Kuwaiti popular history.

Ahmad al Jabir was succeeded by his cousin Abd Allah as Salim Al Sabah (1950–65), who oversaw the distribution of now substantial oil revenues, the consequent emergence of a large bureaucratic state, and the transformation of Kuwait into a wealthy oil-producing shaykhdom. In terms of internal developments, Abd Allah as Salim made two transformative political decisions. The first was to distribute these new revenues broadly throughout the population, primarily through wide-ranging social services, notably education and health care. The second was to introduce a greater degree of political participation to Kuwait in the form of the newly elected National Assembly. This body held its first elections in 1963. Abd Allah as Salim also oversaw Kuwait's transformation into a formally independent state on June 19, 1961, when he and British representatives signed new letters of friendship to replace the treaty of 1899.

When Abd Allah as Salim died in 1965, he was succeeded by his brother Sabah as Salim Al Sabah—a somewhat unusual choice in that he, like Abd Allah as Salim, came from the Salim line rather than the Jabir line of the family, breaking the alternation between the two sides of the family that had existed since the rule of Mubarak's sons Jabir and Salim. Nonetheless, Sabah as Salim's rule proved to be largely a continuation and consolidation of policies set in place by Abd Allah as Salim.

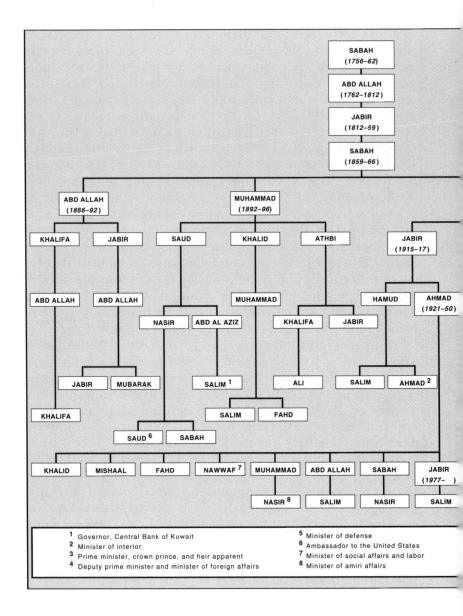

Source: Based on information from Alan Rush, *Al-Sabah: Genealogy and History of Kuwait's Ruling Family, 1752–1986*, Atlantic Highlands, New Jersey, 1987; and United States, Central Intelligence Agency, *Chiefs of State and Cabinet Members of Foreign Governments*, Washington, 1992, 48–49.

Figure 5. Kuwait: Abbreviated Genealogy of the Al Sabah, with Government Positions, Mid–1992

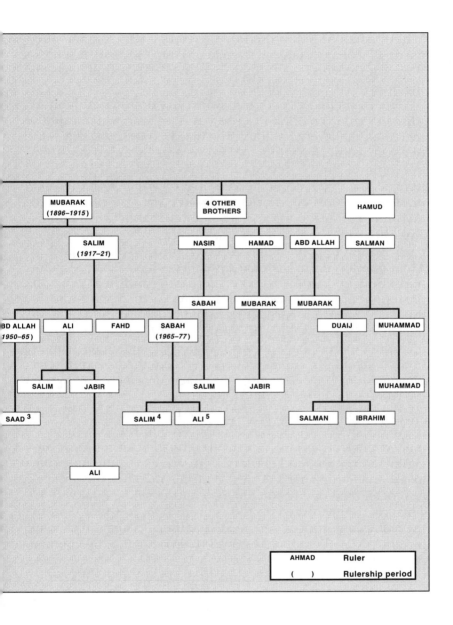

When Sabah as Salim died in December 1977, he was succeeded by Shaykh Jabir al Ahmad al Jabir Al Sabah, a succession that returned the former pattern of alternation between the lines of Jabir and Salim.

The influence of external events has dominated Jabir al Ahmad's rule. The first was the Iran-Iraq War, which rapidly increased the level of political violence in this historically relatively peaceful shaykhdom. Major events included the 1983 bombing of the United States embassy and, probably most notable, the dramatic public assassination attempt on the amir in 1985. The tension associated with the war also exacerbated divisions within Kuwaiti society, notably that between Sunnis and Shia, and prompted the amir increasingly to limit public participation in political life. Although in 1980 Shaykh Jabir al Ahmad restored the National Assembly (which Sabah as Salim had abolished in 1976), the increasing political tension prompted him to do away with it again in 1986 and to introduce new measures curtailing civil and political rights. These measures prompted a wide range of opposition leaders—including old parliamentarians, Islamists (sometimes seen as fundamentalists), and merchants—to form the Constitutional Movement of 1989–90, a prodemocracy movement calling for the restoration of the National Assembly.

The second external event was the Iraqi invasion of Kuwait in August 1990, which, for the first time in Kuwait's history, placed the state under direct foreign rule. Although sovereignty was restored in February 1991, events leading up to the invasion and the amir's behavior during and after the occupation prompted open grumbling about the ruling family itself. The criticism centered on the amir and the fact that most of the ruling family spent the time of the Iraqi occupation in comfortable exile abroad and delayed their return to the country after the war ended.

In 1993 Shaykh Jabir al Ahmad still ruled Kuwait; his designated successor, Prime Minister Saad al Abd Allah as Salim Al Sabah, also came from the Al Sabah ruling family. Although the Al Sabah remained paramount, the family as a ruling institution had changed dramatically since it assumed its leading role in the mid-eighteenth century. First, succession patterns within the family had changed. In the nineteenth century, rule passed regularly from father to son. With the accession of Mubarak in the late nineteenth century, a new pattern was established that excluded all but Mubarak's line from the top position. This custom is formalized in the Kuwaiti constitution and in practice created a new pattern of alternation of rulers between the two lines of Mubarak's sons, Jabir and Salim. It was in keeping with this pattern that Shaykh Jabir al Ahmad (from the Jabir line) named as his crown prince and heir apparent Saad al Abd Allah as Salim, from the Salim line.

The relationship between the ruling family and Kuwaiti society also changed in more subtle ways. Members of the family other than the ruler, once first among equals in a society where merchants and other elites played an important role in decision making, became in the years after oil was discovered far wealthier because their wealth was guaranteed by a civil list—a list of sums appropriated to pay the expenses of a ruler and his household. Ruling family members also became socially more prominent and politically more important as they took over many of the state's highest posts. In part, this transformation occurred as a result of the emergence of a large state bureaucracy and the need Kuwaiti rulers felt to fill the state's highest posts with loyal supporters, notably kin.

Bureaucracy

Kuwait's large state bureaucracy emerged in the post-World War II period as a result of the vast government revenues generated by oil. Under the first oil concession, oil payments went directly from the oil companies to the amir, who, along with his advisers, decided—initially, rather informally—how much of the oil revenues would be spent and in what ways. The historical elite, especially the merchants, objected to this arrangement, most notably in the Majlis Movement of 1938. In time the government instituted ministries, budgets, financial controls, and other aspects of modern public administration, partly in response to such public protests and partly from the practical necessities of carrying out a variety of new state functions related to oil and to popular distribution of revenues through state services.

At the top of this bureaucracy is the cabinet, under the prime minister, a post that historically has been held by the crown prince. The cabinet is appointed by the amir, who has the power to dismiss it along with almost every senior executive official, including the crown prince, local governors, and officers in the armed forces. Members of the Al Sabah play an important role in the cabinet. Twelve of the fifteen members in the original postindependence cabinet appointed in January

1962 were from the ruling family. Although public criticism led to a reduction in their numbers, in the 1970s and 1980s a large number of ministers, including those in the most important posts, came from the ruling family. The remaining cabinet ministers often came from prominent families and from members of the National Assembly (see Legislature, this ch.). These ministers were generally young (in their thirties and forties), highly educated (nearly half with college degrees, some with advanced degrees, especially in economics and business, often from United States universities), and mostly Sunni.

In addition to the cabinet, Kuwait has several autonomous agencies and public corporations. Their employees and those of the various ministries comprise the bulk of the nation's civil servants. The civil service grew tremendously in the years after independence as the state developed a large bureaucracy devoted to spending oil revenues. The largest state institutions are those providing social services, notably education. Historically, this bureaucracy has been staffed largely by foreigners. Although the government's policy has been to staff the civil service with Kuwaitis to the extent possible, and although most employed Kuwaitis work for the state, the government nonetheless relied heavily on foreigners to fill positions at all levels before the Iraqi invasion.

A second factor contributing to the growth of the bureaucracy is the government's guarantee of jobs to all citizens. Not only does the state guarantee jobs, but it also offers Kuwaitis preferential treatment in employment, including higher salaries and preference in advancement over non-Kuwaitis. The government is the largest employer in the country. Many Kuwaitis prefer government employment to other positions even when it means undertaking routine tasks that underuse their skills and time. Others hold jobs in both the public and the private sectors, working in a government office in the morning and working privately in the afternoon. Observers frequently have commented on the country's excessive bureaucracy and overstaffing, to the extent that several people are often assigned to what could be one job. Several efforts to reform the civil service have not reduced the inefficiency and underuse of available labor.

Legislature

One of the most remarkable aspects of Kuwaiti politics in the postindependence period is the National Assembly—one

Jabir al Ahmad al Jabir Al Sabah, ruler of Kuwait
Courtesy Embassy of Kuwait, Washington

of the few elected legislative bodies in the region. Pre-invasion Kuwait was one of the most politically open states in the region and the most open in the gulf. It had a relatively free press and an assembly elected by a small electorate of adult male citizens. The authors of the postindependence constitution of 1962, aware of the precedent set in the 1938 Legislative Assembly, saw the creation of an elected legislative body as an important means to widen the popular consensus and thereby further legitimize the rule of the Al Sabah, especially at a time when the family's position was threatened by the Iraqi claim to the entire territory of the new state. After the January 1963 election of the first National Assembly, the body evolved to serve as a broad forum for discussion and dissent. The men who dominated this assembly, however, were not the historical elite but, with some exceptions, were Kuwaitis who benefited from the state's generous welfare system. The historical opposition, the merchants on whom the amir relied for money in the lean pre-oil years, refrained from politics, devoting themselves instead to investing the money the amir sent their way.

Although the constitution affords the assembly considerable power, the body is limited by two major restrictions: the small size of the electorate as defined by law, which restricts suffrage to most adult male nationals whose ancestors were present in Kuwait in 1920; and the power of the amir to dissolve the assembly virtually at will. Nonetheless, the assembly plays a prominent role in raising issues of public importance, reviewing and challenging government policies and programs, and responding to constituent concerns. It helps give Kuwait a much more open and public political life than that in other gulf states.

The roots of the National Assembly began in the 1961 elections for the Constituent Assembly, which drafted a constitution and laid the groundwork for elections in 1963 to the first National Assembly. The 1963 elections produced a solid opposition in the National Bloc, which challenged government policy in a number of areas. The opposition was so volatile that when elections were next held in 1967, opponents charged the government with widespread election fraud in an effort to restrict the contentious body. The new assembly indeed proved more pliable. However, the 1971 elections returned a more confrontational assembly, one that devoted much of its energies to the nationalization of the oil company. Elections for the fourth assembly took place in 1975 and produced a body more strongly opposed to the government than its predecessor. In August 1976, Sabah as Salim dissolved the assembly and introduced new restrictions on public assembly and speech. But in 1980, because of renewed concern for popular support in light of the Iranian Revolution of 1979 and the regional tension that accompanied the subsequent Iran-Iraq War, the new amir, Shaykh Jabir al Ahmad, allowed elections to be held. The fifth assembly was highly confrontational, as was the sixth, elected in 1985. When in 1986 the assembly began attacking members of the ruling family, primarily in connection with the handling of the 1982 Suq al Manakh stock market crash, the amir again suspended the assembly. The minister of justice, a member of the ruling family, was forced to resign because of allegations he had used public influence for personal gain in resolving the crash. As in 1976, external pressures from Saudi Arabia, which was highly critical of Kuwait's more participatory system, probably played a role in the amir's decision.

Opposition to the decision again to suspend the assembly manifested itself in the Constitutional Movement of 1989–90. In 1989 members of the dissolved assembly began organizing and calling for reinstitution of the assembly and articles of the 1962 constitution that the amir had suspended as well in 1986. They were joined by many merchants, previously politically quiescent—but now alienated by the ruler's inability to provide

City of Kuwait,
capital of Kuwait
Courtesy Embassy of
Kuwait, Washington

the level of economic support they had come to expect owing to the fall in oil prices—and by such others as professionals, liberals, and Islamists. The movement quickly spread through the *diwaniyat* (sing., *diwaniyah*), private weekly social meetings in the homes of prominent families, until it became a series of popular antigovernment demonstrations. As the movement developed, the amir and the crown prince responded with both carrots and sticks. In an effort to divide the opposition, the government announced in 1990 that although it would not restore the National Assembly it would establish a National Council comprising fifty elected members and twenty-five appointed members. The new body would thus be less representative than the old assembly. It would also have less power: for example, it could not enact legislation directly. The opposition opposed such an extra-constitutional council, viewing it not only as an effort to preclude a genuinely representative assembly but also as a way for the government to prepare loyalist candidates in the event that genuine assembly elections were held. (Indeed, when National Assembly elections were eventually scheduled in the postinvasion period, a large number of National Council members announced they would run.) Although opposition leaders and others boycotted the elections, the new body was nonetheless constituted following elections for the nonappointed seats in June 1990. This new body had just begun meeting when the Iraqi invasion rendered it obsolete. The National Council met again on several occasions after the end of the Persian Gulf War in 1991 but was eliminated when the National Assembly was reconstituted by elections in October 1992.

Elections for the National Assembly were held on October 5, 1992, by amiri decree, in accordance with the 1962 constitution. Seven political groups (parties remained banned) backed candidates in the campaign. The groups included the Islamic Constitutional Movement, the Islamic Parliamentarian Alliance, the Islamic National Alliance (a Shia group), and the Democratic Forum (progressive former Arab nationalists). The election proceeded without major incident. Opposition and independent candidates, including many associated with the prodemocracy movement, won the majority, thirty to thirty-five of the assembly's fifty seats. Progovernment candidates won the remaining fifteen to twenty seats, primarily in tribal constituencies. Islamist candidates won nineteen seats, a dramatic increase over the nine they had held in the former assembly. Seventeen of the elected members had served in previous assemblies.

Among the issues the members promised to raise in the new assembly were public spending and related financial concerns, foreign policy and the events leading up to the Iraqi invasion, the political status of women (many of whom demonstrated for suffrage during the elections), and Islamic law. Following the elections, Prime Minister and Crown Prince Saad al Abd Allah announced the formation on October 17 of the new cabinet. The cabinet included fewer members of the ruling family than had previous cabinets and six National Assembly opposition members among the sixteen ministers. The new cabinet, however, still left family members holding key posts, including that of minister of foreign affairs, which was returned to the long-serving but unpopular Sabah al Ahmad Al Sabah.

Constitution

In June 1961, following independence and under the shadow of an Iraqi threat, Amir Abd Allah as Salim announced that he would establish a constitution for Kuwait. In December, elections were held for a Constituent Assembly, which then drafted a constitution promulgated as Law Number 1 on November 11, 1962. Although articles of the constitution have since been suspended twice, the document nonetheless remains the basic statement of intent for the Kuwaiti political system.

The constitution opens with the declaration that Kuwait is "an independent sovereign Arab State," and its people are "a part of the Arab Nation." Islam is "the religion of the state," and the sharia (Islamic law) is "a main source of legislation." The latter phrase has been the source of much debate, with Islamist opposition members pressing to have Islam made "the" source of legislation.

The constitution defines Kuwait as "a hereditary Amirate, the succession to which shall be in the descendants of the late Mubarak Al Sabah." This clause codifies what has become practice: the semiformal alternation of power since 1915 between the lines of Mubarak's two ruling sons: Jabir and Salim.

Although granting the amir substantial power, the constitution also provides for political participation by the citizens. The system of government is defined in Article 6 as "democratic, under which sovereignty resides in the people, the source of all powers." Articles 79 to 122 establish the National Assembly and lay out the rules governing its formation, rights, and duties.

Individual rights protected by the constitution are extensive and include personal liberty and equality before the law, freedom to hold beliefs and express opinions, and freedom of the press. The residences of citizens are inviolable, the torture and the deportation of Kuwaiti citizens are prohibited, and the accused are assumed innocent until proven guilty. Also guaranteed is the freedom to form associations and trade unions. The constitution guarantees the independence of the judiciary and designates the Supreme Council of the Judiciary as its highest body and guarantor of judicial independence.

The constitution also grants citizens a number of social rights, which form the basis for Kuwait's extensive welfare system. The state is constitutionally obligated to care for the young and to aid the old, the ill, and the disabled. It is obliged to provide public education and to attend to public health. The constitution provides for state involvement in the national economy to the degree that these obligations necessitate. However, Articles 16 through 19 protect private property, stating that "private property is inviolable" and reminding citizens that "inheritance is a right governed by the Islamic Sharia." Article 20 stipulates that "the national economy shall be based on social justice. It is founded on fair cooperation between public and private activities. Its aim shall be economic development, increase of productivity, improvement of the standard of living and achievement of prosperity for citizens, all within the limits of the law." Duties of citizens include national defense, observance of public order and respect for public morals, and payment of taxes. These rights and obligations, however, apply only to Kuwaiti citizens. The remainder of the population have few political and civil rights and enjoy only restricted access to the benefits of the state welfare system.

In August 1976, in reaction to heightened assembly opposition to his policies, the amir suspended four articles of the constitution concerned with political and civil rights (freedom of the press and dissolution of the legislature) and the assembly itself. In 1980, however, the suspended articles of the constitution were reinstated along with the National Assembly. In 1982 the government submitted sixteen constitutional amendments that, among other things, would have allowed the amir to declare martial law for an extended period and would have increased both the size of the legislature and the length of terms of office. In May 1983, the proposals were formally dropped after several months of debate. Nonetheless, the issue of constitutional revisions continued as a topic of discussion in both the National Assembly and the palace. In 1986 the constitution was again suspended, along with the National Assembly. As with the previous suspension, popular opposition to this move emerged; indeed, the prodemocracy movement of 1989–90 took its name, the Constitutional Movement, from the demand for a return to constitutional life. This opposition became more pronounced following the Iraqi occupation, which abrogated all constitutional rights, and following Kuwait's return to sovereignty in 1991. In early 1992, many press restrictions were lifted. After the October 1992 election, the National Assembly exercised its constitutional right to review all amiri decrees promulgated while the assembly was in dissolution.

The Media

According to Kuwait's 1991 constitution, "freedom of opinion is guaranteed to everyone . . . within the limits of the law." The 1961 Press and Publishing Law establishes fines and prison terms for the publication of banned material, which includes reports critical of the government. In practice, this provision has been used only rarely, and Kuwait is known for its press freedom. In 1986, however, the government took a number of measures to repress political dissent. New censorship regulations formed a part of these measures. The Ministry of Information requires all publications to submit copy to the ministry in advance for approval and forbids criticism of the ruler and his family, other Arab leaders, or Islam, as well as the acceptance of foreign funding.

As a result of the Iraqi invasion, Iraqi forces took over all media. A few Kuwaiti newspapers and Radio Kuwait managed to operate outside the country. After the war, in April 1991 the six opposition groups joined in calling for a free press. In January 1992, the government lifted censorship, but journalists continued to experience various restrictions. As of 1993, the press, radio, and television were gradually recovering and rebuilding facilities the Iraqis had destroyed.

The Kuwait News Agency (KUNA) is theoretically independent but in practice is an arm of the Ministry of Information. Newspapers are generally privately owned and consist of seven dailies, five in Arabic and two in English (the *Arab Times* and *Kuwait Times*), as well as a number of weeklies. The largest daily is *Al Qabas* (Firebrand), which is independent and had a circulation of about 120,000 before the war. Two smaller dailies, *Al Anba* (News) and *Ar Ray al Amm* (Public Opinion), each with a prewar circulation of 80,000, are more conservative and support the government. With regard to other information media, the Ministry of Information operates the three stations of Radio Kuwait and the Kuwait Television station.

Foreign Relations

As the Iraqi invasion demonstrated, Kuwait's large oil revenues and inherently small defense capabilities gave it tremendous vulnerability. Historically, until the Iraqi invasion, Kuwaiti leaders had always dealt with that vulnerability through diplomacy, trying to find allies that would protect them while maintaining as much independence as possible from those allies by playing them off against each other. Historically, the most important ally was Britain. Kuwait's relationship with Britain came about at the bidding of the early Kuwaiti leader Shaykh Mubarak in an effort to deter a still more troublesome actor, the Ottoman Empire. As one consequence of the 1899 treaty, which gave Kuwait a better status than was the case in British treaties with other possessions, the British presence remained somewhat distant, and British officials meddled less frequently in local politics.

The relationship with Britain continued beyond independence on June 19, 1961, and the new agreement between independent Kuwait and Britain promised continued British protection as necessary. That protection did prove necessary when Iraq, six days after Kuwait's independence, declared Kuwait a part of Iraq and sent troops toward the amirate in support of that claim. Because Kuwait's army was too small to defend the state, British troops arrived, followed soon after by forces from the League of Arab States (Arab League), in the face of which Iraqi forces withdrew.

As Britain increasingly withdrew from the gulf in the 1970s and 1980s, Kuwait was forced to look for other sources of support. Although Kuwaiti leaders tried to maintain a degree of neutrality between the superpowers—Kuwait had an early and sustained economic, military, and diplomatic relationship with the Soviet Union—in the end it was obliged to turn to the United States for support. The Iran-Iraq War was the decisive factor in consolidating closer ties with the United States. Although at the outset of the war Kuwait was an outspoken critic of United States military presence in the gulf, during the war this position changed. When Kuwaiti ships became the target of Iranian attacks, Kuwait's security situation deteriorated, and Kuwait approached the Soviet Union and the United States with requests to reflag and thus protect its beleaguered tankers. As soon as the Soviet Union responded positively to the request, the United States followed. The ground was thus laid for subsequent United States support.

Persian Gulf War

On August 2, 1990, Iraqi forces invaded and occupied Kuwait. On February 26, 1991, United States-led coalition forces restored Kuwaiti sovereignty. These paired events represented both the failure and the success of Kuwait's foreign policy.

The primary impetus for the invasion lay in the dynamics of internal Iraqi politics—economic and political concerns after the long, debilitating, and ultimately unsuccessful Iran-Iraq War. However, economic and political relations between Iraq and Kuwait provided the context for conflict.

Iraq's first financial disagreement with Kuwait related to oil policy. Iraq objected to Kuwait's production beyond OPEC quotas and the consequent contribution that overproduction made to lowering oil prices internationally. Iraq also claimed

Kuwait was siphoning oil from the shared Ar Rumaylah oil field straddling the Iraq-Kuwait border. During the Iran-Iraq War, Iraq ceased production from its side of the field while Kuwait continued operations. Kuwait asserted it had taken oil only from its own side of the field; Iraq claimed its oil had been poached. Another financial disagreement with Kuwait concerned the estimated US$13 billion that Kuwait had lent Iraq during the Iran-Iraq War, a debt that Iraq wished Kuwait to forgive. These financial claims were set in a broader context. The Iraqi government experienced serious financial strains following the war with Iran; nearby Kuwait had apparently ample resources. To obtain these resources, Iraq put forward whatever financial claims it could.

In addition to economic issues, Iraq also disagreed with Kuwait over borders. This claim had two somewhat contradictory dimensions. Iraq first disputed the location of the border and then reaffirmed its claim to all of Kuwait. The latter claim rested on the argument that Iraq had once ruled Kuwait. This assertion to historical sovereignty over Kuwait was not solidly grounded: Kuwait had always been a self-governing political entity. Despite Ottoman Iraq's historic interest in Kuwait, it had never ruled the shaykhdom. When Kuwait was first established, the area was under the control of the Bani Khalid of Arabia, not the Ottomans. For a brief period in the late nineteenth century, Kuwait moved closer to the Ottomans, and for a short time Abd Allah as Salim held the Ottoman title of *qaimaqam,* or provincial governor; part of the Iraqi claim invoked this fact (see Ruling Family, this ch.). After Britain and Kuwait signed the 1899 treaty, Ottoman forces, anxious to overthrow Mubarak, had no place in the shaykhdom. British forces came to Mubarak's support as needed in favor of Kuwaiti independence.

Kuwait's status was again a matter of international discussion in the period around World War I. In 1913 British and Ottoman representatives drew up the draft Anglo-Ottoman Convention in which Britain recognized Ottoman suzerainty over Kuwait but at the same time declared Kuwait an autonomous district of the Ottoman Empire. The convention conditioned recognition of Ottoman interests in Kuwait on the promise of Ottoman noninterference in the internal affairs of Kuwait. The Iraqi government's later assertion that this constituted British recognition of Iraqi jurisdiction in Kuwait was weak. The document specifically recognized Kuwait's historical political autonomy and disallowed Iraqi interference in Kuwait's domestic affairs. In any event, the document was never ratified, and at the beginning of World War I, Britain moved closer to Kuwait, not farther away. At the end of World War I, the Ottoman Empire was dissolved. In the 1923 Treaty of Lausanne, Turkey renounced claims to all former Ottoman provinces.

In the interwar years, the border question again arose. In 1922 the British convened a conference at Al Uqayr in Saudi Arabia that set Saudi Arabia's borders with Kuwait and Iraq but not Kuwait and Iraq's border with each other. However, in 1923 the British high commissioner in Iraq sent a memorandum to the political agent in Kuwait laying out the border between Kuwait and Iraq. When in 1932 Iraq applied to the League of Nations for membership as an independent state, it included information on the borders from the memorandum.

Iraq thus seemed to be moving toward acceptance of its border with Kuwait when the discovery of oil, the promise of more Kuwaiti oil revenues, and the related Majlis Movement occurred. As the Majlis Movement grew, Iraq began to support dissidents in Kuwait and simultaneously put forward claims to Kuwait. Iraq also explored the idea of building a port on Kuwait's coast to give Iraq an alternative to its port of Basra. Iraq began expressing interest in the islands of Bubiyan and Warbah as well. The Majlis Movement in Kuwait failed, however, and Iraq had to await another opportunity.

As long as Britain was there to support Kuwait, Iraq could do little more than assert a verbal claim. When Kuwait became independent in 1961, the Iraqi government tested Britain's resolve by bringing forces to Kuwait's border in support of its claims on the shaykhdom. British and Arab League forces, however, forestalled any Iraqi military action.

In 1963 a new government came to power in Iraq. Anxious to mend fences, this government formally recognized Kuwait and signed an agreement recognizing the borders between the two states as those set forth in Iraq's 1932 application to the League of Nations. Iraq then dropped its objection to Kuwait's membership in the UN and in the Arab League and established diplomatic relations, including the exchange of ambassadors, with Kuwait.

Nonetheless, tensions lingered. During the 1960s and 1970s, a series of border incidents took place, and there was continuing Iraqi pressure for Kuwait to relinquish, or at least offer long-term leases on, the islands of Warbah and Bubiyan. In the 1980s, relations between the two states appeared to improve as Iraq, desperate for Kuwaiti financial support in its war with Iran, was careful not to press its unpopular claims. Both sides claimed sincerity in their historical effort to negotiate the border issue. When the war ended, however, the border issue reappeared.

The dispute itself does not seem to have been a precipitating factor in the invasion. When Iraq entered Kuwait in August 1990, it claimed to do so in support of a Kuwaiti rebellion. When no pro-Iraqi rebellion (or even bloc) emerged, and Iraq found itself unable to set up a pliable Kuwaiti government, it was forced to resort to direct occupation. It was only at this point that the Iraqi claim to Kuwait resurfaced. On August 9, one week after the invasion, Iraq formally annexed Kuwait, adding the northern part of the country, including the Ar Rumaylah oil field and the islands of Warbah and Bubiyan, to Iraq's province of Basra and creating a separate province out of the rest of Kuwait.

After Kuwait's liberation, the UN established a five-member boundary commission to demarcate the Kuwait-Iraq boundary in accordance with UN Security Council Resolution 687, which reaffirmed the inviolability of the Iraq-Kuwait border. In April 1992, the commission announced its findings, which demarcated the Kuwaiti border with Iraq about 570 meters to the north of the old border near the Iraqi town of Safwan and slightly north in the region of the contested Ar Rumaylah oil field. These modifications gave Kuwait six oil wells in the field and part of the Iraqi naval base of Umm Qasr. Kuwait accepted the commission's finding and announced it intended to build a security fence along its border with Iraq as an advance warning system. Iraq responded to the findings with an angry letter in May to the UN secretary general rejecting the commission's findings. Domestically, it continued to refer to Kuwait's territory as an integral part of Iraq. Physical demarcation of the land boundary was completed in November 1992.

The postwar period thus opened with many of the issues still unresolved that had played a role in precipitating the invasion and war. In Iraq the government of Saddam Husayn continued to assert its prewar claim to Kuwait, coloring Kuwait's postwar foreign policy. As long as Saddam Husayn remains at the helm in Iraq, Kuwait can feel no real security. Even were he to be replaced, much of the insecurity that haunts Kuwait and drives its foreign policy would remain. Kuwaitis see the war as one waged by the Iraqi people and remember previous Iraqi promises to respect Kuwait's sovereignty. Kuwait will continue to see Iraq as a serious threat, regardless of what transpires in Iraq's leadership.

Post-Persian Gulf War Foreign Policy

Kuwait's postwar foreign policy is therefore based on two assumptions. The first is that security, notably with regard to Iraq, is its primary concern. The second is that security ultimately can be guaranteed only by the United States. It is clear that Kuwait alone, or even Kuwait with the support of the Gulf Cooperation Council (GCC), established in May 1981, and other Arab members of the coalition—a formal plan, known as the 1991 Damascus Declaration, to include Egypt and Syria in gulf defense arrangements was moribund soon after its issuance—cannot provide for its own defense needs (see Collective Security under the Gulf Cooperation Council, ch. 7). In August 1991, Kuwait and the United States signed a US$81 million Foreign Military Sales agreement. In September 1991, Kuwait signed a formal ten-year defense agreement with the United States that permits the United States to pre-position weapons and conduct military exercises in Kuwait at Kuwaiti expense. However, the agreement does not provide for establishing a permanent United States base there. In 1992 Kuwaiti and United States forces carried out joint exercises under the defense agreement. Kuwait has backed up its formal security arrangements with a close political and economic relationship with the United States. It has given much of its postwar reconstruction business to United States firms, including civil reconstruction contracts that have been awarded through the United States Army Corps of Engineers and many contracts directly related to defense needs. The new pro-United States policy is not without its detractors. In the summer of 1992, the speaker of Kuwait's since-disbanded National Council asserted that the United States ambassador was interfering in internal Kuwaiti affairs. The Kuwaiti government and numerous Kuwaitis, however, condemned these remarks.

Kuwait maintains similarly close ties with other members of the coalition, signing defense agreements with Britain and in 1992 negotiating an agreement with France. It is seeking similar agreements with the remaining Security Council permanent members, Russia and China. It remains very close to

Saudi Arabia. Relations with a regionally resurgent Iran remain ambivalent. Kuwait's relationship with Iran improved dramatically after the Iraqi invasion, which, in drawing attention to Iraq's expansionist ambitions, seemingly vindicated Iran's wartime position. An inevitable conflict remains, however, between Kuwait's postwar aim of maintaining a high and visible level of United States support and Iran's desire to limit United States presence in the gulf. In mid-1992 this tension was seen in a minor dispute over the fate of Kuwait Airways passenger aircraft flown by Iraq to Iran during the war. Kuwait demanded the swift return of the aircraft, whereas Iran demanded US$90 million for servicing them while they remained in Iran.

Kuwaiti policy toward states that had supported Iraq has been unforgiving. One of the hard lessons Kuwait's rulers learned from the Iran-Iraq War is that foreign aid does not buy popularity or enduring political support. Some of its largest aid was to Jordan, Sudan, and Yemen, countries that nonetheless failed to support the coalition. Kuwait cut those countries from its foreign aid program once sovereignty was restored. Kuwait was also a major donor to the Palestine Liberation Organization (PLO). The PLO's wartime support of Iraq also resulted in severance of Kuwaiti monetary and political support. In June 1992, the National Council approved denying economic aid to Arab countries that supported Iraq's invasion. Although foreign aid will continue as a feature of Kuwait's foreign policy, Kuwait's limited postinvasion revenues and its experience during the occupation indicate that such aid would decrease.

Reconstruction after the Persian Gulf War

Postwar Society

The invasion and occupation had a transformative effect on virtually every aspect of Kuwaiti life. Iraqi troops plundered and looted the city of Kuwait. Iraqi occupation forces, according to reports of human rights monitoring groups, tortured and summarily executed those suspected of involvement in the underground opposition movement that quickly emerged.

In the course of the occupation, more than half the population, foreigner and citizen alike, fled Kuwait. After the reestablishment of Kuwaiti sovereignty in February 1991, and the restoration of basic services soon afterward, the population began to return. In May 1991, the government opened the doors to all Kuwaiti citizens who wished to return. The government was far more reluctant to readmit nonnationals, whom it considered a security risk and whom it regarded as not needed in prewar numbers owing to the postwar constriction of the economy. Consequently, relatively fewer nonnationals were allowed to return. A National Bank of Kuwait report estimated the total population of Kuwait in March 1992 at 1,175,000 people, 53 percent of whom were Kuwaitis, compared with an estimated 27 percent Kuwaitis of the 2,155,000 population on the eve of the Iraqi invasion in 1990.

The postoccupation Kuwaiti population differs sharply from that before the invasion. The population is divided psychologically between those who experienced the direct horror of the Iraqi occupation and survived and those who spent the war abroad in what seemed a relatively comfortable exile to many of those who stayed in Kuwait. But the shared experience has unified the country in other ways. Because Kuwait is a small country with large family groups, almost every Kuwaiti lost family members to the Iraqi forces, and there is continuing uncertainty over the 600 or more Kuwaitis that remain prisoners in Iraq. The fate of those who disappeared is an issue of national concern. Regardless of personal losses and experiences during the occupation, the society as a whole has been traumatized by the memory of the invasion and by the uncertain future. A government led by a ruling family that fled in the face of the Iraqi danger can do little to dispel this ambient fear. One expression of the insecurity is a general concern about lawlessness, both a breakdown in some of the peaceable norms that had united prewar Kuwait and a breakdown in the government's ability to enforce those norms owing to the widespread possession of guns (a result of the war) and the reluctance of a still fearful population to return those guns to the state. After the initial lawless months following liberation, the government recovered control of internal security and reinstituted the rule of law.

The position of nonnationals in postwar Kuwait is very different from that of citizens. Perhaps two-thirds of the foreign population fled during the invasion and occupation. Most of those who fled have not been allowed to return, notably the large Palestinian population, who, owing to the public support of Iraq by many prominent Palestinians outside Kuwait, became the target of public and private animosity in the months after liberation. Before the war, Palestinians composed Kuwait's largest foreign population, numbering perhaps 400,000. By 1992 that number had fallen to fewer than 30,000.

In the first postwar days, many Palestinians who remained became victims of private vigilante groups, of which some were apparently linked to members of the ruling family. Human rights monitoring organizations such as Amnesty International and Middle East Watch have reported the murder of dozens of Palestinians and the arrest and torture of hundreds more. The most dramatic transformation is the exodus of the bulk of the Palestinian population. The reaction against Palestinians and other members of groups or states whose leaders had supported Iraq expressed itself in 1991 in a series of show trials of alleged collaborators, carried out, according to international observers and human rights monitoring groups, with little regard for due process. In the face of international criticism, the amir commuted the many death sentences, some given for rather small offenses, that the court had handed down. Trials that took place in late 1992, however, were regarded by international human rights groups as being fair and respecting due process.

One of the first policy decisions the government made on returning to Kuwait was to reduce Kuwait's dependence on foreign labor in an effort to ensure that Kuwaitis would henceforth remain a majority in their country. Former foreign workers are unhappy with this policy, but there is little they can do. Divided between those who oppose Iraq and those who do not, they pose no unified threat. Their energy has been dissipated by individual efforts to arrange to stay. The government and population alike remain deeply suspicious of the nonnational population.

After the war, the government announced it planned to restrict the number of resident foreigners, to keep the nonnational population below 50 percent of the total population, and to ensure that no single non-Kuwaiti nationality would make up more than 10 percent of the total population. In December 1991, the government closed most domestic staff employment agencies and drew up new regulations covering the licensing of domestic staff. In early 1992, the Ministry of Interior announced new rules for issuing visas to dependents of expatriate workers, limiting them to higher wage earners. Looking further into the future, the government approved a resolution in March 1992 doubling to US$14,000 the sum given to young men at marriage in an effort to encourage local population growth. In June 1992, the government announced it had set aside US$842 million for end-of-service payments to foreigners.

The new policy of limiting the number of foreign workers has had serious economic consequences. Foreigners represent many of Kuwait's top technical and managerial workers. The exodus of most of the nonnational population has created special problems for an education system that in 1990 was still heavily dependent on foreign teachers. The direct damage inflicted on school property and looting by Iraqi forces aggravated the education problem. Nonetheless, in September 1991 the university and vocational schools reopened for the first time since the occupation.

The exodus of foreigners also has hampered the health care system, as did the systematic looting of some the country's modern medical equipment by Iraqi forces. The invasion and war added some new health concerns, which include long-term deleterious health effects owing to the environmental damage and to the psychological impact of the war.

Nevertheless, the same forces that generated a prewar need for labor remain operative. A number of years are needed to train Kuwaitis for many of the positions held by foreigners. In the interim, indications are that the preinvasion shift away from Arab and toward Asian labor will continue. One small benefit of the new labor policy is that the government will save some money on services previously provided to the larger foreign population. The basic shortage of sufficient quantities of national manpower, coupled with a political and social reluctance to increase womanpower, limit the extent to which the government can do without imported labor.

Economic Reconstruction

Despite the devastation of the Kuwaiti economy during the invasion and occupation, recovery has proceeded with surprising speed. This was partly because some damage, particularly of the infrastructure, was not as serious as first feared and partly because the government, anxious to restore the population's weakened confidence in its ability to administer, has given reconstruction and recovery of basic services a high priority.

The oil industry, which was badly damaged, has been a top priority because it is the source of revenues to sustain other government spending programs. The most dramatic economic reconstruction effort went toward capping the more than 700 oil wells set afire by retreating Iraqi forces. In addition to an estimated 2 percent of the country's 100 billion barrels of reserves lost in the oil fires, Kuwait had to pay for putting out fires and repairing damaged refineries, pipelines, and other oil infrastructure. By January 1992, oil output had risen to 550,000 bpd. By June 1992, it was back to nearly 1 million bpd. Nineteen new wells were drilled to replace those damaged by the occupation.

The government hoped to raise production to 2 million bpd by the end of 1993. During the invasion, Iraq destroyed or incapacitated Kuwait's entire 700,000 bpd refining capacity at its three refineries. But by April 1992, production levels rose to 300,000 bpd. Nonetheless, there was concern that the rapid return to production might have damaged Kuwait's oil reservoirs beyond the damage done by retreating Iraqi forces, lowering its total future reserves. Accordingly, KOC contracted with several international companies to assess reservoir damage. However, the government also has been under tremendous pressure to increase oil production quickly to pay for war and postwar expenses. In the mid-1980s, overseas investments outstripped oil as the primary source of revenues. The expenses of war, postwar reconstruction, and investment irregularities that were being uncovered in late 1992 have forced the government to use substantial portions of its investment principal, and in the 1990s oil is again expected to be the major revenue source.

Restoring oil operations was expensive. In January 1992, the oil minister announced Kuwait had already spent US$1.5 billion for putting out fires and planned to spend another US$8 to US$10 billion to repair further damage. A National Bank of Kuwait report in mid-1992 estimated that reconstruction expenses in the oil sector for the 1992–95 period would reach US$6.5 billion.

The rest of the economy also suffered, although the effects were not as severe as the oil-well fires. The banking sector, suffering the shock waves of the Suq al Manakh stock market crash in 1982, recovered slowly from the combined effects of that crash and the invasion. The agenda of the returned government included bank reform. In December 1991, the government announced a comprehensive settlement plan for bad debts, the outstanding issue of the Suq al Manakh crash. The plan involved government purchase of the entire domestic loan portfolio of the country's local banking system. The government agreed to buy US$20 billion of domestic debt from eleven commercial banks and investment companies in exchange for bonds. This plan removed the concerns of Kuwaitis, who would be obliged to repay debts, if at all, on more modest terms, and of banks, concerned about nonperforming loans. Although Shaykh Salim al Abd al Aziz Al Sabah, governor of the Central Bank of Kuwait, said the plan is needed to prevent the collapse of banks, it clearly also is intended as part of a series of government payments to Kuwaiti nationals and businesses aimed at restoring confidence in the government prior to the October election. The plan, announced but as yet incomplete, left the entire banking system in a state of limbo in late 1992.

Banks have suffered less from the physical damage of the war and more from the sudden reduction in the number of employees, many of whom in the prewar period were foreigners. Some banks reported postwar staff levels at half those before the invasion. Although there has been speculation that postwar reform will include mergers involving state-controlled banks (notably the Kuwait Investment Company, the Kuwait International Investment Company, and the Kuwait Foreign Trading, Contracting, and Investment Company, known together as the three Ks) and private-sector banks, no formal action had been taken as of late 1992. The bank that survived the invasion in the best shape was the largest commercial bank, the National Bank of Kuwait. It handled the exiled government's finances during the crisis.

According to a National Bank of Kuwait report issued in mid-1992, several additional factors hurt the private sector's recovery. The first was the government's decision to restrict the number of nonnationals, which hampered efforts to import skilled and unskilled labor and left Kuwait with a smaller market. The second was the lower level of government investment in industry as a result of reduced government income and the government decision to invest more in defense and focus in the short run on restoring basic services. The non-oil manufacturing sector, although small, was hurt by the looting and damage done by Iraqi troops. The government has been in no position to subsidize industries at the level it had in the past. Infrastructure projects incomplete before the invasion have not been resumed or have been delayed.

The only sector of the economy to prosper in the immediate postwar period is trade because of the need to replace inventory emptied during the occupation. Returning Kuwaitis and the government have created a small boom for investors. By mid-1992, however, the return demand largely had been met, and many goods, notably automobiles and consumer durables, were available in excess supply. In an effort to boost the private sector, the government approved an offset program in July 1992 requiring foreign companies to reinvest part of their government-awarded contracts locally. Companies with contracts valued at more than US$17 million have been obliged to reinvest 30 percent of the contract sum.

Despite some speculation that the government would turn more functions over to the private sector following its return, widespread privatization has not occurred. In February 1992, the government announced plans to start privatizing the public telecommunications network, a move that was expected to generate US$1 billion for the government. In May the government announced it would privatize seventy-seven local gas stations. There have been, however, no indications of more substantial denationalizations.

Reconstruction costs, which some foreign observers initially put as high as US$100 billion, appear to be more modest, perhaps in the range of US$20 to US$25 billion. The largest postwar expense the government faces is not reconstruction, but the debt it incurred to coalition allies to help pay for Operation Desert Storm, an amount that came to at least US$20 billion, and continuing high defense expenditures (see table 12, Appendix). Reconstruction costs have been met largely from Kuwait's reduced investments (the *Financial Times* estimated in February 1992 that Kuwait had lost as much as US$30 billion of its prewar investment portfolio); from returning oil revenues, which for fiscal year 1992 were only expected to generate US$2.4 billion; and from borrowing on international money markets. In October 1991, the government announced plans to borrow US$5 billion for the first phase of a five-year loan program. The loan would be the largest in history. In mid-1992 one study indicated that as much as 30 percent of 1993 revenue will be needed to pay interest on various government debts, which were expected to exceed US$37 billion by the end of 1992.

Despite the apparently dire economic situation, the government has felt politically obliged to sustain insofar as possible the prewar standard of living. Some of the largest domestic postwar government expenditures have gone directly to Kuwaiti households. The banking debt buyout was but one of a series of measures taken by the government to help nationals hurt by the invasion. The government decided to pay all government employees (the majority of working nationals) their wages for the period of the occupation. In March 1992, the government raised state salaries. The government also agreed to write off about US$1.2 billion in consumer loans, a measure benefiting more than 120,000 Kuwaitis. It wrote off US$3.4 billion worth of property and housing loans made before the invasion. Each Kuwaiti family that stayed in Kuwait through the occupation received US$1,750. In July 1992, the government exempted Kuwaitis from charges for public services due as a result of the occupation, such as bills for electricity, utilities, and telephone service and for rents on housing.

Politics

The invasion also changed the dynamics of Kuwaiti politics. The crisis of invasion, occupation, and exile further solidified the Kuwaiti opposition, which had begun emerging in the Constitutional Movement before the invasion. During the invasion, much of the opposition and the government regrouped in exile in Saudi Arabia. There, opposition leaders reiterated their preinvasion concerns and called on the amir to promise a return to a more democratic system in restored Kuwait.

The showdown came in October 1990 when the ruler met with 1,200 opposition leaders in Saudi Arabia and publicly promised liberalization following liberation. The elite opposition, however, finally unified just as it was losing its popular base to the resistance groups inside Kuwait. Kuwaitis who spent months fighting the occupation had little need for those who spent the war in relatively comfortable exile. To them, opposition leaders in exile became figures as distant as the amir. These divisions surfaced as goods waited in warehouses while resistance leaders argued with returned administrators over the right to feed the population. The opposition, so briefly united, redivided. Several identifiable factions emerged. These included the Democratic Forum, representing the liberal progressives. In defiance of the law, the Democratic Forum declared itself a political party in 1991. The Sunni Islamist opposition broke into the historically Muslim Brotherhood-oriented Islamic Constitutional Movement and the Islamic Alliance. The National Islamic Coalition represented Shia.

Had the amir returned quickly to Kuwait, stood above the factions, and appealed to the natural desire of a population tired by war to retreat from politics to the private world of reunited families, he might have scuttled the prodemocracy movement and reimposed a relatively benign authoritarianism. Instead, the amir hesitated and unwittingly forged a broad united prodemocratic front that could truly challenge his rule. Instead of fracturing, the Kuwaiti opposition came together, voicing a unified demand for a more open, participatory political system. The amir finally agreed to hold elections for the National Assembly in October 1992 (see Legislature, this ch.). In the interim, the National Council continued to meet.

There is little postwar change in the ruling family's dominant position in the country, although probably more grumbling occurs in private about the family's behavior. The Al Sabah continue to control the highest posts, although there have been changes in personnel. In April 1991, the government announced a new cabinet. Whereas the overall presence of the ruling family changed little, the number of cabinet members from the Salim branch rather than the Jabir branch increased, a shift that usually had occurred only after a succession. In the cabinet, Sabah al Ahmad Al Sabah, minister of foreign affairs since the 1960s, was replaced by Salim as Salim Al Sabah, formerly minister of interior. In addition, Minister of Finance Ali al Khalifa Al Sabah stepped down, and Minister of Defense Nawwaf al Ahmad Al Sabah was appointed to the less significant post of minister of social affairs and labor. The opposition hoped that the primary check on the royal family and the cabinet would be the National Assembly. Following the October 1992 election, the Salim and Jabir branches' representation in the cabinet became more balanced.

In 1993 the government continued to express a profound ambivalence about political liberalization. Although it lifted press censorship in January 1992, the government still imposed restrictions on coverage critical of the government. The government has banned several public meetings by opposition groups and private associations. The October 1992 election revealed the basic forces that are likely to continue to shape Kuwait's political future into the twenty-first century. The first force is an historically grounded and popular impulse toward political liberalization. Although the prodemocracy movement may experience times of relative quiescence as it has in the past, it is unlikely to be extinguished. The second is what appeared in the immediate postinvasion period to be a growing impulse toward more authoritarian rule. Whereas Kuwait historically has not experienced heavy-handed government, pockets of its population (some foreigners and Shia) have felt the heavier hand of the state at times. The amir's efforts to develop a larger internal security apparatus to use first against the resident Palestinian population and then against the national opposition threatens Kuwait's prodemocracy movement. These efforts also ran into strong opposition when the National Assembly convened in October 1992. Like the prodemocracy movement, the new security force will not vanish unless compelled to do so. The invasion thus appears to have activated both a more authoritarian impulse in the government and a more prodemocratic impulse among the population. The postinvasion period has seen the struggle between these two forces.

*   *   *

Ahmad Abu-Hakima's *Modern History of Kuwait* provides a good historical overview. Jill Crystal's *Kuwait: The Transformation of an Oil State* offers a general overview of Kuwait; her *Oil and Politics in the Gulf* provides a more analytical survey of Kuwaiti politics. On politics, Hassan Ibrahim's *Kuwait: a Political Study* and John E. Peterson's *The Arab Gulf States* are helpful. On the ruling family, a most useful book is Alan Rush's *Al-Sabah: Genealogy and History of Kuwait's Ruling Family, 1752–1986*. The best general introduction to Kuwait's foreign policy environment is Abdul-Reda Assiri's *Kuwait's Foreign Policy*.

A general sociological introduction to Kuwait is found in Jacqueline Ismael's *Kuwait: Social Change in Historical Perspective*. Suad al-Sabah's *Development Planning in an Oil Economy and the Role of the Woman* looks at women's issues in Kuwait. With regard to expatriates, Shamlan Alessa's *The Manpower Problem in Kuwait* is helpful.

Books on Kuwait's economy include M.W. Khouja and P.G. Sadler's *The Economy of Kuwait*; Y.S.F. al-Sabah's *The Oil Economy of Kuwait*; Ragaei El Mallakh and Jacob Atta's *The Absorptive Capacity of Kuwait*; and Suad al-Sabah's *Kuwait: Anatomy of a Crisis Economy*. Fida Darwiche covers Kuwait's stock market crash in *The Gulf Stock Exchange Crash*.

A wealth of statistical information is available in the annual reports put out by the Kuwait Ministry of Planning's Central Statistical Office in its *Annual Statistical Abstract*. Current economic events can be followed in the *Middle East Economic Digest, Economist, Wall Street Journal,* and *Financial Times* (which usually surveys Kuwait in February). (For further information and complete citations, see Bibliography.)

Chapter 3. Bahrain

Crest of the State of Bahrain

Country Profile

Country

Formal Name: State of Bahrain.

Short Form: Bahrain.

Term for Citizens: Bahraini(s); adjectival form, Bahraini.

Capital: Manama.

Date of Independence: August 15, 1971 .

Geography

Size: 694 square kilometers.

Topography: Archipelago of low desert islands, of which largest is Bahrain.

Climate: Hot and humid, little rainfall.

Society

Population: About 550,000 in early 1992, of which 66 percent Bahrainis; 1992 growth rate 3.1 percent.

Education: Almost all children in six- to eleven-year-old age-group enrolled in primary school system; about two-thirds of all twelve- to fourteen-year-olds enrolled in intermediate schools.

Health: Free, comprehensive public health care system. Two private hospitals and one military hospital. Life expectancy for Bahraini children born in 1990 seventy years for males and seventy-five years for females.

Ethnic Groups: Most Bahrainis are Arabs, although fairly large number of Iranian origin. Foreign residents include other Arabs, Iranians, Indians, Pakistanis, and small groups of East Asians and Europeans.

NOTE—The Country Profile contains updated information as available.

Religion: Population 85 percent Muslim, including about 70 percent Shia and 30 percent Sunni. Non-Muslim foreigners include 7.3 percent Christians and 7.7 percent Hindus and others.

Economy

Gross Domestic Product (GDP): In 1990 about US$4.0 billion; per capita GDP US$7,500; real growth rate 6.7 percent (1988).

Agriculture: Contributed 1.0 percent of GDP (at current prices) in 1990.

Mining and Manufacturing: Hydrocarbons and related industries, mining, and manufacturing contributed 36.3 percent of GDP (at current prices) in 1990.

Electricity, Water, and Construction: Contributed 7.7 percent of GDP (at current prices) in 1990.

Trade, Transportation, and Communications: Wholesale and retail trade, restaurants and hotels, and transportation and communications contributed 18.1 percent of GDP (at current prices) in 1990.

Services: Financial, government, and other services contributed 36.9 percent of GDP (at current prices) in 1990.

Exports: Total exports about US$3.5 billion in 1991. Major exports included crude oil, refined oil products, and aluminum.

Imports: Total about US$3.6 billion in 1991. Major imports included crude petroleum, machinery and transportation equipment, and food.

Currency and Exchange Rate: Bahraini dinar. In 1994 exchange rate US$1 = BD0.376 (fixed rate).

Fiscal Year: Calendar year.

Transportation and Telecommunications

Transportation: In 1994 more than 200 kilometers of paved roads; also twenty-five-kilometer causeway to Saudi Arabia; two major ports: Mina Salman and Sitrah; Bahrain International Airport for airline service.

Telecommunications: In 1994 excellent domestic and international service—telephones, submarine cables, three satellite ground stations, television station, two AM and three FM radio stations.

Government and Politics

Government: Ruler (amir) is head of state and head of government. Shaykh Isa ibn Salman Al Khalifa became amir in 1961; his son and designated successor, Shaykh Hamad ibn Isa Al Khalifa, continued to serve as deputy prime minister in 1993. National Assembly elected in 1973, dissolved in 1975; no plans in 1993 to reestablish it.

Politics: No political parties. Senior members of Al Khalifa and other notable families dominate political and economic decision making.

Foreign Relations: Shaykh Isa ibn Salman continued in 1993 to maintain friendly relations with most countries, Iraq being the principal exception. Major diplomatic activities channeled through Gulf Cooperation Council. Member of United Nations, League of Arab States, Organization of the Petroleum Exporting Countries, and Organization of the Islamic Conference.

National Security

Armed Forces: In mid-1993 personnel strength 7,150: army, 6,000; navy, 500; and air force, 650. Service voluntary. Army in 1991 had eighty-one M–60A3 main battle tanks and armored cars. Navy had two corvettes and four missile craft. Air force had McDonnell Douglas F–5 Tigers, General Dynamics F–16 Fighting Falcons, and Agusta/Bell-212 armed helicopters.

Paramilitary: In mid-1993 coast guard about 400 personnel; police about 9,000.

IN 1993 BAHRAIN CONTINUED to be ruled by the Al Khalifa family. The amir, Shaykh Isa ibn Salman Al Khalifa (b. 1933), was the eleventh ruler of the Al Khalifa dynasty, which has ruled the country since 1783. Originally, the Al Khalifa were a prominent family among the Bani Utub beduin tribes from the interior of the Arabian Peninsula who had settled on the Persian Gulf coast during the eighteenth century. The Al Khalifa initially established a successful commercial port at Az Zubarah on the western coast of the Qatar Peninsula, but this was attacked several times by rulers of Bahrain, at that time part of the Iranian Empire, which intermittently controlled Bahrain from 1602 to 1782. Eventually, with the assistance of a tribal coalition that included the Al Sabah (another Bani Utub family) of Kuwait, the Al Khalifa captured Bahrain from Iran. The first Al Khalifa ruler, Ahmad ibn Muhammad (r. 1783–96), adopted policies that enabled Bahrain's ports to develop into prosperous trade and pearling centers.

During the reign of subsequent Al Khalifa rulers, dynastic feuding among heirs, as well as wars with Oman, adversely affected Bahrain's economy and the security of regional trade. The family rivalries prompted Britain, then the paramount power in the area, to impose a series of treaties that made Bahrain a British protectorate by 1868. An important consequence of Britain's intervention was the regulation of the Al Khalifa succession on the basis of primogeniture. After the death of Shaykh Ali ibn Khalifa Al Khalifa (r. 1868–69) in a dynastic war instigated by his brother and nephew, Britain refused to accept the legitimacy of the victor's rule and forced all factions to acknowledge Ali's son, Shaykh Isa ibn Ali Al Khalifa (r. 1869–1923), as the rightful heir. Since that time, each Al Khalifa ruler has been succeeded by his eldest son. This practice was unlike succession in most other Arab dynasties, which chose the heir apparent from among several able males within the royal family. The principle of primogeniture was codified in the 1973 constitution.

In early 1993, Isa ibn Salman had ruled Bahrain for thirty-two years, having succeeded to the throne in 1961 on the death of his father, Shaykh Salman ibn Hamad Al Khalifa (r. 1942–61). At the time of Isa ibn Salman's accession, Bahrain was still a British protectorate. Isa ibn Salman negotiated the termination of the country's dependent status after Britain announced in 1968 that it would withdraw all its defense forces from the Persian Gulf region. When Bahrain achieved complete independence in 1971, Isa ibn Salman assumed the title of amir.

The Al Khalifa continued to dominate Bahrain's government and society after independence. The amir's brothers, sons, nephews, and cousins controlled the major decision-making positions. For example, Isa ibn Salman's brother, Shaykh Khalifa ibn Salman Al Khalifa, was prime minister and head of government in late 1992; the amir's eldest son, Shaykh Hamad ibn Isa Al Khalifa, was deputy prime minister and heir apparent; and six other members of the ruling family served in the cabinet, including Major General Khalifa ibn Ahmad Al Khalifa, who was minister of defense.

In 1993 Bahrain's economy continued to experience relative prosperity. Before the discovery of oil in 1932, the country's economy had been based on trade and pearling. Fortuitously, oil was discovered in commercial quantities just as the development of the cultured pearl by the Japanese caused the collapse of the Persian Gulf pearling industry. By 1935 oil wells and a small refinery were in operation, thus enabling Bahrain to claim distinction as the first Arab state in the region to benefit from the presence of oil resources. Both Shaykh Hamad ibn Isa Al Khalifa (r. 1923–42) and his son, Shaykh Salman ibn Hamad, used revenues obtained from oil concessions and production royalties to institute education and health care programs and various public services.

Although oil revenues accounted for more than one-half the government budget until the 1980s, the ruling family recognized that Bahrain's oil wells had a limited productive capacity and that oil reserves probably would be exhausted by the end of the twentieth century. Consequently, the government decided to base the country's long-term economic well-being on commercial and industrial diversification. Official efforts to encourage joint-venture projects resulted in the construction of several enterprises, including an aluminum plant (opened in 1972), a ship repair yard (1977), an iron foundry (1984), a chemical factory (1985), and a pharmaceutical facility (scheduled to open in 1993). In addition, Bahrain's efficient communications system and relatively liberal financial policies enabled the island state to emerge in the 1980s as a principal center for regional banking, insurance, and business operations.

The transformation of Bahrain's economy created new occupational groups, in particular an industrial working class and a highly educated professional class. Bahrain's large indigenous labor force was unique in the immediate area because foreign workers constituted the vast majority of the labor force in the neighboring countries of Kuwait, Qatar, Saudi Arabia, and the United Arab Emirates (UAE). Although trade unions and other labor associations were illegal in Bahrain, workers organized their first strike as early as 1943. Labor unrest erupted periodically during the next thirty years but declined after 1974, when the percentage of foreign workers in the industrial labor force began to increase significantly. The growth of an indigenous class of professionals tended to shift societal interest away from working conditions and wages in the oil industry and toward the issue of political participation. Bahrain's professionals were among the most enthusiastic supporters of the brief experiment with an elected legislature in the early 1970s; since the dissolution of the National Assembly in 1975, professionals have been consistent advocates of a return to democratic political institutions.

Two generations of economic and social changes failed to lessen sectarian tensions in Bahrain. The Al Khalifa and their historical political allies are Sunni (see Glossary) Muslims. However, at least two-thirds of Bahrain's population identify themselves as Shia (see Glossary) Muslims. Shia were the original inhabitants of the archipelago when the Al Khalifa seized it from Iranian control in the 1780s. Although the Al Khalifa have not persecuted the Shia, they have habitually excluded them from political power. Shia generally resent their subordinate political status; periodically this resentment flares up as incidents of religious strife. The Iranian Revolution of 1979, which resulted in Shia clergy controlling that country's government, tended to exacerbate Shia-Sunni tensions in Bahrain because events in Iran inspired Shia activists in Bahrain to demand more equitable political representation for their community.

The Iranian Revolution and the subsequent Iran-Iraq War (1980–88) demonstrated how much Bahrain's political stability and economic prosperity depended on overall regional security. The government sought to contain the spillover effects of these crises by joining with Kuwait, Oman, Qatar, the UAE, and Saudi Arabia in the Gulf Cooperation Council (GCC) in 1981. As a result of its membership, Bahrain obtained GCC intelligence assistance in monitoring the activities of local dissident groups suspected of receiving support from Iran and profited from inclusion in regional economic development plans. In addition, it received GCC approval for a program of enhancing its military capability through the purchase of advanced United States weapons. During the Persian Gulf War of 1991, Bahrain participated in the GCC coalition that sent troops to Saudi Arabia to fight against Iraq and permitted the United States Navy to use its port facilities.

Geography and Population

Geography

Bahrain (from the Arabic word for "two seas") comprises an archipelago of thirty-three islands situated midway in the Persian Gulf close to the shore of the Arabian Peninsula. The islands are about twenty-four kilometers from the east coast of Saudi Arabia and twenty-eight kilometers from Qatar. The total area of the islands is 694 square kilometers, or about four times the size of the District of Columbia. The largest island, accounting for 83 percent of the area, is Bahrain (also seen as Al Bahrayn), which has an extent of 572 square kilometers. From north to south, Bahrain is forty-eight kilometers long; at its widest point in the north, it is sixteen kilometers from east to west (see fig. 6).

Around most of Bahrain is a relatively shallow inlet of the Persian Gulf known as the Gulf of Bahrain. The seabed adjacent to Bahrain is rocky and, mainly off the northern part of the island, covered by extensive coral reefs. Most of the island is low-lying and barren desert. Outcroppings of limestone form low rolling hills, stubby cliffs, and shallow ravines. The limestone is covered by various densities of saline sand, capable of supporting only the hardiest desert vegetation—chiefly thorn trees and scrub. There is a fertile strip five kilometers wide along the northern coast on which date, almond, fig, and pomegranate trees grow. The interior contains an escarpment that rises to 134 meters, the highest point on the island, to form Jabal ad Dukhan (Mountain of Smoke), named for the mists that often wreathe the summit. Most of the country's oil wells are situated in the vicinity of Jabal ad Dukhan.

Manama (Al Manamah), the capital, is located on the northeastern tip of the island of Bahrain. The main port, Mina Salman, also is located on the island, as are the major petroleum

refining facilities and commercial centers. Causeways and bridges connect Bahrain to adjacent islands and the mainland of Saudi Arabia. The oldest causeway, originally constructed in 1929, links Bahrain to Al Muharraq, the second largest island. Although the island is only six kilometers long, the country's second largest city, Al Muharraq, and the international airport are located there. A causeway also connects Al Muharraq to the tiny island of Jazirat al Azl, the site of a major ship-repair and dry-dock center. South of Jazirat al Azl, the island of Sitrah, site of the oil export terminal, is linked to Bahrain by a bridge that spans the narrow channel separating the two islands. The causeway to the island of Umm an Nasan, off the west coast of Bahrain, continues on to the Saudi mainland town of Al Khubar. Umm an Nasan is the private property of the amir and the site of his personal game preserve.

The other islands of significance include Nabi Salah, which is northwest of Sitrah; Jiddah, to the north of Umm an Nasan; and a group of islands, the largest of which is Hawar, near the coast of Qatar (see Geography; Foreign Relations, ch. 4). Nabi Salah contains several freshwater springs that are used to irrigate the island's extensive date palm groves. The rocky islet of Jiddah houses the state prison. Hawar and the small islands near it are the subject of a territorial dispute between Bahrain and Qatar. Hawar is nineteen kilometers long and about one and one-half kilometers wide. The other islands are uninhabited and are nesting sites for a variety of migratory birds.

Climate

Bahrain has two seasons: an extremely hot summer and a relatively mild winter. During the summer months, from April to October, afternoon temperatures average 40°C and can reach 48°C during June and July. The combination of intense heat and high humidity makes this season uncomfortable. In addition, a hot, dry southwest wind, known locally as the *qaws*, periodically blows sand clouds across the barren southern end of Bahrain toward Manama in the summer. Temperatures moderate in the winter months, from November to March, when the range is between 10°C and 20°C. However, humidity often rises above 90 percent in the winter. From December to March, prevailing winds from the southeast, known as the *shammal*, bring damp air over the islands. Regardless of the season, daily temperatures are fairly uniform throughout the archipelago.

Bahrain receives little precipitation. The average annual rainfall is seventy-two millimeters, usually confined to the winter months. No permanent rivers or streams exist on any of the islands. The winter rains tend to fall in brief, torrential bursts, flooding the shallow wadis that are dry the rest of the year and impeding transportation. Little of the rainwater is saved for irrigation or drinking. However, there are numerous natural springs in the northern part of Bahrain and on adjacent islands. Underground freshwater deposits also extend beneath the Gulf of Bahrain to the Saudi Arabian coast. Since ancient times, these springs have attracted settlers to the archipelago. Despite increasing salinization, the springs remain an important source of drinking water for Bahrain. Since the early 1980s, however, desalination plants, which render seawater suitable for domestic and industrial use, have provided about 60 percent of daily water consumption needs.

Population

In 1992 an estimated 550,000 people lived in Bahrain. This number included 363,000 Bahraini citizens and 187,000 foreign nationals. Citizens accounted for 66 percent of the total population, a decline from the 70 percent they represented in the 1981 census and the 82.5 percent they represented in 1971. The unofficial estimate indicated that the population had increased by 57 percent, or at an average annual growth rate of 5.2 percent, since 1981. In 1992 the growth rate was 3.1 percent. The non-Bahraini community, which grew from 112,000 in 1981 to 187,000 in 1992, increased by 67 percent, while the number of citizens increased by 52.5 percent in the same eleven-year period.

In 1992 an estimated 58 percent of the population was male and only 42 percent female. The gender disparity resulted from the exceptionally high number of men among Bahrain's foreign residents: 76 percent of foreign residents were male. The male-to-female ratio was more balanced among Bahraini citizens: about 50.3 percent were male and 49.7 percent female. The age distribution also was skewed: about 80 percent of the foreign population was more than fourteen years of age, but less than 60 percent of citizens were more than fourteen. For the total population, 33.4 percent were in the age-group of zero to fourteen; 62.8 percent were in the age-group of fifteen to fifty-nine; and a mere 3.8 percent were in the age-group of sixty years and older. Life expectancy for Bahraini children born in 1990 was seventy years for males and seventy-five years for females.

The population of Bahrain is overwhelmingly urban. About 85 percent of the people live in cities or suburbs. Most working-age men who reside in villages commute to jobs in urban areas. The largest city, Manama, is the principal commercial and cultural center. It had an estimated population of 152,000 in 1992. Manama's expansion since 1960, when its population was only 62,000, resulted in entire villages, fields, and palm and fruit groves—located to the east, north, and south of the city—being incorporated as part of the urban sprawl. Manama also spread to the west through the reclamation of hundreds of hectares from the sea. Traditional brick houses, built with central courtyards and wind towers in the architectural style of southern Iran, and covered bazaars are found in the old sections of the city. In the newer and less congested neighborhoods, multistory apartment complexes, high-rise hotels and office buildings, and supermarkets predominate. Because most of Bahrain's foreign workers tend to live in the city, their presence provides Manama with a cosmopolitan atmosphere.

The city of Al Muharraq, which had an estimated population of 75,000 in 1992, is the country's only other major city. Until the 1930s, the ruler lived in Al Muharraq; thus, for more than a century, the city served as Bahrain's political center, and its commercial importance rivaled that of Manama. Al Muharraq declined after the Al Khalifa family moved to the island of Bahrain, and for nearly forty years the city stagnated. During the 1970s, however, the construction of the US$60 million Arab Shipbuilding and Repair Yard adjacent to the fishing village of Al Hadd, located southeast of Bahrain International Airport, helped to stimulate an investment and development boom in the city.

Bahrain's main towns are Jidd Hafs, Ar Rifaa, Sitrah, and Madinat Isa. Throughout the nineteenth century and during the first half of the twentieth, Jidd Hafs was a relatively prosperous village renowned for its extensive date palm groves and the manufacture of medicinal drugs from the buds, flowers, and pollen of palm trees. By 1975, however, Jidd Hafs had been transformed into Manama's largest suburb. Ar Rifaa, which originally consisted of two adjacent villages—Ar Rifaa ash Sharqi and Ar Rifaa al Gharbi, established in the nineteenth century near natural springs in the central region of Bahrain—grew rapidly after 1952 when Shaykh Salman ibn Hamad established his official residence there. Ar Rifaa's importance as the country's political center has continued under Shaykh Isa ibn Salman, who constructed his palace in the town, as did several other members of the Al Khalifa. The town of Sitrah formerly consisted of several palm-cultivating villages, but extensive residential construction during the 1970s fused the villages into one large suburban town. Madinat Isa was a planned community built to relieve the congestion in Manama and such close suburbs as Jidd Hafs and Sanabis.

Society

Education

Bahrain has the oldest public education system in the Arabian Peninsula. The system was established in 1932 when the government assumed responsibility for operating two preexisting primary schools for boys. Subsequently, separate facilities for girls and various secondary programs were established. Since the 1970s, education has been one of the largest current government expenditures. Despite the intensity of government efforts, however, the literacy rate for adult citizens was only about 75 percent as recently as 1985. The literacy rate for 1990 was estimated by the United Nations Educational, Scientific, and Cultural Organization to be 77 percent for adults (82 percent for males and 69 percent for females). Nevertheless, literacy levels among Bahrainis born since independence in 1971 were high because an estimated 70 percent of primary and secondary school-age children attended school.

In the 1991–92 academic year, 99,348 students attended 129 public schools (see table 13, Appendix). Education in the public system, which included six-year primary schools, three-year intermediate schools, and three-year secular secondary schools, is free. Students receive supplies, uniforms, meals, and transportation to and from school at no charge. Almost all children in the six- to eleven-year-old age-group attend primary school, and about two-thirds of all twelve- to fourteen-year-olds are enrolled in intermediate schools. The number of girls attending public primary and intermediate schools was slightly less than the number of boys but exceeded the number of boys in secondary and vocational public schools.

In addition to the public education system, there are forty-eight private and religious schools, including the United States-operated and accredited Bahrain International School, which offers classes from primary school through secondary school. There were 6,400 public school teachers in the 1988–89 academic year, of whom 65 percent were native Bahrainis. Egyptians constituted the largest group of foreign teachers.

In 1927 the first group of Bahrainis to receive a university education enrolled at the American University of Beirut in Lebanon. The first institution of higher education in Bahrain, the Gulf Polytechnic, was established in 1968 as the Gulf Technical College. In 1984 Gulf Polytechnic merged with the University College of Art, Science, and Education, founded in 1979, to create a national university, the University of Bahrain, offering bachelor of arts and bachelor of science degrees. During the 1991-92 academic year, more than 4,000 students, of whom more than one-half were women, studied at the University of Bahrain.

Bahrain had two additional institutions of higher education in 1993. The College of Health Sciences, established in 1976, offers various medical technology and nurses' training programs. The Hotel and Catering Training Center, established in 1974, offers postsecondary vocational courses in management and culinary arts. No longer an independent entity, the Arabian Gulf University (AGU) was established outside Ar Rifaa in 1984 and funded by the six member countries of the GCC. Construction of AGU facilities, however, was delayed by the decline in oil revenues experienced by all GCC states in the mid-1980s. The first students graduated in 1989. All courses were discontinued in 1991 except for the College of Medicine, which accepted no new students for the 1991–92 academic year.

Health and Welfare

In 1925, when Bahrain was a British protectorate, the government established free medical service, including immunization, outpatient treatment, and hospitalization. The availability of preventive and curative health care led to the virtual eradication of such endemic and infectious diseases as smallpox, trachoma, and dysentery. By the 1980s, life expectancy was estimated at sixty-five years. In 1993 Bahrain's comprehensive health care system included facilities for inpatient and outpatient dental care, general medical care, maternity care, orthopedic care, pediatric care, and psychiatric care. Almost all primary and secondary treatment within the public health system is free to citizens and foreign residents.

The largest public hospital is the 1,000-bed Salmaniya Medical Center, which opened in 1978. The center is a general teaching hospital that has accident and emergency facilities and fully equipped laboratories. More than one-half of Bahrain's 400 physicians work at Salmaniya. The public health system also includes twenty-seven regional health centers that provide such primary care as diagnostic services, minor surgery, dentistry, prenatal and postnatal care, and general family medical care. In addition, the system includes sixteen child welfare centers. The government also maintains the 135-bed Bahrain Military Hospital, which is reserved for members of the armed forces and their families.

In 1992 there were two small private hospitals in Bahrain. The forty-five-bed American Mission Hospital, operated by the United States-based Arabian Mission of the Dutch Reformed Church, is the oldest hospital in the country and is one of the oldest on the Arab side of the Persian Gulf. Many members of the country's ruling elite were born at this hospital, and they continue to come to it for medical care. The newer, twenty-three-bed International Hospital caters to very wealthy patients.

The government established a social security system in 1976. The General Organization of Social Insurance (GOSI) was set up to administer the program, which provides pensions (since 1986) and compensation for work-related accidents. Only Bahraini citizens are eligible for retirement pensions, but both nationals and foreign workers are covered against accidents. GOSI requires all companies employing at least ten persons to participate in the program. GOSI collects 7 percent of an employee's monthly salary for the pension program and requires employers to contribute an additional amount equivalent to 11 percent of a Bahraini's monthly pay. Employers pay an extra 3 percent of their payrolls to cover all employees against accidents.

The Economy

Agriculture and Fishing

Despite the scant rainfall and poor soil, agriculture historically was an important sector of the economy. Before the development of the oil industry, date palm cultivation dominated Bahrain's agriculture, producing sufficient dates for both domestic consumption and export. At least twenty-three varieties of dates are grown, and the leaves, branches, buds, and flowers of the date palm also are used extensively. From the 1950s through the 1970s, changing food consumption habits, as well as the increasing salinity of the aquifers that served as irrigation sources, led to a gradual decline in date cultivation. By the 1980s, a significant number of palm groves had been replaced by new kinds of agricultural activities, including vegetable gardens, nurseries for trees and flowers, poultry production, and dairy farms.

By 1993 Bahrain's cultivated area had been reduced from 6,000 hectares before independence to 1,500 hectares. The cultivated land consists of about 10,000 plots ranging in size from a few square meters to four hectares. These plots are distributed among approximately 800 owners. A minority of large owners, including individuals and institutions, are absentee landlords who control about 60 percent of all cultivable land. The ruling Al Khalifa own the greatest number of plots, including the largest and most productive ones, although public information pertaining to the distribution of ownership among family members is not available. Absentee owners rent their plots to farmers, generally on the basis of three-year contracts. There are approximately 2,400 farmers, 70 percent of whom do not own the land they cultivate.

The small size of most plots and the maldistribution of ownership has tended to discourage investment in agriculture. In addition, the number of skilled farmworkers progressively declined after 1975 because an increasing number of villagers obtained high-paying, nonagricultural jobs. Despite these impediments, official government policy since 1980 has aimed at expanding domestic production of crops through such programs as free distribution of seeds, technical assistance in adopting new and more efficient irrigation technologies, and low-interest credit. Although these programs have contributed to significant increases in the production of eggs, milk, and vegetables, the circumscribed extent of Bahrain's cultivable area limits the island's potential productive capacity. Consequently, agricultural imports remain a permanent aspect of the country's international trade. In 1993 the main food imports included fruits, vegetables, meat, live animals (for slaughter), cereals, and dairy products.

The waters surrounding Bahrain traditionally have been rich in more than 200 varieties of fish, many of which constitute a staple of the diet. Before the development of the oil industry, most males engaged in some form of fishing. In addition, the pearl industry constituted one of the most important bases of the island's wealth, and more than 2,000 pearling boats operated during the late 1920s. After 1935 both fishing and pearling as occupations steadily declined. Although the prospect of steady wages attracted many pearl divers to oil-related jobs, pearling was even more adversely affected by the development in Japan of the cultured pearl. By 1953 only twelve pearling boats remained, and these all disappeared within a decade. Fishing declined more gradually, but by the early 1970s fewer than 1,000 fishermen continued to ply their trade. Fewer fishermen meant less fish available in the market despite rising consumer demand, and this situation led to the annual importation of tons of fish to supplement the local catch. In 1981 the government launched a program to revitalize the fishing industry by introducing trawlers, motorizing the traditional dhows, expanding jetties, constructing cold storage facilities, and offering training courses on the use and maintenance of modern fishing equipment. These initiatives contributed to an increase in the total fish catch, which, according to estimates of the Food and Agriculture Organization of the United Nations, was 9,200 tons in 1989.

Pollution in the Persian Gulf became a problem in the 1970s. Shrimp in the northern gulf seemed particularly sensitive to marine pollution, and by 1979 they had almost disappeared from waters near Bahrain. Pollution was seriously aggravated in 1983 and again in 1991 by major oil slicks that emanated from war-damaged oil facilities and covered several thousand square kilometers of water in the northern Persian Gulf. The slicks were detrimental to the unique marine life in the vicinity of Bahrain, including coral reefs, sea turtles, dugongs (herbivorous sea mammals similar to manatees), oyster beds and shrimp beds, numerous fish species, and water fowl. The oil slicks, especially those of 1991, adversely affected the fishing industry, but as of early 1993, marine biologists remained uncertain about the long-term ecological impact of the pollution.

Petroleum Industry

In 1929 the San Francisco-based Standard Oil Company of California (Socal)—now known as Chevron—set up a subsidiary to acquire an oil exploration and production concession on the island of Bahrain. Socal drilling crews discovered oil in

1932, and two years later the first shipment of crude oil was exported from Sitrah. By 1935, when sixteen oil wells were in production and construction of the Bahrain refinery commenced, the royalties that Socal paid to the government constituted more than 40 percent of the state budget. In 1936 Socal sold half of its oil interest to the Texas Oil Company (Texaco) and, with its new corporate partner, formed the Bahrain Petroleum Company (Bapco). In the years up to independence in 1971, Bapco oil revenues annually averaged 60 percent of government income and helped to finance major development, education, and health programs. The government of Bahrain acquired a 60 percent interest in Bapco in 1975 and assumed control of the remaining 40 percent in 1980.

Bahrain's proven oil reserves are limited in comparison with the other lower Persian Gulf states (see fig. 7). As early as 1965, Bapco estimated that one-half of the island's total oil had been depleted. Oil production peaked in 1977 at 77,000 barrels per day (bpd–see Glossary) and steadily declined thereafter.

During the 1970s and early 1980s, two developments helped to maintain the government's relatively high income from oil revenues despite declining production. First was Bahrain's share of profits from the offshore Abu Safah oil field in the Persian Gulf between Bahrain and Saudi Arabia. When the two countries demarcated their marine boundaries in 1958, Bahrain ceded its claims to an area of the gulf north of the island in return for a Saudi agreement to share the profits from any oil that might be discovered there. Subsequently, oil in commercial quantities was found in the seabed, and from 1968 to 1986, revenues from the Abu Safah field contributed significantly to Bahrain's overall oil income. Since production from the Abu Safah field ceased in early 1987, Saudi Arabia has provided Bahrain with 75,000 bpd of crude oil as compensation for this loss.

The second development was the more than tenfold increase in oil revenues that followed the December 1973 decision by the Organization of the Petroleum Exporting Countries (OPEC) to triple the international price of crude oil. During 1974 and 1975, income from oil accounted for an unprecedented 80 percent of government revenues, although this percentage gradually declined in subsequent years. Nevertheless, as long as oil prices remained high, oil revenues remained high. At the end of 1985, however, Saudi Arabia significantly increased its own oil production, which resulted in a glut of oil on international markets and caused prices to fall by more than 50 percent in just a few months. Bapco could not increase production from its declining oil fields beyond 42,000 bpd, and consequently Bahrain's oil revenues in 1986 were 65 percent less than in 1985. Oil revenues did not increase substantially until 1990, when the regional political crisis that accompanied Iraq's invasion of Kuwait precipitated a rise in oil prices. In 1991 oil revenues constituted about 62 percent of revenues in the government's budget (see table 14, Appendix).

Although Bahrain has had an oil-based economy since 1935, by 1993 proven reserves were estimated at 200 million barrels, and the government anticipated that all oil would be depleted by 2005. Nevertheless, the country's economists expected oil to remain important long beyond that date because of the large refinery Bapco has operated at Sitrah since 1937. Periodically expanded and modernized, the refinery has the capacity to process 250,000 bpd of crude oil, at least five times the amount produced by the island's oil wells (see table 15, Appendix). During 1992 the United States firm Bechtel Corporation began expanding the refinery's capacity to 360,000 bpd. More than 80 percent of the petroleum that the refinery processes comes via pipeline from Saudi Arabia. The Sitrah refinery has been refining Saudi crude oil since 1938 and expects to continue to do so well into the twenty-first century. Its refined petroleum products, most of which are exported, include aviation fuel, fuel oil, and gasoline.

Substantial deposits of natural gas are associated with Bahrain's oil fields. Before 1979, when the government established the Bahrain National Gas Company (Banagas), an estimated 3 million cubic meters per day of this gas were being vented to the atmosphere. Banagas opened a gas liquefaction plant that collected this gas and processed it into propane, butane, and naphtha. There are also large deposits of natural gas in the Khuff field, which is separate from the oil fields. Banagas has drilled more than fifteen wells to tap this gas, which is used for fuel to power the oil refinery, electric generators, and the water desalination plant. Some of the gas is reinjected into the oil fields to maintain reservoir pressure and stimulate production. In 1990 Banagas estimated total natural gas reserves at 209 trillion cubic meters; daily production averaged about 20 million cubic meters.

Other Industry

By 1965 the government recognized that the island's long-term prosperity could not depend on the limited extent of its oil reserves. Accordingly, the government adopted industrial diversification as a primary objective of its economic policy. Tax incentives and low-interest loans encouraged private entrepreneurs to construct several small-scale manufacturing plants, including factories producing plastics, ceramic tiles, paper products, and carbonated beverages. The government assumed a more active role in the establishment of large-scale industry, as a result of which manufacturing contributed 13 percent of the gross domestic product (GDP—see Glossary) in 1986 (see table 16, Appendix). The two most important examples of large-scale industry were the aluminum plant and the ship-repair yard.

Aluminium Bahrain (Alba) was incorporated in 1968 as a joint government and private investment company for the construction of a mill to process imported raw alumina. Located near the Bapco refinery, the Alba plant began production in 1971 with an initial capacity of 99,000 tons of aluminum ingots. Since commencing operations, the Alba facilities have expanded considerably and by 1990 had an annual productive capacity of more than 215,000 tons. Associated with Alba are two other aluminum plants built during the 1980s. The Gulf Aluminium Rolling Mill Company (Garmco), a joint venture of the six member countries of the GCC, produces aluminum strip and sheet. The Bahrain Aluminium Extrusion Company (Balexco), owned 100 percent by the government, produces aluminum doors, window frames, and other products used by the construction industry. A third concern, the jointly owned Bahrain-Saudi Aluminium Marketing Company (Balco), markets Alba's products throughout the Middle East and Asia.

In 1977 the Arab Shipbuilding and Repair Yard Company (ASRY) was inaugurated near Al Hadd. ASRY was a joint venture of Bahrain and the six other members of the Organization of Arab Petroleum Exporting Countries (OAPEC). This large dry-dock facility has accommodations for up to ten supertankers simultaneously, and it annually repairs an average of seventy ships.

Labor

Bahrain's total labor force was estimated at 160,000 in 1992. Foreign workers constituted about 55 percent of the labor force, a slight decline from the 58 percent they had constituted in 1981. Foreign participation in the labor force increased dramatically after 1971, when such workers had constituted 37 percent of the economically active population. The composition of the foreign work force also has changed significantly. During the 1960s, more than one-half of all foreign workers came from Oman and Iran. Since the late 1970s, one-half of all foreign workers have come from South Asia, predominantly from India and Pakistan but also from Bangladesh, the Philippines, Sri Lanka, and Thailand. South Asian workers constituted 13 percent of the total population in 1990 and Iranians, 6 percent. Less than 10 percent of foreign workers come from other Arab countries. Egyptians, about one-half of whom teach in Bahrain's public schools, constitute the largest group of foreign Arabs, followed by Palestinians, most of whom hold Jordanian passports, and Lebanese. Arabs are more likely than Asians to be accompanied by dependents.

The government requires all foreign workers to possess valid residence and work permits. Although work permits are renewable after the expiration of the original contract period, authorities do not encourage long-term residency of foreign nationals. Most of the foreign workers, who are unskilled and semiskilled laborers, have few incentives to live in Bahrain permanently because their families generally remain in their home countries. These workers consequently remit a considerable portion of their employment income to their families in their countries of origin.

As the proportion of citizens declined to less than one-half the labor force, government planners drew up programs and laws designed to replace foreign workers with Bahraini nationals. Within the private sector, which provides jobs for more than two-thirds of all foreign nationals, employers have the option of designing their own special courses for training citizens or providing funds to finance government-operated training courses. Companies pay a special levy, equal to 4 percent of the salary of every employed foreigner but only equal to 2 percent for every local employee. At the completion of a foreign worker's contract, officials of the Ministry of Labor and Social Affairs urge the hiring company to take on more nationals.

Efforts to make employment indigenous encourage the participation of women in the labor force. Women, who constituted about 15 percent of all employees in the early 1990s, work outside the home in far greater numbers in Bahrain than

Worker practicing
traditional craft
of weaving
Courtesy Embassy of
Bahrain, Washington

Members of an oil-
drilling rig at work
Courtesy Embassy of
Bahrain, Washington

in any other state of the Arabian Peninsula. The most dramatic rise in female employment occurred during the decade of the 1970s. Between 1971 and 1981, the proportion of women in the labor force increased from 3.8 to 13.3 percent. Bahraini women predominate in such traditionally female occupations as teaching and nursing, but, since the early 1980s, increasing numbers of women have been employed in administration, banking, commerce, finance, engineering, and the civil service. Despite the trend toward greater female participation in the work force, about 82 percent of Bahraini women do not work outside the home. The overwhelming majority of working women tend to be single women who work for two to five years after completing secondary school or university and before marriage.

In an effort to encourage continued participation of women in the labor force after marriage, the government has enacted labor legislation favorable to working mothers. For example, all employers are required to grant new mothers forty-five days of maternity leave at full pay plus fifteen days at half-pay. In addition, employers are obligated to provide nursing periods for new mothers. The law also forbids discrimination against working mothers.

Transportation and Telecommunications

Bahrain's small size and level terrain made the development of its excellent road system easy. In 1993 the country had more than 200 kilometers of paved roads linking all populated areas of the island. Two paved roads and several gravel roads run through the sparsely inhabited southern half. A twenty-five-kilometer causeway, completed in 1986, allows traffic to cross to Saudi Arabia. A second causeway links the capital with the international airport on the island of Al Muharraq. With its 3,660-meter runway, Bahrain International Airport can handle the largest airplanes in use. In 1993 it was the eastern terminus for British Airways nonstop service from London using the Concorde. Gulf Air, jointly owned by Bahrain, Qatar, the UAE, and Oman, provides regularly scheduled service to more than twenty international destinations.

Bahrain's main port is Mina Salman on the tip of the island of Bahrain. Opened in 1962 and expanded several times thereafter, Mina Salman has sixteen berths and can handle vessels with a draught of up to nine meters. Crude and refined petroleum passes through the port of Sitrah, about ten kilometers southeast of Manama. A dry dock on the southern end of the island of Al Muharraq handles repairs of ships of up to 500,000 tons.

The telecommunications system is modern and has good domestic service and excellent international connections. In 1992 the country had some 98,000 telephones, or eighteen per 100 inhabitants, one of the highest per capita figures in the Middle East. Radio-relay and submarine cables link Bahrain with all its neighbors. Three satellite ground stations—one operating with International Telecommunications Satellite Corporation's (Intelsat) Atlantic Ocean satellite, one operating with Intelsat's Indian Ocean satellite, and one operating as part of the Arab Satellite Communication Organization (Arabsat) system—provide excellent international telephone and data links and live television broadcasts. Two AM and three FM radio stations provide broadcast services in Arabic and English.

*Control tower personnel
at Bahrain
International Airport,
on Al Muharraq,
Bahrain
Courtesy Embassy of
Bahrain, Washington*

*Causeway from Bahrain
to Al Khubar, Saudi Arabia
Courtesy Embassy of
Bahrain, Washington*

A shortwave AM station beams programs in Arabic throughout the Middle East.

Banking and Finance

Bahrain's first commercial bank, a branch of the British-owned Eastern Bank, opened in 1921. Two decades passed before a second bank, the British Bank of the Middle East, set up an office. It was not until 1957 that the first bank wholly owned by Bahraini citizens, the private National Bank of Bahrain, commenced activities. Prior to 1965, when the government introduced the Bahraini dinar (for value of the Bahraini dinar—see Glossary), the Indian rupee had functioned as the most commonly accepted currency for local transactions. The lack of an indigenous currency probably impeded the development of the banking sector. Once the Bahraini dinar replaced the Indian rupee and established itself as a strong, internationally convertible currency, banks began to find the island a more attractive location; by 1974 fourteen commercial banks operated in Bahrain.

The increase in the number of banks after independence prompted the government to consider creating a central monetary authority to regulate banking activities. In 1973 Shaykh Isa ibn Salman issued a decree that established the Bahrain Monetary Agency (BMA) as a legal entity possessing the powers of a central bank. In addition to its regulatory responsibilities, BMA issues currency, sets the official exchange rates for the Bahraini dinar, serves as a depository for government funds from petroleum production and its foreign currency reserves, and manages the government's investments.

In 1975 BMA promulgated regulations for the creation of offshore banking units (OBUs) modeled on those operating in Singapore. OBUs are branches of international commercial banks exempted from foreign-exchange controls, cash reserve requirements, taxes on interest paid to depositors, and banking income taxes that are required of other banks in Bahrain. In return for these privileges, OBUs pay the government annual license fees, are prohibited from accepting deposits from citizens and residents of Bahrain, and must refrain from transactions involving Bahraini dinars. The OBU program has been successful; twenty-six OBUs were established during the first year. The civil war in Lebanon probably stimulated the OBU boom because several international banks based in Beirut transferred their Middle East operations to Bahrain after 1975. By the early 1980s, a total of seventy-five OBUs having assets in excess of US$62 billion were operating out of Bahrain.

Beginning in 1985, falling oil prices and a corresponding decline in oil revenues dramatically reduced the funds deposited in both onshore banks and OBUs. Several banks decided not to renew their OBU licenses, resulting in a net loss of OBUs. Nevertheless, a majority of OBUs, including those that are branches of leading United States, Arab, European, and Japanese banks, continue to operate from Bahrain-based offices. In 1990 a total of fifty-five OBUs were located on the island. Despite the fluctuations in Persian Gulf financial markets of the 1980s, Bahrain is well established as the principal banking and financial center of the gulf region.

Budget

The annual budget is the government's principal instrument of economic development and its barometer of progress. It projects total revenues from all sources, including petroleum, taxes, customs duties, investments, and foreign government transfers. It also includes projected expenditures for government salaries, services, and development projects. The annual budget is supplemented by biennial budgets and six-year development plans. The budget indicated that Bahrain's GDP for 1990 was about US$4.0 billion, or a per capita GDP of US$7,500.

Foreign Trade and the Balance of Payments

Traditionally, Bahrain was the entrepôt and distribution center for the northern Persian Gulf region. Since independence it has lost much of its role as a result of the development of nearby Saudi Arabian ports and strong competition from Dubayy in the UAE in the southern gulf. Oil continues to be the most important item in the country's international trade, representing well over one-half of the total value of both exports and imports. The industrial diversification program has resulted in the creation of non-oil manufactured exports, while investments in agriculture have reduced significantly the importation of certain food commodities.

The total value of imports in 1989 was about US$2.82 billion, a 34 percent decrease from the 1982 total of US$3.7 billion (see table 17, Appendix). The cost of crude petroleum, imported from Saudi Arabia for processing at the Sitrah oil refinery, declined to US$1.5 billion in 1988, compared with US$1.9 billion in 1982 and US$2.5 billion in 1981. This significant drop, however, resulted more from the steady fall in international oil prices than from a decrease in the actual number of barrels imported. The major non-oil imports included machinery and transportation equipment, manufactured goods, alumina, chemicals, food, and live animals.

In 1989 Bahrain's principal trading partners were Britain, the United States, and Japan, accounting for approximately 16.3 percent, 12.4 percent, and 10.5 percent, respectively, of total imports (see table 18, Appendix). Other major import sources included Australia, the Federal Republic of Germany (West Germany), Italy, and Saudi Arabia.

In 1989 the value of Bahrain's exports was US$2.83 billion, down 12 percent from 1984. Depressed oil prices, especially in the 1986-88 period, continued to erode the value of oil and oil products, the principal components of the export trade. Non-oil exports consisted of manufactured goods, in particular aluminum products but also some construction materials. The chief trading partners were Saudi Arabia, the United States, and the UAE, accounting for 18.2 percent, 7.3 percent, and 6.9 percent, respectively, of all exports in 1989. Other export markets included Japan, India, Kuwait, and the Republic of Korea (South Korea).

The value of Bahrain's imports was slightly less than the value of its exports in 1989. Preliminary estimates for 1990 indicated that the trade balance would also have a slight surplus. The favorable balance was attributed to the dramatic rise in oil prices that followed the Iraqi invasion of Kuwait.

Government and Politics

In 1993 Bahrain was a constitutional monarchy in the form of an amirate with an executive-cabinet form of government and a separate judiciary (see fig. 8). The amir is head of state and also supreme commander of the Bahrain Defense Force (BDF); he exercises ultimate authority in all matters pertaining to the government. In addition to the amir, Shaykh Isa ibn Salman, principal government officials include his eldest son and heir apparent, Hamad ibn Isa, who is commander in chief of the BDF and deputy prime minister, and several other members of the ruling Al Khalifa. In accordance with the constitution adopted in 1973, the office of amir passes from father to eldest son unless the amir designates another male relative to succeed him. This clause of the constitution is not subject to amendment.

Although the amir has substantial executive powers, in practice he has delegated decision-making authority to a cabinet since 1956, when an amiri decree created the Administrative Council, an eleven-member body that advised the ruler on policy and supervised the growing bureaucracy. In 1970 Shaykh Isa ibn Salman issued a decree that transformed the Administrative Council into a twelve-member Council of Ministers. The president of the Council of Ministers, the prime minister, serves as the head of government. The amir appoints the prime minister, who then forms a government by selecting members of the Council of Ministers, albeit in consultation with the amir. The ministers are directly responsible to the prime minister, who, like the amir, has authority to veto a decision by any member of the council.

The Council of Ministers gradually expanded to include eighteen members, including the prime minister and the deputy prime minister. In late 1992, the prime minister, deputy prime minister, and six of the sixteen ministers were members of the ruling Al Khalifa. The prime minister, Khalifa ibn Salman, is the brother of the amir. The amir's son holds the cabinet rank of deputy prime minister. The amir's uncle, Major General Khalifa ibn Ahmad, is minister of defense; and the amir's two first cousins, Muhammad ibn Khalifa and Muhammad ibn Mubarak, are minister of interior and minister of foreign affairs, respectively. Khalifa ibn Salman, the son of the amir's second cousin, is minister of labor and social affairs. A more distantly related cousin, Abd Allah ibn Khalid, a first cousin of the amir's grandfather, is minister of justice and Islamic affairs.

The Constitutional Experiment

On December 16, 1971, the day Bahrain formally became independent of Britain (Bahrain technically gained its independence earlier in the year, on August 15), Shaykh Isa ibn Salman announced that the country would have a constitutional form of government. Six months later, he issued a decree providing for the election of representatives to a Constituent Assembly, charged with drafting and ratifying a constitution. The assembly was to consist of twenty-two elected delegates plus twenty additional members, including eight delegates appointed by the amir and the twelve members of the Council

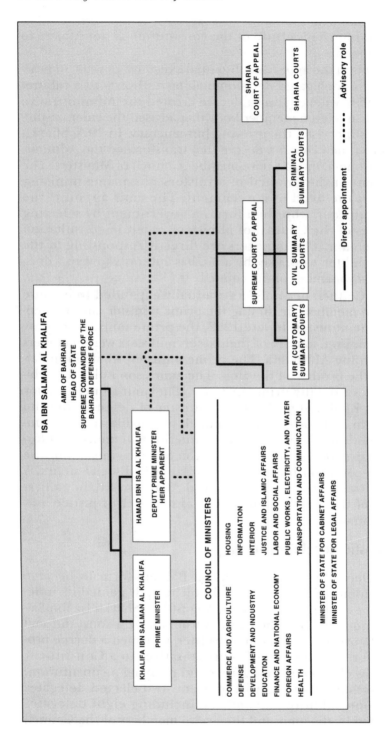

Figure 8. Bahrain: Government Structure, 1992

of Ministers. The election, which was held in December 1972, was the first national election in Bahrain's history. The electorate was restricted, however, to native-born male citizens aged twenty years and older.

The relative openness of political debate permitted during the election campaign for the twenty-two contested Constituent Assembly seats encouraged individuals dissatisfied with the lack of democratic rights to demand more civil liberties. The primary focus of concern was the 1965 Law of Public Security, a series of three amiri decrees that authorized the ruler to maintain indefinitely a virtual state of emergency in order to protect national security from suspected foreign and domestic enemies. A group of mostly university-educated professionals, led by Abd al Aziz Shamlan, unsuccessfully petitioned the amir to rescind the law's harshest provisions, especially those pertaining to arrest and detention. They believed these measures had been used arbitrarily to silence dissent and peaceful opposition. Several women's groups also organized to protest the exclusion of women from the franchise. They presented a petition to the amir requesting support for extending voting rights to female citizens, but they failed to receive a positive response.

The Constituent Assembly was in session during most of 1973. It approved a constitution of 108 articles. The constitution, enacted by amiri decree in December 1973, provided for an advisory legislative body, the National Assembly, consisting of thirty members elected for four-year terms, plus all the members of the Council of Ministers, whose terms were not fixed. The assembly was not empowered to initiate or enact legislation, but it was authorized to give advice and consent to laws proposed by the Council of Ministers. The assembly had the right to question individual ministers about policies and to withdraw confidence from any minister except the prime minister. The constitution stipulated that the amir could dissolve the assembly at his discretion, provided he make public the grounds for so doing. If the assembly were dissolved by decree, new elections had to take place within two months or the dissolution would be invalidated and the dismissed members reinstated.

Elections for the National Assembly took place in December 1973, with the franchise restricted, as in the Constituent Assembly election, to male citizens. In theory, the thirty elected representatives were independents because political parties were not permitted; in practice, several of the assemblymen openly supported the positions and views of banned political organizations, including the National Front for the Liberation of Bahrain, which espoused Marxist economic ideas. Consequently, two distinct coalitions emerged in the assembly: the People's Bloc, consisting of eight members who advocated the legalization of labor unions and the abolition of the 1965 security measures; and the Religious Bloc, consisting of six Shia members who supported labor reforms and various social restrictions, such as a ban on the sale of alcoholic beverages. The majority of elected members—sixteen representatives—comprised a heterogeneous group of independents whose individual positions shifted with the issues. The People's Bloc and the Religious Bloc tended to refer to the independents pejoratively as the Government Bloc because they usually tried to effect compromises between the ministers and their National Assembly critics.

Although the National Assembly lacked authority to prevent the government from enacting legislation that assembly members opposed, this situation did not impede policy debates. The unprecedented public debates attracted wide interest and, from the perspective of the regime, seemed to erode its legitimacy. During the winter and spring of 1975, a prolonged debate over a new state security decree proved especially troublesome for the government. It appeared that most independents, as well as the Religious Bloc, supported the demand of the People's Bloc that the decree, issued in December 1974 without prior consultation with the assembly, be submitted to the legislature for ratification before its implementation. The issue was unresolved as of May 1975, when the assembly recessed for the summer. In August, before the members reconvened, the amir dissolved the National Assembly, citing its inability to cooperate with the government. Although the constitution stipulated that new elections had to take place within two months of a dissolution, this did not occur. One year later, in August 1976, Shaykh Isa ibn Salman announced that the National Assembly would remain dissolved indefinitely.

In January 1993, a new elected body, the thirty-member Consultative Council, met for the first time. The session discussed employment and training matters as groundwork for the formulation of a new labor law.

Although there are no political parties through which citizens can express views, they can petition the amir for redress of grievances. The amir holds a regular majlis, or public meeting,

Shaykh Isa ibn Salman Al Khalifa, ruler of Bahrain
Courtesy Embassy of Bahrain, Washington

Manama, capital of Bahrain
Courtesy Embassy of Bahrain, Washington

at which he listens to views of citizens and accepts petitions for his intervention in dealing with the bureaucracy or some other problem. Officials of the islands' eleven municipalities follow the amir's example and hold local versions of the national majlis.

Legal System

The legal system of Bahrain in 1993 was based on several sources, including customary tribal law (*urf*), three separate schools of Islamic sharia law, and civil law as embodied in codes, ordinances, and regulations. Sharia law includes the Maliki school of Islamic law (from Abd Allah Malik ibn Anas, an eighth-century Muslim jurist from Medina) and the Shafii school of Islamic law (from Muhammad ibn Idris ash Shafii, a late eighth-century Muslim jurist from Mecca). Both of these schools are recognized by Sunni Muslims (see Sunni Islam, ch. 1). The third school is the eighth-century Jaafari (from Jaafar ibn Muhammad, also known as Jaafar as Sadiq, the Sixth Imam) school of Twelve Imam Muslims, recognized by Shia (see Shia Islam, ch. 1). Civil law is heavily influenced by British common law, inasmuch as it was developed by British legal advisers beginning in the 1920s and continuing up to the eve of independence in 1971.

According to the constitution of 1973, the judiciary is an independent and separate branch of government. However, the highest judicial authority, the minister of justice and Islamic affairs, is appointed by, and responsible to, the prime minister. The amir, who retains the power of pardon, is at the pinnacle of the judicial system.

Bahrain has a dual court system, consisting of civil and sharia courts. Sharia courts deal primarily with personal status matters (such as marriage, divorce, and inheritance). Sharia courts of first instance are located in all communities. A single sharia Court of Appeal sits at Manama. Appeals beyond the jurisdiction of the sharia Court of Appeal are taken to the Supreme Court of Appeal, which is part of the civil system (see Bahrain: Internal Security, ch. 7).

The civil court system consists of summary courts and a supreme court. Summary courts of first instance are located in all communities and include separate *urf*, civil, and criminal sections. The Supreme Court of Appeal hears appeals from the summary courts. The Supreme Court of Appeal is the highest appellate court in the country and also decides on the constitutionality of laws and regulations.

The Media

In 1965 the government issued a press law that required all newspapers to be licensed by the Ministry of Information before beginning publication. The same law regulated the contents of reports that could be published, prohibiting, for example, articles deemed offensive to the reputation of the ruling family or harmful to national security. Violations could result in the suspension of a publishing license and prosecution.

In 1993 Bahrain had two daily Arabic newspapers, *Al Ayam* (The Days) and *Akhbar al Khalij* (Gulf News), which had a combined circulation in excess of 45,000. In addition, there was one English-language paper, the *Gulf Daily News*, with a circulation of 11,500. Several weekly and monthly periodicals also are published.

Foreign Relations

Since independence in 1971, one of the most important objectives of Bahrain's foreign policy has been to contain perceived threats to the country's security. As the smallest state in the region, Bahrain feels vulnerable to political influences emanating from more powerful neighbors, in particular Iran and Iraq, and it regards close ties to Saudi Arabia and other Arab monarchial regimes as a means of countering these potentially harmful influences. During the 1970s, for example, the Baath (Arab Socialist Resurrection) Party media in Baghdad frequently denounced Manama as an enemy of Arab nationalism and a puppet of Washington's imperialism because it allowed United States naval vessels to use a naval base in Bahrain. The government also believes that Baghdad has provided financial and other support to Bahraini opposition groups calling for the overthrow of the Al Khalifa dynasty. Although Iraq moderated its policies toward Bahrain in the late 1970s, the Iranian Revolution of 1979 confronted the government with new ideological challenges. Some Shia clergy in Tehran denounced the institution of monarchy as un-Islamic, and some Shia political dissidents in Bahrain embraced this message enthusiastically. During the 1980s, government officials suspected Iranian complicity in four separate plots that it maintained were aimed at the overthrow of the regime.

The outbreak of the Iran-Iraq War in 1980 aroused security concerns that Bahrain shared with the other five Arab monarchies in the gulf: Kuwait, Qatar, the UAE, Oman, and Saudi Arabia. During the 1970s, Bahrain lobbied these countries to cooperate in defense matters, but, other than bilateral agreements, little came from these efforts. By early 1981, when the fighting between Iran and Iraq appeared to have settled into a long-term conflict, attitudes changed, and all five Arabian Peninsula oil-producing states joined Bahrain in the GCC. Ostensibly, the GCC agreement emphasized economic cooperation, but the level of cooperation in security matters increased annually. For Bahrain this meant financial assistance for expanding its defense forces and facilities and the opportunity to participate in joint training maneuvers (see Collective Security under the Gulf Cooperation Council, ch. 7). When fellow GCC member Kuwait was invaded by Iraq in 1990, Bahrain joined the collective military effort against Iraq by sending a small contingent of troops to the front lines in Saudi Arabia. It also permitted United States military forces to use its naval and air facilities (see Bahrain: Role in the Persian Gulf War, ch. 7).

Since 1981 Bahrain's most important foreign relations have been with its GCC allies, although problems with individual members of the GCC have developed. The most serious problems have been with Qatar. Bahrain and Qatar have unresolved territorial disputes stemming from the nineteenth century when the Al Thani of Qatar foreswore allegiance to the Al Khalifa and established a separate amirate. In the twentieth century, the two states have contested sovereignty over Hawar and the adjacent islands, the closest of which is fewer than two kilometers from Qatar's west coast. In 1939, when both countries were still dependencies of Britain, London ruled that the islands belonged to Bahrain. Qatar never accepted this decision and periodically has raised the issue. Incidents connected with this dispute occurred in 1978, in 1982, and in 1986, but each time they were defused by the mediation of other GCC states. The most serious crisis, from April to June 1986, involved Qatari forces raiding the Fasht ad Dibal coral reef island north of Al Muharraq and seizing twenty-nine foreign workers who were building a coast guard station for the government of Bahrain. The workers were released in May, and installations on the island were destroyed. Qatar submitted the dispute to the International Court of Justice in The Hague, but Bahrain refused the jurisdiction of the court in June 1992. The dispute was ongoing as of early 1993. In July 1991, according to reports, Qatari naval vessels violated Bahraini waters, and Bahraini jet fighters flew into Qatari airspace. In August this issue, too, was referred to the International Court of Justice to determine whether it had jurisdiction over the dispute. Other disputes have involved the abandoned town of Az Zubarah on the northwest coast of Qatar. These incidents tended to strain overall relations with Qatar (see Foreign Relations, ch. 4; Territorial Disputes, ch. 7).

Outside the Persian Gulf region, Bahrain has cordial relations with other countries. The two non-Arab countries with which it maintains the closest relations are Britain and the United States. After the Persian Gulf War, Bahrain held negotiations with Washington that culminated in October 1991 in the signing of a defense cooperation agreement. The terms of this agreement permit the United States to pre-position military supplies and equipment in Bahrain and to use its military facilities.

Bahrain is a member of several international organizations, including the United Nations, the International Monetary Fund (IMF—see Glossary), and the World Health Organization. It also belongs to several regional organizations, the most important of which is the League of Arab States, as well as to OPEC and the Organization of the Islamic Conference.

$$*\qquad*\qquad*$$

Bahrain has not received much scholarly attention but generally is covered in books that deal with the Persian Gulf. Nevertheless, the country has been the focus of two important studies since independence. The most important book is Fred H. Lawson's *Bahrain: The Modernization of Autocracy,* which examines the political economy of the state in the 1970s and 1980s. Another valuable book is Fuad I. Khuri's *Tribe and State in Bahrain.* Khuri examines the impact of the oil economy on Bahraini society from the 1930s through 1975. Angela Clarke in *Bahrain: Oil and Development, 1929–1989* presents a historical retrospective of Bapco that contains useful economic data. (For further information and complete citations, see Bibliography.)

Chapter 4. Qatar

Crest of the State of Qatar

Country

Formal Name: State of Qatar.

Short Form: Qatar.

Term for Citizens: Qatari(s); adjectival form, Qatari.

Capital: Doha.

Date of Independence: September 3, 1971.

Geography

Size: 11,437 square kilometers.

Topography: Mostly low-lying, barren terrain.

Climate: Long, hot summers with alternating periods of high and low humidity; mild winters with limited rainfall.

Society

Population: July 1992 estimate 484,387; 1992 growth rate 3.2 percent.

Education: Free in twelve-year public school system, consisting of six-year primary cycle, three-year intermediate cycle, and three-year secondary cycle. Total students in three cycles in 1985–86 academic year 51,350, of whom roughly 50 percent female. University of Qatar free.

Health: Comprehensive system of well-equipped public clinics and hospitals staffed by mainly foreign personnel. Most care provided free to all residents. Several private clinics located in Doha. In 1986 life expectancy at birth 65.2 years for males and 67.6 years for females.

Ethnic Groups: Most Qataris are Arabs; some have Iranian or African ancestry. Large foreign communities of Indians, Iranians, Pakistanis, and Egyptians. Other groups include Filipinos, Bangladeshis, Sudanese, Afghans, other Arabs, Sri Lankans, and Westerners, mostly British.

NOTE—The Country Profile contains updated information as available.

149

Religion: Most Qataris follow Wahhabi interpretation of Sunni Islam. Of remaining Muslims, Arabs, Pakistanis, and Afghans are Sunni, while Iranians are mainly Shia. Other religious groups include Hindus (mostly Indian) and Christians (Indians, Filipinos, and Westerners).

Economy

Gross Domestic Product (GDP): In 1991 GDP US$6.7 billion; per capita GDP US$13,730.

Industry: In 1989 oil and natural gas extraction and processing accounted for 26 percent of GDP and most industrial activity. Other major industries fertilizers, petrochemicals, steel, and cement.

Agriculture: Small-scale, state-subsidized farms and fishing sector, about 1 percent of GDP in 1989, meets small portion of local needs, mostly vegetables and fodder. Some date production. Livestock includes goats, camels, sheep, and horses; also dairy and chicken farms.

Exports: US$2.6 billion in 1989 (mostly oil, gas, and petroleum products). Main destinations Japan (54.4 percent), Thailand (5.0 percent), and Singapore (4.0 percent). Other partners include Persian Gulf and European Community countries.

Imports: US$1.3 billion in 1989 (mostly machinery, manufactured goods, and food). Main sources Japan (18.8 percent), Britain (11.6 percent), United States (8.8 percent), Italy (7.8 percent), and Federal Republic of Germany (West Germany) (7.3 percent). Other partners include Persian Gulf and European Community countries.

Currency and Exchange Rate: Qatar riyal. In 1994 exchange rate US$1 = QR3.64 (fixed rate).

Fiscal Year: April 1 to March 31.

Transportation and Telecommunications

Transportation: In 1994 about 1,500 kilometers of roads, of which 1,000 kilometers paved and rest gravel. Doha main port and Umm Said petroleum export port. Doha has international airport.

Telecommunications: Excellent domestic and international telecommunications with twenty-three telephones per 100 inhabitants in 1992 and satellite ground stations, television, and radio stations.

Government and Politics

Government: Ruler is Shaykh Khalifa ibn Hamad Al Thani, amir since 1972. However, heir apparent, Shaykh Hamad ibn Khalifa Al Thani, has taken over much day-to-day decision making. Government structure based on 1970 provisional constitution with Council of Ministers and Advisory Council.

Politics: Power held by amir and royal family. Political parties banned, and no open opposition tolerated.

Foreign Relations: Closely allied with Saudi Arabia on regional and global issues. Foreign policy efforts channeled through Gulf Cooperation Council and other organizations, such as Organization of Arab Petroleum Exporting Countries, Organization of the Petroleum Exporting Countries, and Organization of the Islamic Conference. Member of United Nations and League of Arab States.

National Security

Armed Forces: In mid-1993 personnel strength 9,500: army, 8,000, of whom 30 percent Qataris; navy, 700; and air force, 800. Army had twenty-four AMX–30 main battle tanks and thirty armored infantry vehicles. Navy had three missile craft. Air force had Alpha Jet and Mirage F1 fighters and armed helicopters.

QATAR IS A SMALL COUNTRY dominated by the Persian Gulf's largest ruling family, the Al Thani. The amir, Shaykh Khalifa ibn Hamad Al Thani, is the country's ruler, but his son, Shaykh Hamad ibn Khalifa Al Thani, in addition to being the heir apparent and minister of defense, wields considerable power in the day-to-day running of the country. The Al Thani regime tolerates no political opposition. The social mores of the country are shaped by a somewhat milder version of Wahhabi (see Glossary) Islam than is found in neighboring Saudi Arabia. Women are permitted to drive if they obtain permits, for example, and non-Qatari women need not veil in public.

Occupying a barren peninsula scorched by extreme summer heat, Qatar was transformed between the mid-1960s and the mid-1980s from a poor British protectorate noted mainly for pearling into an independent state with modern infrastructure, services, and industries. The state was built using mostly foreign labor and expertise, with funding from oil revenues. And as in other states where oil dominates the economy, Qatar's fortunes have followed those of the world oil market. The late 1980s and early 1990s were times of relative austerity, with development projects canceled or delayed. But those years were also a period of significant transition when Qatar began its shift from an economy reliant almost entirely on oil to one that would be supported by the exploitation of natural gas from the North Field, the world's largest natural gas field.

The early 1990s also constituted a watershed period in foreign relations because the invasion of Kuwait by Iraq on August 2, 1990, changed regional and world alignments. Qatar sent troops to fight for Kuwait's liberation and, reversing its previous opposition to the presence of foreign forces in the region, permitted United States, Canadian, and French air force fighter aircraft to operate from Doha (also seen as Ad Dawhah). This placed Qatar firmly on the anti-Iraq side of the great rift that split the Arab world after the invasion and weakened the full support for the Palestine Liberation Organization that the country had previously shown.

Historical Background

Human habitation of the Qatar Peninsula dates as far back

as 50,000 years, when small groups of Stone Age inhabitants built coastal encampments, settlements, and sites for working flint, according to recent archaeological evidence. Other finds have included pottery from the Al Ubaid culture of Mesopotamia and northern Arabia (ca. 5000 B.C.), rock carvings, burial mounds, and a large town that dates from about 500 B.C. at Wusail, some twenty kilometers north of Doha. The Qatar Peninsula was close enough to the Dilmun civilization (ca. 4000 to 2000 B.C.) in Bahrain to have felt its influence. A harsh climate, lack of resources, and frequent periods of conflict, however, seem to have made it inevitable that no settlement would develop and prosper for any significant length of time before the discovery of oil.

The peninsula was used almost continuously as rangeland for nomadic tribes from Najd and Al Hasa regions in Saudi Arabia, with seasonal encampments around sources of water. In addition, fishing and pearling settlements were established on those parts of the coast near a major well. Until the late eighteenth century, the principal towns were on the east coast—Al Huwayla, Al Fuwayrit, and Al Bida—and the modern city of Doha developed around the largest of these, Al Bida. The population consisted of nomadic and settled Arabs and a significant proportion of slaves brought originally from East Africa.

The Qatar Peninsula came under the sway of several great powers over the centuries. The Abbasid era (750–1258) saw the rise of several settlements, including Murwab. The Portuguese ruled from 1517 to 1538, when they lost to the Ottomans. In the 1760s, the Al Khalifa and the Al Jalahima sections of the Bani Utub tribe migrated from Kuwait to Qatar's northwest coast and founded Az Zubarah (see fig. 9). Because the Bani Utub had important trading connections with Kuwait and were close to the rich oyster banks, Az Zubarah became a thriving center of trade and pearling, despite hostilities between the Al Khalifa and the Al Jalahima.

In response to attacks on Az Zubarah by an Omani shaykh who ruled Bahrain from Bushehr in Iran, the Bani Utub of Kuwait and Qatar, as well as some local Qatari tribes, captured Bahrain in 1783. The Al Khalifa claimed sovereignty over Bahrain and ruled it for several years from Az Zubarah. This angered the Al Jalahima, who felt they were deprived of their share of the spoils, and so they moved a few kilometers up the Qatari coast to establish Al Khuwayr, which they used as a stag-

ing point for maritime raids against the shipping of the Al Khalifa and the Iranians.

Most of the Al Khalifa migrated to the more desirable location of Bahrain and established a shaykhdom that endures to this day. That they left only a token presence in Az Zubarah meant initially that the Al Jalahima branch of the Bani Utub could achieve ascendancy in Qatar, with their leader, Rahman ibn Jabir Al Jalahima, earning a reputation as one of the most feared raiders on the surrounding waters. It also meant that with the economic decline of Az Zubarah (because the Al Khalifa shifted their trade connections to Bahrain), the peninsula would once more become a relative backwater. With no dominant local ruler, insecurity and rivalry characterized tribal relations. Settled tribes built walled towns, towers, and small forts to keep raiding beduin at bay.

In the late eighteenth and early nineteenth centuries, continuing bloody conflict involved not only the Al Khalifa, the Al Jalahima, and the Iranians but also the Omanis under Sayyid Said ibn Sultan Al Said, the nascent Wahhabis of Arabia, and the Ottomans. The period also saw the rise of British power in the Persian Gulf as a result of their growing interests in India. Britain's desire for secure passage for East India Company ships led it to impose its own order in the gulf. The General Treaty of Peace of 1820 between the East India Company and the shaykhs of the coastal area—which became known as the Trucial Coast because of the series of treaties between the shaykhs and the British—was a way of ensuring safe passage. The agreement acknowledged British authority in the gulf and sought to end piracy and the kidnapping of slaves. Bahrain also became a party to the treaty, and it was assumed by the British and the Bahrainis that Qatar, as a dependency, was also a party to it.

When, as punishment for piracy, an East India Company vessel bombarded Doha in 1821, destroying the town and forcing hundreds to flee, the residents had no idea why they were being attacked. The situation remained unsettled in 1867, when a large Bahraini force sacked and looted Doha and Al Wakrah. This attack, and the Qatari counterattack, prompted the British political agent, Colonel Lewis Pelly, to impose a settlement in 1868. His mission to Bahrain and Qatar and the peace treaty that resulted were milestones in Qatar's history because they implicitly recognized the distinctness of Qatar from Bahrain and explicitly acknowledged the position of

Muhammad ibn Thani Al Thani, an important representative of the peninsula's tribes. The Al Thani were originally beduin from Najd, but after settling in Qatar, they engaged in fishing, pearling, date palm cultivation, and trade.

With the expansion of the Ottoman Empire into eastern Arabia in 1871, Qatar became vulnerable to occupation. Muhammad ibn Thani opposed Ottoman designs on Qatar, but his son, Qasim ibn Muhammad Al Thani, accepted Ottoman sovereignty in 1872. Although Qasim ibn Muhammad privately complained of the Ottoman presence, he hoped that with Ottoman support he could dominate those shaykhs in other towns who opposed him and rebuff Bahrain's claims on Az Zubarah. The question of Az Zubarah became moot in 1878, however, when Qasim ibn Muhammad destroyed the town as punishment for the piracy of the Naim, a tribe that resided in the north of Qatar but was loyal to the shaykh of Bahrain. Moreover, Qasim ibn Muhammad's ambivalent relations with the Ottomans deteriorated to the point that in 1893 they sent a military force to Doha to arrest him, ostensibly over his refusal to permit an Ottoman customhouse in Doha. Fighting broke out, and Qasim ibn Muhammad's supporters drove out the Ottoman force. This defeat, and Qasim ibn Muhammad's embrace after the turn of the century of the resurgent Wahhabis under Abd al Aziz ibn Saud, marked the de facto end of Ottoman rule in Qatar.

The Ottomans officially renounced sovereignty over Qatar in 1913, and in 1916 the new ruler, Qasim ibn Muhammad's son, Abd Allah ibn Qasim Al Thani, signed a treaty with Britain bringing the peninsula into the trucial system. This meant that in exchange for Britain's military protection, Qatar relinquished its autonomy in foreign affairs and other areas, such as the power to cede territory. The treaty also had provisions suppressing slavery, piracy, and gunrunning, but the British were not strict about enforcing those provisions.

Despite Qatar's coming under British "protection," Abd Allah ibn Qasim was far from secure: recalcitrant tribes refused to pay tribute; disgruntled family members intrigued against him; and he felt vulnerable to the designs of Bahrain, not to mention the Wahhabis. Despite numerous requests by Abd Allah ibn Qasim—for strong military support, for weapons, and even for a loan—the British kept him at arm's length. This changed in the 1930s, when competition (mainly between Britain and the United States) for oil concessions in the region intensified. In a 1935 treaty, Britain made more specific promises of assistance than in earlier treaties in return for the granting of a concession to the Anglo-Persian Oil Company.

The scramble for oil, in turn, raised the stakes in regional territorial disputes and put a dollar value on the question of national borders. In 1936, for example, Bahrain claimed rule over a group of islands, the largest of which is Hawar, off the west coast of Qatar because it had established a small military garrison there. Britain accepted the Bahraini claim over Abd Allah ibn Qasim's objections, in large part because the Bahraini shaykh's personal British adviser was able to frame Bahrain's case in a legal manner familiar to British officials. The question of domain continued in the early 1990s.

Triggered by a dispute involving the Naim, the Bahrainis once again laid claim to the deserted town of Az Zubarah in 1937. Abd Allah ibn Qasim sent a large, heavily armed force and succeeded in defeating the Naim. The British political resident in Bahrain supported Qatar's claim and warned Hamad ibn Isa Al Khalifa, the ruler of Bahrain, not to intervene militarily. Bitter and angry over the loss of Az Zubarah, Hamad ibn Isa imposed a crushing embargo on trade and travel to Qatar.

Oil was discovered in Qatar in 1939, but its exploitation was halted between 1942 and 1947 because of World War II and its aftermath. The disruption of food supplies caused by the war prolonged a period of economic hardship in Qatar that had begun in the 1920s with the collapse of the pearl trade and had increased with the global depression of the early 1930s and the Bahraini embargo. As they had in previous times of privation, whole families and tribes moved to other parts of the gulf, leaving many Qatari villages deserted. Even Shaykh Abd Allah ibn Qasim went into debt and, in preparation for his retirement, groomed his favored second son, Hamad ibn Abd Allah Al Thani, to be his successor. Hamad ibn Abd Allah's death in 1948, however, led to a succession crisis in which the main candidates were Abd Allah ibn Qasim's eldest son, Ali ibn Abd Allah Al Thani, and Hamad ibn Abd Allah's teenage son, Khalifa ibn Hamad Al Thani.

Oil exports and payments for offshore rights began in 1949 and marked a turning point in Qatar. Not only would oil revenues dramatically transform the economy and society, but they would also provide the focus for domestic disputes and foreign relations. This became frighteningly clear to Abd Allah ibn Qasim when several of his relatives threatened armed opposition if they did not receive increases in their allowances. Aged and anxious, Abd Allah ibn Qasim turned to the British, promised to abdicate, and agreed, among other things, to an official British presence in Qatar in exchange for recognition and support for Ali ibn Abd Allah as ruler in 1949.

The 1950s saw the cautious development of government structures and public services under British tutelage. Ali ibn Abd Allah was at first reluctant to share power, which had centered in his household, with an infant bureaucracy run and staffed mainly by outsiders. Ali ibn Abd Allah's increasing financial difficulties and inability to control striking oil workers and obstreperous shaykhs, however, led him to succumb to British pressure. The first real budget was drawn up by a British adviser in 1953. By 1954 there were forty-two Qatari government employees.

A major impetus to the development of the British-run police force came in 1956 when about 2,000 demonstrators, who coalesced over issues such as Gamal Abdul Nasser's pan-Arabism and opposition to Britain and to Shaykh Ali ibn Abd Allah's retinue, marched through Doha. This and other demonstrations led Ali ibn Abd Allah to invest the police with his personal authority and support, a significant reversal of his previous reliance on his retainers and beduin fighters.

Public services developed haltingly during the 1950s. The first telephone exchange opened in 1953, the first desalination plant in 1954, and the first power plant in 1957. Also built in this period were a jetty, a customs warehouse, an airstrip, and a police headquarters. In the 1950s, 150 adult males of the Al Thani received outright grants from the government. Shaykhs also received land and government positions. This mollified them as long as oil revenues increased. When revenues declined in the late 1950s, however, Ali ibn Abd Allah could not handle the family pressures this engendered. That Shaykh Ali ibn Abd Allah spent extravagantly, owned a villa in Switzerland, and hunted in Pakistan fueled discontent, especially among those who were excluded from the regime's largesse (non-Al Thani Qataris) and those who were not excluded but thought they deserved more (other branches of the Al Thani). Seniority and proximity to the shaykh determined the size of allowances.

Succumbing to family pressures and poor health, Ali ibn Abd Allah abdicated in 1960. But instead of handing power over to Khalifa ibn Hamad, who had been named heir apparent in 1948, he made his son, Ahmad ibn Ali, ruler. Nonetheless, Khalifa ibn Hamad, as heir apparent and deputy ruler, gained considerable power, in large part because Ahmad ibn Ali, as had his father, spent much time outside the country.

Although he did not care much for governing, Ahmad ibn Ali could not avoid dealing with family business. One of his first acts was to increase funding for the shaykhs at the expense of development projects and social services. In addition to allowances, adult male Al Thani were also given government positions. This added to the antiregime resentment already felt by, among others, oil workers, low-ranking Al Thani, dissident shaykhs, and some leading individuals. These groups formed the National Unity Front in response to a fatal shooting on April 19, 1963, of a member of a crowd protesting against Al Thani rule by one of Shaykh Ahmad ibn Ali's nephews. The front called a general strike, and its demands included a reduction of the ruler's privileges, recognition of trade unions, and increased social services. Ahmad ibn Ali cracked down by jailing fifty leading individuals and exiling the front's leaders. He also instituted some reforms, eventually including the provision of land and loans to poor Qataris.

Largely under Khalifa ibn Hamad's guiding hand, the infrastructure, foreign labor force, and bureaucracy continued to grow in the 1960s. There were even some early attempts at diversifying Qatar's economic base, most notably with the establishment of a cement factory, a national fishing company, and small-scale agriculture.

In 1968 Britain announced its intention of withdrawing from military commitments east of Suez, including those in force with Qatar, by 1971. For a while, the rulers of Bahrain, Qatar, and the Trucial Coast contemplated forming a federation after the British withdrawal. A dispute arose between Ahmad ibn Ali and Khalifa ibn Hamad, however, because Khalifa ibn Hamad opposed Bahrain's attempts to become the senior partner in the federation. Still giving public support to the federation, Ahmad ibn Ali nonetheless promulgated a provisional constitution in April 1970, which declared Qatar an independent, Arab, Islamic state with the sharia (Islamic law) as its basic law. Khalifa ibn Hamad was appointed prime minister in May. The first Council of Ministers was sworn in on January 1, 1970, and seven of its ten members were Al Thani. Khalifa ibn Hamad's argument prevailed with regard to the federation proposal. Qatar became an independent state on

September 3, 1971. That Ahmad ibn Ali issued the formal announcement from his Swiss villa instead of from his Doha palace indicated to many Qataris that it was time for a change. On February 22, 1972, Khalifa ibn Hamad deposed Ahmad ibn Ali, who was hunting with his falcons in Iran. Khalifa ibn Hamad had the tacit support of the Al Thani and of Britain, and he had the political, financial, and military support of Saudi Arabia.

In contrast to his predecessor's policies, Khalifa ibn Hamad cut family allowances and increased spending on social programs, including housing, health, education, and pensions. In addition, he filled many top government posts with close relatives.

In 1993 Khalifa ibn Hamad remained the amir, but his son, Hamad ibn Khalifa, the heir apparent and minister of defense, had taken over much of the day-to-day running of the country. The two consulted with each other on all matters of importance.

Geography

Qatar occupies 11,437 square kilometers on a peninsula that extends approximately 160 kilometers north into the Persian Gulf from the Arabian Peninsula. Varying in width between fifty-five and ninety kilometers, the land is mainly flat (the highest point is 103 meters) and rocky. Notable features include coastal salt pans, elevated limestone formations (the Dukhan anticline) along the west coast under which lies the Dukhan oil field, and massive sand dunes surrounding Khawr al Udayd, an inlet of the gulf in the southeast known to local English speakers as the Inland Sea. Of the islands belonging to Qatar, Halul is the most important. Lying about ninety kilometers east of Doha, it serves as a storage area and loading terminal for oil from the surrounding offshore fields. Hawar and the adjacent islands immediately off the west coast are the subject of a territorial dispute between Qatar and Bahrain (see Foreign Relations, this ch.).

The capital, Doha, is located on the central east coast on a sweeping (if shallow) harbor. Other ports include Umm Said, Al Khawr, and Al Wakrah. Only Doha and Umm Said are capable of handling commercial shipping, although a large port and a terminal for loading natural gas are planned at Ras Laffan, north of Al Khawr. Coral reefs and shallow coastal waters make navigation difficult in areas where channels have not been dredged.

Qatar shares its land border with the United Arab Emirates (UAE), with which in 1993 it continued to have a dispute in the Khawr al Udayd area. The boundary with Saudi Arabia was settled in 1965 but never demarcated. Qatar's northwest coast is fewer than thirty kilometers from Bahrain.

Doha is the capital of the country and the major administrative, commercial, and population center. In 1993 it was linked to other towns and development sites by a system of about 1,000 kilometers of paved roads. Doha's international airport has an approximately 4,500-meter main runway, capable of receiving all kinds of aircraft.

The long summer (June through September) is characterized by intense heat and alternating dryness and humidity, with temperatures exceeding 40°C. Temperatures are moderate from November through March, although winter temperatures may fall to 17°C, which is relatively cool for the latitude. Rainfall is negligible, averaging 100 millimeters per year, confined to the winter months, and falling in brief, sometimes heavy storms that often flood the small ravines and the usually dry wadis. Sudden, violent dust storms occasionally descend on the peninsula, blotting out the sun, causing wind damage, and momentarily disrupting transport and other services.

The scarcity of rainfall and the limited underground water, most of which has such a high mineral content that it is unsuitable for drinking or irrigation, restricted the population and the extent of agricultural and industrial development the country could support until desalination projects began. Although water continues to be provided from underground sources, most is obtained by desalination of seawater.

Population

The population of Qatar before independence must be estimated because, until oil revenues created a reason to stay on the peninsula, individuals and whole tribes migrated when the economic or security situation became intolerable. Some sought work elsewhere; others joined neighboring branches of their tribe. In 1908 a British observer estimated there were 27,000 inhabitants; 6,000 were described as foreign slaves and 425 as Iranian boatbuilders. (By 1930 the number of Iranians had increased to 5,000, or almost 20 percent of the population.) The population probably remained fairly stable until the

1930s and 1940s, when economic hardship and regional insecurity caused people to migrate to other areas, leaving Qatar with a population of only 16,000 in 1949, according to one estimate.

After oil exports increased in the 1950s, employment opportunities attracted Arabs from other Persian Gulf countries and foreign workers (mostly Indians at first) to Qatar. In 1970 the Qatari government, assisted by British experts, carried out a census that reported a population of 111,113, of whom 45,039, or more than 40 percent, were identified as Qataris. With the oil boom of the 1970s and the resultant influx of foreign workers came the largest population growth, so that by 1977 it was estimated that 200,000 people lived in the country, about 65 percent of whom were non-Qataris. During the 1960–75 period, the population grew at an average annual rate of 8.9 percent; in the 1970–75 period it grew at 12.7 percent.

The census of March 16, 1986, counted a population of 369,079. The July 1992 estimate was 484,387, with a 1992 growth rate of 3.2 percent. The 1989 birth rate was 31.8 per 1,000 population and the death rate 2.5 per 1,000, for a natural increase per 1,000 of 29.3, a high rate for a developing country.

The 1986 census showed that 84 percent of the population was concentrated in Doha and in the neighboring town of Ar Rayyan. Other towns included Al Wakrah (population 13,259) and Umm Said (population 6,094). In total, 88 percent of the population was urban. Reflecting the huge influx of foreign workers, about 67 percent of the population was male. The age breakdown was as follows: under fifteen, 27.8 percent; fifteen to twenty-nine, 29.3 percent; thirty to forty-four, 32.3 percent; forty-five to fifty-nine, 8.6 percent; and sixty and over, 2.0 percent.

South Asians (mainly Indians, Pakistanis, Bangladeshis, and Filipinos) made up about 35 percent of the population; Qataris, 20 percent; other Arabs, 25 percent; Iranians, 16 percent; and others, 4 percent. Roughly 90 percent of the population was Muslim (mostly Sunni—see Glossary), and the remainder were Christian, Hindu, Bahai, and other.

Education

Before oil was discovered, there was no formal education system in Qatar. Instead, some children in villages and towns memorized passages from the Quran and learned to read and write in a *kuttab*, an informal class taught in mosques or homes by literate men and women knowledgeable about Islam. Based on the custom of keeping women in a milieu shut off from the political, social, and economic opportunities afforded men, the development of education in Qatar focused mainly on the male population. From 1918 to 1938, for example, an Islamic school for adult males was run by Muhammad Abd al Aziz al Mana, an eminent scholar who had studied under Muhammad Abduh of Egypt and Al Alusi of Baghdad. According to a 1970 study, only 9 percent of the population born between 1895 and 1910 were literate, as were 15 percent of those born between 1910 and 1920 and 14 percent of those born between 1920 and 1930.

In 1949 Shaykh Hamad ibn Abd Allah opened a somewhat more modern school. The school, the Islah al Muhammadiyyah, had one teacher and fifty boys. In 1951 the school received funding from the ruling family, and the number of students and teachers increased. Subjects included Islamic religion and history, Arabic, arithmetic, geography, and English. By 1954 there were four such schools, with a total of 560 male students and twenty-six teachers. The first girls' school funded by oil money was a small *kuttab* that had been run by Amina Mahmud since 1938. After it was reorganized in 1956 as the first public school for girls in Qatar, four teachers taught 122 students the Quran, Arabic, arithmetic, ethics, and health. In the same year, the Department of Education was established. The budget for education increased from QR1 million (for value of the Qatari riyal—see Glossary) in 1955 to QR25 million in 1960. Not only was all public schooling free, but between 1956 and 1962 students received a monthly stipend. Despite inequality during the 1950s between the number of boys and the number of girls attending school, attendance was almost equal by gender in the late 1970s, with girls outperforming boys academically.

In the early 1990s, the education system consisted of six years of primary school, three years of intermediate school, and three years of secondary school (see table 19, Appendix). The secondary education program includes schools specializing in religion, commerce, and technical studies in which only males are allowed. Females, however, may attend teacher-training institutions. Instruction throughout the system is in Arabic, but English is introduced in the last two years of primary school, and there are special language-training programs for government personnel. Private facilities are available for kindergarten instruction. In addition, many foreign communities have established schools for their children; the largest are the schools for the Indian community. Although the government offers assistance to private schools, they are funded mainly through tuition and private sources.

In the 1975–76 academic year, 21,402 children attended primary school; by the 1985–86 academic year, that number had risen to 31,844. Students continue to be segregated by gender. In 1986 approximately 5.6 percent of the gross national product (GNP—see Glossary) went toward public education. The state in the 1990s continued to cover education costs, including school supplies, clothing, meals, and transportation to and from school.

In the 1988–89 academic year, there were 48,097 students in ninety-seven primary schools taught by 2,589 teachers and 22,178 intermediate and secondary students in seventy-eight schools taught by 2,115 teachers. At the three secular vocational schools, there were 924 students and 104 teachers. In the 1989–90 academic year, there were 5,637 students at the University of Qatar, which had 504 instructors, mostly Egyptians and non-Qatari Arabs.

The first institutions of higher education in Qatar were separate teacher-training colleges for men and women that opened in 1973. Before that, those wishing to pursue advanced degrees either studied abroad (mainly in Egypt and Lebanon) or took correspondence courses. A decree establishing the University of Qatar was passed, and in 1977 faculties of humanities, social studies, Islamic studies, and science joined the education faculty of the teacher-training colleges. In the 1985–86 academic year, about 1,000 Qataris received government scholarships to pursue higher education abroad, mostly in other Arab countries and in the United States, Britain, and France.

Health

Before oil was discovered, health care consisted of traditional medicine: barbers performed circumcisions and other minor procedures, and herbalists dispensed natural remedies. A one-doctor "hospital" opened in Doha in 1945. In 1951 Shaykh Ali ibn Abd Allah agreed to a British doctor and a small staff. The first state hospital, Rumailah Hospital, opened in 1959 with 170 beds. A 165-bed maternity hospital was established in 1965. The health budget was abused by Shaykh Ahmad ibn Ali's son and minister of health, Abd al Aziz ibn

Ahmad Al Thani. He apparently sent thousands of Ahmad ibn Ali's supporters abroad for luxurious and, in many cases, unnecessary health care in the 1960s.

The development of social services, including health care, accelerated after the accession in 1972 of Shaykh Khalifa ibn Hamad, who dramatically altered the allocation of oil revenues. This included transferring the ruler's 25 percent of oil revenues to the state budget. But the health budget suffered because of the downturns in oil revenues. In 1986, for example, there were cuts of 10 percent in clinic staff.

There are three hospitals in Doha, with a total of about 1,100 beds. Hamad General Hospital, which opened in 1982, has modern facilities for emergency care, cardiovascular surgery, tomography, nuclear medicine, and plastic surgery. Rumailah Hospital, once the only general hospital, has become a center for geriatric, psychiatric, and rehabilitative care. It also has dental and dermatology departments and a burn unit. The Women's Hospital has 314 beds. In addition, dozens of clinics throughout the country ensure accessible primary care to most of the population. For example, 90 percent of births in the late 1980s were attended by a health professional. There are 752 government physicians and many other support staff. In the 1980s, several private clinics also opened in the capital.

Life expectancy at birth in 1986 was 65.2 years for males and 67.6 years for females. The infant mortality rate in 1989 was thirty-one per 1,000 live births. In the 1988–89 period, 81 percent of one- to three-year-olds were immunized. Major causes of death in 1989 were diseases of the circulatory system, injuries and poisonings, tumors, and perinatal conditions.

The Economy

Oil and Natural Gas

Oil

In 1935, after years of behind-the-scenes wrangling involving the shaykh, British and United States oil companies, the British, and the Saudis, an onshore concession was granted to the Anglo-Persian Oil Company, which transferred the concession to Petroleum Development (Qatar), an affiliate of the Iraq Petroleum Company (IPC). British, French, and United States oil companies held shares in IPC. Petroleum Development

(Qatar) was renamed the Qatar Petroleum Company (QPC) in 1953.

As a result of adequate crude oil supplies at the time, exploratory drilling in Qatar did not begin until 1938. Oil was discovered in Dukhan, on the west coast, in 1939. By 1940 about 4,000 barrels per day (bpd—see Glossary) were being produced. World War II and its aftermath brought development to a halt between 1942 and 1947, and exports did not begin until 1949. The Dukhan field extends south from Dukhan along the west coast and has three oil reservoirs layered progressively deeper between limestone formations and a natural gas field underlying them all. Dukhan crude has an American Petroleum Institute (API) rating of 40° and a sulfur content of 1.2 percent. A pipeline carries crude oil from the Dukhan fields to storage, refining, and terminal facilities on the east side of the peninsula at Umm Said.

In 1952 a Royal Dutch Shell subsidiary, Shell Company of Qatar (SCQ), obtained a concession for offshore exploration on the continental shelf. Most offshore discoveries centered on the island of Halul, about ninety kilometers east of Doha. The major offshore fields and the dates they were discovered are Idd ash Sharqi (1960) and Maydan Mahzam (1963). Offshore production began in 1964. Because both Qatar and Abu Dhabi claimed the Al Bunduq field, the two parties agreed to exploit it jointly starting in 1969. Another offshore field was discovered in the summer of 1991 by Elf Aquitaine Qatar. Offshore crude had an API rating of 36° and a sulfur content of 1.4 percent. Offshore crude is stored at facilities on the island of Halul, which also has pumping stations and two single-buoy moorings for loading tankers. Combined offshore and onshore reserves as of January 1990 were 4.5 billion barrels, offering thirty-two years of production at 1989 levels.

Both concessions were for seventy-five years and gave the oil companies the right to explore, produce, refine, transport, and market all oil found in the stipulated area. In addition, the concessionaire companies were exempt from taxes and duties on imports and exports but were required to hire local labor where possible. The Anglo-Persian Oil Company (after a down payment of 400,000 rupees in 1935) was required to pay Shaykh Abd Allah ibn Qasim 150,000 rupees annually thereafter (see Money and Banking, this ch.). (During World War II, when oil operations were suspended, the annual payment was 300,000 rupees.) Before commercial production could begin,

View of heavy industry area in Umm Said, south of Doha
Courtesy Qatar Today
Khalifa ibn Hamad Al Thani, ruler of Qatar, inaugurates Phase One
of North Field natural gas development project , September 1991
Courtesy Qatar Today

an industry had to be assembled. The company built a jetty at Bir Zikrit and shipped in water, foodstuffs, and almost 100,000 tons of equipment and supplies from Bahrain before the first drop of oil was pumped. Once exports began, oil became extremely profitable in Qatar and in the rest of the Persian Gulf as a result of favorable concession terms, cheap labor, relatively inexpensive drilling and pumping costs, and easy access to transportation.

In 1952 the 1935 concession agreement was revised (in line with others in the region) to split profits fifty-fifty between the company and the ruler. Shaykh Ali ibn Abd Allah's share rose from about US$1 million in 1950 to US$61 million in 1958, after which his profits dipped to US$53 million in 1959 and did not rise to the 1958 level until 1963. Some money reached the local economy, but the initial impact of oil exports consisted mainly of high incomes for the Al Thani and high inflation on basic commodities.

From its initial concession in 1935, QPC kept aloof from the shaykh and was seen by the ruler and workers as high-handed and inept; for example, it triggered strikes by forgetting to issue workers' coffee rations or inadvertently forcing them to work during Muslim holidays. In the 1950s, the company had its own infrastructure (power, water, communications, and housing) and provided health care to workers and police protection to its facilities.

To gain some leverage over the oil company with regard to revenues, pricing, and production, Qatar joined the Organization of the Petroleum Exporting Countries (OPEC) in 1961, one year after it was formed. Qatar has stayed close to its OPEC production quota when it has been in its economic interest but has often exceeded its quota to compensate for soft markets or to take advantage of the price increases that resulted from the Iraqi invasion of Kuwait in August 1990.

Between 1960 and 1970, annual oil production more than doubled, from 60.4 million barrels (165,000 bpd) to 132.5 million barrels (363,000 bpd). Production peaked in 1973 at 208.2 million barrels (570,000 bpd). Between 1974 and 1980, production leveled off in the range of 410,000 bpd to 520,000 bpd. The early 1980s saw a steady decline, apart from a small recovery in 1984, with an average annual production of 151.5 million barrels (415,000 bpd). After another flat period in the mid 1980s, production levels rose once again in the late 1980s and early 1990s, with 146.7 million barrels (402,000 bpd) produced in 1990 (see table 20, Appendix). The 395,000 bpd production levels of 1989 and the first eight months of 1990 exceeded OPEC quotas.

After independence in 1971, the Qatar National Petroleum Company was created in 1972 to handle oil operations. In 1973 the government held 25 percent each of QPC and SCQ. Two years later, the Qatar General Petroleum Corporation (QGPC) was established, and the government signed new agreements with the oil companies giving QGPC 60 percent ownership. By 1977 onshore and offshore operations were fully nationalized, and service contracts were given to former concessionaires.

Production of petroleum products began in 1953 when a QPC-owned refinery started up with a capacity of 600 bpd. By 1975 refining capacity had expanded to 6,000 bpd, and by the early 1980s another 4,000-bpd-capacity had been added. A refinery opened in 1983 and added 50,000 bpd in capacity, bringing the national total to more than 60,000 bpd. The National Oil Distribution Company refined an average of 62,000 bpd in 1990; 75 percent of production was exported. As a result of the jump in prices caused by the Iraqi invasion of Kuwait, 1990 profits were 40 percent higher (US$1 billion) than in 1989. Most of the refined products are consumed locally.

Natural Gas

The Qatari government celebrated twenty years of independence in September 1991 with the inauguration of Phase One of the North Field development project. The gas project, in a 6,000-square-kilometer field off Qatar's northeast coast, is supervised by Bechtel of the United States and by Technip Geoproduction of France. The project marks a major step in Qatar's switch from a reliance on oil to gas for most of its revenues. The North Field is the world's largest natural gas field, and its exploitation will place Qatar in the top ranks of the world's gas producers. Natural gas from other fields provides fuel for power generation and raw materials for fertilizers, petrochemicals, and steel plants. With the expected depletion of oil reserves by about 2023, planners hope natural gas from the North Field will provide a significant underpinning for the country's economic development.

In the early 1970s, Qatar flared about 80 percent of the 16.8 million cubic meters of natural gas produced daily in association with crude oil liftings. In that decade, the country made progress in using its natural gas resources despite several set-backs. Whereas nearly 66 percent of onshore gas was flared in 1974, by 1979 that proportion had fallen to less than 5 percent.

Two natural gas liquids (NGL) plants began operation in Umm Said in 1981. NGL–1 used gas produced from the Dukhan field, and NGL–2 processed gas associated with off-shore fields. The combined daily capacities were 2,378 tons of propane, 1,840 tons of butane, 1,480 tons of condensate, and 2,495 tons of ethane-rich gas. However, repeated difficulties prevented the plants from coming on-line as scheduled and operating at full capacity. A massive explosion at the precursor of NGL–1 in 1977 killed six people and caused US$500 million in damage. NGL–2 had problems with the pipelines that con-nected the plant with offshore fields. The sharp drop in oil pro-duction in the 1980s meant that lack of feedstock caused plant shutdowns and underproduction. As a result, downstream (see Glossary) users suffered as well. In 1982 the two plants pro-duced 500,000 tons of propane and butane—slightly more than one-half of plant capacity. Condensate production lagged even further at 138,000 tons, or 40 percent of capacity.

This gloomy outlook is mitigated to some degree by hope for development of the massive natural gas reserves in the North Field. Discovered in 1972 by SCQ, its proven reserves of 4.6 million cubic meters (as of 1989) will be productive well into the twenty-first century. The Qatar Liquefied Gas Com-pany (Qatargas) was established in 1984 as a joint venture with QGPC and foreign partners to market and export liquefied natural gas (LNG) from the North Field.

Phase One of the US$1.3 billion project was officially inau-gurated on September 3, 1991. By the end of the month, it was pumping 23 million cubic meters of gas per day from sixteen wells. This is expected to meet an estimated 17 million cubic meters per day of domestic demand.

QGPC plans a massive development at Ras Laffan in associa-tion with the North Field project. In addition to a new port with LNG, petroleum products, and container loading berths, project plans include a 2,500-ton per year methanol plant and a 450,000-ton per year petrochemical complex. The develop-ment is scheduled for completion in the late 1990s.

In line with its desire to diversify the firms engaged in devel-oping its resources, Qatar signed a letter of intent in February 1991 with Chubu Electrical Power Company of Japan to supply 4 million tons per year of North Field gas for twenty-five years, starting in 1997. This amount represents two-thirds of Qatar-gas's expected capacity of about 6 million tons per year.

Industry

The government has established heavy industry to diversify Qatar's economy. The pattern has been to allow foreign firms to provide expertise in planning, construction, management, and marketing in return for minority shares in the companies. Oil revenues have funded the construction of plants and the development of infrastructure; natural gas has been used as a source of power and as feedstock. The country's main power generation and water desalination plants are at Ras Abu Abbud and Ras Abu Fintas. Electrical generating capacity in 1990 was 1,095 megawatts, and there were plans to add an additional 234 megawatts in the early 1990s. Power consumption in 1990 stood at 4,818 million kilowatt-hours and peak demand at 987 megawatts. Bureaucratic delays stalled many projects, and poor market conditions and technical problems doomed others to unprofitability. Major construction projects such as factories are seldom completed on schedule.

The Industrial Development Technical Centre (IDTC), formed in 1973, directs much of Qatar's industrialization, apart from petroleum extraction. The IDTC identifies industries to meet Qatar's medium- and long-term needs and coordinates industrial planning. In addition, the IDTC monitors the performance of all industries on a monthly basis. In the early 1980s, the center began assessing the environmental impact of industrial plants and production. The IDTC has also been involved in pilot manufacturing programs: in 1989 it announced the formation of the Qatar Industrial Manufacturing Company, owned partly by the government and designed to establish small- and medium-sized enterprises and to buy shares in existing companies.

The country's center for heavy industry is Umm Said. Smaller industries and businesses are concentrated in the As Salwa Industrial Area. The government encourages business and industry by offering, among other things, low-interest loans; free road, water, and electrical hookups; subsidized electricity and water; land leases at minimal cost; and protective tariffs and tax incentives.

The three largest enterprises are the Qatar Fertilizer Company (Qafco), Qatar Steel Company (Qasco), and Qatar Petrochemical Company (Qapco). Qafco was established in 1969 and since 1975 has been owned by QGPC (75 percent) and Norsk Hydro of Norway (25 percent). The government took over Qafco's management in 1991. The Qafco facility, which uses methane-rich natural gas from the Dukhan field as feedstock to produce ammonia and urea, has been less affected by periodic drops in oil production than plants relying on offshore natural gas. Production increased steadily in the 1970s, and a second plant opened in 1979. Nonetheless, because of a steep decline in world fertilizer prices, in 1986 Qafco faced its first operating losses since 1977, despite record levels of production (660,000 tons of ammonia and 744,000 tons of urea). In 1990 Qafco produced 710,000 tons of ammonia (down from 714,000 tons in 1989) and 760,000 tons of urea (down from 778,561 tons in 1989). It had profits of US$40 million in that year. India and China are Qafco's main customers.

Qasco was established in 1974 with 70 percent state ownership. Kobe Steel Company (20 percent) and Tokyo Boeki (10 percent) of Japan hold the remaining shares. Japanese companies initially handled construction, production, marketing, and export. The Qasco plant, which began producing in 1978, has consistently outproduced its 330,000-ton per year design capacity. Its main products are steel bars used to reinforce structural concrete.The plant uses imported iron ore and local scrap; its direct reduction and rolling stages are rated as highly efficient. Despite high levels of output, lack of demand and low prices have contributed to millions of dollars in losses.

Production levels have risen steadily from the outset, with 1979 production at 378,544 tons of steel bars. Because of declines in world steel prices, in 1982 the plant registered its first losses despite a 485,000-ton production level. The mid-1980s saw a sharp decline in demand and increased foreign competition. The company registered a loss of US$13.7 million in 1985. In response to cheaper Japanese and Korean imports, the government imposed a 20 percent tariff on bars similar to those produced domestically. The plant returned to profitability in 1988. Qasco took over management of the plant in 1989; Kobe Steel Company remained as consultant. In 1990 Qasco produced a record 565,000 tons of steel bars, up from 556,538 tons in 1989. Plans to expand the plant were approved. Saudi Arabia has been the principal customer, followed by the UAE and other gulf countries.

Qapco's petrochemical complex in Umm Said started production in 1981 with an annual output of 132,679 tons of ethylene, well below its 280,000-ton capacity. The plant also has a capacity to produce 140,000 tons of linear low-density polyethylene (LLDPE) and small amounts of sulfur and propylene. QGPC holds 84 percent of the company, and ORKEM of France holds the remaining 16 percent.

Shortages in feedstock caused by troubles in 1982 with gas pipelines from the offshore fields caused production to drop by one-half. Such difficulties, combined with sluggish sales in the early and mid-1980s, contributed to large operating losses: QR69 million in 1984; QR156 million in 1985; and QR57 million in 1986. The end of the decade, however, saw significant improvement, with profits of around QR420 million in 1989 and production of ethylene at 295,000 tons, LLDPE at 181,000 tons, and sulfur at 52,000 tons.

As a result of the 1989 cabinet reshuffle, the Supreme Council for Planning (SCP) was formed to coordinate the diversification of Qatar's economy by, among other things, encouraging industries linked to the North Field gas project (see Oil and Natural Gas, this ch.). There are plans for a US$500 million petrochemical complex and also a 240,000-ton per year aluminum smelter at Umm Said that will use North Field gas.

Some industries that are smaller but important suppliers of the domestic market include a flour mill and several cement companies. The Qatar Flour Mills Company processes flour and bran from wheat. It began production in 1969, and output in the 1980s was 700 tons per day. The Qatar National Cement Company (QNCC), owned jointly by the government and private shareholders, uses local gypsum in cement production. QNCC was established in 1965 with a production capacity of 100,000 tons per year. By 1982 the plant had a capacity of 330,000 tons per year. Annual production varied as a result of the competition of cheap imports, and after achieving an output of 319,740 tons in 1985, production declined steadily. Following a low of 160,000 tons in 1988, in 1990 the plant produced 327,000 tons of cement in 1990.

Labor

The discovery of oil brought wage labor to Qatar, removing many pearl divers, fishermen, and herders from reliance on a subsistence economy that was plagued with privation, debt, and other hardships and setting them in a new system of relatively steady labor for cash. But the work force did not consist entirely of free males. In the early 1950s, there were about

3,000 slaves, brought from Africa, in the peninsula. The 250 slaves who were working for Petroleum Development (Qatar) in 1949 turned over 80 to 95 percent of their wages to their owners. (After the British political agent expressed his disapproval of the practice to the shaykh, the ruler decreed reluctantly that slaves could keep 50 percent of their wages.)

Because there were no labor regulations in the 1940s and 1950s, hours, conditions, and wages varied widely. Some workers were paid less than one rupee per day, whereas others received as much as four rupees per day. (In contrast, a man working on a pearl boat might earn only sixty rupees in six months.) Sometimes overtime was compensated; at other times it was not. In the late 1930s and into the 1940s, workers put in seven-day weeks, with only one day off per month. Workers were often dismissed for minor infractions and endured humiliating treatment and difficult, dangerous conditions to hold their jobs.

The special skills of the pearl divers were used to help set up offshore rigs. Other workers were employed as drivers, cooks, and houseboys for British personnel, and still others were employed as roustabouts. There were four levels of salaries and amenities in Petroleum Development (Qatar). At the top were the British engineers and foremen, next the clerks (mostly Indians), then the drivers, and finally the laborers at the bottom of the pay and accommodation scale. Local merchants acted as representatives of the oil company and collected one rupee from Qataris and forty to fifty rupees from foreigners for work certificates.

At the outset, the unskilled laborers were Qataris and other gulf Arabs. They had frequent disagreements with the oil company's management, most of whom were non-Qataris, and some disagreements flared into strikes. Early strikes focused on wages, conditions, and benefits. In addition, the shaykh often encouraged strikes to pressure concessions from the oil company at the times he was negotiating new contracts.

During one strike in 1951, Qatari workers opposed those from the Dhofar region in present-day Oman. To resolve the matter, the Dhofaris were deported (a solution to labor disputes that, along with imprisonment, continued to be used in the early 1990s). Shaykh Ali ibn Abd Allah freed the slaves in 1952 and paid 1,500 rupees each to 660 of them. A major strike in 1955 by Qatari workers induced the shaykh to form a Qatari riot squad to be used against them. In 1956 well-organized oil workers joined opposition forces in demonstrations against the regime and against the British. In response, the government inserted clauses in labor contracts banning political activity.

In 1959 a labor department was established to deal with oil workers. In 1962 a labor law was enacted that gave preference in hiring first to Qataris, then to other Arabs, and finally to other foreigners. Strict controls existed on foreign workers, whose visas stipulated that they must work for a specific Qatari sponsor at a specific job. In practice, there was some fluidity in employment. Trade unions were banned, but Qatari workers had workplace-based organizations, known as workers' committees, that dealt with grievances. The country's labor court was the first in the Persian Gulf. The government has sought to encourage Qataris to take jobs in the industrial work force (the process of "Qatarization"). In 1993, however, the majority of laborers and middle-level employees were foreigners.

All foreign workers require sponsorship by a Qatari, some of whom illegally charge their employees high fees for renewing sponsorship. Other abuses include breach of contract and physical or sexual abuse.

Regulations govern safety in the workplace, but these are unevenly enforced. The labor force represents 42 percent of the population, with 7 percent of the force made up of women. Those women who work outside the home are often teachers, nurses, clerks, or domestic servants. Service industries absorb 69 percent of the work force, industry 28 percent, and agriculture 3 percent.

Agriculture and Fishing

Small-scale farming, nomadic herding, pearling, and fishing were the predominant means of subsistence in the region for the centuries before the discovery of oil. Although the relative importance of these activities has declined as a means of livelihood (with commercial pearling disappearing completely), the government has attempted to encourage agriculture and fishing to provide a degree of self-sufficiency in food.

Between 1960 and 1970, agriculture grew. The number of farms, for example, increased fourfold to 411. Qataris who own agricultural land or properties generally hold government jobs and hire Iranians, Pakistanis, or non-Qatari Arabs to manage their farms. The government operates one experimental farm. Of land under cultivation in 1990, about 48 percent was used for vegetables (23,000 tons produced), 33 percent for fruit and date production (8,000 tons), 11 percent for fodder (70,000 tons), and 8 percent for grains (3,000 tons). In 1990 the country had approximately 128,000 head of sheep, 78,000 goats, 24,000 camels, 10,000 cattle, and 1,000 horses. There are also dairy farms and about 2,000 chickens for poultry. All but 20 percent of local demand for eggs is met domestically. Despite the encouragement of agriculture and fishing, these two elements of the economy together produced only about 1 percent of the gross domestic product (GDP—see Glossary) in 1989 (see table 21, Appendix).

Severe conditions, such as extremely high temperatures and lack of water and fertile soil, hinder increased agricultural production. The limited groundwater that permits agriculture in some areas is being depleted so rapidly that saltwater is encroaching and making the soil inhospitable to all but the most salt-resistant crops. According to estimates, groundwater will be depleted about the year 2000. As a partial solution, the government plans to expand its program of using treated sewage effluent for agriculture. Parkland and public gardens in Doha are already watered in this way.

The Qatar National Fishing Company was incorporated in 1966 to fish for shrimp in territorial waters and to process catches in a refrigerated factory. Japan is a large market for Doha's commercial fish. The total catch of fish and other aquatic animals for 1989 was 4,374 tons.

Transportation and Telecommunications

In 1993 Qatar had 1,500 kilometers of roads, 1,000 kilometers of which were paved and the rest gravel. Most paved highways are centered in the Doha area or radiate from the capital to the northern end of the peninsula, to Dukhan on the west coast, or southwest to the border with Saudi Arabia to connect with the Saudi highway system. Outside the capital and the principal highways, however, large stretches of country are accessible only by vehicles with four-wheel drive.

Facilities for air and water transportation are located in or near the capital. Doha is the main port, having four berths capable of handling ships up to nine meters in draught and five additional berths that can accommodate ships requiring 7.5 meters of water. Forty kilometers south of Doha, Umm Said handles petroleum exports. Doha International Airport, with a 4,500-meter runway, accommodates all types of airplanes. Qatar is part owner of Gulf Air, the flag carrier for

*Fishing harbor, Doha, capital of Qatar; the fishing industry is a main
source of food and income for the Persian Gulf states.*
Courtesy Anthony Toth

Qatar, Bahrain, the UAE, and Oman. Most international air
traffic to and from Qatar is shunted through Bahrain, but
Gulf Air and a few international carriers offer nonstop service from Doha to other points in the Middle East, South
Asia, the Philippines, and France.

Domestic and international telecommunications are
excellent. In 1992 Qatar had 110,000 telephones, or twenty-
three per 100 inhabitants, a per capita figure higher than
many European nations. Radio-relay and submarine cables
link Qatar with all the Arab states around the Persian Gulf.
Three satellite ground stations, one operating with the International Telecommunications Satellite Organization's (Intelsat) Atlantic Ocean satellite, one operating with Intelsat's
Indian Ocean satellite, and one operating as part of the Arab
Satellite Communication Organization (Arabsat) system,
provide excellent international telephone and data links and
live television broadcasts. Seven AM and three FM radio stations have programs in Arabic, French, Urdu, and English. A
powerful shortwave station with broadcasts in Arabic and
English is heard worldwide.

Money and Banking

The Indian rupee was the principal currency until 1959, when the government replaced it with a special gulf rupee in an effort to halt gold smuggling into India. In 1966 Qatar and Dubayy jointly established a currency board to issue a Qatar-Dubayy riyal. In 1973 Qatar introduced its own riyal, which was pegged to the International Monetary Fund's (IMF—see Glossary) special drawing rights (SDR—see Glossary). The exchange rate is tied to the United States dollar at a rate of QR3.64 per US$1.00.

The Qatar Monetary Agency (QMA), established in 1973, has most of the traditional powers and prerogatives of a central bank. The QMA regulates banking, credit, and finances; issues currency; and manages the foreign reserves necessary to support the Qatari riyal. Unlike many central banks, the agency shares control over the country's reserves with what was in 1973 the Ministry of Finance and Petroleum. QMA does not act as the state's banker, which is the preserve of the Qatar National Bank (QNB).

QMA's long-time governor, Majid Muhammad al Majid as Saad, was replaced in January 1990 by Abd Allah Khalid al Attiyah, who had been general manager of QNB. The position of governor was upgraded to ministerial level, signaling a more assertive future role for QMA in the country's banking sector.

Banks give loans at rates between 7 and 9 percent, and they pay 7 percent on deposits. About fifteen local and foreign banks operate in Qatar. Two banks—Qatar Islamic Bank, licensed in 1989, and Qatar International Islamic Bank, licensed in 1990—reflect a trend toward Islamic banking that started in Saudi Arabia.

Banking in the gulf has been vulnerable to the shaky regional security situation. As a result of the Iraqi invasion of Kuwait, banks in Qatar lost an estimated 15 to 30 percent of deposits in late 1990.

Budget

Oil and gas revenues make up 90 percent of government revenue, and government spending is the primary means of injecting these earnings into the economy. Given the small size of the local market, government spending generates most of the economic activity. Because of increased involvement in the

Employees and clients at one of Qatar's numerous commercial banks
Courtesy Qatar Today

international economic scene, in April 1989 Qatar's fiscal year was changed from the Islamic to the Gregorian calendar.

Large budget surpluses in the 1970s funded major development projects, with government spending leveling off and dropping in the 1980s, years of more modest oil revenues. After years of surpluses, the government had a deficit of nearly QR8 billion in 1983. The government has attempted to keep deficits down by reducing the number of new projects and delaying those under way. In addition, the fiscal situation of the regime can often be gauged by the amount of time required to pay contractors.

Budgets offer only a rough estimate of actual government spending. Many significant items, such as military and amirate expenses, do not appear. Projections are consistently conservative, and deficits often are lower than predicted. In the 1986–87 period, when oil prices plummeted, the government did not even announce a budget. Restrained spending in recent years has meant frustration for contractors relying on government contracts, but the policy has also led to ever-shrinking deficits. The budget continued to show a deficit in the early 1990s (see table 22, Appendix).

181

Overseas assets are estimated at between US$10 and US$14 billion. These assets have been periodically tapped to make up for shortfalls in oil revenues.

Trade

The main export and source of revenue is oil, although the government's efforts to diversify Qatar's industrial base have resulted in the growth of other exports. Crude oil, petroleum products, and LNG accounted for 82 percent of exports in 1989, chemicals (ammonia and urea) accounted for 12.4 percent, and manufactures (mainly steel) accounted for 5.1 percent. Total earnings for the year were QR9.7 billion (see table 23, Appendix). Japan was the largest customer at 54.4 percent of purchases, followed by Thailand (5.0 percent) and Singapore (4.0 percent) (see table 24, Appendix).

Because imports are financed by oil revenues, the level of goods coming into the country rises and falls with the oil economy. Between 1969 and 1979, for example, the value of imports grew an average of 40 percent annually. Imports declined in the early to mid-1980s, sinking to a low of QR4.0 billion in 1986, then rising gradually until they reached QR4.8 billion in 1989.

Machinery and transportation equipment accounted for 37.0 percent of imports in 1989, manufactured goods for 23.9 percent, food and live animals for 15.1 percent, and chemicals and chemical products for 6.0 percent. The main import sources were Japan (18.8 percent), Britain (11.6 percent), the United States (8.8 percent), Italy (7.8 percent), and the Federal Republic of Germany (West Germany) (7.3 percent).

In keeping with a Gulf Cooperation Council (GCC) agreement, Qatar raised tariffs from 2.5 to 4.0 percent in 1984. In addition, there is a 20 percent duty on steel products similar to those produced by Qasco. Qatar plays a small role in the region's entrepôt trade. Most imports arrive by sea and are for local use, with only a small percentage reexported to Saudi Arabia and the UAE.

Government and Politics

The 1970 provisional constitution (sometimes called the basic law) declares Qatar a sovereign Arab, Islamic state and vests sovereignty in the state. In fact, sovereignty is held by the amir, but, although he is supreme in relation to any other individual or institution, in practice his rule is not absolute. The constitution also provides for a partially elected consultative assembly, the Advisory Council. The first council's twenty members were selected from representatives chosen by limited suffrage. The size of the council was increased to thirty members in 1975. Among the council's constitutional prerogatives is the right to debate legislation drafted by the Council of Ministers before it is ratified and promulgated.

The amir is also obliged to rule in accordance with Islamic precepts, which include fairness, honesty, generosity, and mutual respect. Islamic religious and ethical values are applicable to both the ruler's personal life and his rule. Thus, the ruler must retain the support of the religious community, which often asserts itself in such areas as media censorship, education regulations, and the status of women.

The state political organs include the ruler, the Council of Ministers, and the Advisory Council. The ruler makes all major executive decisions and legislates by decree. The constitution institutionalizes the legislative and executive processes in the functions of the ruler, in effect formalizing his supremacy. Among the ruler's constitutional duties are convening the Council of Ministers, ratifying and promulgating laws and decrees, commanding the armed forces, and appointing and dismissing senior civil servants and military officers by decree. The constitution provides that the ruler possess "any other powers with which he is vested under this provisional constitution or with which he may be vested under the law." This means that the ruler may extend or modify his powers by personal decree.

The constitution also provides for a deputy ruler, who is to assume the post of prime minister. The prime minister is to formulate government programs and exercise final supervisory control over the financial and administrative affairs of the government. When the constitution was promulgated, Khalifa ibn Hamad was concurrently prime minister and heir apparent, but the constitution did not specify that the post of prime minister must be held by the heir apparent.

The Council of Ministers, which resembles similar bodies in the West, forms the amir's cabinet. A major government reshuffle in July 1989 reorganized several ministries, bringing in younger men loyal to Khalifa ibn Hamad's son, Shaykh Hamad ibn Khalifa. The Al Thani continued to dominate the government, with the most influential (after the amir and heir appar-

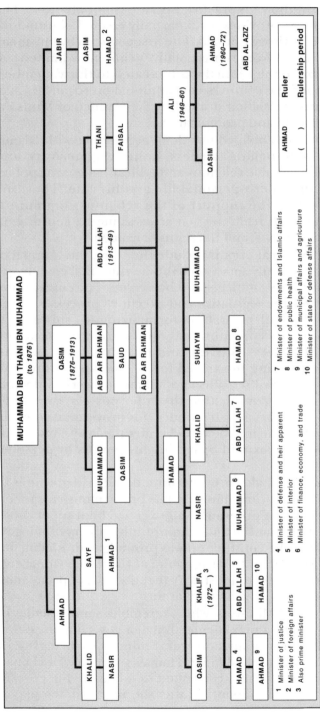

Source: Based on information from John Duke Anthony, *Arab States of the Lower Gulf,* Washington, 1975, 78; United States, Central Intelligence Agency, *Chiefs of State and Cabinet Members of Foreign Governments,* Washington, 1992, 72; and "Qatar," in *The Middle East and North Africa, 1993,* London, 1992, 758.

Figure 10. Qatar: Abbreviated Genealogy of the Al Thani, with Government Positions, 1992

ent) being Shaykh Abd Allah ibn Khalifa, minister of interior; Shaykh Ahmad ibn Hamad, minister of municipal affairs and agriculture; and Shaykh Muhammad ibn Khalifa, minister of finance, economy, and trade (see fig. 10). In October 1992, of the eighteen Council of Ministers posts, ten were occupied by the Al Thani and eight by commoners.

The Council of Ministers is responsible collectively to the ruler, as is each minister individually. The ruler appoints and dismisses ministers (technically on the recommendation of the prime minister when that post is occupied by someone other than the ruler). Only native-born Qataris can become ministers, and the constitution prohibits the prime minister and other ministers from engaging in business or commercial activities while holding state office.

The Advisory Council debates laws proposed by the Council of Ministers before they are submitted to the ruler for ratification. If approved by the ruler, a law becomes effective on publication in the official gazette. In 1975 the amir empowered the Advisory Council to summon individuals to answer questions on legislation before promulgation. The Advisory Council also debates the draft budgets of public projects and general policy on political, economic, social, and administrative affairs referred to it by the prime minister. The Advisory Council can request from the Council of Ministers information pertaining to policies it is debating, direct written questions to a particular minister, and summon ministers to answer questions on proposed legislation. Ministers have the right to attend and address Advisory Council meetings in which policy matters within their purview are being discussed; in practice, no use has been made of this constitutional guarantee because members of the Council of Ministers are also members of the Advisory Council.

As the constitution stipulates, Qatar is divided into ten electoral districts for the purpose of forming the Advisory Council. Each district elects four candidates, of whom the ruler selects two, making a total of twenty; they constitute the relatively representative portion of the council. The members represent all Qataris, not just those in their districts. The Advisory Council was increased to thirty members in December 1975 and to thirty-five members in November 1988. Membership is limited to native-born citizens at least twenty years of age. The constitution states that members are to serve three-year terms, but in May 1975 members' terms were extended for an additional three years and then for additional four-year terms in 1978, in 1982, in 1986, and in 1990.

Before the implementation of the constitution, the ruler's legislative authority frequently overlapped or encompassed judicial functions because he personally adjudicated disputes and grievances brought before him. The constitution marks the beginning of an attempt to organize the judiciary. The secular courts include a higher and lower criminal court, a civil court, an appeals court, and a labor court. Civil and criminal codes, as well as a court of judicial procedure, were introduced in 1971. All civil and criminal law falls within the jurisdiction of these secular courts. A labor court was created in 1962, primarily because few of the country's existing judicial customs and codes were applicable to contemporary labor relations.

The sharia court is the oldest element in Qatar's judiciary. The court's law is based on the Hanbali legal school of Islam, wherein judges (qadis) adhere to a strict interpretation of the Quran and sunna, or traditions of the Prophet Muhammad (see Sunni Islam, ch. 1). Originally, the sharia court's jurisdiction covered all civil and criminal disputes between Qataris and between all other Muslims. Beginning in the 1960s, the court's jurisdiction was successively restricted by decree. In the early 1990s, its responsibilities were confined primarily to family matters, including property, inheritance, divorce, and Islamic ethics. Non-Muslims were tried in secular courts unless they were married to Muslims.

The constitution establishes the legal presumption of innocence and prohibits ex post facto laws. It also stipulates that "judges shall be independent in the exercise of their powers, and no party whatsoever may interfere in the administration of justice." The judiciary is nominally independent, not so much as a result of a constitutional guarantee but because its jurisdiction is unlikely to confront the ruler's exercise of power. Secular courts adjudicate on the basis of the ruler's past decrees, and religious courts are restricted to questions of personal status. No provision exists for judicial review of the constitutionality of legislation.

According to the preamble to the 1970 constitution, the government was undergoing a transitional stage of development. The constitution was thus provisional and was to be replaced with a new constitution after the transitional period ended. Shaykh Khalifa ibn Hamad has usually legitimated government changes that he decrees by reference to the constitu-

*Khalifa ibn Hamad
Al Thani,
ruler of Qatar
Courtesy Embassy of Qatar,
Washington*

tion. As of early 1993, however, there had been no indication that the full implementation of the constitution was imminent (for example, the electoral aspects of selection to Advisory Council membership) or that the transitional period was ending and a new constitution forthcoming.

In addition to describing and delineating governmental authority, the constitution sets forth such protections as equality among Qataris regardless of race, sex, or religion; freedom of the press; sanctity of the home; and recognition of both private and collective ownership of property. Such guarantees, however, are limited by the public interest and must be in accordance with the law—which is determined by the ruler. In practice, freedom of the press means that incoming foreign publications are screened by a government office for potentially objectionable material, and the indigenous press exercises self-censorship and is subject to sanction if it fails to deal appropriately with political and religious issues (see The Media, this ch.).

The constitution also includes a commitment to certain economic, social, and cultural principles, including state provision of health care, social security, and education. Housing, pension, education, and medical programs were begun in the 1960s and expanded by Shaykh Khalifa ibn Hamad as oil reve-

187

nues permitted throughout the years. There were no state taxes on individuals, and the state subsidized the prices of basic commodities to minimize the effects of inflation. Although these programs appeared to reflect West European statism, they were manifestations of the ruler's sense of duty, based on obligations inherent in Islamic ethics.

The Al Thani

In the early 1990s, the Al Thani ruling family comprised three main branches: the Bani Hamad, headed by Khalifa ibn Hamad (r. 1972–); the Bani Ali, headed by Ahmad ibn Ali; and the Bani Khalid, headed by Nasir ibn Khalid (minister of economy and commerce in 1984). The family had 20,000 members, according to one estimate.

The two preindependence rulers, Ali ibn Abd Allah (r. 1949–60) and his son, Ahmad ibn Ali (r. 1960–72), had no particular interest in supervising daily government, content to hunt in Iran and Pakistan and spend time at their villa in Switzerland. Thus, somewhat by default, those duties were assumed, beginning in the 1950s, by Ahmad ibn Ali's cousin, Khalifa ibn Hamad, the heir apparent and deputy ruler. By 1971 Khalifa ibn Hamad not only had served as prime minister but also had headed the ministries or departments of foreign affairs, finance and petroleum, education and culture, and police and internal security.

On February 22, 1972, with the support of the Al Thani, Khalifa ibn Hamad assumed power as ruler of Qatar. Western sources frequently refer to the event as an overthrow. Qataris regarded Khalifa ibn Hamad's assumption of full power as a simple succession because leading members of the Al Thani had declared Khalifa ibn Hamad the heir apparent on October 24, 1960, and it was their consensus that Ahmad ibn Ali should be replaced.

The reasons for the transfer of power were not entirely clear. Khalifa ibn Hamad reportedly stated that his assumption of power was intended "to remove the elements that tried to hinder [Qatar's] progress and modernization." Khalifa ibn Hamad has consistently attempted to lead and to control the process of modernization caused by the petroleum industry boom and the concomitant influx of foreigners and foreign ideas so that traditional mores and values based on Islam can be preserved. He and other influential members of the ruling family are known to have been troubled by the financial excesses of many members of the Al Thani. Ahmad ibn Ali reportedly drew one-fourth, and the entire Al Thani between one-third and one-half, of Qatar's oil revenues in 1971. The new ruler severely limited the family's financial privileges soon after taking power.

Family intrigue may also have played a part in the change of rulers. Factionalism and rivalries are not uncommon, particularly in families as large as the Al Thani. Western observers have reported rumors that Khalifa ibn Hamad acted to assume power when he learned that Ahmad ibn Ali might be planning to substitute his son, Abd al Aziz, as heir apparent, a move that would have circumvented the declared consensus of the Al Thani.

The Merchant Families

The merchant sector in Qatar differed from other gulf Arab countries before the exploitation of oil in its small size (Doha was an insignificant port compared with ports in Kuwait, Bahrain, or Dubayy), in the absence of foreigners (the Indians were forced out in the late 1800s, leaving Qatar the only gulf amirate without Indians until the 1950s), and in the dominant role of a single family, the Al Thani. Although there were merchants before oil, there was no merchant class as in Dubayy or Kuwait. Two important families before oil were the Darwish and the Al Mana, who made their living through trade, pearling, and smuggling and who competed for favor with the ruler. The Darwish and the Al Mana maintained their influence by trading loans and advice to the shaykh for monopolies and concessions.

With the arrival of Petroleum Development (Qatar), the Darwish reaped huge profits through their monopoly on supplying labor, housing, water, and goods to the oil company. This monopoly ended, however, when workers, small merchants, and anti-British Qataris used Abd Allah Darwish, the patriarch of the Darwish family, as one of several convenient targets for an antiregime strike in 1956. By this time, however, with oil revenues growing, the shaykh could remove himself from financial dependence on the merchants, who lost a measure of political influence.

A series of citizenship and commercial laws promulgated in the 1960s helped to channel economic benefits in the direction of Qatari nationals in general and the merchants and ruling family in particular. Only Qataris were permitted to own land, for example, and companies were required to be at least 51 percent Qatari owned. In the 1970s, some laws were enacted that worked against merchant interests by limiting prices and profits.

As they had before the discovery of oil, the Al Thani continued engaging in trade and in other enterprises. Sometimes they used their family connections to win lucrative contracts for themselves or for firms in which they had more common business partners, such as the Jaidah, the Attiyah, and the Mannai families.

Opposition

Because no public dissent is tolerated in Qatar, opposition usually manifests itself in royal family intrigue or behind-the-scenes grumbling by aggrieved parties. The apparent public tranquillity is cultivated by the amir and by the private but closely controlled media. Incidents in the 1980s, however, demonstrated that opposition to the regime existed.

In September 1983, for example, a conspiracy to assassinate the ruler or a GCC head of state was uncovered by Qatari authorities, and seventy people were arrested. Contradictory press reports said that either some military people were involved or that the plot reflected a squabble among members of the ruling family. Qatari security forces learned of the plot from Egyptian intelligence via the Saudi Arabians. Informed that the plotters were backed by Libya, Qatar declared the Libyan chargé d'affaires persona non grata. The target of the plot, according to conflicting reports, was either Shaykh Khalifa ibn Hamad or one of the GCC heads of state who were coming to Doha for a November summit. Since then, there have been other reported assassination attempts.

In August 1985, it was reported that Shaykh Suhaym ibn Hamad Al Thani, one of the amir's brothers, disappointed that the position of crown prince was given to Shaykh Khalifa ibn Hamad's son, Hamad ibn Khalifa, plotted a coup and maintained a cadre of supporters and a cache of weapons in the northern part of the country. When Shaykh Suhaym ibn Hamad died suddenly, his sons blamed Minister of Information and Culture Ghanim al Kuwari for not responding promptly to the call for medical help. After supporters of Suhaym ibn Hamad and his sons attempted to kill Ghanim al Kuwari, they were imprisoned.

Soon after the Iraqi invasion of Kuwait, Palestinians and Iraqis living in Qatar came under intense government scrutiny. Dozens were deported, and many more were forced to leave after their contracts were not renewed.

The Media

Qatar has no official censorship, but newspapers recognize the need for self-censorship in not publishing material critical of the ruling family, the government, or religious issues. The privately owned press consists of three Arabic dailies—*Ar Rayah* (The Banner), *Al Arab* (The Arab), and *Ash Sharq* (The East)— and an English daily, *Gulf Times*. The Ministry of Information and Culture operates the Qatar News Agency, the Qatar Broadcasting Service, and the Qatar Television Service.

Foreign Relations

The Iraqi invasion and occupation of Kuwait and the resulting threat to other small Persian Gulf states forced Qatar to alter significantly its defense and foreign policy priorities. For example, whereas Qatar had supported Iraq financially in its 1980–88 war against Iran, Qatar quickly joined the anti-Iraq coalition after the invasion. Formerly a political and economic supporter of the Palestine Liberation Organization (PLO), Qatar bitterly condemned the alliance between the PLO and many Palestinians on the one hand and Saddam Husayn on the other hand. Moreover, Qatar's previous opposition to superpower naval presence in the gulf turned into an open willingness to permit the air forces of the United States, Canada, and France to operate from its territory.

The GCC, which for years had been aimed, in part, at dealing with a perceived Iranian threat (both external and, in the cases of Kuwait, Bahrain, and Saudi Arabia, internal), became a forum for condemnation of Iraq and a venue for building a concerted defense against further Iraqi advances. After the Iraqi defeat, Qatar and other GCC members focused their energies on improving cooperation and coordination on mutual defense issues while also continuing to work together in social, cultural, political, and economic spheres. Qatar, like Saudi Arabia, has been historically sensitive to outside military intervention in the gulf and was eager to bolster regional security measures.

The war also drew Qatar and other GCC members closer to Egypt and Syria, the two strongest Arab members of the anti-Iraq coalition. The Qatari-Egyptian rapprochement began in 1987 when the two countries resumed diplomatic relations after the League of Arab States (Arab League) summit that adopted the resolution allowing members to reestablish diplomatic links at their discretion. After the war, Egypt and Syria received large sums from the Persian Gulf states in appreciation for their roles. Qatar and Syria signed an agreement on trade and economic and technical cooperation in January 1991.

Even before August 1990, Qatar historically had close relations with its larger and more powerful neighbor, Saudi Arabia. Because of geopolitical realities and the religious affinity of the two ruling families (both adhere to the conservative Wahhabi interpretation of Islam), Qatar followed the Saudi lead in many regional and global issues. Qatar was one of the few Arab countries that observed the full forty-day mourning period after the assassination of Saudi Arabia's King Faisal ibn Abd al Aziz Al Saud in March 1975 and the death of King Khalid ibn Abd al Aziz Al Saud in 1982. The two countries signed a bilateral defense agreement in 1982, and on several occasions Saudi Arabia acted as mediator in territorial disputes between Qatar and Bahrain.

Qatar also has had cordial relations with Iran, despite Qatar's support of Iraq during the Iran-Iraq War. In 1991 Shaykh Hamad ibn Khalifa welcomed Iranian participation in Persian Gulf security arrangements. Iran was one of the first countries to recognize Shaykh Khalifa ibn Hamad in 1972. Relations were based partially on proximity (important trade links exist between the two countries, including a ferry service between Doha and Bushehr) and partly on mutual interests. Plans were being formulated in 1992 to pipe water from the Karun River in Iran to Qatar. The Iranian community in Qatar, although large, is well integrated and has not posed a threat to the regime. Iran's claim in May 1989 that one-third of Qatar's North Field gas reservoir lay under Iranian waters apparently was resolved by an agreement to exploit the field jointly.

Relations with Bahrain continue to fluctuate between correct and strained, with tensions rising regularly over territorial disputes dating back for decades. Most of the friction involves Hawar and the adjacent islands, which both countries claim. Tensions rose most recently in July 1991 when, according to reports, Qatari naval vessels violated Bahraini waters, and Bahraini jet fighters flew into Qatari airspace. The issue was referred in August to the International Court of Justice in The Hague to determine whether it had jurisdiction over the dispute. Other disputes have involved the abandoned town of Az Zubarah, on the northwest coast of Qatar. The most serious crisis took place in the spring of 1986, when Qatari forces raided Fasht ad Dibal, a coral reef in the gulf north of Al Muharraq in Bahrain that had been artificially built up into a small island. They took into custody twenty-nine workers who were sent by Bahrain to build a coast guard station. The workers were released in May, and installations on the island were destroyed. Qatar submitted the dispute to the International Court of Justice at The Hague, but Bahrain refused the jurisdiction of the court in June 1992. The dispute was ongoing as of early 1993 (see Foreign Relations, ch. 3).

Britain's historical role in the Persian Gulf has guaranteed a special relationship with its former protectorates. Qatari-British relations are tempered by a complex blend of suspicion and cordiality. On the one hand, Qataris are wary of the former colonial power because they remember instances when they were ill-served by their "protector," especially regarding the exploitation of oil. On the other hand, the long-term British presence in the gulf has fostered many fruitful political, economic, and cultural ties between the two countries. The British Embassy in Doha, for example, is the only foreign mission that owns its land outright. In addition, many Britons advise or work for the Qatari government at high levels. British banks and other businesses are well represented in Doha. Many Qataris attend university in Britain, own homes there, and visit regularly.

Relations with the United States have been generally proper but took a sudden turn for the worse in March 1988 when United States-made Stinger missiles (obtained through unsanctioned channels) were observed at a military parade in Doha. When the Qatari government refused to relinquish the weapons to the United States or to allow an inspection, the United States instituted a policy of withholding military and economic cooperation. The Stinger issue was settled when Qatar destroyed the missiles in question in 1990. Furthermore, both sides acknowledged the need to cooperate militarily in the face of Iraq's invasion of Kuwait. Operation Desert Shield and Operation Desert Storm greatly improved Qatar's image of the

United States as a desirable security partner and resulted in changed bilateral military relations. On June 23, 1992, Qatar and the United States signed a bilateral defense cooperation agreement that provided for United States access to Qatari bases, pre-positioning of United States matériel, and future combined military exercises.

Following Saudi Arabia's lead, Qatar refused for many years to have diplomatic relations with the Soviet Union. This changed in the summer of 1988, when Qatar announced the opening of relations at the ambassadorial level with the Soviet Union and with China. In the wake of the dissolution of the Soviet Union in 1991, Qatar established relations with newly independent Russia.

Qatar became a member of the United Nations in September 1971, soon after it proclaimed independence. It is a member of several of its specialized agencies, including the International Civil Aviation Organization, the Food and Agriculture Organization, the International Labour Organisation, the World Health Organization, the Universal Postal Union, and the United Nations Educational, Scientific, and Cultural Organization.

*   *   *

A number of books on Qatar appeared in the 1980s. The most useful, particularly in its interpretation of history and politics, based largely on British Foreign Office records, is Jill Crystal's *Oil and Politics in the Gulf.* Less analytical but still helpful, especially for understanding the disputes concerning Az Zubarah and Hawar and the adjacent islands, is Rosemarie Said Zahlan's *The Creation of Qatar.* Information on the oil industry is presented uncritically in *Qatar: Energy and Development* by Ragaei El Mallakh. Zuhair Ahmed Nafi gives a similarly sanguine appraisal in *Economic and Social Development in Qatar.* Somewhat more enlightening is Sheikha al-Misnad's *The Development of Modern Education in the Gulf,* which contains a wealth of statistical information. Naser al-Othman's *With Their Bare Hands* gives a Qatari's proud view of his country's history and includes several fascinating interviews with Qataris who worked in the first years of oil exploration. Abeer Abu Saud gives a personal view in *Qatari Women, Past and Present.*

For an encompassing overview of the country, the "Qatar" section in *The Middle East and North Africa* is an informative annual reference. An excellent source of statistics is the "Qatar" section in another annual, the *Britannica Book of the Year.* P.T.H. Unwin compiled the *Qatar* volume of the World Bibliographical Series and wrote a helpful historical introduction. Up-to-date information on business and economic matters appears in the indispensable *Middle East Economic Digest.* (For further information and complete citations, see Bibliography.)

Chapter 5. United Arab Emirates

Crest of the United Arab Emirates

Country Profile

Country

Formal Name: United Arab Emirates.

Short Form: UAE.

Term for Citizens: No generally accepted term.

Capital: Abu Dhabi.

Date of Independence: December 2, 1971.

Geography

Size: Approximately 77,700 square kilometers (excluding islands), but land borders undemarcated.

Topography: Largely flat or rolling desert, although mountains in northeast.

Climate: Hot and dry in desert regions; frequent high humidity along Persian Gulf coast.

Boundaries: Land boundaries with Oman, Qatar, and Saudi Arabia mostly undefined; several internal boundaries subject of disputes between and among seven constituent amirates.

Society

Population: Estimated at 2.0 million in mid-1993; 1993 growth rate 5.1 percent. Foreigners, of whom majority male workers, accounted for 88 percent of population.

Education: In 1990–91 academic year, more than 388,000 students (half of them female) attended primary and secondary schools. Education compulsory at primary level and free at all levels. Most of 22,000 teachers and administrators foreigners. In 1990–91 academic year, more than 8,900 students, of whom 65 percent women, attended United Arab Emirates University.

Note—The Country Profile contains updated information as available.

Health: Comprehensive public health care system, free for citizens but charges for some services provided foreigners. Majority of medical personnel foreigners, primarily from Egypt, India, and Pakistan. In 1990 life expectancy at birth 68.6 years for males and 72.9 years for females.

Ethnic Groups: Almost all citizens indigenous Arabs. Foreign population included other Arabs (especially Egyptians, Omanis, Palestinians, and Yemenis), Indians, Pakistanis, and Iranians.

Religion: Most citizens Sunni Muslims. About 60 percent of foreign population Sunnis; 20 percent Shia Muslims; 20 percent Hindus, Christians, and other.

Economy

Gross Domestic Product (GDP): US$34.9 billion in 1992, about US$14,000 per capita.

Oil Industry: Contribution of petroleum sector to GDP dropped from 63 percent in 1980 to 47 percent in 1990. Petroleum products accounted for 79 percent of exports in 1990. Abu Dhabi had largest reserves and most of production. Crude oil production in 1992 averaged 2.3 million barrels per day.

Industry: Oil refining and gas processing most important, followed by petrochemicals, utilities, and cement, all using oil or gas as fuel and feedstock. Government owned at least one-half interest in these plants. Non-oil manufacturing constituted 7.3 percent of GDP in 1990. Dubai Dry Docks one of world's largest and most modern. Majority of industrial workers foreigners.

Agriculture and Fishing: Represented less than 2 percent of GDP in 1990. Production mostly vegetables, fruit, livestock, and poultry. Water shortages restrict farming. Fishing industry being developed.

Exports: US$23.4 billion in 1992, of which US$14.0 billion oil and gas. Remainder largely propane and butane and reexports. Japan, Singapore, and Republic of Korea (South Korea) primary petroleum markets.

Imports: US$11.2 billion in 1990. Principal imports manufactured goods, machinery, transportation equipment, food, and live animals. Japan, United States, and Western

Europe major sources of imports.

Currency and Exchange Rate: UAE dirham. In 1994 exchange rate US$1 = Dh3.67 (fixed rate).

Fiscal Year: Calendar year.

Transportation and Telecommunications

Transportation: About 2,000 kilometers of roads, of which 1,800 kilometers paved as of 1993. Principal road is highway from Ash Sham via all main coastal cities to Qatar and Saudi Arabia. Dubayy major regional and international sea and air traffic center. UAE has several ports, of which largest is Mina Jabal Ali near city of Dubayy. Dubayy has major international airport, but Abu Dhabi, Al Fujayrah, Ras al Khaymah, and Sharjah also have international airports.

Telecommunications: International telecommunications excellent via satellites, radio relay, and telephone. All populated areas receive radio and television transmissions.

Government and Politics

Government: Federation of seven amirates, as defined in 1971 provisional constitution. Powers divided between federal and amirate governments. Head of state is UAE president, Shaykh Zayid ibn Sultan Al Nuhayyan, chosen by Supreme Council of the Union composed of rulers of seven amirates. Federal National Council has consultative function.

Politics: No political parties. Amirs and their families, particularly those of Abu Dhabi and Dubayy, most important political actors; technocrats and commercial interests play lesser role.

Foreign Relations: Member of United Nations, League of Arab States, Organization of the Islamic Conference, Gulf Cooperation Council, Organization of the Petroleum Exporting Countries, and Organization of Arab Petroleum Exporting Countries.

National Security

Armed Forces: Known as Union Defense Force. In mid-1993 personnel strength 57,500: army, 53,000; navy, 2,000; and air force, 2,500. Army uses French and Italian main battle tanks and wide assortment of other armored vehicles. In addition to several gun boats, navy operates six Exocet-equipped guided missile boats. Combat aircraft include Mirages, Hawks, and Aeromacchi MB–326s.

THE UNITED ARAB EMIRATES (UAE) in 1993 was a federation of seven separate amirates that had joined together in the winter of 1971–72 to form a single independent country. The new nation was created out of the British dependencies that had been known as the Trucial Coast states (also seen as Trucial Oman or Oman Coast) since 1853 when Britain and the local rulers signed the Treaty of Maritime Peace in Perpetuity, an agreement that ceded to London responsibility for foreign affairs. The individual amirates of the UAE include Abu Dhabi (also seen as Abu Zaby), Ajman, Al Fujayrah, Dubayy (also seen as Dubai), Ras al Khaymah, Sharjah (also seen as Ash Shariqah), and Umm al Qaywayn.

The UAE's oil resources make it one of the wealthiest countries in the world. The oil and the revenues it generates, however, are not equitably distributed. Revenues from petroleum exports accrue principally to the government of Abu Dhabi, where more than 80 percent of the oil is located. Three other amirates—Dubayy, Ras al Khaymah, and Sharjah—account for the remainder of the UAE's oil production. Nevertheless, since the formation of the UAE, Abu Dhabi has made significant annual contributions to the federal budget. Federal expenditures on development projects in the amirates lacking oil enable them to benefit, albeit modestly, from the overall oil wealth.

The UAE's oil-fueled economic growth has been accomplished with the assistance of thousands of foreign workers. Citizens composed only 12 percent of the 2.0 million people living in the UAE in 1993 and constituted only 7 percent of the labor force. The foreign workers come from other Arab countries and from Afghanistan, Bangladesh, Britain, India, Iran, Pakistan, the Philippines, Sri Lanka, Thailand, Turkey, the United States, and Western Europe. The presence of such a large and diverse foreign community provides a cosmopolitan atmosphere in the cities of Abu Dhabi and Dubayy. However, throughout the 1980s, there was growing resentment of foreigners among many UAE citizens, who felt uncomfortable being a minority, although a very privileged one, within their own country.

The rulers have been conscious that their country's small size and population, combined with relatively large oil revenues, make the UAE vulnerable in the context of regional politics. During the 1980s, the UAE tried to maintain its neutrality in the Iran-Iraq War (1980–88) by providing modest loans for the Iraqi war effort and permitting Dubayy to serve as a major port of entry for goods being transshipped to Iran. The UAE also joined the Gulf Cooperation Council (GCC), a collective security and cooperation association, established in 1981, of the six oil-producing Arabian Peninsula states. After Iraq invaded and occupied fellow GCC member Kuwait in 1990, the UAE joined the international military coalition that opposed and eventually defeated Iraq. In 1992 tensions with Iran over disputed islands in the Persian Gulf induced the UAE to expand its military cooperation with the United States.

Geography

The UAE lies between 22°50' and 26° north latitude and between 51° and 56°25' east longitude. It shares a nineteen-kilometer border with Qatar on the northwest, a 530-kilometer border with Saudi Arabia on the west, south, and southeast, and a 450-kilometer border with Oman on the southeast and northeast. The land border with Qatar is one over which in 1993 the UAE continued to have a dispute in the Khawr al Udayd area. The total area of the UAE is approximately 77,700 square kilometers. The country's exact size is unknown because of disputed claims to several islands in the Persian Gulf, because of the lack of precise information on the size of many of these islands, and because most of its land boundaries, especially with Saudi Arabia, remain undemarcated. The largest amirate, Abu Dhabi, accounts for 87 percent of the UAE's total area (67,340 square kilometers). The smallest amirate, Ajman, encompasses only 259 square kilometers (see fig. 11).

The UAE stretches for more than 1,400 kilometers along the southern shore of the Persian Gulf. Most of the coast consists of salt pans that extend far inland. The largest natural harbor is at Dubayy, although other ports have been dredged at Abu Dhabi, Sharjah, and elsewhere. Numerous islands are found in the gulf, and the ownership of some of them has been the subject of international disputes with both Iran and Qatar. The smaller islands, as well as many coral reefs and shifting sandbars, are a menace to navigation. Strong tides and occasional windstorms further complicate ship movements near the shore.

The UAE also extends for about ninety kilometers along the Gulf of Oman, an area known as the Al Batinah coast. The Al Hajar al Gharbi (Western Al Hajar) Mountains, rising in places to 2,500 meters, separate the Al Batinah coast from the rest of the UAE. Beginning at the UAE-Oman border on the Persian Gulf coast of the Musandam Peninsula (Ras Musandam), the Al Hajar al Gharbi Mountains extend southeastward for about 150 kilometers to the southernmost UAE-Oman frontier on the Gulf of Oman. The range continues as the Al Hajar ash Sharqi (Eastern Al Hajar) Mountains for more than 500 kilometers into Oman. The mountain slopes tend to run right to the shore. Nevertheless, there are small harbors at Diba al Hisn, Kalba, and Khawr Fakkan on the Gulf of Oman. In the vicinity of Al Fujayrah, where the mountains do not approach the coast, there are sandy beaches.

South and west of Abu Dhabi, vast, rolling sand dunes merge into the Rub al Khali (Empty Quarter) of Saudi Arabia. The desert area of Abu Dhabi includes two important oases with adequate underground water for permanent settlements and cultivation. The extensive Al Liwa Oasis is in the south near the undefined border with Saudi Arabia. About 200 kilometers to the northeast of the Al Liwa Oasis is the Al Buraymi Oasis, which extends on both sides of the Abu Dhabi-Oman border.

Prior to withdrawing from the area in 1971, Britain delineated the internal borders among the seven amirates in order to preempt territorial disputes that might hamper formation of the federation. In general, the rulers of the amirates accepted the British intervention, but in the case of boundary disputes between Abu Dhabi and Dubayy, and also between Dubayy and Sharjah, conflicting claims were not resolved until after the UAE became independent. The most complicated borders were in the Al Hajar al Gharbi Mountains, where five of the amirates contested jurisdiction over more than a dozen enclaves.

The climate of the UAE generally is hot and dry. The hottest months are July and August, when average maximum temperatures reach above 48°C on the coastal plain. In the Al Hajar al Gharbi Mountains, temperatures are considerably cooler, a result of increased altitude. Average minimum temperatures in January and February are between 10°C and 14°C. During the late summer months, a humid southeastern wind known as the *sharqi* makes the coastal region especially unpleasant. The aver-

age annual rainfall in the coastal area is fewer than 120 millimeters, but in some mountainous areas annual rainfall often
reaches 350 millimeters. Rain in the coastal region falls in
short, torrential bursts during the summer months, sometimes
resulting in floods in ordinarily dry wadi beds. The region is
prone to occasional, violent dust storms, which can severely
reduce visibility.

Population

A harsh environment and marginal economic conditions
kept the population of the region low and economically
depressed until the exploitation of oil. According to estimates,
between 1900 and 1960 there were 80,000 to 95,000 inhabitants
in the amirates, mostly in small coastal settlements. Although
the population of the amirates probably did not increase a
great deal during this period, there were considerable shifts
within the territories, caused by changes in economic and
political conditions. Whereas Sharjah was dominant in the
nineteenth century, by 1939 Dubayy was the most populous
amirate, with an estimated population of 20,000, one-quarter
of whom were foreigners. The largest minorities were Iranians
and Indians in Dubayy and in other amirates. Abu Dhabi's
onshore oil exports began in 1963, bringing wealth and a
demand for foreign labor. The 1968 census, conducted under
the British, was the area's first; it enumerated 180,226 inhabitants. Ever greater demands for labor and expertise fueled a
population boom throughout the 1970s and early 1980s, but
population growth has slowed since 1985.

The UAE had an officially estimated population of nearly 2.0
million in early 1993. Only about 12 percent of the total actually were UAE citizens. The number of foreign workers has
increased dramatically since 1968, when they constituted 36
percent of the total population. By 1975 foreigners accounted
for 70 percent of the population, increasing to 80 percent in
1980 and to 88 percent in 1985. Since 1985, the percentage of
foreigners has leveled at 88 percent. Asian workers from the
Indian subcontinent (Bangladesh, India, Pakistan, and Sri
Lanka) constituted about 45 percent of the total population in
1993. Iranians, who accounted for an estimated 17 percent of
the population, were the next largest ethnic group. Non-UAE
Arabs, primarily Egyptian nationals, accounted for 13 percent
of the population. Other Asians and Africans made up 8 per-

cent of the population, and foreigners from Europe and North America accounted for 5 percent.

Although the population density was about twenty-five persons per square kilometer in 1991, the population was unevenly distributed among the seven amirates. The three most populous amirates—Abu Dhabi, Dubayy, and Sharjah—together accounted for roughly 84 percent of the total population. The remaining 16 percent lived in Ras al Khaymah, Ajman, Al Fujayrah, and Umm al Qaywayn (see table 25, Appendix).

The population of the UAE is overwhelmingly urban, with more than 90 percent of the people living in cities. The largest city, Abu Dhabi, the federal capital, had an estimated population of 530,000 in 1993. Dubayy, the second largest city and the UAE's main port and commercial center, had an estimated population of 402,000. The residential neighborhoods along the Persian Gulf coast north of the center of Dubayy were contiguous with those of the city of Sharjah (estimated population of 130,000). Sharjah in turn flowed into the city of Ajman (estimated population of 60,000). About fifty kilometers north of Ajman is the city of Ras al Khaymah (estimated population of 45,000). The largest inland population concentration is in the contiguous villages and residential developments at Al Ayn (estimated population of 105,000) in Abu Dhabi's Al Buraymi Oasis.

Religion

Most of the citizens of the UAE are Sunni (see Glossary) Muslims who adhere to the Maliki legal tradition (see Sunni Islam, ch. 1). Some Sunnis of the Wahhabi sect (followers of a strict interpretation of the Hanbali legal school) live in the Al Buraymi Oasis, and some who follow the Shafii legal school live along the Al Batinah coast. The foreign population includes Sunni and Shia (see Glossary) Muslims, Hindus, and Christians.

Although varying from amirate to amirate, the degree of religious freedom afforded non-Muslims is greater in the UAE than in Saudi Arabia and Qatar. For example, non-Muslims are permitted to worship but not to proselytize. There are several large Christian churches and schools in the UAE, primarily in Dubayy and Abu Dhabi.

Education

In the early 1900s, three major schools were established by pearl merchants in Dubayy, Abu Dhabi, and Sharjah. The schools were staffed by foreign teachers who taught reading, writing, and Islamic studies. The economic crises of the 1920s and 1930s forced some of these and other schools to close, but some reopened when the economy improved.

The British built the first school offering a comprehensive curriculum in Sharjah in 1953. Staffed by teachers from other Arab countries, the school had 450 boys between the ages of six and seventeen that year. Shortly after, the first modern primary school for girls was established in Sharjah. The British government also built schools in Abu Dhabi, Ras al Khaymah, and Khawr Fakkan and established an agricultural school in Ras al Khaymah in 1955 and a technical school in Sharjah in 1958. In 1958 Kuwait started to build schools in the amirates, including facilities in Ajman and Umm al Qaywayn. Kuwait also funded teacher trainees from the amirates to go abroad for training. Until the amirates could afford to pay teachers, Bahrain, Qatar, and Egypt paid teachers to work in the amirates.

After Abu Dhabi began earning oil revenues in the early 1960s, it developed and funded its own educational system, while the other amirates continued to rely on outside assistance. By the 1964–65 academic year, Abu Dhabi had six schools attended by 390 boys and 138 girls, taught by thirty-three teachers. In the same year, there were thirty-one schools outside Abu Dhabi, twelve of which were for girls. Dubayy had 3,572 students in ten schools and 137 teachers, most of whom came from Kuwait and Egypt.

After the founding of the UAE, there was tremendous expansion of public education facilities. Section 17 of the constitution states that education is fundamental to the progress of society and is to be compulsory at the primary level and free at all levels. Uniforms, books, equipment, and transportation are also free. In the first seven years of the UAE's existence, education was second only to defense in the federal budget. In 1989 the budget allocated Dh2.0 billion (for value of the the UAE dirham—see Glossary) for education.

The education system in the UAE includes six years of primary school and six years of secondary school (see table 26, Appendix). By 1972–73, the first full academic year following the formation of the UAE, the government operated an estimated 140 schools, twelve of which offered boarding facilities.

Most schools are segregated according to gender, but some through the primary level are coeducational. In 1990–91 there were about 760 schools with 49,904 pupils in preschool, 227,083 students in primary school, and 111,611 in secondary school. One-third of the pupils attended private or religious schools. Beginning in the 1991–92 academic year, military courses were compulsory in federal secondary schools.

United Arab Emirates University opened in 1977 at Al Ayn with four faculties: arts, science, education and political science, and business administration. First-year enrollment was 400. A sharia (Islamic jurisprudence) faculty was added in 1978; faculties in agriculture and engineering were added in 1982. In 1988 four higher colleges of technology (two for men and two for women) opened. By the 1990–91 academic year, enrollment stood at 8,941 students. In the previous academic year, 65 percent of university students were women. Many UAE nationals go abroad for university and graduate studies to other Arab countries and to Britain and the United States.

In the early 1990s, United Arab Emirates University was being expanded, at an estimated outlay of Dh3 to Dh5 billion, to accommodate up to 16,000 students by the year 2000. The existing campus will become a technical college after the expansion is completed.

The Women's Federation of the UAE provides adult literacy classes. There were twenty-six adult education centers in 1992. The United Nations (UN) estimated the UAE's literacy rate in 1988–89 as 53.5 percent overall, 58.4 percent for males and 38.1 percent for females. The government also operates several vocational training centers, which in the 1987–88 academic year had 2,614 students.

Status of Women

The role of women in UAE society has gradually expanded since the discovery of oil. Before 1960 there were few opportunities for them outside the realm of home and family. The president, Shaykh Zayid ibn Sultan Al Nuhayyan, has acknowledged the validity of women participating in the work force as well as in the home. The president's wife, Shaykha Fatima, heads the Women's Federation and promotes training, education, and the advancement of the status of women. In the early 1990s, there were five women's societies promoting various issues of importance to women, including literacy and health.

Women constituted 6.2 percent of the work force in 1988. A study by the Administrative Development Institute found that a majority of female workers who are UAE citizens work under the Ministry of Education and the Ministry of Health. In 1988 they accounted for 82 percent of UAE national employees in these ministries. Since the late 1980s, women graduates have outnumbered men by a ratio of two to one at United Arab Emirates University.

Health and Welfare

In the years before the discovery of oil, the health situation in the amirates was poor. Those who could afford it obtained modern treatment abroad; those who could not had to make do with traditional remedies. Britain became interested in the region's welfare when it perceived that the United States would gain local influence in the scramble for oil through the successes of United States missionary doctors, who, in Muscat and Bahrain, operated the only hospitals in the region. As a result, in 1938 Britain appointed a medical officer for the Trucial Coast and sent an Indian physician to serve in a dispensary in Dubayy the following year.

In 1949 the British government built Al Maktum Hospital, a small hospital in Dubayy, and appointed a British physician from the Indian Medical Service to initiate modern medical service. Contributions to health care also came from Kuwait, Iran, and the Trucial States Development Fund. Earlier suspicions by the British notwithstanding, in the 1950s and 1960s American Mission hospitals were established in Sharjah, Al Ayn, and Ras al Khaymah.

In 1965 the Abu Dhabi government employed one physician; three others were in private practice. The amirate also received technical and material assistance from Egypt. After federation in 1971, rapid, uncoordinated growth characterized the health system. Although cooperation among amirates in the health field had improved by the early 1990s, oil companies and the military continued to have their own medical facilities.

All residents received free medical care until 1982. In that year, escalating costs, shrinking oil revenues, and a change in attitude toward foreign residents caused the UAE to begin charging noncitizens for all services except emergency and child and maternity care.

Student nurses at Abu Dhabi nursing school; the United Arab Emirates has stressed academic and professional education.
Courtesy Embassy of the United Arab Emirates, Washington

In 1985 there were 2,361 physicians, 6,090 nurses, 242 dentists, and 190 pharmacists, almost all of whom were foreigners. In 1986 the UAE had forty public hospitals with 3,900 beds and 119 clinics. In 1990 life expectancy at birth was 68.6 years for males and 72.9 years for females. The major causes of death registered in Abu Dhabi in 1989 per 100,000 population were accidents and poisonings, 43.7; cardiovascular diseases, 34.3; cancer, 13.7; and respiratory diseases, 8.1. As of December 1990, eight cases of acquired immune deficiency syndrome (AIDS) were reported in the UAE. Infant mortality declined dramatically from 103 per 1,000 live births in 1965 to twenty-three per 1,000 live births in 1990. In 1985 a health worker attended 96 percent of births.

In the early 1990s, the UAE had a modern health care system with facilities and professionals capable of providing excellent care and performing advanced procedures such as organ transplants and complex heart surgery. Although facilities are concentrated in the cities of Abu Dhabi and Dubayy, most of the population has access to at least basic facilities. The federation's first hospital specializing in pediatric and maternity care, the 374-bed Al Wasl Hospital in Dubayy, opened in the late 1980s. The New Medical Centre in Abu Dhabi, a private facility, is equipped to treat diving accidents. Most hospitals are run by the government.

The UAE also has created an extensive social welfare network that includes family care centers aimed at solving domestic problems and training women in domestic skills and handicrafts. Psychological care is available for troubled youths. The National Assistance Law provides benefits to victims of catastrophic illnesses and disasters. Widows, orphans, the elderly, the disabled, and others unable to support themselves receive social security payments. In 1975 nearly 24,000 citizens benefited from Dh87.7 million in such social aid; in 1982 approximately 121,000 persons received a total of Dh275 million.

Other benefits given UAE citizens are free housing and subsidized furnishings. However, the Ministry of Public Works and Housing reported in 1992 that 70 percent of 15,000 government-built low-income houses had deteriorated to the point of being uninhabitable. Among the causes were damage from groundwater salinity, failure to grant proprietary rights, and withdrawal of a Dh10,000 per house maintenance grant.

Economy

Before the discovery of oil, the separate amirates that now constitute the UAE had similar economies. The raw materials of these economies were the fish and pearls of the gulf and the meager soil and scarce water onshore. In this forbidding milieu, the rich and poor fought heat, disease, and famine to make a living. Occupations ranged from slaves who dived for pearls and artisans who hammered coffee pots or stitched sandals to wealthy pearl merchants and powerful shaykhs. Among the sources of revenue for ruling shaykhs were the collection of customs fees, the issuance of fishing licenses, and the imposition of levies on date groves. Pearl merchants, many of whom were also landholders and moneylenders, gained political influence through their wealth and connections. In addition, there were cultivators of dates in oases, nomadic livestock herders, and small-scale traders.

Pearls from the rich banks off the amirates' coast were probably the single largest source of wealth until the 1930s and 1940s. In 1905 the pearling trade involved 22,000 men from the amirates working in about 1,300 boats, and income amounted to £600,000. Trade and fishing were also important maritime activities. Sharjah, the principal port and political power in the nineteenth century, was in the twentieth century eclipsed by Dubayy. A large boatbuilding industry, using timber imported from India, developed along the coast; the industry supplied vessels of varying sizes and designs for pearling, fishing, and transport. The Great Depression of the 1930s, coinciding with the development of the Japanese cultured pearl industry, severely disrupted markets for Persian Gulf pearls. At about the same time, large numbers of men from the amirates began to migrate to work in the fledgling oil industries of Kuwait, Bahrain, and later Qatar and Saudi Arabia.

Agriculture is limited to those few locations where fresh water is available. In the Al Buraymi and Al Liwa oases and the plains of Ras al Khaymah, relatively abundant water resources permit settled agriculture, especially the cultivation of date palms and fodder crops. The wells of the oases also provide water for the nomadic population, who migrate with their animal herds throughout the desert areas in search of seasonal forage.

British hegemony in the Persian Gulf had positive and negative economic consequences for the inhabitants. British suppression of maritime raiding, for example, meant that pearling fleets could operate in relative security. (The fleet had previously been unable to sail during periods of unrest, losing vital income for divers and merchants alike.) Some shaykhs and merchants benefited from regular visits by steamships from Britain and from other countries. For a period of time, local Indian merchants received deferential treatment as a result of Britain's control of India. On the negative side, however, the British prohibition on raiding and trading in slaves and arms meant an important source of income was lost to some shaykhs and merchants. In addition, because non-British powers were kept out of the gulf, trade and development opportunities were lost.

British development assistance began piecemeal in the 1940s and 1950s, prompted by fears that the United States and other countries would gain a foothold in the region and compete for oil concessions. Total outlays in 1954–55 were £50,300 and funded a water resources study, an irrigation restoration project, improvements at the hospital in Dubayy, and school construction in Sharjah. In 1961–62 the amount rose to £550,000. The total British investment between 1955 and 1965 was £1 million. Neighboring Qatar provided a freshwater system for Dubayy and the first bridge across Dubayy Creek. Saudi Arabia built a road from Sharjah to Ras Al Khaymah. Britain also paid Sharjah's ruler to allow the establishment of a military base there in 1966.

Trade began to grow, especially in Dubayy, in the 1950s and 1960s. Imports increased from £3 million in 1958 to £8 million in 1963 and £41.7 million in 1967. Gold, often smuggled into India, greatly enriched Dubayy merchants and bankers during this period. An estimated 250 tons of gold brought revenues of about £80 million in 1970.

The discovery and export of petroleum resulted in a major transformation of the amirates' economies. Before federation, oil revenues enriched the royal families who ruled the amirates in which production occurred and provided funding for local economic development. After the formation of the UAE, oil revenues, especially from Abu Dhabi and Dubayy, continued to fuel local development but increasingly became the main engine of growth for the national economy.

Oil revenues became significant in Abu Dhabi in 1963, in Dubayy in 1970, in Sharjah in 1975, and in Ras al Khaymah in 1984. The disparity in resource endowment and timing of oil discoveries led to uneven economic development before and after federation. The governments of Abu Dhabi and Dubayy, which together in 1991 accounted for 99 percent of the UAE's production, expend significant portions of their oil revenues on infrastructure development, including airports, highways, and port facilities. Nonetheless, Abu Dhabi's economic predominance has created tensions with the other amirates. Lack of coordination in economic development and duplication in facilities and industries are problems that political federation had not solved as of 1993.

The rapid pace of development brought other problems. In the early and mid-1970s, the distribution system could not keep up with the massive amounts of imports. Shortages resulted, and inflation exceeded 30 percent per year. By 1982, however, the rate of inflation had declined to about 10 percent. Between 1975 and 1980, the gross domestic product (GDP—see Glossary) in constant 1980 prices increased by an average of 16 percent per year. Although oil production declined after 1977, sharp increases in world oil prices in the 1979–80 period brought windfall revenues to the amirates, pushing per capita GDP up to US$29,000 in 1981, one of the world's highest.

During the early 1980s, the economy began to contract. This economic slowdown was caused by several factors, including lower oil revenues, the completion of several large industrial

Offshore oil rig; oil is the major revenue source of the United Arab Emirates.
Courtesy Embassy of the United Arab Emirates, Washington

Mina Jabal Ali, southwest of Dubayy, a major port engaged in the transshipment trade
Courtesy Embassy of the United Arab Emirates, Washington

and infrastructure projects, and the Iran-Iraq War (1980–88). By 1983 GDP had fallen to an estimated US$26.7 billion, down from US$32.5 billion in 1981.

The mid-1980s were a period of recession, with GDP falling from a little less than US$29 billion in 1982 to US$21.5 billion in 1986, caused in large part by a 40 percent drop in oil revenues. Exports fell by 33.5 percent in 1986, and the federation's trade surplus dropped 58 percent compared with 1985. As a result of the austere conditions, the 1986 federal budget allocated funds mainly for current expenditures, stalling many new projects.

The late 1980s and early 1990s saw improving conditions, with oil exports increasing. A spurt in oil prices as a result of Iraq's invasion of Kuwait helped push GDP to almost US$34 billion in 1990. Contracts to help rebuild Kuwait after its liberation aided the UAE economy. But the invasion also had negative effects. Banks lost between 15 and 30 percent of their deposits, and development projects were halted. Trade declined as a result of uncertainty and higher insurance premiums. And the UAE paid out about US$6 billion to the United States and Britain to help defray the military costs of the war and to contribute to a fund that supported countries whose economies were severely hurt by the war.

The collapse of the Bank of Credit and Commerce International (BCCI) in the summer of 1991 caused ripples throughout the UAE economy (see Banking, ch. 6). The BCCI collapse became a major international scandal because the bank had become a significant financial institution in several countries, including Britain and the United States, and because members of Abu Dhabi's ruling family were major shareholders in the bank.

Oil and Natural Gas

Abu Dhabi became a member of the Organization of the Petroleum Exporting Countries (OPEC) in 1966. When the amirates federated in 1971, membership was transferred to the UAE. Although Abu Dhabi officials represented the other amirs, the officials exercised no power over the amirs because each maintained control of his amirate's underground wealth. Each ruler oversaw arrangements for concessions, exploration, and oil field development in his own territory and published limited information about such arrangements. Thus, the federal Ministry of Petroleum and Mineral Resources has limited power to set policy and engage in overall planning. In 1988 a presidential decree abolished the Department of Petroleum and dissolved the board of directors of the Abu Dhabi National Oil Company (ADNOC). The functions of these bodies (administration and supervision of the country's petroleum affairs) were taken over by the newly formed Supreme Petroleum Council, whose eleven members were led by Shaykh Khalifa ibn Zayid Al Nuhayyan.

Discoveries in the 1980s and 1990s greatly increased the UAE's oil and gas reserves. By 1992 the four oil-producing amirates had total estimated proven crude oil reserves of 98 billion barrels and natural gas reserves of 5.2 trillion cubic meters, with the majority of both reserves lying within Abu Dhabi.

Based on the relative size of their reserves and on their long-term development plans, Abu Dhabi and the other oil-producing amirates have pursued differing policies. Abu Dhabi, with massive reserves, has on the whole based its production and economic development plans on long-term benefits, occasionally sacrificing production and price to meet this end. The other amirates, less well endowed with oil and gas, have sought to exploit their meager resources to produce short-term gains.

In the early 1980s, Abu Dhabi adhered to OPEC production ceilings while Dubayy routinely exceeded them. After 1987, however, both Abu Dhabi and Dubayy habitually produced above OPEC levels. In early 1987, for example, when Abu Dhabi's OPEC quota was set at 682,000 barrels per day (bpd—see Glossary) and Dubayy's at 220,000 bpd, Abu Dhabi produced 1,058,000 bpd (64 percent above quota) and Dubayy produced 365,000 bpd (60 percent above quota) (see table 27, Appendix). As a result, OPEC established a committee to promote greater adherence to quotas by chronic overproducers such as the UAE. For its part, the federation argued that its quotas were too small in relation to its large reserves and to the quotas of other producers.

The UAE's quota was raised several times by OPEC, and it was at almost 1.1 million bpd in March 1990. Not recognizing the OPEC figure, UAE production at the time was 2.1 million bpd. By July 1990, oil prices had fallen to US$14 per barrel, and the UAE agreed to a compromise proposal that raised its OPEC quota to 1.5 million bpd. Meanwhile, among Iraq's public accusations was that both Kuwait and the UAE had deprived

Iraq of much-needed revenues by driving down world oil prices through production above their OPEC quotas.

After Iraq invaded Kuwait in August 1990, OPEC suspended quotas to allow member states to compensate for the lost production of Kuwait and Iraq. Producing an average of 2.1 million bpd, the UAE earned US$15 billion in oil revenues in 1990. In the following year, producing an average of about 2.4 million bpd, the federation earned US$14 billion. In March 1992, OPEC raised the UAE's quota to slightly more than 2.2 million bpd, which the UAE appeared to be observing. In March 1991, the UAE announced that it would expand its oil production capacity to 4 million bpd by the mid-1990s as part of a multibillion dollar development program.

Abu Dhabi

Abu Dhabi granted its first oil concession, covering its entire territory, in 1939 to the Trucial Coast Development Oil Company (renamed the Abu Dhabi Petroleum Company, or ADPC, in 1962). The company discovered oil in 1960; production and export commenced in 1962 offshore and in 1963 onshore. ADNOC acquired 60 percent of ADPC in the early 1970s. In 1978 ADPC was reconstituted as the Abu Dhabi Company for Onshore Oil Operations (Adco). In the late 1980s, the remainder of Adco's shares were divided: British Petroleum (BP), Royal Dutch Shell Oil, and Compagnie Française des Pétroles (CFP) received 9.5 percent each; Mobil Oil and Exxon, 4.75 percent each; and Participations and Explorations (Partex), 2.0 percent. The principal onshore fields were Bu Hasa, Bab, and Asab. Onshore production totaled 267 million barrels in 1980.

In 1953 the amirate granted a concession to the D'Arcy Exploration Company of Britain to look for oil in offshore and submerged areas not covered in the ADPC concession. Abu Dhabi Marine Areas (ADMA), a multinational consortium, took over this concession in 1955. The company made its first commercial strike in 1958, and production and export started in 1962. In 1977 ADMA and ADNOC agreed to form the Abu Dhabi Marine Areas Operating Company (ADMA-Opco) for offshore work. In the late 1980s, ADNOC owned 60 percent of ADMA-Opco; Japan Oil Development Company, 12.0 percent; BP, 14.7 percent; and CFP, 13.3 percent. Offshore fields included Umm ash Shayf, Az Zuqum, Sath ar Ras Boot, Dalma, and Umm ad Dalkh. The island of Das, northeast of the island of Dalma, became the center for offshore operations.

Unlike most gulf countries, as of the end of 1992 Abu Dhabi had not claimed 100 percent ownership of its oil industry. ADNOC was established in 1971 and, in addition to holding majority shares in Adco and ADMA-Opco, was involved in producing, refining, distributing, and shipping gas. ADNOC owned 51 percent of the Abu Dhabi Gas Liquefaction Company, whose Das facility has sent most of its liquefied natural gas (LNG) and liquefied petroleum gas (LPG) to Japan since 1977. In 1988 the Das facility produced nearly 2.5 million tons of LNG from offshore fields. ADNOC also holds 68 percent of Abu Dhabi Gas Industries, which extracts propane, butane, and condensate at the Ar Ruways plant from associated gas produced by the onshore Bu Hasa, Bab, and Asab fields.

Abu Dhabi's refining, at plants in Umm an Nar and Ar Ruways, is also controlled by ADNOC. Total refining capacity in 1991 was 185,000 bpd, of which 100,000 bpd was available for export. Marketing and distribution are carried out by the Abu Dhabi National Oil Company for Distribution, an ADNOC subsidiary. To buy refineries and gas stations in Europe and Japan, ADNOC and the Abu Dhabi Investment Authority formed a joint venture, the International Petroleum Investment Corporation (IPIC). In 1989 IPIC held a 20 percent share in a Madrid-based refining company.

The amirate's exports are pumped through terminals at Jabal az Zannah and on the island of Das. There is a smaller terminal at Al Mubarraz.

Dubayy

The Iraq Petroleum Company (IPC) held a concession for Dubayy from 1937 to 1961. CFP and Compañía Española de Petróleos (Spanish Petroleum Company—Hispanoil) obtained an onshore concession in 1954 and formed Dubai Marine Areas (Duma). Continental Oil Company acquired the IPC concession in 1963 and formed the Dubai Petroleum Company (DPC). That same year, DPC acquired 50 percent of Duma and released some of its shares to other companies. Oil was discovered offshore in 1966, and production commenced in late 1969. The Dubayy government acquired a 60 percent share in Duma-DPC in 1975.

Dubayy's oil reserves in 1991 were estimated at 4 billion barrels, which will run out by 2016 if 1990 levels of production continue. Dubayy's production policy has been to ignore OPEC quotas for the most part, concentrating on exploiting the amirate's fields as efficiently as possible. This has meant producing at or near capacity most of the time. The principal fields are Fath, Rashid, and Falah offshore, and Margham onshore. The amirate has two refineries, with a third planned for the mid-1990s.

The Dubayy government established the Dubai Natural Gas Company (Dugas) in 1975 to process gas from offshore oil fields. By the early 1990s, the company also planned to process associated gas from the onshore Margham field. Dugas's foreign partner was Scimitar Oils (Dubai), a subsidiary of Canada's Sunningdale Oils. The Dugas processing facilities at Mina Jabal Ali came on-line in 1980 with a capacity of 20,000 bpd of natural gas liquids (propane, butane, and heavier liquids) and 2.1 million cubic meters of dry gas (methane) a day. The dry gas is piped to the Dubai Aluminum Company (Dubal), where it fuels a large electric power and desalination plant. A small part of the natural gas liquids is locally bottled and consumed, but most is exported to Japan. A special gas terminal at Mina Jabal Ali that can handle tankers of up to 48,000 tons opened in 1980. The amirate's gas reserves are estimated at 125 billion cubic meters.

Sharjah

In 1969 the amir of Sharjah granted a forty-year concession for offshore exploration and production to a consortium of small United States oil companies known as Crescent Oil Company. Oil was discovered in 1973 in the Mubarak field off the island of Abu Musa, and production began in 1974. Because of conflicting territorial claims, Sharjah has production and drilling rights but shares production and revenue with Iran (50 percent), Umm al Qaywayn (20 percent), and Ajman (10 percent). By 1984, Iran reportedly ceased transferring to Sharjah its half-share of oil revenues, presumably because of the financial drain of the war with Iraq, as well as Arab support of Iraq. In 1988 Iran attacked the facilities at Mubarak, causing their closure for two months.

In 1980 the American Oil Company (Amoco—later Amoco Sharjah) announced a major discovery onshore of oil and gas in the Saghyah field. By late 1983, output reached 35,000 bpd of condensate, which was exported. In 1984 total production reached 62,000 bpd. In the same year, the Emirates General

Petroleum Corporation completed a 224-kilometer pipeline to supply dry gas to power plants in the northern amirates. The pipeline had a capacity of 60,000 bpd of condensate and 1.1 million cubic meters per day of gas. After Dubayy and Sharjah settled their border dispute in 1985, a pipeline was built to supply gas from the Saghyah field to the power and desalination plant of the Dubai Electrical Company at Mina Jabal Ali. An LPG processing plant that came on-line in 1986 was producing 11.3 million cubic meters of wet gas per day in 1987. The amirate's outlook was optimistic in 1992, with Amoco Sharjah announcing a new onshore gas and condensate field and increased reserves at existing fields.

Other Amirates

Ras al Khaymah has limited oil and gas reserves, which were initially exploited in the early 1980s. By 1986 production was about 10,000 bpd, with most of the revenues plowed back into exploration and development. In that year, the amirate had completed pipelines from its offshore As Sila field to the mainland and had established separation and stabilization facilities, storage facilities capable of holding 500,000 barrels, and a 1,000-bpd LPG plant. By 1991 production had plummeted to 800 bpd.

Exploration and drilling in Ajman, Umm al Qaywayn, and Al Fujayrah have not yielded significant finds. Some of this activity has been funded by the federal government.

Industry

Non-oil industries have had a checkered history. On the positive side, federal and local governments have initiated many industrial projects that have aided in the development of the UAE. Local and foreign private capital found numerous opportunities in the friendly business climate of the amirates, with the result that by 1987 manufacturing contributed 9 percent to GDP (see table 28, Appendix). However, because of the lack of a unified planning mechanism and outright competition among amirates, redundancy has been a recurring problem. For example, there are nine cement factories in the UAE with a total capacity of 8.5 million tons per year. Local demand was estimated in 1986 at only 2 million tons. In addition, out of five steel rolling mills, three have had to close. Plastics and certain foods are overproduced. A 1988 study by the Ministry of Economy and Industry reported that local industry suffered

Downtown Dubayy, capital of the amirate of Dubayy
Courtesy Embassy of the United Arab Emirates, Washington

from low wage levels, a lack of new technology, and a low level of value added in many industries. In 1983 the Emirates Industrial Bank was established; one of its roles is to assist ailing industries financially.

Dubayy, with its long history of entrepôt trading, has the most developed non-oil industrial sector. Abu Dhabi, however, has focused on using its oil resources in downstream (see Glossary) facilities. Some of the northern amirates are developing their mineral resources. By 1990 total manufacturing output had a value of about US$2.6 billion, with 80 percent of the UAE's factories located in Abu Dhabi, Dubayy, and Sharjah.

Dubayy

The first major factory in the amirate was the aluminum smelter opened by Dubal at Mina Jabal Ali in 1979. It had a capacity of 135,000 tons of aluminum ingots per year, which was reached in 1982. In 1991, after expansion, it produced 290,030 tons of aluminum ingots. The five gas turbines that generate power for the plant are fueled by Dugas's neighboring gas treatment plant. A desalination plant associated with the turbines supplies 40 percent of Dubayy's drinking water requirements.

Dubayy became a strong magnet for industries, large and small, with the opening in 1985 of the Mina Jabal Ali Free Zone. Starting with about forty companies in the first year, the zone hosted 382 firms by 1992, including multinational giants Mitsubishi, Minnesota Mining and Manufacturing, Union Carbide, and Xerox, and scores of small Indian firms, many producing textiles. Local firms include National Flour Mills and the National Cement Company. Among the inducements to firms are a large pool of cheap labor, no taxes, no import or export duties, the right to 100 percent foreign ownership, and the right to repatriate profits and capital.

Another major facility in the free zone is the Dubai Dry Docks, owned by the Dubayy government. One of the largest and most modern in the world, the facility has three dry docks that can handle vessels up to 1 million deadweight tons. The dry docks have well-equipped workshops for plate and pipe, machinery, rigging, and electric repair, as well as a sophisticated laboratory. Completed in 1979, the docks lay idle, incurring substantial maintenance costs, until 1983 when a contract for an operator was signed. The delay was attributed in part to indecision and the amir's poor health.

By 1985, however, 111 ships with a total capacity of 10 million deadweight tons had been repaired. In 1988 the dock was fully occupied by vessels damaged in the Iran-Iraq War.

Abu Dhabi

The principal industrial facilities are located at Ar Ruways, 224 kilometers from the capital. The Ruways Fertilizer Industries plant came on-line in 1983 and uses natural gas as fuel and feedstock. ADNOC owns two-thirds of the plant, and Total-CFP owns the remainder. The plant was built with a capacity to produce 100 tons per day of ammonia and 1,500 tons per day of urea. Its customers have been mainly India and China. Sulfur extracted through oil and gas processing is exported from a special bulk terminal. A smaller industrial area exists at Al Musallah, just outside the city of Abu Dhabi.

The Northern Amirates

According to a 1987 study, Sharjah was the site of 35 percent of the UAE's industrial installations. The amirate has an industrial zone with factories producing a variety of items, including furniture and household utensils. A fodder factory at Mina Khalid run by the Gulf Company for Agricultural Development opened in 1982. Other plants in the amirate include a cement factory, a plastic pipe factory, and a rope factory.

The gulf's first explosives factory opened in Ras al Khaymah in 1980. A pharmaceutical plant opened the following year. The amirate has several factories that use local stone and minerals. In addition to three cement factories, there is an asphalt company, a lime kiln, and a thriving export business by the Ras al Khaymah Rock Company in aggregate, the stone used in making concrete.

Al Fujayrah and Ras al Khaymah have capitalized on resources from the Al Hajar al Gharbi Mountains, building plants that produce aggregate, marble, tile, asbestos insulation, and concrete blocks. Although lack of local energy sources has hindered industrial development, Al Fujayrah's development plans for the 1990s include provision for investment by other GCC states.

Umm al Qaywayn has relied on cement and related industries as a source of revenue but has suffered because of overproduction in the UAE. In 1987 it established a free zone modeled on that of Dubayy. Among Ajman's facilities are a dry dock, a ship repair yard, and a cement factory.

Electricity and Water

The demands of a rapidly growing population and a developing industrial base have necessitated a concomitantly speedy expansion of the capacity to provide electrical power and potable water. As in other areas, Abu Dhabi and Dubayy have had the funds to provide public utilities at a faster pace than the northern amirates. When the UAE was formed and the Ministry of Electricity and Water created, Abu Dhabi, Dubayy, Sharjah, and Ras al Khaymah had their own electric companies. The creation of the federation has seen some progress in unifying the national electrical grid and assisting the smaller amirates with power and water supply.

Abu Dhabi's generating capacity expanded from eight megawatts in 1973 to 845 megawatts in 1982. One study found that between 1973 and 1982, Abu Dhabi's demand for electricity expanded by 25 percent per year, while Dubayy's grew by 15 percent per year. The other amirates were not as well supplied with electricity and needed additional generating capacity. Sharjah and Ras al Khaymah suffered power disruptions in 1983 because of overloaded facilities. By 1988 installed generating capacity for the entire UAE had risen to 3,850 megawatts, up from 1,724 megawatts in 1979.

Unable to meet demand from natural sources of freshwater, the UAE has had to use desalination plants, many of which run in tandem with power stations. In 1985 there were twenty-two desalination plants in the amirates. Water production in 1989 amounted to about 327 billion liters, up from about 312 billion liters in 1987.

Labor

There was no significant foreign labor force before the sharp rise in oil revenues in the 1970s. Most work was done by local Arabs, some by slaves brought from Africa; Indians and Iranians were mainly merchants. The slave trade, most of which ended by about 1945, was a major point of contention in relations between Britain and the rulers of the Trucial Coast. For example, if the British resident was opposed by a shaykh on a specific matter, the resident in some cases might accuse the shaykh of violating treaty bans on the slave trade and threaten to destroy his pearling fleet or invalidate the travel documents of the shaykh and his subjects.

The massive influx of foreign workers and professionals in the 1970s and 1980s, mainly from other Arab countries and from India, Pakistan, and Iran, fundamentally changed the face of UAE society. (The UAE's population increased 86 percent between 1975 and 1980.) Working conditions of foreign workers in the UAE vary. Professionals, managers, and clerical workers are attracted by contracts offering good salaries, comprehensive benefits, and high living standards. Unskilled and semiskilled workers are in a more precarious situation. In their home countries, they might be cheated or misled by unscrupulous labor contractors who supply workers to the gulf countries. Although many obtain safe work at reasonable wages (much of which they remit to their families abroad), others work long hours in conditions not regulated for safety and health as stringently as they should be. In the 1980s, however, the government attempted to improve the labor law, which covered conditions of employment, compensation, inspection of the workplace, and enforcement procedures. Job security can be capricious, often depending on the whims of the oil market and the national mood. In the early 1980s, for example, during a period of economic decline, authorities increased their efforts to discover foreign workers without proper credentials and deported them as illegal aliens. By 1986, however, Dubayy tried to reverse the outward flow of labor by encouraging immigrant workers to bring their families with them.

In addition, labor is not permitted to organize, strike, or engage in collective bargaining. Individuals or groups of workers may bring grievances to the Ministry of Labor and Social Affairs, which has been known to settle matters with fairness. Although the law prohibits the employment of youths under eighteen and restricts hours of work to eight hours per day six days per week, the law is widely violated. There is no minimum wage.

In 1986, according to one set of government figures, the size of the labor force was 890,941. About 25 percent worked in construction, 14 percent in trade, 7 percent in transportation and communications, and 6 percent in manufacturing. According to the Ministry of Labor and Social Affairs, in 1992 UAE citizens accounted for 7 percent of the total work force and about 1 percent of the private-sector work force.

Transportation

Oil revenues have helped finance a modern transportation

infrastructure consisting of roads, ports, and airports. These facilities have helped make the UAE, and Dubayy in particular, a major hub of regional and international air and sea traffic. The UAE has about 2,000 kilometers of roads, of which 1,800 kilometers were paved as of 1993. The principal road is a highway via the main coastal cities, from Ash Sham to the northwestern border of the UAE, where it connects with roads to Saudi Arabia and Qatar.

Dubayy's port at Mina Jabal Ali, with sixty-seven berths in 1988, is one of the largest man-made harbors in the world. Located fifty-three kilometers southwest of the city of Dubayy, it handled nearly 10 million tons of cargo in 1989. Mina Rashid, also in Dubayy, in 1984 had thirty-five berths. The Dubayy Ports Authority was established in 1991 to operate the two ports. In addition to Mina Jabal Ali and Mina Rashid in Dubayy, the UAE's other ports are Mina Zayid in Abu Dhabi, Mina Khalid in Sharjah, Mina Saqr in Ras al Khaymah, Khawr Fakkan, and Mina al Fujayrah, the port at Al Fujayrah.

During periods of regional conflict, such as the Iran-Iraq War of 1980–88 and the Persian Gulf War of 1991, high insurance premiums for gulf shipping periodically reduce the amount of traffic handled at the UAE's ports, although Mina al Fujayrah and Khawr Fakkan have the advantage of lying outside the Persian Gulf on the Gulf of Oman. Abu Dhabi National Tankers Company operates about fifty ships, another aspect of UAE port traffic.

The international airport in Dubayy is the region's busiest, serving 4.3 million passengers in 1988 and handling 144,282 tons of cargo in 1990. Other international airports, which have had difficulty attracting traffic, operate in Sharjah, Ras al Khaymah, and Al Fujayrah. The New Abu Dhabi International Airport opened in 1982, and the Al Ayn International Airport was scheduled to open in the early 1990s. Emirates Airlines is the UAE's international airline.

Telecommunications

The UAE has a modern telecommunications network that provides its citizens with good telephone and broadcast services. In 1992 the country had 386,000 telephones, or about eighteen telephones per 100 inhabitants. About one-third of the telephones are in the Dubayy area. Service is entirely automatic. International direct dial is available to all customers. A

*Bridge across Dubayy Creek; the United Arab Emirates boasts
many modern highways.*
Courtesy Embassy of the United Arab Emirates, Washington

domestic network of high-capacity radio-relay stations and coaxial cable links all major towns.

International telecommunications are excellent. Radio-relay and undersea cables link the UAE with neighboring countries, and two satellite systems provide links to the rest of the world. Telecommunications to Saudi Arabia and to Bahrain go via high-capacity radio-relay links. Submarine cables laid in the late 1980s carry telephone calls to Qatar, Bahrain, India, and Pakistan. Telephone, television, and data communication to Europe, Asia, and the Americas go via three satellite groundstations, working with the International Telecommunications Satellite Corporation's (Intelsat) Atlantic Ocean and Indian Ocean satellites. In the early 1990s, television viewers in the UAE and throughout the Persian Gulf began receiving the twenty-four-hour news broadcasts of the Atlanta-based Cable News Network (CNN) via Intelsat. Television transmission and telephone calls to other countries in the Middle East are routed through a ground station linked to the Arab Satellite Communication Organization (Arabsat) satellite. Arabsat provides telephone, data transmission, telex, and facsimile service. Arabsat also is used for live broadcasts of prayers from Mecca and Medina and for viewing inter-Arab sports events.

In early 1993, broadcast facilities were adequate, and all populated areas of the country received television transmissions and radio broadcasts. Eight AM radio stations broadcast in Arabic, English, Urdu, and Sinhalese, in addition to three FM radio stations. Two powerful shortwave stations with broadcasts in Arabic and English can be received worldwide. Television broadcasts reach throughout the country via twelve large transmitters. The country has an estimated 400,000 radios and 170,000 television sets.

Agriculture and Forestry

Agriculture, including fishing, was a minor part of the UAE economy in the early 1990s, contributing less than 2 percent of GDP. Since the formation of the UAE, the availability of capital and the demand for fresh produce have encouraged agricultural development. The main farming areas are Diqdaqah in Ras al Khaymah, Falaj al Mualla in Umm al Qaywayn, Wadi adh Dhayd in Sharjah, Al Awir in Dubayy, and the coastal area of Al Fujayrah. Total cultivable land is around 70,000 hectares.

Most of the UAE's cultivated land is taken up by date palms, which in the early 1990s numbered about 4 million. They are cultivated in the arc of small oases that constitute the Al Liwa Oasis. Both federal and amirate governments provide incentives to farmers. For example, the government offers a 50 percent subsidy on fertilizers, seeds, and pesticides. It also provides loans for machinery and technical assistance. The amirates have forty-one agricultural extension units as well as several experimental farms and agricultural research stations. The number of farmers rose from about 4,000 in the early 1970s to 18,265 in 1988.

Lack of arable land, intense heat, periodic locust swarms, and limited water supplies are the main obstacles to agriculture. The drive to increase the area under cultivation has resulted in the rapid depletion of underground aquifers, resulting in precipitous drops in water tables and serious increases in soil and water salinity in some areas. As a result, several farms have been forced to cease production. Despite the creation in 1983 of a federal authority to control drilling for water, development pressures in the 1980s and 1990s increased the exploitation of underground water supplies.

Between 1979 and 1985, agricultural production increased sixfold. Nevertheless, the UAE imported about 70 percent of its food requirements in the early 1990s. The major vegetable crops, supplying nearly all the country's needs during the season, are tomatoes, cabbage, eggplant, squash, and cauliflower. Ras al Khaymah produces most of the country's vegetables. In addition to dates, the major fruit crops are citrus and mangoes. A vegetable canning facility in Al Ayn has a processing capacity of 120 tons per day.

Poultry farms provided 70 percent of local requirements for eggs and 45 percent of poultry meat needed in 1989. Local dairies produced more than 73,000 tons of milk in 1991, meeting 92 percent of domestic demand.

Considerable revenues have been devoted to forestation, public landscaping, and parks. Trees and shrubs are distributed free to schools, government offices, and residents. Afforestation companies receive contracts to plant plots in the range of 200 to 300 hectares. The goals are to improve the appearance of public places as well as to prevent the desertification process in vulnerable agricultural areas.

Fishing

The government has supported traditional fishing in the rich waters off the UAE, an activity that has provided livelihood for centuries along the coast. The government offers a 50 percent subsidy on fishing boats and equipment and has opened marine workshops that offer free repair and maintenance. Cooperatives assist fishermen in marketing their catch. The number of fishermen rose from 4,000 in 1980 to 10,611 in 1990. The total catch in 1989 of 91,160 tons (up from 70,075 tons in 1982) supplied most local demand. Moreover, prawns and fish are raised in fish farms at the National Mariculture Center—operated with Japanese assistance—in Umm al Qaywayn.

Banking and Finance

The Indian rupee was the principal medium of exchange in the amirates until 1966, when Abu Dhabi began using the Bahraini dinar and Dubayy and the northern amirates switched to the Qatar-Dubayy riyal. The federal Currency Board was established in 1973 to manage the new national currency (the UAE dirham, divided into 100 fils). The UAE dirham was officially linked in 1978 to the special drawing rights (SDR—see Glossary) of the International Monetary Fund (IMF—see Glossary); in practice, however, the UAE dirham was pegged to the United States dollar. The rate of Dh3.67 to US$1 has held constant since the end of 1980.

Reluctant to transfer financial accountability over local banks (including ones in which they had major interests) to outsiders, the ruling amirs refused to give the Currency Board, managed mainly by foreigners, any control over banking. In the midst of an oil boom, banks proliferated, credit expanded, and real estate speculation was rampant, creating a chaotic financial environment. In 1975 a moratorium on the opening of new banks was imposed, temporarily lifted, then reimposed. The board's lack of foreign exchange meant it could not support the UAE dirham in 1977 when a massive run on the currency led to a financial crisis and the collapse of two banks. In late 1980, a law converting the Currency Board into a central bank took effect. Although the Central Bank had more authority than the Currency Board, it encountered opposition from various members of amirate ruling families when it attempted to put new policies and regulations in place.

The Central Bank's responsibilities include issuing currency, maintaining gold and foreign currency reserves, regulating banks, and controlling credit to encourage balanced economic growth. It also advises the government on monetary and finan-

Fisherman and his wares; Persian Gulf waters provide abundant fish.
Courtesy Embassy of the United Arab Emirates, Washington

cial policy. In 1981 the moratorium on new banks was lifted once again. But in an effort to rein in the proliferation of banks, the Central Bank announced the same year that foreign banks would receive no new branch licenses and that foreign banks already operating in the country would be restricted to eight branches each by 1984.

The Central Bank took several measures in the early 1980s to strengthen the banking structure. It expanded audits and inspections, increased bank reporting requirements, established a computerized loan risk department, and set minimum capital requirements. The Central Bank also created a regulation that limited the size of a bank's loans to its directors. As a result of a violation of this regulation, administrators appointed by the Central Bank in 1983 took over the UAE's third largest bank, the Union Bank of the Middle East. The Central Bank and the Dubayy government bailed out the bank in the amount of US$380 million. Another bank, the Emirates Industrial Bank, was established in 1983 with capital of Dh500 million as a source of loans for new industries.

As a result of uncertainty in the wake of Iraq's August 1990 invasion of Kuwait, between 15 and 30 percent of customer bank deposits were transferred out of the UAE. At least two banks required injections of funds from the Central Bank to maintain liquidity, but confidence and deposits gradually returned. The Central Bank's governor was replaced in 1991 in the wake of the failure of the National Investments and Security Corporation.

Another crisis rocked the UAE banking sector in 1991 when the Luxembourg-registered Bank of Credit and Commerce International (BCCI) was shut down in most of the sixty-nine countries in which it operated. BCCI's troubles began in 1988 when two of its United States subsidiaries were accused of laundering profits from the illegal drug trade. Abu Dhabi's ruler and UAE president, Shaykh Zayid ibn Sultan Al Nuhayyan, is a founding shareholder in BCCI and in 1990 had purchased, along with others in Abu Dhabi, a 77 percent share in the bank. Having moved the bank's headquarters from London to Abu Dhabi, Shaykh Zayid ibn Sultan was in the process of restructuring the troubled bank when an audit commissioned by the Bank of England alleged major and systematic fraud by BCCI. That audit triggered the closing of most of BCCI's banks worldwide.

The ripples of the crisis spread throughout the UAE business community. In addition to its massive obligations worldwide, BCCI owed agencies in Abu Dhabi US$1.4 billion and private investors US$600 million. In October 1992, a Luxembourg court approved a US$1.7 billion compensation agreement between the bank's liquidators and the majority shareholders. The agreement called for the shareholders to pay 30 to 40 cents on the dollar to BCCI depositors.

Budget

The provisional constitution stipulates that each amirate contribute to the federal budget. In practice, however, Abu Dhabi was the only contributor in the 1970s; Dubayy began to contribute in the early 1980s. In 1991 Abu Dhabi provided 77.5 percent of the federal budget and Dubayy, 8.5 percent. The government levies taxes on oil companies and banks in Abu Dhabi and Dubayy but not on other businesses and individuals.

The poorer amirates benefit from federal expenditures on defense, infrastructure, education, and social services, but they draw up their own budgets (which are seldom published) for municipal expenditures and industrial projects. Some of these projects have been motivated more by prestige than practicality. For example, Dubayy, Sharjah, and Ras al Khaymah have built large international airports, even though they are a one-half-hour drive from each other and less than a two-hour drive from Abu Dhabi's large international airport.

Ras al Khaymah and Sharjah have borrowed heavily to finance facilities and industries, resulting occasionally in economic and political problems. Sharjah, for example, suffered a coup attempt in 1987 carried out by opponents critical of the amir's alleged financial mismanagement. The amirate's debt burden at the time was estimated at US$920 million.

The revenue and spending estimates for the UAE's first and only five-year plan (1981–85) were based on strong oil revenues in the late 1970s. Petroleum revenues fell in the early 1980s, however, rendering many of the plan's goals unattainable. The federation's first budget deficit (Dh3.9 billion) occurred in 1982. Since that time, government planners have opted for a more flexible approach, keeping in mind the vagaries of the world oil market and tending to be more conservative in revenue and spending projections. Even so, sudden drops in oil revenues have repeatedly forced the government to put new projects on hold and to freeze current projects. Deficits generally are funded by Abu Dhabi and Dubayy and by borrowing from the Central Bank.

Although there is no attempt at long-term, coordinated development planning, three main objectives have guided federal government spending. These include strengthening the federation's physical infrastructure and social services network, diversifying the economy, and expanding entrepôt trade.

Despite slowdowns in world oil markets and amirs jealous of their local sovereignty, the UAE has been able to finance massive infrastructure projects (roads, utilities, communications, ports, and airports); modern education, health, and welfare systems; and improvements in agriculture and fishing. The lion's share of the federal budget, however, goes to defense (see table 29, Appendix). As a result of the continuing potential for conflict in the gulf in the 1990s, defense will probably continue to absorb between 40 and 50 percent of federal outlays and will not face the same cuts as do other sectors if the economy contracts.

After battling budget deficits during most of the 1980s, the UAE saw budget surpluses in 1990 and 1991. Deficits were projected to return in 1992 and 1993, with an almost US$710 million shortfall expected in 1993 (the figure includes US$245 million rolled over from the previous year's deficit).

Abu Dhabi is one of the world's most generous donors of foreign aid in terms of GDP and population. In 1981 foreign grants and loans amounted to US$2.7 billion, or 8 percent of GDP. Even in leaner times, aid in 1983 was US$1 billion, or 4 percent of GDP. The Abu Dhabi Fund for Arab Economic Development, with paid-up capital of US$500 million, extends loans and grants mainly to Arab and Muslim countries. Recipients have included Bangladesh, Egypt, Jordan, Mauritania, Morocco, Syria, and Yemen. The level of annual outlays depends on oil revenues. In 1989 the fund's committed capital was US$2.2 billion. Loans in 1988 amounted to US$41.1 million, up from US$4.2 million in 1987.

Trade

The UAE, in particular Dubayy, epitomizes trade. The federal government promotes open and free trade as an official policy, and a thriving source of income and full employment has resulted. The oil economy (world prices and demand as well as local production) and regional security strongly influence trade. Oil and gas exports account for about three-fourths of all exports. The UAE's balance of trade surplus grew during the boom years of the 1970s but leveled off in the 1980s with decreased oil production. Although the Iran-Iraq War buffeted the oil economies of the region, Dubayy's fruitful trade links with Iran helped it to have exports and reexports of US$354 million in 1987.

The end of the Iran-Iraq War in 1988 led to a 20 percent increase in UAE imports, reducing the trade surplus from its 1987 level of US$5.2 billion (Dh19 billion) to US$3.7 billion (Dh13.4 billion) (see table 30, Appendix). But oil price increases and production increases resulting from Iraq's invasion of Kuwait in 1990 created a windfall for the UAE and drove the federation's trade surplus to US$9.3 billion (Dh34.1 billion).

Administering customs and setting rates are functions reserved to the individual amirates, and duties and regulations therefore vary among them. In 1982 Dubayy and Sharjah reduced their customs duties from 3 percent to 1 percent, bringing them on a par with Abu Dhabi's tariffs. In 1983 a 4 percent general import tariff was imposed to conform to agreements among GCC members on minimum duties.

Principal imports are manufactured goods, machinery, transportation equipment, food, and live animals. Leading suppliers in 1988 were Japan, Britain, and the United States. Non-petroleum exports include basic manufactures, aluminum, and cement. The reexport trade overshadows national exports. Federal exports, which consist largely of petroleum, go mainly to Japan (see table 31, Appendix). In 1988 national exports amounted to US$518 million while reexports stood at more than US$2 million. Iran, Qatar, and Saudi Arabia are the principal recipients of reexports. The view along bustling Dubayy Creek gives ample evidence of the vibrant reexport trade. Scores of large, motorized dhows tied up four and five deep line the wharf, their decks and holds packed with refrigerators, television sets, clothing, toys, and even automobiles. In 1991 Dubayy's imports (much of which was destined for reexport) arrived from Japan, the United States, China, Britain, and the Republic of Korea (South Korea).

Government and Politics

Executive and Legislative Branches

On July 18, 1971, rulers of six amirates from those known as the Trucial Coast states, ratified the provisional constitution of the UAE. A product of more than three years of discussion and debate among the rulers, the document was promulgated on December 2, 1971, on the UAE's independence. (Ras al Khaymah joined the union in February 1972.) Originally, the provisional constitution was to be replaced after five years with a permanent document, pending the resolution of issues standing in the way of full integration among the federation's amirates. These issues included individual amirates' contributions to the federal budget and defense integration. Reflecting a lack of progress in resolving these matters and a grudging preference for the status quo, however, the provisional constitution was extended for five-year periods in 1976, 1981, 1986, and 1991.

The provisional constitution of the UAE provides for the separation of powers into executive, legislative, and judicial branches. Additionally, it separates legislative and executive powers into federal and amirate jurisdictions. Certain powers are expressly reserved for the central government, including foreign policy, defense, security, immigration, and communications. The individual amirates exercise residual powers.

The separation of powers remained nominal in 1993. The Supreme Council of the Union (SCU), also seen as the Federal

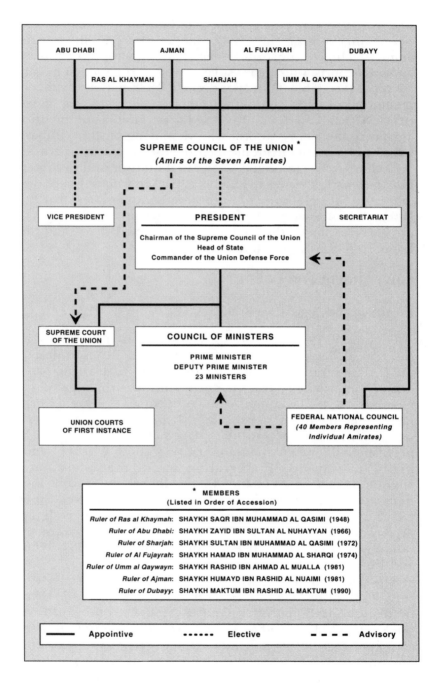

Figure 12. United Arab Emirates: Government Structure, 1992

Supreme Council, functions as the highest federal authority in executive and legislative capacities. Narrowly, the executive branch consists of the SCU, the Council of Ministers (the cabinet), and the presidency (see fig. 12). The SCU consists of the rulers of the seven amirates; it elects from among its members a chairman and a vice chairman, who serve for a term of five years. Article 150 of the provisional constitution defines the powers of the SCU as formulation of general policy; legislation on all matters of state; ratification of federal laws and decrees, including those relating to the annual budget and fiscal matters; ratification of international treaties and agreements; and assent to the appointment of the prime minister and Supreme Court of the Union judges.

The rulers make decisions by a simple majority vote, except on substantive issues. Substantive issues require a two-thirds majority (five of seven rulers), including the votes of both Abu Dhabi and Dubayy. The SCU carries out its work through a secretariat and whatever ad hoc committees it chooses to appoint.

The president serves as chairman of the SCU, head of state, and commander of the Union Defense Force. The president convenes the SCU and appoints the prime minister, deputy prime minister, cabinet ministers, and other senior civil and military officials. He has the power to proclaim martial law and to carry out a variety of functions usually associated with the chief executive.

The Council of Ministers administers federal affairs. In 1992 there were twenty-five ministers, including the prime minister and deputy prime minister. UAE citizenship is a requirement for appointment as a minister. All ministers are individually and collectively answerable to the president and the SCU. In addition to its executive duties, the Council of Ministers is responsible for drafting bills for formal enactment.

Under the provisional constitution, the Federal National Council (FNC) is the principal legislative authority, but its actual role in the governmental process is limited to consultation. Its forty members are appointed for two-year terms by the respective amirate rulers, in accordance with a constitutionally fixed quota that allots proportionately more members to the wealthiest and most populous amirates. Thus, Abu Dhabi and Dubayy each appoint eight members to the FNC; Ras al Khaymah and Sharjah each appoint six members; and Ajman, Al Fujayrah, and Umm al Qaywayn each appoint four members. Members of the FNC must be citizens of the amirates they represent, twenty-one years of age or older, and literate. They may not hold any other public office.

The FNC meets in regular session for a minimum of six months, beginning in November. The UAE president may call a special session if necessary. The president opens the regular session with a speech on the state of the union. The FNC can reply to the state of the union address in the form of "observations and wishes," but the reply has no legal effect. The FNC also makes recommendations on legislative matters to the Council of Ministers, the president, and the SCU. The FNC can discuss any government bills drafted by the Council of Ministers; it can agree with, amend, or reject such bills, but it cannot veto them.

The laws of the UAE are divided into two main categories: union laws and decrees. A bill drafted by the Council of Ministers for nonbinding deliberation by the FNC and then submitted to the president for his assent and the SCU for ratification becomes a union law when promulgated by the president. Decrees are issued jointly by the president and the Council of Ministers between sessions of the SCU; a decree must be confirmed by the SCU to remain valid.

The Judiciary

Article 94 of the provisional constitution guarantees the independence of the judicial branch under the Supreme Court of the Union. This body consists of a president and up to five judges appointed by the UAE president, following approval by the SCU. The Supreme Court is vested with the power of judicial review and original jurisdiction over federal-amirate and interamirate disputes. It also is empowered to try cases of official misconduct involving cabinet and other senior federal officials.

The provisional constitution also provides for the establishment of union courts of first instance to adjudicate civil, commercial, criminal, and administrative cases. Judgments of these courts can be appealed to the Supreme Court. Local courts in each of the seven amirates have jurisdiction over matters that the provisional constitution does not specifically reserve to the union courts.

The provisional constitution designates the sharia (Islamic law) as the basis of all legislation. Three of the four legal schools of Sunni Islam have adherents in the UAE. Most citizens follow the Maliki legal school, but a minority follow the

Hanbali and Shafii schools. The Twelve Imam Shia (see Glossary) legal school of Shia Muslims also has adherents in the federation (see Sunni Islam; Shia Islam, ch.1).

Ruling Families

In 1993 the most important political figures in the UAE were the senior members of the ruling families of the individual amirates—the Al Nuhayyan family of Abu Dhabi, the Al Nuaimi of Ajman, the Al Sharqi of Al Fujayrah, the Al Maktum of Dubayy, the Al Qasimi of Ras al Khaymah and Sharjah, and the Al Mualla of Umm al Qaywayn. The most powerful amir is Shaykh Zayid ibn Sultan Al Nuhayyan (b. ca. 1920), the ruler of Abu Dhabi and the president of the UAE (reelected to a five-year term in 1991). Shaykh Zayid ibn Sultan has ruled Abu Dhabi since 1966, when his older brother, Shaykh Shakhbut Al Nuhayyan (r. 1928–66), was deposed by the British.

The Al Nuhayyan originally were beduin of the Bani Yas tribe and were based in the Al Liwa Oasis. An ancestor of the current ruler migrated to the island of Abu Dhabi in the late 1770s and established a commercial port there. Prior to 1966, Abu Dhabi remained a small town and residence site of the ruler, but it had not attracted most Al Nuhayyan shaykhs, who preferred to live in the interior oases. Even Shaykh Zayid ibn Sultan favored the beduin lifestyle as a young man, and for several years under his brother's rule he was governor of Al Ayn in the Al Buraymi Oasis. Beginning in the late 1960s, the oil boom-induced transformation of Abu Dhabi into a cosmopolitan city prompted politically ambitious Al Nuhayyan members to settle in the capital, where many of them obtained positions in the expanding amirate and federal bureaucracies.

Shaykh Zayid ibn Sultan designated his son, Shaykh Khalifa ibn Zayid Al Nuhayyan (b. 1949), as crown prince. Khalifa ibn Zayid acquired progressively more responsibilities as he matured. In 1992 he served as president of Abu Dhabi's Executive Council (the amirate equivalent of the Council of Ministers) and as head of the Department of Social Services. In addition, he was deputy commander in chief of the federal Union Defense Force. Shaykh Zayid ibn Sultan had more than forty-five other children, although most of them were not involved actively in politics; one son was a colonel in the Union Defense Force air force. Several of Shaykh Zayid ibn Sultan's cousins were prominent in government, especially the sons of his cousin Muhammad ibn Khalifa Al Nuhayyan: Tahnun ibn

Muhammad Al Nuhayyan was head of ADNOC; Hamdan ibn Muhammad Al Nuhayyan was deputy prime minister; and Sarur ibn Muhammad Al Nuhayyan was chief of the ruler's diwan (court).

Until his death on October 7, 1990, Shaykh Rashid ibn Said Al Maktum (b. 1912), as ruler of Dubayy and vice president and prime minister of the UAE, was the second most powerful amir. His eldest son, Shaykh Maktum ibn Rashid Al Maktum, succeeded him in all his offices. The Al Maktum are a branch of the same Bani Yas tribe that includes the Al Nuhayyan. The Al Maktum emigrated from Abu Dhabi to Dubayy's creek in the 1830s and established there the port that eventually became Dubayy. The late Shaykh Rashid ibn Said succeeded to the rule of Dubayy in 1958 following the death of his father, Shaykh Said ibn Maktum Al Maktum (r. 1912–58). During the 1960s and 1970s, Shaykh Rashid ibn Said presided over the transformation of Dubayy into a wealthy oil amirate. Since the mid-1980s, however, his sons effectively have ruled the amirate because of Rashid ibn Said's serious and chronic illnesses.

Before taking over his father's offices, Shaykh Maktum ibn Rashid (b. 1941) was crown prince and had several other governmental responsibilities. Shaykh Maktum ibn Rashid's brother, Muhammad ibn Rashid Al Maktum, is UAE minister of defense and head of Dubayy's armed forces. Two other brothers also hold important positions in the Dubayy or federal administrations. In addition, several of Shaykh Rashid ibn Said's nephews and cousins are politically prominent.

Two branches of the Al Qasimi tribe rule Sharjah and Ras al Khaymah. The Al Qasimi, based at Ras al Khaymah, emerged as a major maritime power during the eighteenth century; the Al Qasimi control of trade in the Persian Gulf area led to conflict with Oman and eventually with Britain, which was consolidating its colonial empire in India (see Treaties with the British, ch. 1). Following several naval battles, the British finally defeated the Al Qasimi in 1819, burning their ships and the town of Ras al Khaymah. Because of this history, the Al Qasimi inherited a historical hostility toward the British.

The Al Qasimi family of Sharjah is the larger of the two ruling houses. Shaykh Sultan ibn Muhammad Al Qasimi (b. 1942) of Sharjah became ruler in 1972, following the assassination of his brother, Shaykh Khalid ibn Muhammad Al Qasimi (r. 1965–72), killed in an unsuccessful coup to restore his cousin, Shaykh Saqr ibn Sultan Al Qasimi (r. 1951–65), whom the British had

Zayid ibn Sultan Al Nuhayyan,
president of the
United Arab Emirates and ruler
of Abu Dhabi
Courtesy Embassy of the
United Arab Emirates,
Washington

deposed. Shaykh Sultan ibn Muhammad has a reputation for being relatively progressive and for being an enthusiastic supporter of strengthening the powers of the federal government.

The ruler also has a reputation for initiating extravagant construction projects for the amirate. Since assuming power, Shaykh Sultan ibn Muhammad had amassed a debt estimated in 1987 at US$920 million, creating discontent among some members of the royal family and precipitating a coup attempt in June 1987. While Shaykh Sultan ibn Muhammad was out of the amirate, his elder brother, Shaykh Abd al Aziz Al Qasimi, issued a statement through Sharjah's news agency that Shaykh Sultan ibn Muhammad had abdicated because he had mismanaged the amirate's economy. Despite initial Abu Dhabi support for the pretender, the coup failed when Dubayy called a meeting of the SCU. Through mediation it was decided to return Shaykh Sultan ibn Muhammad to power, but to give Shaykh Abd al Aziz a seat on the SCU and the title of crown prince. Somewhat chastened, Shaykh Sultan ibn Muhammad initiated administrative and financial reforms, but he had the last word when, in February 1990, he removed his brother from the post of crown prince, revoked his brother's right to succeed him, and exiled him.

The Al Qasimi family of Ras al Khaymah is smaller than the branch in Sharjah. Shaykh Saqr ibn Muhammad Al Qasimi (b. 1920) has ruled the amirate since 1948. As do his cousins in Sharjah, he has acquired a reputation for being sympathetic to Arab nationalist issues. He is a contemporary of the former ruler of Sharjah, Shaykh Saqr ibn Sultan, and, like him, tends to be suspicious of the British. In 1971 he refused to accept Britain's compromise for resolving Iran's claims to Tunb al Kubra (Greater Tumb) and Tunb as Sughra (Lesser Tumb), two tiny islands in the Persian Gulf (see Foreign Relations, this ch.). Shaykh Saqr ibn Sultan has designated his son, Khalid ibn Saqr Al Qasimi, as crown prince; Khalid ibn Saqr was educated in the United States.

The rulers of the other three amirates have limited influence within the UAE. Ajman, Al Fujayrah, and Umm al Qaywayn are relatively small, poor, and dependent on their wealthier neighbors for development grants. Shaykh Humayd ibn Rashid Al Nuaimi has ruled Ajman since 1981. Shaykh Rashid ibn Ahmad Al Mualla has ruled Umm al Qaywayn since 1981 as well. In Al Fujayrah, where a majority of the population claims membership in the dominant Al Sharqi tribe, Shaykh Hamad ibn Muhammad Al Sharqi has ruled since 1974.

The Media

Provided the media do not criticize the ruling families and the government, they are relatively free. Abu Dhabi publishes two dailies, one in Arabic, *Al Ittihad* (Unity), and one in English, *Emirates News*, at a government-owned press. The Dubayy government publishes one Arabic daily, *Al Bayan* (The Official Report). In addition, the UAE has three other Arabic dailies and two English dailies.

The government-owned UAE Broadcasting Service airs radio programs mainly from Abu Dhabi, which also has a television station, and from Dubayy. Other amirates also have radio stations, and Sharjah airs a small amount of television time.

Foreign Relations

Since obtaining full independence at the end of 1971, the UAE has focused on security concerns in its foreign relations. Indeed, it was uncertain in the early 1970s whether the UAE would endure as a viable state. Saudi Arabia, for example, refused to recognize the new federation because of a border dispute with Abu Dhabi over the Al Buraymi Oasis, subsequently resolved in 1974. Iran and Oman also contested UAE claims to certain territories. In addition, the discovery of extensive petroleum deposits in the 1960s prompted Iraq and other states to challenge the legitimacy of the UAE's ruling families. Because the UAE was a relatively small state, its leaders recognized that defending the country's security from both internal and external threats depended on skillful management of diplomatic relations with other countries, particularly larger and more powerful neighbors such as Iran, Iraq, and Saudi Arabia.

A principal goal of the UAE's foreign policy has been to contain the spillover effects of various regional crises. For example, during the initial years of UAE independence, a major insurrectionary movement threatened to overthrow the government in neighboring Oman. This movement also supported a group known as the Popular Front for the Liberation of Oman and the Arab Gulf, which aimed at establishing a republican regime in the UAE. During the mid-1970s, repercussions of the escalating civil war in Lebanon reverberated throughout the Persian Gulf. Subsequently, the Iranian Revolution of 1979, the civil war and Soviet intervention in Afghanistan, and the Iran-Iraq War all affected the UAE in various ways.

Despite its criticisms of United States policies toward the Palestinians, the UAE perceives its evolving relationship with the United States as providing a measure of protection from these crises. Thus, by 1990–91, when it joined with the United States in the military effort to force Iraq out of Kuwait, the UAE already had become a de facto member of the United States strategic umbrella over the region.

The Iraqi invasion and occupation of Kuwait were a shock to the UAE. Prior to that crisis, the UAE had tried to demonstrate solidarity on inter-Arab issues. In particular, it had supported the cause of Palestinian Arabs, both within the League of Arab States (Arab League), of which it was a member, and within international forums. In practical terms, this meant that the UAE did not recognize Israel. When Egypt signed a separate peace agreement with Israel in 1979, the UAE joined other Arab states in breaking diplomatic relations with Egypt. The UAE did not, however, expel the thousands of Egyptian workers in the UAE or interfere with their transfer of remittances home. For the UAE, the crisis over Kuwait demonstrated a lack of Arab unity on a critical Arab issue. The UAE joined the Arab states that opposed the Iraqi invasion and supported the use of force to compel Iraq's withdrawal of troops.

More fundamental for the UAE, this crisis exposed the failure of the GCC, of which the UAE had been a founding member in 1981, as a deterrent collective security organization. Although it was not prepared to abandon the GCC—it derived other benefits from this alliance with Bahrain, Kuwait, Oman, Qatar, and Saudi Arabia—the UAE believed that new security arrangements were necessary. The UAE initially supported expanding the GCC framework to include formal military ties with Egypt and Syria. When this option seemed unrealistic, the UAE concluded that a security relationship with the United States should be continued. Consequently, negotiations began during the summer of 1991 and continued for more than a year. In late 1992, officials of both countries signed an agreement that permitted the United States to use some UAE bases temporarily and to pre-position supplies on UAE territory.

The negotiations with the United States may have been a factor in the UAE's 1992 problems with Iran, a country that opposed a continuing United States military presence in the region. Like Iraq, Iran is a large neighbor—and a much closer one—with a recent history of policies that discomfited the UAE. Throughout the 1980s, the UAE had striven with difficulty to maintain neutrality in the Iran-Iraq War. That conflict was also a source of internal UAE tension because Abu Dhabi tended to support Iraq while Dubayy was more sympathetic to Iran. After the war ended in 1988, Iran appeared to single out the UAE for special and friendly attention. By 1992 the UAE was the Arab country with which Iran had the closest commercial relations. Thus, the crisis that erupted in April 1992 over disputed islands in the Persian Gulf seemed unexpected.

The dispute with Iran over the sovereignty of three small islands—Abu Musa, Greater Tumb, and Lesser Tumb—had been dormant for twenty years. It was rekindled in 1992 when Iranian officials on Abu Musa refused to permit UAE contract workers to disembark, in apparent contravention of a shared sovereignty agreement. Iran had claimed all three islands in 1970, before the UAE was formed. On the eve of independence in 1971, the amirate of Sharjah, which had jurisdiction over Abu Musa, accepted an agreement negotiated between London and Tehran that permitted Iran to establish a military garrison in the northern part of the island and allowed Sharjah to administer the civilian population living in the southern part. The agreement provided for Iran and Sharjah to share the proceeds from an offshore oil field but otherwise left the question of ultimate sovereignty to be resolved at some unspecified future time.

Greater Tumb and Lesser Tumb are two uninhabited islands claimed by Ras al Khaymah but occupied by Iran since 1971. Unlike Sharjah, Ras al Khaymah never accepted an Iranian claim to the islands and protested Britain's failure to interfere with Iran's occupation. Indeed, it was the amirate's anger over the 1971 occupation that caused it to refrain from joining the UAE for several months. In the midst of the 1992 crisis over Abu Musa, Ras al Khaymah resurrected its grievance over Greater Tumb and Lesser Tumb, thus enflaming an already delicate situation. At the end of the year, Iran and Sharjah quietly agreed to a restoration of the status quo ante the crisis, but the incidents left the UAE feeling wary of Iranian intentions.

In 1993 the UAE maintained relatively cordial relations with countries outside the Middle East. It was a member of the United Nations and its specialized agencies. It also was a member of the Organization of the Petroleum Exporting Countries and the Organization of the Islamic Conference.

*   *   *

The body of scholarly literature on the UAE gradually increased in the 1980s. A recent book, Malcolm C. Peck's *The United Arab Emirates*, provides a good account of UAE society, politics, and economy. Hassan Hamdan al-Alkim's *The Foreign Policy of the United Arab Emirates* gives a solid introduction to the subject. The history of the region from World War I until independence is presented with insight by Rosemarie Said Zahlan in her book, *The Origins of the United Arab Emirates*. A.O. Taryam's *The Establishment of the United Arab Emirates, 1950–85* gives a detailed discussion of the years immediately before and after the UAE's creation.

There are also informative chapters about the UAE in several earlier books, including Ali Mohammad Khalifa's *The United Arab Emirates: Unity in Fragmentation* and Enver Khoury's *The United Arab Emirates: Its Political System and Politics*. (For further information and complete citations, see Bibliography.)

Chapter 6. Oman

Crest of the Sultanate of Oman

Country

Formal Name: Sultanate of Oman.

Short Form: Oman.

Term for Citizens: Omani(s); adjectival form, Omani.

Capital: Muscat.

Geography

Size: About 212,000 square kilometers, although estimates vary.

Topography: Mostly desert; 15 percent of land mountainous. Four major regions: Musandam Peninsula, Al Batinah coastal plain, Oman interior, and Dhofar region.

Climate: Hot and dry, except for Dhofar, which has light monsoons.

Boundaries: Oman and Saudi Arabia signed agreement in 1990 to demarcate borders; Oman and Yemen signed agreement in 1992 to demarcate borders.

Society

Population: In 1992, for planning purposes, government estimated 2 million; actual figure may be closer to 1.5 million. Growth rate 3.5 percent in 1994. Foreigners estimated at 23.3 percent of population in 1992.

Education: Free public schools consist of primary level of six years, lower secondary level of three years, and upper secondary level of three years. Most teachers (60 percent) foreign.

NOTE—The Country Profile contains updated information as available.

Health: Improvement and expansion of health care facilities major ongoing government priority. In 1994 infant mortality estimated at thirty-seven per 1,000 population. In 1994 life expectancy at birth sixty-eight years on average, with sixty-six years for males and seventy years for females.

Ethnic Groups: Most Omanis are Arabs, although numerous citizens of non-Arab African origin. Foreign community includes Egyptians, Pakistanis, Indians, and others.

Religion: Most Omanis are Muslims; Ibadis constitute largest group.

Economy

Gross Domestic Product (GDP): In 1991 GDP about RO4.0 billion, or US$10.5 billion; per capita income RO2,696, or US$7,000.

Oil Industry: In 1991 accounted for about 43 percent of GDP, 95 percent of export earnings, and 82 percent of government revenues.

Agriculture and Fishing: Contributed about 3.8 percent of GDP in 1991.

Currency and Exchange Rate: Omani riyal. In 1994 exchange rate US$1 = RO0.3845 (fixed rate).

Fiscal Year: Calendar year.

Transportation and Telecommunications

Transportation: In 1992 about 6,000 kilometers paved roads and 20,000 kilometers gravel or earthen roads. Four-lane highway from Muscat along Gulf of Oman runs to Dubayy in United Arab Emirates. Major airport As Sib International Airport near Muscat. Major port Mina Qabus, near Muscat, being expanded in 1994; other major port at Raysut.

Telecommunications: Telecommunications internationally via satellites; domestic telephone service very limited but being expanded. Television available throughout Oman, but radio broadcast facilities limited.

Government and Politics

Government: Sultan Qabus ibn Said Al Said as head of state and prime minister presides over Council of Ministers. Consultative Council has advisory role but no legislative powers. No constitution.

Politics: No political parties. Important political actors are persons close to sultan, including Western-educated administrators and special advisers.

Foreign Relations: Member of United Nations and its specialized agencies, League of Arab States, Organization of the Islamic Conference, and Gulf Cooperation Council. June 1980 agreement allows United States use of military facilities in Oman.

National Security

Armed Forces: In mid-1993 Royal Armed Forces personnel strength 36,700, including 3,700 foreign personnel, as follows: Royal Oman Land Forces, 20,000; Royal Oman Navy, 3,500; Royal Oman Air Force, 3,500; and Royal Household, 6,000 (including Royal Guard of Oman, 4,500; Special Forces, 700; Royal Yacht Squadron, 150; and other, 650). Army primarily infantry force but has some tanks and armored cars. Navy a coastal patrol force, expanding and modernizing by acquiring guided missile (Exocet) craft and new gunboats. Air force has more than fifty combat aircraft, all of British manufacture.

SINCE 1970, WHEN OMAN'S RULER, Sultan Qabus ibn Said Al Said, assumed power, the sultanate has moved from a poor underdeveloped country toward a modern nation state. Indexes of development measuring per capita gross national product, infant mortality, literacy rates, and availability of social services validate the government's claim that its policies have effected positive change. Although the government's administrative structure expanded to accommodate public services, change in the political system has been slow. Oman remains a conservative monarchy, with the sultan relying on the support of a traditional political elite comprising the Al Said ruling family, established merchant families, and, to a lesser extent, tribal shaykhs.

Until the commercial production and export of oil in 1967, Oman's budget was exclusively dependent on religious taxes (*zakat*), customs duties, and British loans and subsidies. The bulk of this revenue served as a mechanism through which the sultan could co-opt his traditional allies among the merchant families and tribal shaykhs. By transferring income from the state treasury, the sultan was able to draw in influential segments of Omani society and ensure continuance of Al Said rule. Post-1970 economic developments were in part constructed on these antecedents. Income distribution remained a principal mechanism for ensuring political stability, but the network involved a state administrative structure rather than the more direct and personal individual-ruler relationship. Also, the system expanded to incorporate the average Omani through the creation of a public sector. The net effect has been the establishment of a salaried middle class whose economic interests are closely tied with the government.

Since the development of the country's infrastructure in the 1970s, national development plans have given priority to reducing dependency on oil exports and encouraging income-generating projects in non-oil sectors (diversification), promoting private-sector investment, and effecting a wider geographical distribution of investments to correct regional imbalances. Such a wider distribution is intended to narrow the gap in the standard of living in different regions, develop existing areas of population, and discourage migration to densely populated urban centers, such as Muscat (also seen as Masqat), the capital. Equally important are the national goals to develop local human resources, to increase indigenous participation in the private sector, and to improve government management and organization.

Constraints on the government in implementing its economic diversification program include the limited growth potential of alternative sectors, such as agriculture, fishing, and industry. Constraints also include the limited involvement of the private sector in businesses other than trade, the low-skilled labor force, the limited water resources, and the inability of government ministries to manage and expand services.

Sultan Qabus ibn Said, therefore, faced different challenges in 1993 than those he confronted when he assumed power in 1970 through a palace coup d'état. Then, the rebellion of tribes in the southern Dhofar (also seen as Zufar) region and the exploitation of the country's oil reserves had taken precedence.

Opportunities in urban centers stimulated a rural-urban shift, reducing the number of individuals engaged in agricultural labor and contributing to the key role of the oil sector in the economy. On the one hand, an increasingly urbanized population has the potential to be better educated and better enumerated. On the other hand, the small indigenous population has necessitated the presence of a large foreign labor force. This has contributed to an informal caste system, with Omanis clearly ranked highest in the hierarchy, followed by Westerners, with non-Western foreigners at the bottom.

Economic development has resulted in social transformation, not only in terms of diminishing the importance of the tribal element in Oman and stratifying Omani society but also in terms of inadvertently engendering a sense of entitlement among the public, common to social welfare states. In doing so, the government has been under increasing pressure to provide suitable employment for new migrants to the cities from village communities and to new graduates from colleges, to expand its social services, and to maintain the security of the country.

To fulfill these expectations, the government must ensure sustainable economic growth. Therefore, the policies of diversification and indigenization have taken on greater importance. Diversification is needed to ensure growth in the post-oil era; indigenization potentially eliminates the demand for foreign labor and increases opportunities for Omani nationals. The problems of the 1990s are resistant to change, however. The depletion of the country's proven oil reserves (at the production rate of 1992, reserves will be depleted within seventeen years) heightens the need for economic diversification, but so far, non-oil sectors have shown limited potential.

The net effect of the government's policies has been to link economic conditions with political stability. The suppression of the Dhofar rebellion in the first half of the 1970s provided a lesson for Sultan Qabus ibn Said. By addressing the gross economic neglect of the south, the government was able to ensure some political quiescence. In providing the majority of Omanis with adequate income through employment in the public sector, health and medical services, education, and other social services, the government has similarly ensured a modicum of public political support.

Geography and Population

Geography

Oman is located in the southeastern quarter of the Arabian Peninsula and, according to official estimates, covers a total land area of approximately 300,000 square kilometers; foreign observer estimates, however, are about 212,000 square kilometers, roughly the size of the state of Kansas. The land area is composed of varying topographic features: flat or rolling terrain covered with desert accounts for 82 percent of the land mass; mountain ranges, 15 percent; and the coastal plain, 3 percent.

The sultanate is flanked by the Gulf of Oman, the Arabian Sea, and the Rub al Khali (Empty Quarter) of Saudi Arabia, all of which contributed to Oman's isolation. Historically, the country's contacts with the rest of the world were by sea, which not only provided access to foreign lands but also linked the coastal towns of Oman. The Rub al Khali, difficult to cross even with modern desert transport, formed a barrier between the sultanate and the Arabian interior. The Al Hajar Mountains, which form a belt between the coast and the desert from the Musandam Peninsula (Ras Musandam) to the city of Sur at Oman's easternmost point, formed another barrier. These geographic barriers kept the interior of Oman free from foreign military encroachments (see fig. 13).

Natural features divide the country into seven distinct areas: Ruus al Jibal, including the northern Musandam Peninsula; the Al Batinah coastal plain; the Muscat-Matrah coastal area;

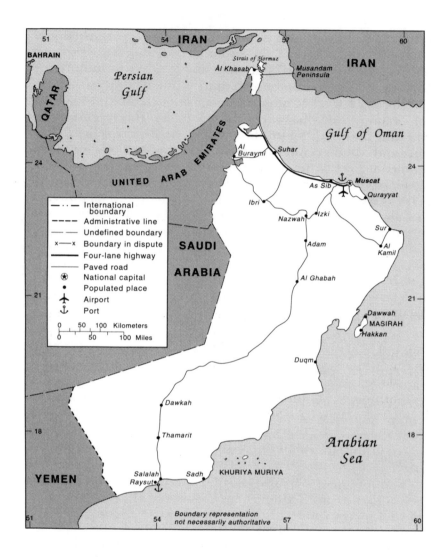

Figure 13. Oman, 1993

the Oman interior, comprising Al Jabal al Akhdar (Green
Mountain), its foothills, and desert fringes; the barren coastline south to Dhofar; the Dhofar region in the south; and the
offshore island of Masirah.

The northernmost area, Ruus al Jibal, extends from the
Musandam Peninsula to the boundary with the United Arab
Emirates (UAE) at Hisn Diba. It borders the Strait of Hormuz,

which links the Persian Gulf with the Gulf of Oman, and is separated from the rest of the sultanate by a strip of territory belonging to the UAE. This area consists of low mountains forming the northernmost extremity of the Al Hajar al Gharbi (Western Al Hajar) Mountains. Two inlets, Elphinstone (Khawr ash Shamm) and Malcom (Ghubbat al Ghazirah), cleave the coastline about one-third the distance from the Strait of Hormuz and at one point are separated by only a few hundred meters of land. The coastline is extremely rugged, and the Elphinstone Inlet, sixteen kilometers long and surrounded by cliffs 1,000 to 1,250 meters high, has frequently been compared with fjords in Norway.

The UAE territory separating Ruus al Jibal from the rest of Oman extends almost as far south as the coastal town of Shinas. A narrow, well-populated coastal plain known as Al Batinah runs from the point at which the sultanate is reentered to the town of As Sib, about 140 kilometers to the southeast. Across the plains, a number of wadis, heavily populated in their upper courses, descend from the Al Hajar al Gharbi Mountains to the south. A ribbon of oases, watered by wells and an underground channel (*falaj*) system, extends the length of the plain, about ten kilometers inland.

South of As Sib, the coast changes character. For about 175 kilometers, from As Sib to Ras al Hadd, it is barren and bounded by cliffs almost its entire length; there is no cultivation and little habitation. Although the deep water off this coast renders navigation relatively easy, there are few natural harbors or safe anchorages. The two best are at Muscat and Matrah, where natural harbors facilitated the growth of cities centuries ago.

West of the coastal areas lies the tableland of central Oman. The Al Hajar Mountains form two ranges: the Al Hajar al Gharbi Mountains and the Al Hajar ash Sharqi (Eastern Al Hajar) Mountains. They are divided by the Wadi Samail (the largest wadi in the mountain zone), a valley that forms the traditional route between Muscat and the interior. The general elevation is about 1,200 meters, but the peaks of the high ridge known as Al Jabal al Akhdar—which is considered a separate area but is actually part of the Al Hajar al Gharbi Mountains— rise to more than 3,000 meters in some places. Al Jabal al Akhdar is the only home of the Arabian *tahr*, a unique species of wild goat. In the hope of saving this rare animal, Sultan Qabus ibn Said has declared part of Al Jabal al Akhdar a national park. Behind the Al Hajar al Gharbi Mountains are two inland regions, Az Zahirah and inner Oman, separated by the lateral range of the Rub al Khali. Adjoining the Al Hajar ash Sharqi Mountains are the sandy regions of Ash Sharqiyah and Jalan, which also border the desert.

The desolate coastal tract from Jalan to Ras Naws has no specific name. Low hills and wastelands meet the sea for long distances. Midway along this coast and about fifteen kilometers offshore is the barren island of Masirah. Stretching about seventy kilometers, the island occupies a strategic location near the entry point to the Gulf of Oman from the Arabian Sea. Because of its location, it became the site of military facilities used first by the British and then by the United States, following an access agreement signed in 1980 by the United States and Oman and most recently renewed in 1990.

The Dhofar region extends from Ras ash Sharbatat to the border with Yemen. Its exact northern limit has never been defined, but the territory claimed by the sultan includes the Wadi Mughshin, about 240 kilometers inland. The southwestern portion of the coastal plain of Dhofar is regarded as one of the most beautiful in Arabia, and its capital, Salalah, was the permanent residence of Sultan Said ibn Taimur Al Said and the birthplace of the present sultan, Qabus ibn Said. The highest peaks are about 1,000 meters. At their base lies a narrow, pebbly desert adjoining the Rub al Khali to the north.

Climate

With the exception of the Dhofar region, which has a light monsoon climate and receives cool winds from the Indian Ocean, the climate of Oman is extremely hot and dry most of the year. Summer begins in mid-April and lasts until October. The highest temperatures are registered in the interior, where readings of more than 50°C in the shade are common. On the Al Batinah plain, summer temperatures seldom exceed 46°C, but, because of the low elevation, the humidity may be as high as 90 percent. The mean summer temperature in Muscat is 33°C, but the *gharbi* (literally, western), a strong wind that blows from the Rub al Khali, can raise temperatures from the towns on the Gulf of Oman by 6°C to 10°C. Winter temperatures are mild and pleasant, ranging between 15°C and 23°C.

Precipitation on the coasts and on the interior plains ranges from twenty to 100 millimeters a year and falls during mid- and late winter. Rainfall in the mountains, particularly over Al Jabal al Akhdar, is much higher and may reach 700 millimeters. Because the plateau of Al Jabal al Akhdar is porous limestone, rainfall seeps quickly through it, and the vegetation, which might be expected to be more lush, is meager. However, a huge reservoir under the plateau provides springs for low-lying areas. In addition, an enormous wadi channels water to these valleys, making the area agriculturally productive in years of good rainfall. Dhofar, benefiting from a southwest monsoon between June and September, receives heavier rainfall and has constantly running streams, which make the region Oman's most fertile area.

Population

A comprehensive population census has never been conducted, but in 1992 the sultanate solicited help from the United Nations (UN) Fund for Technical and Financial Assistance in taking a full census. For planning purposes, the government in 1992 estimated the population at 2 million, but the actual figure may be closer to 1.5 million, growing at a rate of 3.5 percent per annum. The population is unevenly distributed; the coastal regions, the Al Batinah plain, and the Muscat metropolitan area contain the largest concentration.

Omanis live mainly in rural areas, but urban locations also exist. The major city is Muscat, the capital. In the Al Batinah plain in the north, the largest town is Suhar. Farther south, in the hilly region of Al Jabal al Akhdar, lies the town of Nazwah. Salalah is a major center for the Dhofar region.

The population is heterogeneous, consisting of an ethnic and religious mix derived in large part from a history of maritime trade, tribal migrations, and contacts with the outside world. Although Arabs constitute the majority, non-Arab communities include Baluchis—from the Makran coast of Iran and Pakistan—who are concentrated in Muscat and the Al Batinah coast and play a significant role in the armed forces; ex-slaves (a legacy of Oman's slave trade and East African colonies); and Zanzibari Omanis, who are well represented in the police force and the professions. The integration of Omanis of African descent is often circumscribed by a language barrier (they often speak Swahili and English but not always Arabic). The presence of Omanis of Indian descent in Muscat reflects the historical commercial ties between the sultanate and the Indian subcontinent. The Khoja community in Matrah, of Indian origin, is perhaps the richest private group in Oman, and its members are among the best educated. The Shihuh of the northern Musandam Peninsula numbered about 20,000 in the early 1990s. They speak Arabic and a dialect of Farsi and engage primarily in fishing and herding.

Because of the small indigenous population, the government has been obliged to use foreign labor. In 1992 about 60 percent of the labor force was foreign. Some 350,000 foreign workers and their families (primarily Indians, Pakistanis, Bangladeshis, Filipinos, and Sri Lankans) live in Oman. The high percentage of foreigners in the work force, combined with improvements in the country's education system, has prompted the government to institute a program of indigenization whereby Omani nationals gradually replace foreigners (see Labor, this ch.).

Society

Religion

The majority of Omanis are Ibadi Muslims, followers of Abd Allah ibn Ibad (see Shia Islam, ch. 1). Approximately 25 percent are Sunni (see Glossary) Muslims and live primarily in Sur and the surrounding area and in Dhofar. They form the largest non-Ibadi minority. The Shia (see Glossary) minority lives along the Al Batinah coast in the Muscat-Matrah region. This minority includes the Khoja, the Baharina of Iraqi or Iranian descent, and the Ajam, of vague origin but generally considered to originate in Iran.

Ibadism is an outgrowth of the Kharijite movement, a variant form of Islam practiced by descendants of a sect that seceded from the principal Muslim body after the death of the Prophet Muhammad in A.D. 632. Kharijites reject primogeniture succession of the Quraysh, the tribe of Muhammad, and assert that leadership of Islam, the caliphate, should be exercised by an imam (see Glossary) elected by the community from candidates who possess spiritual and personal qualities. Ibadi leadership is vested in an imam, who is regarded as the sole legitimate leader and combines religious and political authority. The imam is elected by a council of prominent laymen or shaykhs (see Glossary). Adherence to Ibadism accounts in part for Oman's historical isolation. Considered a heretical form of Islam by the majority Sunni Muslims, Ibadis were not inclined to integrate with their neighbors.

Education

As in other sectors of Omani society, the education system was radically altered after the accession of Sultan Qabus ibn Said. Prior to 1970, there were only three primary schools in the sultanate—in Muscat, Matrah, and Salalah. These were reserved for approximately 900 boys personally selected by the sultan from among many applicants. Additionally, in Muscat there was a religious institute with an enrollment of fifty boys, three private schools for Hyderabadis (Indians), and one United States missionary school serving fifty foreign girls. Sultan Qabus ibn Said initiated a shift in the government's policies and priorities from neglect to expansion of the school system, increasing the public's access to general education.

The education system is guided by the policy-making body of the Council for Education chaired by the sultan and operated by the Ministry of Education and Youth. General education is divided into three levels: primary (grades 1–6); lower secondary (grades 7–9); and upper secondary (grades 10–12). Teacher-training colleges provide training programs for primary and lower secondary school teachers.

Education accounted for a modest 11.2 percent of the government's current expenditures in 1990, up from only 2.4 percent in 1975 but still considerably less than the 28 percent planned and less than the proportion recorded by other countries in the process of expanding their school systems. By the 1989–90 academic year, the percentage of students enrolled in primary schools was almost 100 percent in the respective age-group, compared with 53 percent in 1977–78 (see table 32, Appendix). The percentage of girls attending primary schools also rose rapidly during this period, from 37 percent in 1977–78 to 97 percent in 1989–90. The student-teacher ratio at the primary level was twenty-seven to one in 1988–89. Secondary school enrollment lagged behind primary school attendance and rose from 8 percent of secondary-school-age youth in 1977–78 to 48 percent in 1989–90. In 1986 Sultan Qabus University opened at Al Khawd, west of Muscat, with faculties of agriculture, education, engineering, Islamic studies, medicine, and science. Faculties for commerce, economics, and the arts are planned.

Rapid expansion and enrollment have exceeded the capacity of the ministry to plan and administer the system. This has produced problems in planning, budgeting, curriculum development, and teacher training. Often, inappropriate sites for facilities are selected, and programs are of poor quality or unavailable. Lower secondary education remains underdeveloped, contributing to the low enrollment rates in upper secondary school, particularly for females.

The government emphasizes teacher training for Omanis, in order to create an indigenous teaching force. The dependency on foreign staff, and hence the high turnover rate and lack of continuity, further compromises the quality of education. In the 1980–81 academic year, 618 of a total 5,663, or 11 percent of the teaching staff, were Omanis. By the 1985–86 academic year, the number had increased to 18 percent. The majority of ministry employees (55 percent in 1990) are non-Omanis, of whom more than 70 percent are Egyptians; the balance consists of Jordanians, Pakistanis, Sudanese, Indians, Filipinos, and others. As of 1990, there were six teacher-training colleges providing a two-year program and enrolling a total of about 700 students. Secondary school teachers receive training at the Faculty of Education at Sultan Qabus University.

The government's medium-term objectives are to ensure that all six-year-olds are enrolled in primary school and to expand access to primary and secondary education in rural areas. The government also seeks to expand teacher-training facilities; to increase the number of trained nationals staffing schools by increasing the number of teacher-training colleges; to improve teacher-class ratios and school-building operations; and to introduce student testing and new programs.

Health

Developments in the health and medical sector paralleled those in education. In 1970 there was one twelve-bed hospital operated by United States missionaries and nine government health centers. In 1990 there was a total of forty-seven hospitals, compared with fourteen in 1980. The number of doctors increased from 294 to 994 in the same ten-year period, and the number of nurses more than quadrupled from 857 to 3,512.

The government's health policy is directed at achieving a level of health care that approaches its goal of Health for All by the Year 2000. Included among the health priorities of the Ministry of Health are strengthening curative services, particularly in urban areas, and improving preventive services, with the emphasis on communicable diseases and immunization. The Public Health Department of the Ministry of Health is responsible for mass immunizations for smallpox and other infectious

Sultan Qabus University at Al Khawd, west of Muscat
Sultan Qabus ibn Said Al Said presenting gifts to the first graduates of
Sultan Qabus University
Courtesy Embassy of the Sultanate of Oman, Washington

diseases. The government stresses delivering maternal and child health care at the village level to decrease the infant mortality rate, estimated in mid-1992 at forty-four per 1,000 population. Life expectancy in mid-1992 was sixty-four years for males and sixty-eight years for females. The government is also expanding its education program, especially with regard to maternal and child health care. In July 1987, the country held its first workshop on acquired immune deficiency syndrome (AIDS) to increase awareness of the problem in the medical community. Contraceptives are available at private hospitals and dispensaries and through commercial outlets. Abortion is illegal except when the mother's life is endangered.

Although adequate health facilities exist in urban centers, coverage in rural areas remains insufficient. As a result, the government is continuing to develop health services as an integral part of national development. The Fourth Five-Year Development Plan (1991–95) allocated RO48 million (for value of the Omani riyal—see Glossary), which is equivalent to US$124.7 million, for this purpose. Ministry of Health plans include a 100-bed hospital in Al Buraymi and a 200-bed hospital at Ar Rustaq, southeast of Qurayyat, to replace the existing medical facility in Ar Rustaq and to serve as a central, referral hospital for the region. Other projects include replacing all outpatient clinics at the Royal Hospital polyclinic in the capital and building a new 200-bed hospital at Ibri and a 200-bed hospital at Tanam, in the interior north of Ibri.

The Economy

Omani economic development may be divided into three phases: a period of rapid expansion between 1970 and 1986; economic retrenchment and rationalization between 1986 and 1989 as a result of the 1985–86 oil price collapse; and a period of stabilized growth since 1990. Economic growth and structural change have proceeded rapidly in Oman during the rule of Sultan Qabus ibn Said. Oman, however, lagged behind such neighboring gulf amirates as Kuwait and the UAE as a result of the late discovery of oil, financial constraints, and political instability in the first half of the 1970s. Nonetheless, increased government expenditure as a result of the commercial production and export of oil transformed the standard of living in Oman. By the latter half of the 1980s, Oman emerged as a middle-income country after entering the development process as one of the poorest Arab states. Per capita income rose from US$360 in 1970 to US$3,140 in 1980 and to US$7,000 in 1991.

When Sultan Qabus ibn Said assumed power in 1970, he immediately implemented an economic development and modernization program. Priority was given to expanding the country's almost nonexistent infrastructure. In the early 1970s, substantial progress was made in developing physical and social infrastructure, mainly in the form of roads, a new deepwater port, an international airport, electricity-generating plants, desalination plants, and schools, hospitals, and low-cost housing. Government revenue derived almost exclusively from oil receipts made this possible.

Economic growth was accompanied by uneven structural development, however. In 1960 agriculture accounted for 75 percent of the gross domestic product (GDP—see Glossary); by Oman's fiscal year 1991, its share had fallen to less than 3 percent. By contrast, industry (including petroleum), which accounted for only 8 percent of GDP in 1960, increased to 59 percent by 1985. Manufacturing increased only from 1 percent to 3 percent and services from 18 percent to 38 percent in the same period.

As a result, in 1993 Oman's economy was dominated by the petroleum and the services sectors. Aware of the vulnerability produced by dependency on a depletable natural resource, the government has increased funding for sectors based on renewable natural resources that can provide sustainable economic growth. The government is concentrating on the agriculture and fishing sectors, encouraging tourism, and constructing light industrial parks with the objective of exporting consumer goods to its Gulf Cooperation Council (GCC) partners.

Public Finance and the Five-Year Development Plans

Prior to 1970, the financial position of the sultan was virtually synonymous with the public finances of the sultanate. After Qabus ibn Said's accession to the throne, a formal separation was initiated. The first government budget was announced in 1971, and the First Five-Year Development Plan was initiated in 1976.

After recovering somewhat in 1987 after the collapse of oil prices in 1986, government revenue fell again in 1988 to RO1,198 million (see table 33, Appendix). Iraq's invasion of Kuwait resulted in a sharp rise in oil prices: average crude oil spot prices increased from US$16 per barrel in July 1990 to almost US$40 per barrel in September. Higher oil prices resulted in increased 1990 oil revenues, up 38 percent from 1989. The restoration of the Al Sabah monarchy in Kuwait and the defeat of Iraqi forces by an allied coalition stabilized the international oil market's uncertainty about supplies, and prices collapsed to precrisis levels. Omani government revenues dropped to RO1,570 million in 1991, from RO1,859 million in 1990. The government budget for 1992 was based on an estimate that total revenues would increase to RO1,628 million as a result of slightly higher oil income and as a result of increases in gas revenues and other domestic indirect taxes.

Although the government stresses investment, government expenditures are largely current expenditures, suggesting the importance the government places on maintaining its security, against both internal and external threats, and on its civil administration. Public corporations and ministries have provided a mechanism for income distribution and the creation of a salaried middle class. Reducing expenditures through public-sector cuts is regarded as politically sensitive and therefore has been avoided, even after the oil price collapse in the mid-1980s and the associated loss of income.

The 4.3 percent per annum increase in total expenditures after 1986 largely resulted from these concerns. Between 1987 and 1991, total government spending rose from RO1,576 to RO1,853 million. During this period, current expenditures grew at 5 percent per annum. Although barely keeping pace with domestic inflation and increasing at a slower growth rate than that of the preceding ten years—when current outlays rose at 19.7 percent per annum—maintaining domestic income and defense and security expenditures prevented any retrenchment, despite wild fluctuations in income. Capital expenditures, however, had to be reduced between 1987 and 1990 and fell by 4 percent per annum. Higher oil prices in 1991 allowed the government to boost investment spending to pre-1986 levels, with a 37 percent increase over 1990. This adjustment restored the share of capital outlays in total government spending to 23 percent, after falling to about 12 percent in 1990. The 1992 budget called for further increases in spending to RO1,876 million, of which capital expenditures were slated to rise to RO404 million, or 22 percent of the total.

With the exception of a short period in the early 1980s, the government budget has registered sizable deficits. During 1986 the deficit (RO700 million) peaked at 28 percent of GDP. It was sharply reduced during the latter half of the 1980s but has continued to hover close to 10 percent of GDP. A lag in increased spending to match the rise in oil revenues late in 1990 permitted the government almost to balance the budget. But in 1991 spending more than offset oil revenues, and the actual budget deficit rose to RO283 million, or 10 percent of GDP. The 1992 budget forecast indicated another deficit of this magnitude.

The government has financed these budget deficits by drawing down on the Contingency Fund and by small amounts of commercial borrowing. Economic difficulties have compelled the government to raise money on international capital markets. In 1986 the government received a US$500 million syndicated Euroloan, the major sponsors of which were Gulf International Bank (in which the government is a shareholder) and Chase Investment Bank. In 1988 the government obtained a Japanese yen-denominated loan valued at US$130 million and a second US$100 million loan. Balanced fiscal conditions permitted the authorities to pay some of Oman's debt outstanding in 1990. During 1991 and 1992, authorities instituted a domestic development bond scheme, which has financed roughly one-half the fiscal shortfall.

The Fourth Five-Year Development Plan (1991–95) projected government revenue at RO8,571 million, up 22.8 percent from the previous plan. Oil revenue is expected to account for more than 76 percent of total revenue and to increase by an average of about 5 percent each year, reaching RO1,785 million in 1995 on a gross basis and RO1,429 million on a net basis (that is, gross oil revenues less subventions to the State General Reserve Fund and the Contingency Fund). The plan was based on an assumed average oil price of US$20 per barrel in the five years. During the first two years of the plan, total revenues roughly kept pace with planned earnings because oil prices held at those levels.

Expenditures during the Fourth Five-Year Development Plan were set at RO9,450 million, with current expenditures accounting for 76 percent of the total, investment expenditures set at 22 percent, and additional support to the private sector set at 1.4 percent. Defense and national security and civil ministries continue to make up the bulk of current expenditures. With expenditures exceeding revenues, the government projects a cumulative deficit of RO879 million. The government plans to finance the deficit by issuing RO430 million in government bonds on the Muscat securities market and by further drawdowns on the Contingency Fund.

The State General Reserve Fund is to be strengthened by allocating 15 percent of oil revenues to the fund, up from the previous 5 percent. This policy change was made possible after the creation of the Contingency Fund in 1990, which receives 7.5 percent of net oil revenues if the oil price is US$18 to US$20 per barrel and 10 percent if the oil price rises to US$20 to US$22 per barrel. Both policies are directed toward smoothing out the effects of oil price fluctuations and reducing the economy's vulnerability to unexpected changes in the international oil market.

Foreign Trade and the Balance of Payments

Oman's exports are dominated by oil earnings. Total exports peaked in 1985 at almost US$5.0 billion before the oil price collapse in 1986. During the preceding decade, exports rose by a factor of 3.5, largely because of the higher volume of crude and refined product sales overseas and the sustained rise in international oil prices. Petroleum exports constituted 98 percent of foreign merchandise earnings in 1985. Exports declined to US$2.9 billion in 1986 but have steadily risen since then as a result of further increases in the volume of oil shipped and higher oil prices. In 1990 total exports rose to US$5.5 billion, of which oil exports were just under US$5.2 billion (see table 34, Appendix). Non-oil exports accounted for only 3.4 percent of total exports in 1990, up from 2 percent in 1986. The bulk of non-oil exports includes livestock and some metals. Oman also made considerable strides in increasing textile and mineral exports during the early 1990s. Most exports go to other Middle Eastern countries, followed by Japan and other Asian countries (see table 35, Appendix).

Domestic government expenditures and rising incomes have stimulated a steady increase in merchandise imports. Total imports rose from US$907 million in 1975 to a peak of US$3 billion in 1985 before economic retrenchment and weaker domestic economic conditions caused a slight reduction in foreign purchases. After falling to below US$2 billion in 1987, imports increased to US$3.3 billion in 1991 because of the improved oil revenue situation and the onset of the Fourth Five-Year Development Plan. Development goods, notably machinery and transportation equipment, and defense items dominate the imports profile. In 1991 machinery and transportation items constituted 42 percent of the total import bill, and other manufactured goods made up 18 percent. Oman's total food imports fell in 1991 to 18 percent from a mid-1980s average of 20 percent. Imports came mostly from other Middle Eastern countries and from Japan.

Despite the vagaries of international oil markets and sharp fluctuations in oil prices, Oman has succeeded in maintaining a surplus on its merchandise trade account, except in 1986. A deficit in the services account, however, continues to constitute a leakage in the government's external position. Workers' remittances and payments on external debt account for more than one-half of the services deficit. Although the net outflow from workers' remittances slowed after the mid-1980s because of the recessionary climate in the region and the reduction in the number of foreign workers, the value of workers' remittances constituted just under US$1 billion per annum on the balance of payments. The program of indigenization was intended to reduce this leakage, but limited local manpower skills remain a bottleneck for indigenization. Interest on the foreign debt is the second largest item of services imports. It peaked at US$320 million in 1990 but declined in 1991 as a result of lower international interest rates and some repayment of the foreign debt. Interest receipts on official and commercial bank assets abroad (totaling US$350 million in 1991) are insufficient to offset services outflows.

During the 1980s, Oman registered sizable surpluses on its current account. In 1981 the surplus reached just over US$1 billion; it tapered off rapidly thereafter with the decline in oil prices. In 1986 Oman registered a deficit just over US$1 billion on its current account, recovered to a US$784 million surplus in 1987, a smaller deficit in 1988, and a surplus in 1989. Higher oil prices in 1990 boosted the balance to a record US$1.2 billion surplus, but a rapid rise in imports and some weakening in external earnings left the current account in balance in 1991.

Before 1986 the capital account was dominated by increases in external reserves. The cumulative increase in external assets of the government was US$2.5 billion between 1978 and 1985. Despite a shrinking surplus on the current account, the government could raise foreign assets because of a sizable program of foreign borrowing and direct foreign investment, mainly in the oil sector. In 1986 the government had to reduce foreign reserves by US$612 million to fortify the capital account. This was necessary despite nearly US$765 million in loans secured on international markets. Since then, continued access to international loan markets and a steady rise in foreign direct investment, not to mention higher oil prices, have permitted the government to replenish foreign assets. At the end of 1991, the government's published foreign assets totaled US$1.6 billion; the World Bank (see Glossary) estimate of Oman's foreign debt at the end of 1990 was US$2.5 billion.

Hydrocarbon Sector

Since the first commercial field was discovered at Jibal, west of Adam, in 1962, the petroleum industry has dominated the economy. In 1991 the industry contributed about 43 percent of GDP and 82 percent of government revenues. The government's heavy reliance on crude oil export earnings to maintain its income distribution system and political stability made continued development of this sector a priority.

By early 1977, the newly organized Ministry of Petroleum, Fisheries, and Agriculture prematurely assumed that production had probably peaked at more than 350,000 barrels per day (bpd—see Glossary) and would decline. Exploration activity in the south was insignificant, deterred by political instability in the region, and production at the main fields of Petroleum Development Oman (PDO) in the north, including Jibal, was in decline (see fig. 14). The suppression of the Dhofar rebellion in the mid-1970s helped reverse an output decline. Foreign exploration companies, satisfied with the restoration of political stability, began to sign area exploration and production agreements with the government. Enhanced oil recovery (EOR) techniques at existing fields, combined with new fields coming onstream, raised average output to 708,000 bpd in 1991.

The principal problem the government faced in the early 1990s was a diminishing reserve base. Proven reserves were estimated at 4.6 billion barrels in 1992, small in comparison with other gulf states. At the mid-1992 rate of production of 725,000 bpd, Oman's crude reserves are sufficient to permit seventeen years of output, compared with nearly 350 years for Saudi Arabia.

Oil prospecting began in 1924 when the Anglo-Persian Oil Company (later renamed British Petroleum) obtained a concession; however, unsuccessful exploratory drilling discouraged further interest. Discoveries in Bahrain and Saudi Arabia during the 1930s stimulated exploration activity. The first concession agreement was signed with Petroleum Concessions, a Western consortium formed by the owners of the Iraq Petroleum Company (IPC). In 1951 the concessionaire's name was changed to Petroleum Development Oman (PDO). In 1993 PDO remained the principal operating company and controlled the bulk of oil reserves and output.

After several years of costly and unsuccessful exploratory drilling, most IPC partners wanted to withdraw from their concession area. In 1960 Royal Dutch Shell acquired an 85 percent interest in PDO; Participations and Explorations (Partex) held the remaining 15 percent share. In 1967 the French firm Total-Compagnie Française des Pétroles acquired 10 percent of Partex's 15 percent interest. In December 1973, the government of Oman, following the participation agreements negotiated by several gulf countries, acquired a 25 percent share of PDO. In July 1974, the government's stake was raised to 60 percent, retroactive to January 1, 1974. Since 1974 the remaining 40 percent has been held by Royal Dutch Shell with 34 percent, Total-Compagnie Française des Pétroles with 4 percent, and Partex with 2 percent.

PDO operates two main production areas: a group of northern oil fields, including Jibal, Fuhud, and Sayh Nuhaydah, that produce lighter grades of crude oil; and a group of southern fields, including Rima, Mamul, Amal, Nimr, Mukhaizna, and Sayyala, that produce heavier crudes. Development of the southern fields took place after the suppression of the Dhofar rebellion and the reestablishment of political stability in the sultanate.

Reserves

As of January 1992, official proven crude reserves were estimated at 4.6 billion barrels, up almost 6 percent from 1991 and up 83 percent from the oil reserve estimate in 1980. The relatively gradual increments to Oman's reserve base since 1980 were attributable to the discovery of new, smaller oil fields and revised estimates for existing fields.

More than one-half of Oman's total reserves are concentrated in the northern region, where six fields—Jibal, Natih, Fuhud, Al Huwaysah, Al Khuwayr, and Shaybikah—are part of a single geological structure containing recoverable reserves of more than 2 billion barrels. Similarly, in the south, eight principal producing fields also come from a single geological structure.

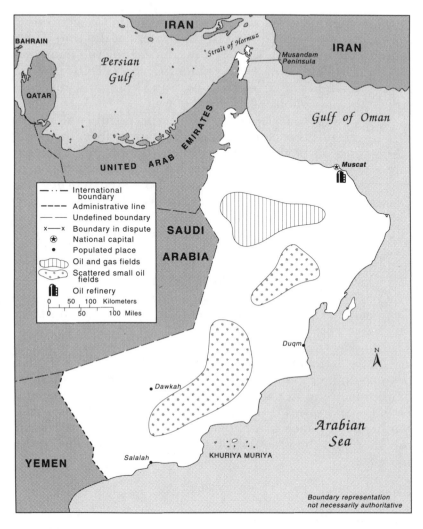

Figure 14. Oman: Oil Fields, Gas Fields, and Refineries, 1993

Several foreign companies that are engaged in exploration and production activities, such as France's Elf Aquitaine Oman, the Occidental Petroleum Corporation (Occidental Oman), and the American Oil Company (Amoco), signed agreements in the 1970s. Others, such as the Japan Exploration Company (Japex Oman) and Canada's International Petroleum, followed in 1981 and 1984, respectively.

Oil Production and Exports

During the period from 1967 to 1980, crude oil production peaked in 1976 at 365,000 bpd but subsequently declined. Producing fields are concentrated in the northern region around Jibal, Fuhud, and Natih, all three of which were discovered in the 1960s. The Dhofar rebellion inhibited exploration farther south and suspended development activity around Mamul, discovered in 1957 and holding 600 million barrels of gross proven and probable oil reserves. Because of the declining production from northern fields, total output fell. In 1979 average output was 285,000 bpd.

Once hostilities ceased in 1975 and confidence in the authority of the central government returned, southern exploration and production activities resumed, facilitating new discoveries in the late 1970s and 1980s. The Rima field, with gross proven and probable reserves estimated at 270 million barrels, was discovered in 1979; Amal, with 145 million barrels of reserves, was discovered in 1982; and Mukhaizna, with 130 million barrels, was discovered in 1985. All were brought onstream by PDO. As a result, oil output increased throughout the 1980s. Crude oil production averaged 708,000 bpd in 1991, compared with 685,000 bpd in 1990 (see table 36, Appendix). Output for 1992 averaged 745,000 bpd. Most of this, about 670,000 to 680,000 bpd, was lifted by PDO. According to Minister of Petroleum and Minerals Said Ahmad ash Shanfari, there are plans to maintain output at that level into the twenty-first century.

Apart from PDO, which contributes the bulk of the output, three other groups have interests in the producing fields. These are Occidental Oman (28,000 bpd), Elf Aquitaine Oman (15,000 bpd), and Japex Oman (8,000 bpd).

To maintain output at current levels and avoid future declines, the government is pursuing a two-pronged strategy of developing smaller fields and applying EOR and secondary techniques at existing fields. The strategy appears successful because 1992 was the twelfth consecutive year in which production increased. However, a pattern has emerged whereby the number of fields discovered holding large (greater than 500 million barrels of gross proven and probable) reserves has been declining. The potential for discovering fields with a reserve base and production rates comparable to Jibal appears remote, given Oman's mature exploration history.

EOR techniques are applied to the mature fields. In the north, additional wells have been drilled, and water injection facilities have been constructed at the Jibal field. Gas injection is used at Fuhud and Natih. At Mamul, in the south, high-pressure steam injection techniques have been used since 1985.

Most of the increase in output will come from PDO's Al Khuwayr field in north-central Oman, where a US$500 million development project was designed to increase the field's output from 25,000 bpd to more than 120,000 bpd when completed in 1993. The project involves gas lift and water injection facilities. Output will compensate for falling output from existing producing fields. Apart from the pilot waterflood project at Al Khuwayr, near Izki, the Sayh Nuhaydah gas-condensate field is a potential candidate for an analogous waterflood development program.

More than 90 percent of oil production is exported. The majority of Oman's exports are destined for the Far East market. Japan, the Republic of Korea (South Korea), Singapore, China, Taiwan, Thailand, and the Philippines accounted for 85 percent of total crude exports in 1990. Japan accounted for 40 percent of total exports, South Korea for 26 percent, and Singapore for 7 percent. Less than 7 percent of crude exports was destined for the United States market.

All crude oil from the northern and southern fields is collected and blended into Omani export blend. The country's only refinery and terminal is at Mina al Fahl, near Muscat. The refinery, completed in 1982 with an initial throughput capacity of 50,000 bpd and expanded to 80,000 bpd in 1987, was designed to meet domestic demand for petroleum products. Operated by the Oman Oil Refinery Company, in which the Ministry of Petroleum and Minerals holds a 99 percent share and the Central Bank of Oman holds 1 percent, the refinery produces liquefied petroleum gas (LPG), butane, jet fuel, and two grades of gasoline.

Foreign Downstream Ventures

The Oman Oil Company (OOC), established in the late 1980s, is responsible for the government's foreign petroleum activities. The board of directors consists of former government officials and private advisers and is responsible to the Ministry of Petroleum and Minerals. The OOC engages in international oil trading, including the purchase and sale of Omani crude oil, and in acquiring foreign downstream (see Glossary) holdings. Acquiring foreign downstream holdings is the most recent development in the ministry's oil policies, lagging behind such other Arab oil producers as Kuwait, Saudi Arabia, and Libya, which have actively pursued foreign downstream ventures to ensure a secure market for crude oil sales.

As of late 1992, the OOC was negotiating equity interest in a foreign downstream venture, the acquisition of a 20 percent stake in Thailand's fifth refinery, in Rayong Province in the south. The refinery is designed to process up to 120,000 bpd of crude and will cost US$600 million. Operations are scheduled to begin in 1996 and will involve Oman's supplying part of the refinery's feedstock. Also, as a member of a consortium including Chevron Corporation of the United States, the OOC has committed itself to build an export pipeline to transport oil from the Tengiz and Korolyov fields in Kazakhstan to international markets. The pipeline complements an agreement signed on June 18, 1992, by the government of Oman with Kazakhstan for exploration and production of oil and gas in the former Soviet republic. The Tengiz and Korolyov fields are said to have a potential output of 700,000 bpd by 2010.

Gas Development and Production

The depletion of the sultanate's crude oil reserves accelerated the government's bid to increase the use of gas in electric power generation and industry. In the early 1970s, the sultanate began to use gas in electric power generation. Gas pipelines were laid, and generators were converted from diesel to gas. This was done in the Muscat metropolitan area just before the second oil price shock despite resistance by importers of diesel. Plans were to increase gas use by extending the government gas grid linking the south and the east to the north. Power generation facilities north of Muscat in 1992 were using gas as a feedstock, and plans were to increase gas-fired units elsewhere.

Although the government has promoted the industrial use of gas, oil firms remain the principal consumers, using a total of 8.5 million cubic meters per day of associated gas. Gas is required for reinjection, compression fuel, and power generation to support facilities at producing fields. This is likely to continue in the short term, given the slow pace of switching industrial use from petroleum. The government's focus in the 1990s on exploiting natural gas reserves and increasing output to meet rising demand complements its priority in maintaining current oil output levels. It seeks to do this without depleting crude reserves by using gas produced in association with oil output for reinjection at mature fields to increase production and, by substituting gas for oil, to release greater volumes of crude oil for export.

On February 8, 1992, the Ministry of Petroleum and Minerals signed a cooperation protocol with Royal Dutch Shell for a comprehensive evaluation of Oman's gas reserves, estimated in June 1992 at 482 billion cubic meters, the bulk of which is in nonassociated form. According to the minister of petroleum and minerals, some studies indicate a reserve base as high as 935 million cubic meters. A preliminary feasibility study conducted by Royal Dutch Shell indicated the potential for exploiting gas reserves at a rate of 142,000 cubic meters per year as exports over a twenty-year period and for meeting domestic demand for the next fifty years.

Most of the gas produced is in associated form and comes from PDO's Jibal field; smaller volumes come from the Natih and Sayh Nuhaydah fields in northern Oman and the Birba field in the south. Gas plants have been constructed in Jibal, Fuhud, Sayh Nuhaydah, Sayyala, and Rima, providing Oman with a gas-processing capacity of almost 18 million cubic meters per day. Despite increased gas production, gas throughput at these plants ran at about one-half of total capacity in 1989.

Evaluation of the commercial viability of the northern offshore Bukha natural gas and condensate field, discovered in 1986 by its concession operator, the International Petroleum Company of Canada, was completed in June 1992. The company estimates the life expectancy of the Bukha field at fifteen years, a capacity of 28 million cubic meters per day of gas and 5,000 to 10,000 bpd of condensate, and a requirement of an approximately US$60 million capital investment to bring the field onstream. Production was scheduled to begin in 1993.

The government planned to drill wells in the central fields (Sayh Rawl, Sayh Nuhaydah, Barik, and Mabruk) at a cost of RO47 million (US$18 million) between 1992 and 1995. Output from these structures will supply the US$9 billion LNG project, which was finalized on May 6, 1992, by a memorandum of understanding. In this project, the government will be responsible for all upstream (see Glossary) activities. A new consortium was established, comprising the Omani government at 51 percent, PDO's foreign shareholders (Royal Dutch Shell, Total-Compagnie Française des Pétroles, and Partex) at 42 percent, and three Japanese firms (Mitsubishi, Mitsui, and C. Itoh) at the remaining 7 percent, undertaking downstream operations under a service contract. Deliveries of LNG are not expected to begin before 1999. The Japanese market is expected to be the most probable destination for output.

If increasing volumes of gas are lifted, the government may consider new gas-based industries such as methanol, fertilizers, and methyl tertiary-butyl ester (MTBE). During 1992 talks were conducted with Iran concerning joint development of the Bukha and Henjam offshore fields, where limited drilling has indicated a gas and gas liquids potential. Omani officials have also conducted talks with Qatar regarding the purchase of natural gas from Qatar's North Field. The proposal to build a gas line from Qatar to Dubayy may be expanded to include a spur line to Oman. Minister of Petroleum and Minerals Shanfari indicated that Oman is prepared to purchase a volume up to 113 million cubic meters per day of gas from Qatar if an acceptable price can be negotiated. The regional gas line proposal was being considered among gulf countries for much of the 1980s. As of early 1993, a definitive decision on a regional (Arabian Peninsula) coordinated, long-term gas plan that would rationalize supply and demand for decades had not been completed.

Agriculture and Fishing

The government's economic development policy emphasizes the expansion of such non-oil sectors as agriculture, fishing, industry, and mining in its bid to diversify the economy and diminish its dependence on oil exports. The goal is to establish a sustainable economic base in preparation for the time when hydrocarbon reserves are depleted. The government launched several economic campaigns, naming 1988 and 1989 as Years of Agriculture and 1991 and 1992 as Years of Industry. Through these campaigns, the government has encouraged private-sector investment by allocating generous amounts of cash support for private industry to be disbursed mainly through official development banks. For example, the Oman Bank for Agriculture and Fisheries, created in 1981, extends loans at concessionary rates to individuals for whom farming or fishing is the principal activity. The bank acts as a distributive institution, receiving an interest subsidy from the government. In 1990 there were 1,308 loans, totaling RO4.7 million. Development programs also incorporate the government's policy of indigenization, with a large component of funds allocated for domestic technical training and academic training, often in the United States or in developing countries.

Agriculture

Oman has five distinct agricultural regions. Going roughly from north to south, they include the Musandam Peninsula, the Al Batinah coast, the valleys and the high plateau of the eastern region, the interior oasés, and the Dhofar region, along the narrow coastal strip from the border with Yemen to Ras Naws and the mountains to the north.

In the early 1990s, interior farming areas accounted for more than one-half of the country's cultivated land. Rainfall, although greater in the interior than along the coast, is insufficient for growing crops. Most of the water for irrigation is obtained through the *falaj* system, in which a vertical shaft is dug from the surface to reach water in porous rock. From the bottom of this shaft, a gently sloping tunnel is dug to tap the water and allow it to flow to a point on the surface at a lower level or into a cistern or underground pool from which it can be lifted by bucket or pump.

A *falaj* may be many kilometers in length and require numerous additional vertical shafts to provide fresh air to the workers digging the tunnels and to permit the removal of the excavated rock and soil. A *falaj* requires tremendous expenditure of labor for maintenance as well as for construction. Because private maintenance efforts during the 1970s and early 1980s proved inadequate, the government initiated repair and maintenance of the *falaj* system to increase the quantity of water available to cultivated areas.

The cooler climate on the high plateau of the Al Jabal al Akhdar enables the growing of apricots, grapes, peaches, and walnuts. The Al Batinah coastal plain accounts for about two-fifths of the land area under cultivation and is the most concentrated farming area of the country. Annual rainfall along the coast is minimal, but moisture falling on the mountains percolates through permeable strata to the coastal strip, providing a source of underground water only about two meters below the surface. Diesel motors are used to pump water for irrigation from these shallow wells.

By the mid-1980s, the water table along the Al Batinah coast had dropped to a low level, and salinity of the wells had increased, significantly reducing the water quality. This was caused by the combined effect of cultivating land too close to the sea and pumping more well water than was being recharged by nature, thereby permitting seawater to encroach.

Falaj Alin at Al Jabal al Akhdar; the falaj *is an ancient underground channel used for irrigation in Oman.*
Al Jabal al Akhdar, showing terraced farming in one of Oman's main agricultural areas
Courtesy Embassy of the Sultanate of Oman, Washington

Overfarming and attendant water problems caused the government to establish the Ministry of Water Resources in 1990 with the mandate of limiting water consumption and improving irrigation. A freeze on new wells was imposed in addition to delimiting several "no drill zones" in areas where groundwater supplies are low. The ministry is also considering the installation of water meters. Recharge dams are designed to hold rainwater in the wadis for a period of time to facilitate the trickling of water down into the ground; replenishing aquifers have been built mainly in the northeastern Al Batinah region, where the groundwater levels are up to five meters below sea level.

Apart from water problems, the agricultural sector has been affected by rural-urban migration, in which the labor force has been attracted to the higher wages of industry and the government service sector, and by competition from highly subsidized gulf producers. As a result, agriculture and fishing have declined in relative sectoral importance. In 1967 the two sectors together contributed about 34 percent of GDP; by 1991 they accounted for 3.8 percent of GDP (see table 37, Appendix). The government encourages farming by distributing land, offering subsidized loans to purchase machinery, offering free feedstock, and giving advice on modern irrigation methods. As a result, the area under cultivation has increased, with an accompanying rise in production. But extensive agricultural activity has also depleted freshwater reserves and underground aquifers and has increased salinity.

The area under cultivation increased by almost 18 percent to 57,814 hectares over the period from 1985 to 1990. Fruits were grown on 64 percent, or 36,990 hectares, of the area under cultivation in crop year 1989–90. Dates accounted for 45 percent of the total area, or 70 percent of the area under fruit cultivation. Grains such as barley, wheat, and corn accounted for 19.2 percent, or 11,092 hectares, and vegetables accounted for 16.8 percent, or 9,732 hectares, of the total area under cultivation.

In the same five-year period, overall agricultural production increased by 3 percent to 699,000 tons. Field crops, largely alfalfa, accounted for more than one-half of total production, or 354,300 tons, a 40 percent increase in the five-year period. Fruit production (including dates and limes) was 182,400 tons, up from 154,500 tons. Vegetable production totaled 162,300 tons, an increase of almost 50 percent.

Fishing

Historically, fishing was second only to farming as an economic activity in pre-oil Oman. Both the Gulf of Oman and the Arabian Sea offer a variety of catch, including sardines, bluefish, mackerel, shark, tuna, abalone, lobsters, and oysters. Fishermen harvest their catch in the waters near the coast, using the traditional, small seagoing canoe, to which an outboard motor has been added.

The fishing sector (along with agriculture) is considered one of the most promising areas for commercial attention and accounts for the highest non-oil export revenue. However, sales in 1990 totaled RO17.3 million, dwarfed by oil export earnings of RO1.9 billion. The GCC provided the largest fish export market. The fishing sector also provided employment opportunities to 19,296 registered fishermen in 1990, of whom 18,546 were employed in traditional fisheries and 750 in industrial fisheries. Like agriculture, fishing has been affected by the diminishing number of people employed in the sector. As increasing numbers of fishermen turn to more remunerative employment, there has been a gradual decrease in the amount of fish caught.

The government has stressed modernizing and expanding the fishing industry and developing its export potential. The Joint United States-Oman Commission funded the Oman Fisheries Development and Management Project to strengthen the technical, administrative, and management skills of the Directorate General of Fisheries Resources (DGFR). In strengthening the DGFR, the government hopes to increase private-sector confidence in the fishing industry and, in the long term, to create private-sector-led development of the industry.

The government is following a dual strategy—internally, to improve the capacity of the DGFR to manage Oman's fishing resources and, externally, to provide incentives for fishermen to remain in their occupations. The government provides subsidies to purchase fiberglass boats and outboard engines; to construct workshops, cold storage facilities, and jetties along the coastline; and to establish companies to market fish both domestically and internationally.

Non-oil Minerals

The sultanate produces copper, chromite, gold, and silver. Oman's main copper reserves are in the Suhar area on the Al Batinah coast. The processing of ore at the Suhar complex, operated by the government-owned Oman Mining Company, began in 1983. The production of chromite by the Oman Mining Company also began in 1983 in the Suhar area. Exports of the Oman Mining Company are primarily destined to the Far East market. In 1990 Taiwan accounted for 38.5 percent of exports, followed by Japan with 11.1 percent and South Korea with 2.9 percent.

In July 1991, the government established the Oman Chrome Company (OCC), in which it holds a 15 percent share. The remainder of the shares are held by the private sector. The OCC was created to develop the country's chromite reserves— estimated by the Robertson Group of Britain and the Bureau des Recherches Géologiques et Minières of France at 2 million tons of chromite—at 600 sites throughout the country. The public offering of OCC shares reflects the government's official policy of encouraging private-sector participation in industry and manufacturing.

Limestone for cement production is mined in both the northern and the southern areas to supply the Oman Cement Company's plant in the Rusayl Industrial Estate near As Sib and the Raysut Cement Corporation's plant near Salalah. Tile and marble are also produced for local construction.

Surveys have indicated deposits of numerous other materials—asbestos, coal, iron ore, lead, manganese, nickel, silver, and zinc. Large deposits of metal ores are located at the Sayh Hatat area (northeast of Izki) and the Al Jabal al Akhdar area. Substantial deposits of zinc and lead are known to exist in Dhofar, Jalan, and Hawshi Huqf (southwest of Al Ghabah). The feasibility of exploiting coal reserves at Al Kamil, near Sur, to replace oil in electric power generation, is being studied. A preliminary study on coal completed in 1990 by the UN Department of Technical Cooperation for Development estimates coal reserves in the sultanate at 22 million tons, a figure considered adequate for domestic use but not for export.

Industry

The government's program to diversify from the oil industry emphasizes the industrial sector, with a steady increase in small and medium-sized industries based on heavily subsidized industrial parks. The first industrial estate, at Ar Rusayl, fifteen kilometers from As Sib International Airport, was developed in the mid-1980s and housed about sixty enterprises, including manufacturers of cement, soap, crackers, and copper cathodes. The

Copper mine near Suhar; copper has been mined in Oman since ancient times.
View of multiple-highway system near Al Khuwayr, linking the sultanate's major cities
Courtesy Embassy of the Sultanate of Oman, Washington

287

sultanate's second industrial estate, a 100-hectare site at Raysut, was developed in the early 1990s by the local firm of Shanfari and Partners. The sultanate's third industrial estate is a planned fifty-hectare project at Suhar. Other estates are planned at Nazwah, Sur, Al Khasab, and the Al Buraymi Oasis. The government is also studying the feasibility of establishing cottage industries to produce such items as pottery, rose water, and frankincense. As a result of these efforts, by 1991 manufacturing contributed 3.5 percent of Oman's GDP.

A few small-scale traditional industries use primitive methods, such as in the production of ghee (clarified butter) and the drying of fish, dates, and limes. Some handicraft industries remain, but their importance is steadily being eclipsed. Silversmiths practice their trade, and artisans work with clay at Bahla, just west of Adam, an important center for the production of household pottery. Goldsmiths follow their trade in the Muscat metropolitan area and its environs. In several regions, workers fashion low-quality, hand-made cloth from locally produced wool. The coastal towns remain boat-building centers.

Whereas the industrial sector during the 1970s and 1980s was aimed at import-substitution industrialization (see Glossary), the objective in the 1990s is to encourage export industries for the Persian Gulf market. However, this assumes that Oman will be able to operate effectively in an increasingly competitive market, attract foreign investors, and increase the role of private-sector industry.

To increase its ability to compete with its Persian Gulf neighbors, particularly Dubayy, where the Mina Jabal Ali Duty-Free Zone permits fully owned foreign subsidiaries, Oman needs to overhaul its commercial and economic laws. The Ministry of Commerce and Industry set up three working teams in early 1992 to recommend amendments to existing laws for discussion with the Oman Chamber of Commerce and Industry (OCCI) and the Consultative Council. The government revised laws to permit GCC nationals to own up to 49 percent of the shares in twenty specified Omani companies, ten of which are banks. The OCCI has introduced an industrial consultations unit, computer-linked with the Vienna-based United Nations Industrial Development Organization, offering investment advice on twenty industrial sectors as well as data on equipment suppliers and training needs.

Tourism

The government promotes tourism, consistent with its policy of economic diversification, with emphasis on the Muscat metropolitan area and on coastal towns where principal hotels are located. The Ministry of National Heritage and Culture is restoring historical sites at Muscat and in the coastal towns. The forts at Nazwah, Ar Rustaq, Al Hazm, Bidbid, and Jabrin in the interior are accessible by automobile.

Oman has seven international hotels, the majority located in the Muscat metropolitan area. AZD Enterprises, set up by Qais ibn Tariq Al Said, Sultan Qabus ibn Said's first cousin, is planning a new tourism project at Bandar Jissah, a weekend coastal retreat in the north. The site of the planned hotel and sports facilities, including a large golf course, will be near the Al Bustan Palace Hotel, the most luxurious hotel in Oman.

Transportation

The Omani transportation system, as with virtually all the sultanate's physical infrastructure, is a post-1970 development. It includes an expanding highway network, two modern deepwater ports, an oil port at Mina al Fahl, and an international airport facilitating international, intraregional, and domestic service. By 1992 there were 6,000 kilometers of paved roads and 20,000 kilometers of gravel or earthen roads, in a contrast to 1970, when there was one ten-kilometer paved highway and limited coastal and air traffic.

The sultanate's modern transportation system links all significant populated places within Oman and gives easy access to many international destinations. A four-lane highway runs west from Muscat along the Gulf of Oman to Dubayy in the UAE. A second major paved highway in the interior connects locations from just east of Al Ayn in the UAE to Salalah on Oman's south coast. Good land connections link Oman only with the UAE, however. No roads extend across the Saudi or Yemeni borders. The sultanate's principal airport, As Sib International Airport, has regularly scheduled flights to numerous cities worldwide and also to five domestic destinations. Muscat's natural harbor has long been a haven for ships, and its port facilities are among the best in the eastern part of the Arabian Peninsula.

Transportation planning and administration, with the exception of the Muscat metropolitan area highways, are administered by the Ministry of Communications through the northern and southern directorates general of roads. The Development Council is responsible for recommending and monitoring overall sectoral objectives and priorities and reports directly to the Council of Ministers. Laying pipelines and certain roads and port facilities related to oil production are under the direction of PDO.

With the major infrastructure in place by the mid-1980s, there was a shift from construction to maintenance and improvement of the existing network. Until 1984 ministry budgets reflected a marginal outlay for maintenance as a result of the relatively new paved road system. However, starting in 1984, maintenance of paved roads became important, and a program of bituminous surface treatment and regraveling was begun. The emphasis in the early 1990s has been on maintaining and upgrading the present highway infrastructure, but the government continues to allocate substantial resources to the development plan for the Muscat metropolitan area, where severe urban traffic problems are being addressed by the construction of interchanges and expansion of some highways to four-lane systems.

Further expansion of the existing transportation system includes enlarging both As Sib International Airport and Mina Qabus, the port near Muscat. Mina Qabus is expected to be inadequate to accommodate the projected increase in cargo traffic by the year 2000. An expansion project is designed to increase port capacity from 1.6 million tons to 2.6 million tons. The project involves converting two berths to container berths, building a new berth for the Royal Yacht Squadron, creating a storage area, and building a sea wall. The expansion is partially funded by the Kuwait Fund for Arab Economic Development. The possibility of a port at Suhar, to be used as a transshipment site for destinations farther up the gulf, is under consideration.

Telecommunications

Modern telecommunications facilities were introduced in 1975, but major investment in such facilities occurred only after 1982. In 1989 the sultanate had almost 87,000 telephones, or about 6.8 telephones per 100 inhabitants, a figure considerably lower than for Oman's Persian Gulf neighbors. Service is unevenly distributed; more than 50 percent of the telephones are in the Muscat area. Service is entirely automatic, with international direct dial available to all customers.

International telecommunications to Europe, Asia, and the Americas go via a satellite ground station, working with the International Telecommunications Satellite Corporation's (Intelsat) Indian Ocean satellite. Calls to other countries in the region are routed through a ground station linked to the Arab Satellite Communication Organization (Arabsat) satellite. A third system of eight ground stations is used for domestic calls.

In 1992 broadcast facilities were limited. Television service was more widespread than radio. There are only two AM radio stations, one in Muscat and one in Salalah, and three FM radio stations, two in Muscat and the other in Al Khasab in northernmost Oman. A powerful shortwave station that broadcasts in Arabic and English can be received worldwide. Television service is available throughout the country; seven large transmitters are located in major towns, and twenty-five smaller relay stations broadcast in rural areas.

The government's priorities in the 1990s are to expand the local telephone facilities in existing telephone switching centers, to provide telephone service to rural communities without service, and to expand domestic long-distance and international telephone facilities. The Fourth Five-Year Development Plan allocated RO93 million (US$242 million) to telecommunications projects. Plans of the state-owned General Telecommunications Organization include launching public paging, data communications, and telephone expansion services.

Labor

A foreign work force was the key to the development of Oman's physical and administrative infrastructure. In 1992 about 60 percent of the labor force consisted of foreigners. However, indigenization is among the government's principal priorities. Only 23 percent of the private-sector work force is Omani, whereas the public-sector work force is dominated by Omani nationals. In 1990 Omanis made up 80 percent of public corporation employees, 52 percent of diwan, or court, employees, and 65 percent of the civil service. In certain organizations and ministries—such as the Oman News Agency and the ministries of foreign affairs; interior; justice, *awqaf* [religious endowments], and Islamic affairs; national heritage and culture; and social affairs and labor—Omanis exceed 90 percent of the work force.

In the banking sector, 70.8 percent of the work force was Omani in 1990; in the oil sector, it was 61.0 percent, with a large disparity between producing and nonproducing companies. Of PDO's work force, 61.0 percent was Omani, compared with 53.4 percent of Elf Aquitaine Oman, 20.0 percent of Occidental Oman, and 21.0 percent of Japex Oman (see Hydrocarbon Sector, this ch.). In non-oil-producing companies, Omanis averaged 31.6 percent of the work force. In 1990 only 24.0 percent of insurance-sector workers and 19.0 percent of hotel-sector workers were Omanis.

The government hopes that an increasing number of Omanis will enter trade and industry, increasing the number of Omanis in the private sector to 45.2 percent by 1995. RO40 million (US$104 million) was allocated to training in 1990, with the intent of training 100,000 individuals and creating 160,000 job opportunities. In March 1991, the Higher Committee for Vocational Training and Labor was established to generate employment for Omanis and to establish other policies for the indigenous and foreign work force.

Institution building has been largely a foreign initiative. The professional core of the civil administration has consisted mainly of British and United States citizens, influencing the development of ministries, the judiciary, development planning, and resource management. The dependency on foreign advisers in the 1990s is likely to grow, given increasing Western, notably United States, involvement in the gulf after Operation Desert Shield and Operation Desert Storm, particularly in defense and security areas. Also, the emphasis of the Joint United States-Oman Commission on institution building and privatization has resulted in sustained foreign influence in the sultanate (see International Relations, this ch.).

The government not only faces a skills barrier to its indigenization program but also a psychological obstacle. As a result of the initiation of a civil administrative structure, a sense of entitlement has arisen in the public psyche. By ensuring positions in the public sector for Omani nationals, the government inadvertently created the notion that it was the universal provider for its citizens. This notion may be difficult to reverse and perhaps will become a source of political instability if the government proves unable to fulfill its obligations should an economic downturn and consequent financial difficulties occur.

Water and Power

The country's water resources are a key to its economic

future, and continued development will require much more water than has been available. Rainfall is so scant that crop production is impossible without irrigation. Livestock raising is restricted to areas having a dependable supply of drinking water for animals. Any substantial expansion of agricultural production will therefore require developing new water sources. Industrial expansion, increased tourism, and an improved standard of living combine to increase the requirements for water.

In the 1990s, water sources include wells for village water supplies, the *falaj* system, and desalination plants. Although the Muscat metropolitan area, Salalah, and Raysut are supplied with adequate water distribution and sewerage systems, such systems remain underdeveloped in many rural areas.

In 1969 Oman had only one electric power generating station, which produced one megawatt of electricity for the Muscat metropolitan area. Since then, electricity has been introduced in an increasing number of areas: Salahin in 1970; the island of Masirah in 1976; and Nazwah, As Sahm, and Ibri in 1978. In 1990 in the sultanate, 4,503 million kilowatt-hours were produced in comparison with 787 million kilowatt-hours in 1980. The Muscat metropolitan area represents 67.4 percent of the sultanate's electricity consumption, followed by the Al Batinah area at 14.7 percent and Dhofar at 9.4 percent. The government's diversification program and its plans to develop infrastructure across the country to balance economic development and to correct the regional disparities between the less developed south and interior and the more developed north require greater attention to water and power. Several large infrastructure projects are being considered in the Fourth Five-Year Development Plan: a new power station and grid network for the interior; improvement in Muscat's sewerage network; and construction of another desalination plant, which was completed by 1992. However, the water problem requires greater attention to the management of existing installations.

Banking

The Omani banking sector is largely the product of a November 1974 banking law that established the Central Bank of Oman (CBO), effective April 1975. The law also facilitated the entry of foreign-owned banks and permitted an increase in the number of local banks in the sultanate. As of September 1992, there were twenty-one commercial banks in comparison with three registered in 1972. In addition, there were three specialized development banks: the Oman Development Bank (1977); the Oman Housing Bank (1977); and the Oman Bank for Agriculture and Fisheries (1981). However, the Omani banking market is the smallest in the GCC. Of the twenty-one commercial banks, eleven are foreign owned and concentrate primarily on financing trade. Ten are local banks operating in an increasingly competitive market. Because of competition, the government seeks to encourage consolidation. The expectation is that five or six local banks will emerge as the core, with those facing financial difficulties ceasing operations or merging with more profitable institutions. A similar pattern may apply to foreign banks, of which only five or six would continue to undertake significant business.

The CBO effectively replaces the Oman Currency Board, which was created in 1972 to issue currency, manage government accounts, and execute banking transactions with commercial banks and international institutions. A board of governors appointed by the sultan manages the CBO. The board's responsibilities include management of the government's foreign assets. The CBO is empowered to make advances to the government to cover temporary deficiencies in current revenues; to purchase government treasury notes and securities with a maximum maturity of ten years; to make advances to commercial banks; and to buy, sell, discount, and rediscount commercial paper. In 1991 the banking law was amended to empower the CBO to withdraw the license or suspend the activities of banks under its jurisdiction, allowing the CBO to liquidate, reorganize, or manage a bank directly.

The CBO exercised these expanded powers with regard to the takeover of the Bank of Credit and Commerce International (BCCI) branches in the sultanate. BCCI was incorporated in Luxembourg in 1972 and established a presence in Oman in July 1974. After 1974 it expanded its local operations to include twelve branches having total assets of RO67 million (US$174 million) as against total deposit liabilities of RO57 million (US$148 million). Gross mismanagement of assets resulted in a decision by central banks of various countries to freeze BCCI operations on July 5, 1991. Accordingly, the CBO suspended BCCI operations in the sultanate on July 6, 1991, and its board of governors offered BCCI branches for sale to locally incorporated banks. An agreement was signed with Bank Dhofar al Omani al Fransi, effective February 15, 1992, to assume all assets and liabilities of BCCI Oman. Bank Dhofar al Omani al Fransi received a grant of RO15 million to cover BCCI's frozen assets abroad and a guarantee of RO4 million against future claims. The arrangement made Bank Dhofar al Omani al Fransi the second largest capitalized bank in the sultanate. The sale did not affect the National Bank of Oman, the largest bank in the sultanate, in which BCCI was a 40 percent shareholder.

In 1992 this sale was the most recent in a series of restructuring arrangements of the Omani banking market. The Union Bank of Oman was restructured in June 1990 and thereafter was called the Omani European Bank. Kuwaiti institutions lost their shares in the bank, the shares of France's Banque Indosuez increased, and several Omani groups held the remaining shares: Zubair Enterprises, Royal Oman Police Pension Trust, Oman International Development and Investment Company, Oman Aviation Services, and the Port Services Corporation. In January 1989, the Bank of Muscat purchased the assets and liabilities of the Oman Banking Corporation, which itself was a product of the restructuring of the Bank of Oman and the Gulf.

Consumer loans rose to 31.3 percent of total loans in 1990 from 18.8 percent in 1985. There was an accompanying decline in the share of construction and trade to 44.8 percent from 57.3 percent in the same period, reflecting the shift in commercial bank lending from commerce and real estate to personal loans. The decline also indicated the different development needs within the sultanate. During the early 1980s, large-scale infrastructural growth prompted banks to extend loan facilities for construction and real estate. The 1986 oil price collapse and the subsequent economic retrenchment contributed to repayment difficulties, and nonperforming loans diminished the net profits of banks.

In its declared interest in promoting mergers in the banking industry, in 1991 the government placed a ceiling on the amount banks could lend to their directors. Banks could lend up to 15 percent of their net capital to related individuals or their business interests, in comparison with the previous ceiling of 20 percent. An amendment to the 1974 banking law announced in May 1992, increasing the minimum required capitalization for banks to RO10 million for local banks and RO3 million for branches of foreign banks, was similarly designed to encourage mergers and rationalization of the banking sector.

The three specialized development banks serve as mechanisms to promote government policies of economic diversification, private-sector development, and indigenization of the work force. The Oman Housing Bank is a joint venture developed by the government, Kuwait's Ministry of Finance, and the Oman Development Bank. In 1991 the Oman Housing Bank recorded a net profit of RO4.1 million (US$10.7 million), as compared with RO3.4 million (US$8.8 million) the previous year.

The Oman Development Bank extends loans to industrial development projects. The government holds 40 percent of the shares, and regional and foreign institutions hold 40 percent; the remaining 20 percent is open for private Omani subscription. In March 1991, the bank offered five- to six-year interest-free loans of up to RO50,000 (US$131,600) for establishing small businesses if all employees were Omanis. Businesses employing foreigners were to be levied 3 percent interest.

The government holds 98 percent of the capital of the Oman Bank for Agriculture and Fisheries, which, as its name implies, is authorized to extend loans to individuals or enterprises to finance activities in agriculture and fishing. By March 31, 1992, the bank had thirteen operating branches.

Government and Politics

Historical Patterns of Governance

Until 1970 the political title for the Al Said rulers was sultan of Muscat and Oman, implying two historically irreconcilable political cultures: the coastal tradition, the more cosmopolitan, secular, Muscat tradition of the coast ruled by the sultan; and the interior tradition of insularity, tribal in origin and ruled by an imam according to the theological tenets of Ibadism (see Religion, this ch.). The more cosmopolitan has been the ascending political culture since the founding of the Al Said dynasty in 1744, although the imamate tradition has found intermittent expression.

Several millennia ago, Arab tribes migrated eastward to Oman, coinciding with the increasing presence in the region of peoples from present-day Iran. In the sixth century, Arabs succeeded in repelling encroachments of these ethnic groups;

the conversion of Arab tribes to Islam in the seventh century resulted in the displacement of the settlers from Iran. The introduction of Ibadism vested power in the imam, the leader nominated by tribal shaykhs and then elected by public acclamation.

The Ibadis had five imamates before the founding of the Al Said dynasty. The first imamate in the ninth century became the example of the ideal Ibadi state. The fifth imamate, the Yarubid Imamate, recaptured Muscat from the Portuguese in 1650 after a colonial presence on the northeastern coast of Oman dating to 1508. The Yarubid dynasty expanded, acquiring former Portuguese colonies in East Africa and engaging in the slave trade.

A civil war broke out in the first half of the eighteenth century between two major tribes: the Hinawi, who claimed descent from an eponymous ancestor Qahtan, and the Ghafiri, who claimed descent from an eponymous ancestor Nizar. The war ended in the 1740s with the election of Ahmad ibn Said Al Said as imam. Ahmad ibn Said had previously served as governor of Suhar under the Yarubid imam, whom he replaced. By 1749 Ahmad ibn Said had become imam of Oman, Zanzibar, and part of what now constitutes Tanzania. Following Ahmad ibn Said's death in 1775, his son, Sultan ibn Ahmad Al Said, became ruler.

The successors of Ahmad ibn Said were known initially as *sayyids*, a title of respect for a Muslim of noble lineage, and later as sultans. Like its predecessors, Al Said dynastic rule has been characterized by a history of internecine family struggle, fratricide, and usurpation. Apart from threats within the ruling family, there was the omnipresent challenge from the independent tribes of the interior who rejected the authority of the sultan, recognizing the imam as the sole legitimate leader and pressing, by resort to arms, for the restoration of the imamate.

Schisms within the ruling family were apparent before Ahmad ibn Said's death and were later manifest with the division of the family into two main lines, the Sultan ibn Ahmad Al Said (r. 1792–1806) line controlling the maritime state, with nominal control over the entire country; and the Qais branch, with authority over the Al Batinah and Ar Rustaq areas. During the period of Sultan Said ibn Sultan Al Said's rule (1806–56), Oman cultivated its East African colonies, profiting from the slave trade. As a regional commercial power in the nineteenth century, Oman held territories on the island of Zanzibar off the coast of East Africa, in Mombasa along the coast of East Africa, and until 1958 in Gwadar (in present-day Pakistan) on the coast of the Arabian Sea. But when the British declared slavery illegal in the mid-1800s, the sultanate's fortunes reversed. The economy collapsed, and many Omani families migrated to Zanzibar. The population of Muscat fell from 55,000 to 8,000 between the 1850s and 1870s.

The death of Sultan Said ibn Sultan in 1856 prompted a further division: the descendants of the late sultan ruled Oman (Thuwaini ibn Said Al Said, r. 1856–66) and Zanzibar (Mayid ibn Said Al Said, r. 1856–70); the Qais branch intermittently allied itself with the ulama to restore imamate legitimacy. In 1868 Azzam ibn Qais Al Said (r. 1868–71) emerged as self-declared imam. Although a significant number of Hinawi tribes recognized him as imam, the public neither elected him nor acclaimed him as such.

Imam Azzam understood that to unify the country a strong, central authority had to be established with control over the interior tribes of Oman. His rule was jeopardized by the British, who interpreted his policy of bringing the interior tribes under the central government as a move against their established order. In resorting to military means to unify Oman, Imam Azzam alienated members of the Ghafiri tribes, who revolted in the 1870–71 period. The British gave Imam Azzam's rival, Turki ibn Said Al Said, financial and political support. Turki ibn Said succeeded in defeating the forces of Imam Azzam, who was killed in battle outside Matrah in January 1871.

The deteriorating economy resulting from the suppression of the slave trade rendered Sultan Turki ibn Said's rule susceptible to opposition from the interior. For a brief period, Turki ibn Said appeased his opposition with cash payments and British backing. His authority extended from the Al Batinah coast to Suhar, with the rest of the country operating autonomously. Sultan Turki ibn Said suffered a stroke in the early 1870s and was incapacitated. He was succeeded in 1888 by his son, Faisal ibn Turki Al Said, who was the first ruler of the Al Said family in the nineteenth century to assume power peacefully, without resort to arms or political subterfuge.

Four sultans of the Al Said family have ruled Oman in the twentieth century: Faisal ibn Turki Al Said (1888–1913), Taimur ibn Faisal Al Said (1913–32), Said ibn Taimur Al Said (1932–70), and the present sultan, Qabus ibn Said Al Said

(1970–). In large part, Omani political developments in the twentieth century followed the temperament and priorities of successive sultans. Each, to varying degrees, responded to threats to his authority from the interior; each had to balance independent action with an indirect role by Britain, with which Oman had treaties of friendship. The initial British-Omani treaty, similar to British treaties with other Persian Gulf states, was signed in 1891.

The process of state formation in Oman and the centralization of political power within the ruling family followed the same pattern found in other gulf shaykhdoms, particularly Kuwait, Bahrain, and Qatar. Oil revenues and income redistribution facilitated a pattern of continuity of political power within the ruling family and the traditional political elite as well as change with the modest creation of new institutions and expanded administration engaging an increasingly diverse segment of Omani society.

Faisal ibn Turki, 1888–1913

On assuming power in 1888, Faisal ibn Turki gradually found his authority over the interior weakened as tribal leaders increasingly perceived his dependence on British advisers as an inherent weakness. In 1895 he was forced to seek refuge at Jalali fort after Muscat was captured. British political agents frustrated his efforts to recapture Muscat, compelling him to court the French. He granted the French coaling facilities for their fleet at Bandar Jissah near Muscat.

Determined to thwart any growth in French presence in what Britain considered its sphere of influence, Britain presented Faisal ibn Turki with an ultimatum in 1899 ordering the sultan to board the British flagship or Muscat would be bombarded. Having little recourse, Faisal ibn Turki capitulated. Publicly humiliated, his authority was irreversibly damaged. In 1903 he asked Lord George Nathaniel Curzon, viceroy of India, for permission to abdicate, but his request was denied. Responsibility for the capital was delegated to Said ibn Muhammad Al Said, while affairs of the interior fell to an ex-slave, Sulayman ibn Suwaylim. By 1913 control over the interior was completely lost, and a reconstituted imamate was again a threat to Muscat. In May 1913, Salim ibn Rashid al Harthi was elected imam at Tanuf and spearheaded a revolt against the sultan that combined both Hinawi and Ghafiri tribal groups.

Taimur ibn Faisal, 1913–32

Taimur ibn Faisal succeeded his father as sultan in October 1913. When he assumed suzerainty over the country, he inherited an external public debt and widespread rebellion among the tribes. Between 1915 and 1920, the sultan's forces were aided by British financial and matériel support against the rebel tribes, ensuring adequate resistance but not total victory. An uneasy situation of no war, no peace existed, with the sultan controlling Muscat and the coastal towns and the imam ruling the interior. This was tacitly codified in the Treaty of As Sib in 1920, brokered by the British political agent in Muscat. The treaty was between the sultan and the tribes, represented by Shaykh Isa ibn Salih al Harthi, leader of the Al Harth tribe.

In return for full autonomy, the tribes in the interior pledged to cease attacking the coast. The Treaty of As Sib was, de facto, a partition agreement between Muscat and Oman, serving Britain's interest in preserving its power through the office of the sultan without dispatching British troops to the region. The Treaty of As Sib ensured political quiescence between Muscat and Oman that lasted until the 1950s, when oil exploration in the interior reintroduced conflict. In return for accepting a truncation of his authority, the sultan received a loan from the government of British India with an amortization period of ten years, sufficient to repay his debts to merchants. When Sultan Taimur ibn Faisal abdicated for financial reasons in 1932, the twenty-two-year-old Said ibn Taimur inherited an administration that was in debt.

A United States Department of State bulletin on the sultan of Muscat and Oman in February 1938 describes the situation in which Sultan Said ibn Taimur found himself after assuming power: "The young Sultan found the country practically bankrupt and his troubles were further complicated by tribal unrest and conspiracy by certain of his uncles, one of whom immediately profited by the occasion to set up an independent regime. The Sultan tackled the situation with resolution and within a short time the traitorous uncle had been subdued, unrest quelled, and most important of all, state finances put on much more solid footing."

Said ibn Taimur, 1932–70

Between 1932 and 1970, Said ibn Taimur ruled Oman and impressed on it his own myopic vision. Said ibn Taimur was an

Anglophile who was compelled, in order to alleviate the country's debt, to integrate the interior with Oman and create an independent state. To create a financially independent state, he needed oil export revenues. But the acquiescence of the interior tribes was indispensable for exploration activities.

The dilemma materialized in 1954 when the PDO sent exploration teams to the interior. The move was interpreted by the tribal shaykhs as a violation of the 1920 Treaty of As Sib. This coincided with the death of Imam Muhammad ibn Abd Allah al Khalili, who had ruled the interior of the country, and the election in 1954 of a new imam, who led a breakaway movement seeking independence from coastal Oman. The new imam's brother solicited political and material support from Saudi Arabia and established a secessionist movement called the Omani Liberation Movement, with the goals of establishing an independent Omani state in the interior and forcing the withdrawal of foreign troops. The British intervened on behalf of the sultan and by 1959 reestablished the sultan's authority. The British abrogated the Treaty of As Sib and ended the office of imam.

After 1958 Said ibn Taimur established his residence at Al Hisn near Salalah, in Dhofar, where he remained permanently except for periodic visits to London. By retiring to the south from Muscat, Said ibn Taimur was not only more secure from assassination but was also no longer obligated to meet frequently with tribal shaykhs and distribute subsidies and thereby avoided depleting the treasury. He married Dhofari wives, one of whom bore him his only son, Qabus ibn Said, and two daughters. Above all, Said ibn Taimur created his personal fiefdom and sought to arrest modernization by enforcing antiquated laws, public executions, and slavery of people of African descent. The isolation and xenophobia that he forced on the country in general and on Dhofar in particular left Oman grossly underdeveloped, despite increasing oil export revenues in the late 1960s.

Qabus ibn Said spent his early years isolated within the royal palace. At the instigation of his father's British advisers, Qabus ibn Said was permitted to go to Britain in 1958 for his education. He spent two years at a small private school, where he acquired mastery of the English language. In 1960 he was enrolled in the Royal Military Academy at Sandhurst and, after graduating from a two-year course of study, served for several months with British units stationed in the Federal Republic of

Germany (West Germany). After a world tour and studies in London, he returned to Oman in December 1964. His father, however, refused to entrust him with a responsible role in the government or military and instead sequestered him in the palace in Salalah. Qabus ibn Said's more cosmopolitan and progressive views were incompatible with his father's conservatism and isolationism, which Qabus ibn Said considered detrimental to the country's development. With the tacit endorsement of the British, who saw thirty-year-old Qabus ibn Said as an agreeable alternative, Qabus ibn Said and a number of alienated political elite overthrew Said ibn Taimur in a palace coup d'état on July 23, 1970. Said ibn Taimur withdrew to London, where he died in 1972.

Qabus ibn Said: The Emergence of a Modern State

After assuming power in 1970, Qabus ibn Said concentrated on restoring control over the southern Dhofar region, which had been in rebellion against his father's oppressive rule. He used economic and military means, believing that poor economic conditions had helped motivate the Dhofar rebellion. By 1975 he succeeded in suppressing militarily the Marxist-inspired rebellion, and the sultan could turn to development issues and the establishment of modern governmental and administrative institutions. By the mid-1980s, virtually all regions of the country were linked by a transportation system and a telecommunications network. Ministerial government and the civil service were expanded, and limited participation in the political process was created in 1981 with the establishment of the State Consultative Council and in 1991 with the formation of the Consultative Council, an advisory body that superseded the State Consultative Council.

The Dhofar Rebellion

The Dhofar rebellion combined economic grievances with political ideology. Placed in a regional context, Arab nationalism, the principal ideology of the 1950s and 1960s, indicted the conservative monarchs of the gulf and demanded their overthrow. Oman was susceptible to these populist stirrings, and, given Dhofar's economic backwardness, Dhofar was a tinderbox. Dhofaris resonated with the Marxist ideology of the People's Democratic Republic of Yemen (PDRY, also seen as South Yemen) during the late 1960s. The primary objective of the Omani liberation movement named the Popular Front for the

*Sultan Qabus ibn Said Al Said,
ruler of Oman
Courtesy Embassy of the
Sultanate of Oman,
Washington
(Photo Mohamed Mustafa)*

*Muscat, capital of Oman, with
Jilali and Mirani forts in the
background
Courtesy Embassy of the
Sultanate of Oman, Washington*

Liberation of the Occupied Arabian Gulf (in 1972 renamed the Popular Front for the Liberation of Oman and the Arab Gulf and in 1974 further renamed the People's Front for the Liberation of Oman) was the removal of Sultan Said ibn Taimur. The government's policies and strategy after Sultan Qabus ibn Said's ascent to power diffused much of this opposition. Pacification occurred through the dual strategy of carrot and stick—military pressure and economic rewards.

Qabus ibn Said engaged neighboring states, apprehensive of the growth of left-wing movements in the region, in dispatching economic and military assistance. In 1973 the shah of Iran, fulfilling his self-perceived role as guardian of the Persian Gulf following the departure of the British, dispatched ground forces (eventually numbering more than 3,000) and air units to Dhofar to assist the sultan. Oman received annual financial aid of about US$200 million from Abu Dhabi to assist military and civil development projects and about US$2.5 billion from Saudi Arabia, with which relations had improved. Britain, Jordan, Saudi Arabia, Egypt, and Pakistan provided training in military schools for armed forces personnel. The UAE and Jordan occasionally provided troop units for guard duty in the north, thereby releasing Omani units for service in Dhofar.

To erode the Dhofaris' political will, Qabus ibn Said directed a disproportionate percentage of government revenues to the Dhofar region. The shift was designed in part to augment military capabilities in the event of a resumption of hostilities and in part as economic appeasement. The construction of schools, hospitals, roads, and other infrastructure ameliorated the underprivileged status of the south.

Almost 25 percent of the approximately RO600 million (US$1.8 billion) allocated for development between 1971 and 1975 went to Dhofar to improve transportation, education, rural health, and religious facilities. This amount was spent on projects in Dhofar, although the population only numbered about 50,000, in comparison with the population of the rest of Oman of 400,000 in the mid-1970s.

The government also benefited from factionalization within the insurrectionary movement. The movement in the region had originally been organized in 1963 under the Dhofar Liberation Front, led largely by Arab nationalists and religious conservatives who could enlist support of tribal shaykhs in a common struggle against Sultan Said ibn Taimur. In 1968 the Marxists took over leadership, having the support of the PDRY, the Soviet Union, and China. Conservative Dhofaris broke with the movement, and when Qabus ibn Said seized power in 1970, many agreed to support him against the insurgency. By the mid-1970s, as many as 2,000 rebels had surrendered and had been retrained and incorporated into the Sultan's Armed Forces (SAF) as pledged under the terms of the amnesty declared shortly after the 1970 coup.

The government based its new administration and distribution networks on preexisting tribal structures. The government established centers headed by local representatives, usually minor tribal leaders elected by the population of their respective districts but who had to be endorsed by the governor of Dhofar before assuming office. In the larger coastal settlements, local deputy governors managed the district administration independent of the governor of Dhofar. Most of these were major tribal shaykhs, who received a monthly stipend from the government and additional allowances, usually on state or religious holidays. The government's financial allowances to the shaykhs, irrespective of whether or not the shaykh held an administrative position, served to ensure allegiance to authorities in Muscat. Two state institutions distributed these allowances: the finance section of the *wali* (governor) and the palace administration, popularly known as Diwan Affairs.

State Formation and Politically Influential Groups

The process of state formation facilitated by Oman's commercial production and export of hydrocarbon resources transformed the relationship between the ruler and the traditional political elite comprising the ruling family, established merchant families, and tribal shaykhs. While reinforcing some linkages, such as the central role of the Al Said and the political influence of the merchant families, other linkages, particularly the tribes, have diminished in importance. Society outside the capital and urban centers remains tribal, with tribal leaders exercising political authority locally. But the power of tribes as regional pressure groups declined steadily as a result of the incorporation of rural areas into the government-administered sector.

Oil revenues facilitated the transfer of some of the income from the state to society, creating a broader base. Pre-oil stratification of Omani society, wherein the ruler depended on the tribal shaykhs to ensure popular support, has partially been superseded by the establishment of a social welfare state through which the government fosters a direct relationship between the state and the individual. Government clinics, agricultural and industrial projects, schools, and employment in the public sector reinforce this new linkage.

The Al Said Dynasty

Members of the Al Said family have historically played a central role in the state apparatus, not only because of hereditary succession to the sultanate but also because much of the ruler's bureaucracy has consisted of his relatives. Before 1932 there was an implicit division between Muscat and Oman, with the ruler rarely able to extend his authority over the whole geographical area of Oman. Not only was the interior outside his sphere of influence, but frequently the ruler could not exercise authority over the Al Batinah coast. Relatives often controlled towns such as Suhar and Ar Rustaq autonomously, creating individual fiefdoms.

By the time Sultan Said ibn Taimur assumed power in 1932, these independent power centers had disappeared, coinciding with an increasing role of family members in the administration of the state. This nepotism has been practiced since the nineteenth century when members of the Al Said served in such positions as representative (*wakil*), deputy (*wazir*), governor (*wali*), field general, and council minister. Yet, the practice was not without its risks, and often rulers were sensitive to the potential for relatives to become contenders for power. Sultan Said ibn Taimur recognized the risk his half-brothers Tariq ibn Taimur Al Said and Fahar ibn Taimur Al Said and his son Qabus ibn Said presented, and he delegated only minor responsibilities, if any, to Qabus ibn Said.

Sultan Qabus ibn Said has similarly incorporated members of the Al Said family into the state apparatus, particularly in sensitive ministerial positions. The sultan reserved major ministerial positions for himself. In 1993 he held the posts of prime minister, minister of defense, minister of finance, and minister of foreign affairs, although the functions of the prime minister were often entrusted to the minister of state for foreign affairs. In the 1993 cabinet, two members of the Al Said served as deputy prime ministers: Fahar ibn Taimur Al Said for security and defense and Fahd ibn Mahmud Al Said for legal affairs; Faisal ibn Ali Al Said served as minister of national heritage and culture. The Al Said also controlled the Ministry of Interior, the governorship of Muscat, and the governorship of Dhofar. Sultan Qabus ibn Said's cousin, Thuwaini ibn Shihab Al Said, was the sultan's special personal representative, and some considered him the most likely candidate to succeed Qabus ibn Said. Shabib ibn Taimur Al Said, Qabus ibn Said's uncle, assumed the role of special adviser to the sultan for environmental affairs (see fig. 15).

Despite his progressive rule on some fronts, Sultan Qabus ibn Said has been slow to delegate real political authority. One of his first acts as sultan was to return his father's half-brother, Tariq ibn Taimur, from exile in West Germany and appoint him prime minister. Tariq ibn Taimur was educated in West Germany, married a German national, and had extensive experience working in the Middle East as the representative of a construction firm. He had been an outspoken critic of Sultan Said ibn Taimur's rule, when forced into exile in 1958.

Tariq ibn Taimur formed his first cabinet on August 16, 1970, and brought the notion of political reform. He supported the establishment of a constitutional monarchy and parliamentary system and as a result came into direct conflict with Sultan Qabus ibn Said, who preferred the status quo, with real power remaining in the office of the sultan. As of 1993, power remained centralized with the Al Said, and, although departing from his father's conviction that to maintain the ruler's power the people must remain uneducated, real decision making remained the exclusive privilege of a narrowly based elite that the Al Said dominated.

The centralization of power with the sultan and the absence of a mechanism for succession left speculation open concerning Oman after Qabus ibn Said. Qabus ibn Said has no heir, although he was married briefly in 1976 to Tariq ibn Taimur's daughter. The Al Said family is small, numbering fewer than 100 male members. Since the death in 1980 of Tariq ibn Taimur, no individual within the ruling family has distinguished himself or demonstrated any exceptional ability to rule. Likely candidates to succeed Qabus ibn Said include his two uncles, Fahar ibn Taimur and Shabib ibn Taimur; three cousins, Thuwaini ibn Shibab, Fahd ibn Mahmud, and Faisal ibn Ali; and, among the junior princes, Haitham ibn Tariq Al Said, son of Oman's former prime minister. The issue of succession is sensitive, and, in the absence of a designated crown prince, the door is open for political struggle.

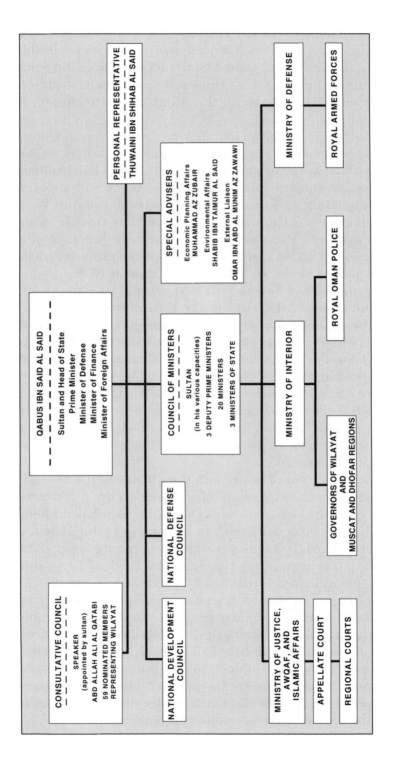

Figure 15. Oman: Government Structure, 1992

Established Merchant Families

Among the most important groups, in terms of political influence, are a number of merchant families whose economic wealth is predicated on old, established links with the ruling family. The merchant families live primarily in Muscat and the coastal region and include both Hindus and Muslims from the Indian subcontinent and Shia from Iran. These families consolidated their power during the reign of Sultan Said ibn Taimur and continued to amass fortunes after 1970, largely through monopolistic or quasi-monopolistic franchises. None is directly involved in the oil business, but together they are the principal suppliers of goods to the government, local contractors, foreign firms, local consumers, and the oil industry. Valuable distributorships for consumer and capital services are under their aegis.

Close cooperation between the merchants and Sultan Said ibn Taimur evolved into a mutually protective relationship with civil servants in the Qabus ibn Said government. Included in this group are the Zawawis, whose roots are in Saudi Arabia. Qais ibn Abd al Munim az Zawawi, for example, as of 1991 served as deputy prime minister for economic and financial affairs. Apart from his ministerial position, Qais ibn Abd al Munim is a prominent Muscat businessman. He was educated in India, has no hereditary relationship with the ruling family, and is well connected in the Arab world. His brother, Omar ibn Abd al Munim az Zawawi, a Harvard-educated physician, is considered the second wealthiest man in Oman next to the sultan. In addition to being president of Omar Zawawi Establishment (the Omzest Group), which comprises about seventy companies and joint ventures, he is special adviser for external liaison to the sultan. The Omzest Group represents multinational companies, such as Daimler-Benz and Mitsui Engineering and Shipping Company, which is contracted to build the oil refinery near Muscat.

Another example of a merchant family drawn into the ministerial level is Said Ahmad ash Shanfari, the minister of petroleum and minerals, whose family origins are Dhofari and who has held the portfolio since 1974. The Shanfari family is related to Qabus ibn Said's mother and controls Shanfari and Partners, a contracting company involved in building infrastructure. Its bid was selected from among six contractors to build the new industrial estate at Raysut.

Khimji Ramdas, who heads the Khimji Ramdas Group, which holds international franchises ranging from consumer products and soft drinks to insurance and construction, is also in this circle. Yahya Muhammad Nasib, chairman of Yahya Enterprises, provides defense and communications equipment to the Ministry of Defense and other ministries. Other influential families include those of Muhsin Haidar Darwish and Suhail Bahwan, chairman of the Bahwan Group, Muscat.

Government Institutions

Government institutions on the national level include the Council of Ministers and two other bodies: the National Defense Council and the National Development Council. In 1992 the Council of Ministers had twenty-seven members, including the prime minister and three deputy prime ministers—for security and defense, legal affairs, and financial and economic affairs. The sultan occupied the sensitive posts of prime minister, minister of defense, minister of foreign affairs, and minister of finance. Sultan Qabus ibn Said controls all ministerial appointments and cabinet reshuffles. Policy formulation remains largely the product of person-to-person negotiations between the sultan and individual ministers.

The National Defense Council, working in conjunction with the Ministry of Defense and the Ministry of Interior, coordinates the activities of the Royal Armed Forces (formerly called the Sultan's Armed Forces) and the Royal Oman Police. The National Development Council manages national development planning, and all projects involving more than a certain minimum expenditure require its review.

Consultative Council

In 1991 Qabus established the Consultative Council (Majlis ash Shura), a sixty-member body. The Consultative Council superseded the fifty-five-member State Consultative Council (SCC; Majlis al Istishari lil Dawlah) created in 1981 with significant regional and popular as well as official representation.

Whereas the concept of consultation is an integral part of Ibadi Islam and the imamate, it was not a tradition incorporated into Oman's contemporary sultanate until Qabus ibn Said established the SCC by royal decree on October 18, 1981. Initially, the SCC consisted of forty-three members but was expanded to fifty-five in 1983 with representation of the seven geographic regions weighted according to population size and development needs. Nineteen members were government officials, and of the nineteen, eleven—undersecretaries of social service ministries—were the only permanent members of the SCC. The remaining seven government officials could serve a maximum of two terms (four years), as could other SCC members.

Like the SCC, the Consultative Council lacks legislative powers but plays a consultative role. Its representatives come from Oman's forty-one *wilayat* (governorates; sing., *wilayah*). Candidates are selected by the *wali* (Muscat-appointed governor) and can be nominated by friends or themselves. After the nomination process, names of three candidates are submitted to the deputy prime minister for legal affairs in Muscat, who selects the final candidates, who must then be endorsed by the sultan.

Unlike the SCC, members of the Consultative Council cannot include government officials or civil servants. Although this condition automatically excludes a pool of politically experienced individuals, it is intended to circumvent potential allegations of conflict of interest. The inclusion of eleven undersecretaries in the SCC tended to strengthen it as a body codifying the status quo rather than offering legitimate criticism and alternative policies. The SCC's recommendations did not include defense, foreign affairs, or the petroleum sector. It convened three times annually, with each session lasting three days to a week. The restricted format, infrequent meetings, and lack of veto power or legislative role combined to tie the SCC's hands. Despite these shortcomings, the news reports and televised broadcasts of the SCC exposed the public to a limited part of the government structure. It also modestly introduced the concept of accountability, although the ultimate authority of the sultan remained unquestioned.

The role of the new Consultative Council can perhaps best be understood in the framework of Oman's graduated development process. In 1970 Qabus ibn Said rejected a constitutional monarchy and parliamentary system in favor of preservation of the status quo. Subsequently, the SCC evolved from an earlier advisory body, the Council on Agriculture, Fisheries, and Industries, established in April 1979. The council was largely successful in serving as an "outside" body offering policy recommendations to the sultan and the ministers, although the scope of its consultation was relatively narrow. It was abolished in October 1981, and seven of its twelve members were incorporated into the SCC. The Consultative Council has modestly opened the political system.

Judicial System

Oman's legal system is based on the Ibadi interpretation of the sharia (Islamic law), which is similar to that of the four orthodox schools of Sunni Islam (see Sunni Islam, ch. 1). Jurisprudence is administered regionally by the *wali*, in conjunction with the qadi, a judge who has attained that position either by graduating from an Islamic law college or by taking advanced study with local religious experts. Although primarily guided by the sharia, the system aims at arriving at a fair decision or compromise acceptable to all parties. Invariably, tribal law has become mixed with religious law. Modern commercial law, borrowed from other parts of the Middle East and Europe, also operates in the business sphere.

The Media

The media sector remained rudimentary in 1993. There are three Arabic-language dailies: *Al Watan* (The Nation), *Khalij Times,* and *Oman Daily Newspaper.* The Muscat daily, *Times of Oman,* and the *Oman Daily Observer* are two English-language newspapers. Rather than a forum for open discourse, the media serve primarily as benign commentators on local and international news.

Foreign Relations

Oman's foreign policy since the 1970s has been influenced by Qabus ibn Said's determination to reverse the isolationism of Sultan Said ibn Taimur's rule and guardedly to integrate Oman both regionally and internationally. The geostrategic position of the country on the southern shore of the Strait of Hormuz, the imperatives of an oil-dependent economy, and the threats posed by stronger, neighboring regimes, notably Saudi Arabia and Iran, have also shaped the sultan's foreign policy. Oman's foreign policy, as a result of the sultan's goals and the regime's ties to Britain and the United States, has been nonconfrontational and conciliatory to Western interests in the region.

Nonetheless, the regime has displayed an uncommon independence of action in comparison with other Arab gulf states. On several occasions, Oman has acted as a broker in regional disputes. During the Iran-Iraq War (1980–88), the two belligerents conducted cease-fire talks secretly in Muscat. Although no formal agreement resulted, the talks reduced mistrust between the parties. Similarly, after 1988 Oman acted as mediator in the restoration of diplomatic relations between Iran and Britain and Iran and Saudi Arabia.

Regional Relations

Since 1970, when Qabus ibn Said assumed power, Oman's role in regional political dynamics has increased. Although remaining outside the Organization of the Petroleum Exporting Countries (OPEC), it has been a member of the GCC since its formation in May 1981. Relations between Oman and other Persian Gulf countries have improved since 1970 as long-standing territorial disputes have been resolved. Oman and Saudi Arabia signed a treaty in 1974 ending a long-standing territorial dispute concerning the Al Buraymi Oasis; in March 1990, the two countries concluded a border agreement. Oman and the UAE resolved a border dispute in 1981. And in 1982, Oman and the PDRY normalized relations; in October 1992, Oman and reunited Yemen signed a border demarcation agreement, ending a twenty-five-year border dispute.

The resolution of the Al Buraymi Oasis territorial dispute, concerning a cluster of nine villages claimed by Saudi Arabia and administered by Abu Dhabi and Oman, improved regional relations. With the discovery of oil reserves in the Persian Gulf, the revenue potential for the Al Buraymi Oasis prompted Saudi Arabia to press its claim to the disputed territory. Riyadh dispatched troops, which occupied the area in 1952. After failing to win their claim in international arbitration, the British, using the sultan's army and the Trucial Oman Scouts, reoccupied the oasis in 1955. Although the United States protested the British action, the United States was not prepared to extend military assistance to Saudi Arabia to reverse the situation. From the early 1950s onward, Saudi Arabia provided a base from which the Ibadi imam of the interior continued to challenge the authority of the Al Said dynasty.

After the 1970 coup d'état, Qabus ibn Said sought to improve and normalize relations with Saudi Arabia. Formal relations were established following a state visit by the sultan to the kingdom in December 1971. An agreement on July 29, 1974, among Oman, Saudi Arabia, and the UAE settled the Al Buraymi dispute. It stipulated that Oman would receive three villages in the region and Abu Dhabi six and that the two countries would share the oil field at Shaybah. The agreement provided Saudi Arabia with an outlet to the gulf through UAE territory.

In the course of the Dhofar rebellion, Oman received substantial financial support from Saudi Arabia, the UAE, and Kuwait, countries that feared the growth of left-wing, antimonarchist movements in their own territories. In March 1990, Saudi Arabia and Oman formalized a border pact legitimating the existing declared line separating the two countries.

The Iranian Revolution of 1979 and the fear of militant Islam among Arab leaders, combined with the Iran-Iraq War and the potential interruption of tanker traffic through the Strait of Hormuz, catalyzed the formation of the GCC, consisting of Bahrain, Kuwait, Oman, Qatar, Saudi Arabia, and the UAE (see Collective Security under the Gulf Cooperation Council, ch. 7). The GCC is theoretically a means to ensure collective security of the member states. In practice, as Iraq's 1990 invasion of Kuwait showed, it proved ineffectual in deterring and responding to aggression by neighboring states.

After the Persian Gulf War, Sultan Qabus ibn Said suggested the creation of a multilateral 100,000-strong collective defense force. However, Saudi Arabia scuttled the proposal, which was unpopular in Oman and in other gulf states. Objections ranged from the matter of costs and manpower needs of such a force, given the small populations of GCC member states, to the question of who would command such a force. The smaller gulf states feared a dominant Riyadh dictating terms and foreign policy.

International Relations

Reciprocity has characterized Oman's relationship with foreign powers. Historically, Oman has relied on foreign powers to ensure political stability, domestically and regionally. In turn, Oman's geostrategic location at the entry point of the Strait of Hormuz and its long coastline have guided the interests of foreign powers.

Relations with the British date back to 1798 when the first treaty of friendship was concluded between the sultan of Muscat and the British government of India. British interests in Oman were predicated on Whitehall's concern with the defense of India and the imperative of maintaining secure trade routes and containing the expansion of other European powers in the Indian Ocean. Following the discovery of the potential for using oil as fuel, and later the conversion of the British naval fleet from coal-fired ships to oil-fired ships in 1911, the security of tanker traffic through the Strait of Hormuz gained increasing importance. Britain's Royal Air Force had staging and diplomatic telecommunications facilities on the island of Masirah from 1932 to 1977.

The British largely facilitated the extensive military buildup and modernization of Oman's armed forces during the course of the Dhofar rebellion in the 1960s and 1970s. Without British military assistance in suppressing the rebellion, the sultanate probably could not have contained the threat, even with troops from Iran and advisers from Jordan. This close military relationship continued after the suppression of the insurrection. The chief of the general staff and the commanders of the air force and navy were British officers through the mid-1980s.

United States influence in Oman has been felt more strongly since the 1970s. Britain's disengagement east of Suez in 1971 opened up the region to greater competition for influence, primarily from the United States. When Sultan Qabus ibn Said assumed power, there was no United States diplomatic presence in Oman. A United States consular officer made at least an annual visit, with contacts managed by the British, who had full control of Oman's foreign relations and defense matters. A United States missionary medical doctor was prominent in the health program. In addition, a United States archaeologist, explorer, and oilman briefly extended his exploration from the PDRY into Dhofar in the 1970s.

United States interests in regional security and in maintaining local allies, particularly after the fall of the shah of Iran in 1979, called for the reinforcement of close security links to the sultanate. Since the 1970s, Sultan Qabus ibn Said has quietly asserted his independence and engaged United States petroleum professionals to advise the government. The selection of United States citizens to manage the development programs in the Musandam Peninsula and the Al Buraymi Oasis and to develop water resources in the sultanate was a dramatic departure from the sultanate's exclusive reliance on British advisers. Relations between Oman and the United States strengthened as Qabus ibn Said supported United States peace initiatives in the Middle East, manifest in Muscat's support of the Camp David Accords signed in 1979 by Egypt and Israel and mediated by the United States.

United States influence in Oman widened with the signing of a facilities access agreement in June 1980 (most recently renewed in 1990) providing United States military access to Omani bases under specified conditions. This was part of a larger regional strategy that also included facilities in Somalia and Kenya. The air bases at As Sib and Thamarit and on Masirah (the latter abandoned by the British in 1977) were upgraded with United States assistance.

The Joint United States-Oman Commission was established in 1980 with the mandate to fund and administer economic assistance programs in the country. Activities funded through the commission reflect sectoral priorities and include a school construction project, a scholarship and training project, a fisheries development project, a management project, and a water resources project.

The activities funded reflect United States Agency for International Development (AID) priorities. In the 1990s, AID development assistance focused on the agency's interest in privatization and institution building. The annual Omani budget proposal for fiscal year 1993 allocated US$5 million (or 33 percent of the total program) to private-sector development, US$9.5 million (or 63 percent) to institution building, and US$8.8 million (or 58 percent) to develop education facilities.

Despite these programs promoting economic development and education, Oman faced significant problems in the early 1990s. A wealthier, better-educated population will demand greater participation in the political process. As of early 1993, the sultan was unwilling to relinquish real power, and he carefully preserved his political autonomy. A new Consultative Council was established in late 1990 but was essentially an advisory body without legislative power. To serve as a mechanism for true political reform, the council must be empowered with a legislative role; as of early 1993, this had not occurred.

*   *   *

The literature on Oman is scarce and varies in quality. Most works were published in the late 1970s or 1980s and concentrate on contrasting the periods before and after Qabus ibn Said came to power. Although such comparative analysis is valid, it seems dated because more than twenty years have elapsed since the accession of the sultan. Government publications, such as the annual *Statistical Yearbook*, provide information on every sector of the society and economy and are helpful tools in determining economic and social trends.

Monographs offer a general framework for understanding Oman's contemporary scene and also provide a detailed history. Among the more useful is John E. Peterson's *Oman in the Twentieth Century.* Also valuable is a work by John Townsend, former adviser to sultans Said ibn Taimur and Qabus ibn Said, *Oman: The Making of a Modern State,* which focuses on institution building in the post-1970 period.

Various journal articles provide more up-to-date material. General economic information is reported weekly in *Middle East Economic Survey* and *Middle East Economic Digest* and periodically in London's *Financial Times* country surveys. Current information on the hydrocarbon sector is best found in industry journals, particularly the *Oil and Gas Journal, Petroleum Intelligence Weekly,* and *Petroleum Economist.* (For further information and complete citations, see Bibliography.)

Chapter 7. Regional and National Security Considerations

Crossed scimitars

ANY THREAT TO THE STABILITY of the Persian Gulf endangering the region's oil flow greatly concerns the rest of the world. The Iranian Revolution of 1979 was the opening stage in more than a decade of upheaval. The outbreak of war between Iran and Iraq in 1980, the expansion of the war to nonbelligerent shipping, and the presence of foreign naval flotillas in the gulf followed. When general hostilities eventually broke out, they arose from an unexpected quarter—Iraq's sweep into Kuwait in August 1990 and the possibility of Iraqi forces continuing down the gulf coast to seize other oil-rich Arab states. The smaller Arab regimes volunteered use of their ports and airfields as bases for the coalition of forces in Operation Desert Storm to defeat Iraq.

The overwhelming concentration of military power that enabled Iraq to invade and occupy Kuwait underscored the vulnerability of the territory and oil facilities of the other gulf states. To the extent that their military resources permitted, each of the Arab states participated in the coalition that defeated Iraq and drove it out of Kuwait. It was clear, nonetheless, that they played a subordinate role in the vast operation in which the United States, Britain, and France predominated, supported by Egypt and Syria.

After its sharp setback, Iraq in early 1993 remained a major regional power and a littoral state of the Persian Gulf, along with Iran and Saudi Arabia. None of the five other Persian Gulf littoral states—Kuwait, Bahrain, Qatar, the United Arab Emirates, or Oman—is in a position to defend its borders or territorial waters alone. In the face of their fragility, these Persian Gulf states continue to take measures to reinforce their individual and collective security. Relative to size and population, they have been among the world's most lavish spenders on the needs of their armed forces. Nevertheless, their military potential is limited by small manpower pools, sectarian divisions, limited area, and little experience in the effective use of modern weaponry.

A few months after the start of the Iran-Iraq War in 1980, the six regional nonbelligerents—the five gulf states and Saudi Arabia—in 1981 banded together to form the Gulf Cooperation Council (GCC). Although the GCC had economic, social, and political aims, its main purpose was the creation of a defensive military alliance. The GCC leaders feared that a decisive

Iranian military victory would fuel the drive of the revolutionary government of Iran to spread its Islamic revolution. Concurrently, the GCC states accelerated their individual military efforts by purchasing modern aircraft, armored vehicles, air defense systems, and missile-armed naval vessels.

The GCC members are determined to construct a collective self-defense system without the direct involvement of foreign powers. For both political and practical reasons, however, the military goals of the GCC—standardization of equipment, coordination of training, integration of forces, and joint planning—have been achieved only to a limited degree. The gulf states have also been forced to restrain their military purchases as a result of declining oil revenues.

In the immediate aftermath of the Persian Gulf War, agreement was reached with the GCC to station Egyptian and Syrian troops in Kuwait to ensure the military stability of the northern gulf. By 1993, however, this plan seemed to have been abandoned. Instead, Kuwait and most other gulf states turned to cooperation with the West to develop a new security framework. The United States concluded agreements to permit prepositioning of United States equipment for combat units, port access, and joint exercises and training. Britain and France also negotiated military cooperation arrangements. The effect was to spread a Western strategic umbrella over the region without the permanent stationing of foreign forces, although a United States and British naval presence is expected to continue.

In early 1993, two years after the gulf war ended, the danger of renewed violence in the region had receded, although no reconciliation among the antagonists had occurred. Iraq has not fully recovered from its humiliating defeat; nevertheless, its reduced army and air force still overshadow the combined forces of the GCC. Iran's military strength was depleted during its eight-year struggle with Iraq, and recovery is proceeding slowly. Although it appears to have shifted to more moderate policies, Iran's ambition to be a factor in regional gulf security has been treated with suspicion.

Traditional rivalries and territorial disputes among the smaller gulf states still linger but have steadily diminished as sources of tension. Subversion and terrorist incidents, often linked to Iran, have abated, as has the potential for disruption by foreign workers manipulated by external forces. The police vigilantly control internal dissent that can threaten the stability of the existing regimes. Nevertheless, resistance to democratic reforms by some members of the conservative ruling families of the gulf increases the likelihood of future destabilization and upheaval.

Historical Overview

According to archaeologists, warfare was a common activity 5,000 years ago among the peoples of the area of the Middle East that in modern times became known as Iran, Iraq, Saudi Arabia, and the smaller gulf states. Sargon, Hammurabi, Nebuchadnezzar II, and Alexander the Great were among the best known kings who led warring armies in the 2,500 years before the birth of Christ. During the centuries of Greek and Roman domination, the gulf region was of limited interest to the major powers, but the area's importance as a strategic and trading center rose with the emergence of Islam in the seventh century A.D. The caliphate's naval strength was concentrated at Hormuz (present-day Bandar-e Abbas in Iran). Strategically sited at the mouth of the Persian Gulf, its authority extended over ports and islands of the Arabian Sea and the Persian Gulf (see fig. 16).

The strategic importance of Hormuz, however, did not survive the appearance of Western powers, initially the Portuguese who came to the gulf in the late fifteenth century after Vasco da Gama's discovery of the route to India via the Cape of Good Hope. The Ottomans and the Iranians also tried to dominate the gulf but faced opposition from local tribes in Bahrain and Muscat, reluctant to cede authority over their territories, which by then were the most important areas on the coast. Increasing British involvement in India beginning in the late eighteenth century quickened British interest in the Persian Gulf region as a means of protecting the sea routes to India. The principal challenge to Britain arose from the Al Qasimi confederation originating in the area of the present-day United Arab Emirates (UAE). The Al Qasimi, who amassed a fleet of about 900 vessels, demanded tribute for the passage of merchant vessels and were regarded as pirates by the Europeans. Between 1809 and 1820, British sea power gradually brought about the destruction of the Al Qasimi fleet. This in turn led to the signing of agreements with Britain by the Al Qasimi and other shaykhs (see Glossary; see Treaties with the British, ch. 1). The amirates promised to have no direct dealings with other foreign states and to abstain from piracy. Britain in turn assumed responsibility for the foreign relations of the amirates and promised to protect them from all aggression by sea and to lend its support against any land attacks. Before the end of the century, Britain

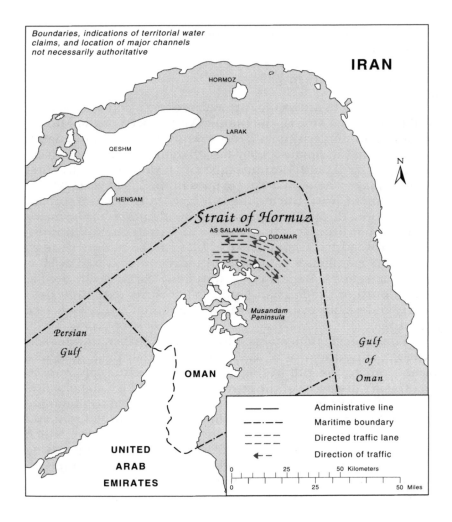

Boundaries, indications of territorial water
claims, and location of major channels
not necessarily authoritative

Figure 16. Strait of Hormuz, 1993

extended protection to Bahrain and Kuwait. Qatar entered the
trucial system as well, in 1916, and received Britain's military
protection from Ottoman encroachment in return for relinquishing its autonomy in foreign affairs and certain other
areas.

Although Muscat was traditionally a center of the slave
trade, its sultan made concessions to the British in this regard
in return for British help in building a navy. In the early nineteenth century, the sultan's efficient fleet of sloops, corvettes,
and frigates enabled him to support a maritime empire extend-

ing from East Africa to the coast of present-day Pakistan. With the eventual decline of this empire, owing in part to its division into two states—Zanzibar and Oman—Britain's influence grew, and it signed a treaty in 1891 similar to those with the gulf amirates.

The strategic importance of the Persian Gulf became increasingly apparent as the oil industry developed in the twentieth century. Saudi Arabia, Iraq, and Iran all claimed some of the territory of the gulf states during the years between World War I and World War II, but Britain's firm resistance to these claims enabled the amirates to maintain their territorial integrity without resort to arms. Except for a small force of the British Indian Navy to ensure observance of the treaty conditions and maintain maritime peace in the gulf, Britain abstained from direct military involvement. As the wealth of the gulf's oil resources became clear, the size of the British military establishment expanded. By the end of the 1960s, Britain had about 9,000 men in Oman, Sharjah (an amirate of the Trucial Coast states, which became the UAE in 1971), and Bahrain, where British military headquarters was located. The Trucial Oman Scouts, a mobile force of mixed nationality that Britain supported and British officers commanded, became a symbol of public order in the Trucial Coast states until Britain's withdrawal from the Persian Gulf in 1971.

Impact of the Iran-Iraq War, 1980–88

The first major threat to the security of the Persian Gulf states followed the outbreak of war between Iran and Iraq in 1980. The war began after a period of deteriorating relations between these two historic rivals, dating from the fall of Mohammad Reza Shah Pahlavi in 1979 and his replacement as Iranian leader by Ayatollah Sayyid Ruhollah Musavi Khomeini. Full-scale warfare erupted in September 1980 as Iraqi military units swept across the Shatt al Arab waterway—which forms the confluence of the Tigris and Euphrates rivers—into the province of Khuzestan, Iran's richest oil-producing area. Iraqi president Saddam Husayn hoped to overthrow Khomeini, who had been overtly attempting to spread his Islamist (also seen as fundamentalist) revolution into Iraq, where the secular Baath (Arab Socialist Resurrection) Party regime feared Iran's influence among Iraq's disaffected Shia (see Glossary) Muslims.

By November 1980, the Iraqi offensive had lost its momentum. Rejecting an Iraqi offer to negotiate, Iran launched a series of counteroffensives in 1982 that resulted in the recapture of the Iranian city of Khorramshahr. The destruction of huge oil facilities caused both belligerents sharp declines in oil revenues. Iraq was able to obtain substantial financial aid from Saudi Arabia and other gulf states. In early 1986, an Iranian offensive across the Shatt al Arab resulted in the fall of the Iraqi oil-loading port of Faw and the occupation of much of the Faw Peninsula almost to the Kuwait border. But the Iranians could not break out of the peninsula to threaten Basra, and their last great offensive, which began in December 1986, was ultimately repelled with heavy losses. In the spring of 1988, the freshly equipped Iraqi ground and air forces succeeded in retaking the Faw Peninsula. Iranian battlefield losses, combined with Iraqi air and missile attacks on Iranian cities, forced Khomeini to accept a cease-fire, which took effect in August 1988.

Initially, the fighting between Iran and Iraq only peripherally affected the Persian Gulf states. In May 1981, Bahrain, Kuwait, Oman, Qatar, Saudi Arabia, and the UAE banded together in the GCC to protect their interests and, if necessary, to defend themselves (see Collective Security under the Gulf Cooperation Council, this ch.). In 1984 Iran reacted to Iraqi air attacks on its main oil terminal on the island of Khark by attacking ships destined for ports in gulf countries that assisted Iraq's war effort. In addition, the Arab states of the gulf suspected Iranian involvement in several destabilizing incidents, including an abortive coup in Bahrain in 1981, terrorist activity in Kuwait in 1983, and the violence in Mecca during the 1987 pilgrimage resulting in the deaths of more than 400 pilgrims.

Iran stepped up the tanker warfare in early 1987 by introducing high-speed small craft armed with Italian Sea Killer missiles. Kuwait had already sought the protection of United States naval escorts through the gulf for reflagged Kuwaiti vessels. Determined to protect the flow of oil, the United States began tanker convoys in July 1987. Eleven Kuwaiti ships—one-half of the Kuwaiti tanker fleet—were placed under the United States flag. Other Kuwaiti tankers sailed under Soviet and British flags. Although United States escorts were involved in a number of clashes with Iranian forces and one tanker was damaged by a mine, Iran generally avoided interfering with Kuwaiti ships sailing under United States protection.

Persian Gulf War, 1991

Despite its huge losses in the Iran-Iraq War, Iraq was unchallenged as the most powerful military presence in the gulf area.

Reviving Iraq's old territorial claims against Kuwait, Saddam Husayn demanded leases for the islands of Bubiyan and War-bah at the mouth of the Shatt al Arab to give Iraq a clear pas-sage to the gulf. He also accused Kuwait of illegally siphoning off oil from Ar Rumaylah field, one of the world's largest oil pools, which the two countries shared. Saddam Husayn threat-ened to use force against Arab oil producers, including Kuwait and the UAE, that exceeded their oil quotas, charging them with colluding with the United States to strangle the Iraqi econ-omy by flooding the market with low-priced oil.

Although Iraq had accompanied its threats by moving troops to the border area, the world was largely taken by sur-prise when, on August 2, 1990, the Iraqi army invaded and occupied Kuwait. A force of about 120,000 soldiers and approx-imately 2,000 tanks and other armored vehicles met little resis-tance. The Kuwaiti army was not on the alert, and those troops at their posts could not mount an effective defense. Some air-craft operating from southern Kuwait attacked Iraqi armored columns before their air base was overrun, and they sought ref-uge in Saudi Arabia. Of the 20,000 Kuwaiti troops, many were killed or captured, although up to 7,000 escaped into Saudi Arabia, along with about forty tanks.

Having completed the occupation of Kuwait, the Iraqi armored and mechanized divisions and the elite Republican Guard advanced south toward Kuwait's border with Saudi Ara-bia. Intelligence sources believed that the Iraqis were position-ing themselves for a subsequent drive toward the Saudi oil fields and shipping terminals, possibly continuing toward the other gulf states.

In the first of a series of resolutions condemning Iraq, the United Nations (UN) Security Council on August 2 called for Iraq's unconditional and immediate withdrawal from Kuwait. In the ensuing months, a coalition force of more than 600,000 ground, sea, and air force personnel was deployed to defend Saudi Arabia and to drive the Iraqis out of Kuwait. Command of the coalition force was divided: the commander in chief of the United States Central Command, General H. Norman Schwarzkopf, headed United States, British, and French units; his Saudi counterpart, Lieutenant General Khalid ibn Sultan ibn Abd al Aziz Al Saud, commanded units from twenty-four non-Western countries, including troops from Saudi Arabia, Egypt, Syria, Kuwait, and the other Persian Gulf states. In addi-tion to 20,000 Saudi troops and 7,000 Kuwaiti troops, an esti-mated 3,000 personnel from the other GCC states took part in the land forces of the coalition offensive, which was known as Operation Desert Storm.

When the massive coalition ground assault of Operation Desert Storm got under way on February 24, 1991, troops of the Persian Gulf states formed part of two Arab task forces. The first, Joint Forces Command North, consisting of Egyptian, Saudi, Syrian, and Kuwaiti troops, deployed on Kuwait's western border. Joint Forces Command East deployed along the gulf immediately south of Kuwait and consisted of about five brigades (each well below the strength of a regular Western brigade) from Saudi Arabia, Kuwait, Bahrain, and Qatar. The main attack was a sweeping movement by United States, British, and French forces in the west designed to cut the links between the Iraqi forces in Kuwait and their bases in Iraq. The Saudis and Kuwaitis on the western border of Kuwait, composed of about four brigades organized as the Khalid Division, together with an Egyptian regiment, breached Iraqi defenses after allied bombing and engineer operations blasted passages. Iraqi troops, although in strong positions, surrendered or streamed to the north. Units of Joint Forces Command East advanced up the coastal road, capturing the city of Kuwait on the third day of the offensive after light fighting and the surrender of thousands of Iraqi soldiers.

Territorial Disputes

Before the oil era, the gulf states made little effort to delineate their territories. Members of Arab tribes felt loyalty to their tribe or shaykh and tended to roam across the peninsula's desert areas according to the needs of their flocks. Official boundaries meant little, and the concept of allegiance to a distinct political unit was absent. Organized authority was confined to ports and oases. The delineation of borders began with the signing of the first oil concessions in the 1930s. The national boundaries had been defined by the British, but many of these borders were never properly demarcated, leaving opportunities for contention, especially in areas of the most valuable oil deposits. Until 1971 British-led forces maintained peace and order in the gulf, and British officials arbitrated local quarrels. After the withdrawal of these forces and officials, old territorial claims and suppressed tribal animosities rose to the surface. The concept of the modern state—introduced into the gulf region by the European powers—and the sudden importance of boundaries to define ownership of oil deposits kindled acute territorial disputes.

Iran has often laid claim to Bahrain, based on its seventeenth-century defeat of the Portuguese and its subsequent occupation of the Bahrain archipelago. The Arab clan of the Al Khalifa, which has been the ruling family of Bahrain since the eighteenth century, in turn expelled the Iranians in 1783. The late shah, Mohammad Reza Pahlavi, raised the Bahrain question when the British withdrew from areas east of Suez, but he dropped his demand after a 1970 UN-sponsored plebiscite showed that Bahrainis overwhelmingly preferred independence to Iranian rule.

In 1971 Iranian forces occupied the islands of Abu Musa, Tunb al Kubra (Greater Tumb), and Tunb as Sughra (Lesser Tumb), located at the mouth of the Persian Gulf between Iran and the UAE. The Iranians reasserted their historic claims to the islands, although the Iranians had been dislodged by the British in the late nineteenth century. Iran continued to occupy the islands in 1993, and its action remained a source of contention with the UAE, which claimed authority by virtue of Britain's transfer of the islands to the amirates of Sharjah and Ras al Khaymah. By late 1992, Sharjah and Iran had reached agreement with regard to Abu Musa, but Ras al Khaymah had not reached a settlement with Iran concerning Greater Tumb and Lesser Tumb.

Another point of contention in the gulf is the Bahraini claim to Az Zubarah on the northwest coast of Qatar and to Hawar and the adjacent islands forty kilometers south of Az Zubarah, claims that stem from former tribal areas and dynastic struggles. The Al Khalifa had settled at Az Zubarah before driving the Iranians out of Bahrain in the eighteenth century. The Al Thani ruling family of Qatar vigorously dispute the Al Khalifa claim to Az Zubarah, as well as lay claim to the Bahraini-occupied Hawar and adjacent islands, a stone's throw from the mainland of Qatar but more than twenty kilometers from Bahrain. The simmering quarrel reignited in the spring of 1986 when Qatari helicopters removed and "kidnapped" workmen constructing a Bahraini coast guard station on Fasht ad Dibal, a reef off the coast of Qatar. Through Saudi mediation, the parties reached a fragile truce, whereby the Bahrainis agreed to remove their installations. However, in 1991 the dispute flared up again after Qatar instituted proceedings to let the International Court of Justice in The Hague decide whether it had jurisdiction. (Bahrain refused the jurisdiction of the court, and as of early 1993 the dispute was unresolved.) The two countries exchanged complaints that their respective naval vessels had harassed the other's shipping in disputed waters.

As one pretext for his invasion of Kuwait in 1990, Saddam Husayn revived a long-standing Iraqi claim to the whole of Kuwait based on Ottoman boundaries. Ottoman Turkey exercised a tenuous sovereignty over Kuwait in the late nineteenth century, but the area passed under British protection in 1899. In 1932 Iraq informally confirmed its border with Kuwait, which had previously been demarcated by the British. In 1961, after Kuwait's independence and the withdrawal of British troops, Iraq reasserted its claim to the amirate based on the Ottomans' having attached it to Basra Province. British troops and aircraft were rushed back to Kuwait. A Saudi-led force of 3,000 from the League of Arab States (Arab League) that supported Kuwait against Iraqi pressure soon replaced them.

The boundary issue again arose when the Baath Party came to power in Iraq after a 1963 revolution. The new government officially recognized the independence of Kuwait and the boundaries Iraq had accepted in 1932. Iraq nevertheless reinstated its claims to Bubiyan and Warbah in 1973, massing troops at the border. During the 1980–88 war with Iran, Iraq pressed for a long-term lease to the islands in order to improve its access to the gulf and its strategic position. Although Kuwait rebuffed Iraq, relations continued to be strained by boundary issues and inconclusive negotiations over the status of the two islands.

In August 1991, Kuwait charged that a force of Iraqis, backed by gunboats, had attacked Bubiyan but had been repulsed and many of the invaders captured. UN investigators found that the Iraqis had come from fishing boats and had probably been scavenging for military supplies abandoned after the Persian Gulf War. Kuwait was suspected of having exaggerated the incident to underscore its need for international support against ongoing Iraqi hostility.

A particularly long and acrimonious disagreement involved claims over the Al Buraymi Oasis, disputed since the nineteenth century among tribes from Saudi Arabia, Abu Dhabi, and Oman. Although the tribes residing in the several settlements of the oasis were from Oman and Abu Dhabi, followers of the Wahhabi (see Glossary) religious movement that originated in Saudi Arabia had periodically occupied and exacted tribute from the area. Oil prospecting began on behalf of Saudi oil interests, and in 1952 the Saudis sent a small constabulary force to assert control of the oasis. When arbitration efforts broke down in 1955, the British dispatched the Trucial Oman Scouts to expel the Saudi contingent. After new negotiations, a settlement was reached in 1974 whereby Saudi Arabia recognized claims of Abu Dhabi and Oman to the oasis. In return, Abu Dhabi agreed to grant Saudi Arabia a land corridor to the gulf and a share of a disputed oil field. Other disagreements over boundaries and water rights remained, however.

The border between Oman and Yemen remained only partially defined, and, as of early 1993, border clashes had not occurred since 1988. Improving relations between Oman and the People's Democratic Republic of Yemen (PDRY, also seen as South Yemen)—which was reunited with the Yemen Arab Republic (YAR, also seen as North Yemen) in 1990—offered some hope that the border would be demarcated. Earlier, the physical separation of the southern portion of Oman from its territory on the Musandam Peninsula (Ras Musandam) was a source of friction between Oman and the various neighboring amirates that became the UAE in 1971. Differences over the disputed territory appeared to have subsided after the onset of the Iran-Iraq War in 1980.

Regional Security Problems

The Persian Gulf is a relatively constricted geographic area of great existing or potential volatility. The smaller states of the gulf are particularly vulnerable, having limited indigenous populations and, in most cases, armed forces with little more than symbolic value to defend their countries against aggression. All of them lack strategic depth, and their economies and oil industries depend on access to the sea. Conflicts involving the air forces and navies of the larger gulf powers inevitably endanger their critical transportation links. Closure of the Strait of Hormuz, which was threatened but which never actually occurred during the Iran-Iraq War, would have a catastrophic effect on regular ship movements.

The oil drilling, processing, and loading facilities of the Persian Gulf states, some of them on offshore platforms, are vital to their economies. In an era of highly accurate missiles and high-performance aircraft, the protection of these exposed resources against surprise attack presents enormous difficulties. Even those states that can afford the sophisticated weaponry to defend their installations can ensure their effectiveness only through proper training, manning, and maintenance.

Most of the Arab gulf states, although vulnerable by air and by sea, are relatively immune from ground attack. Because of their geographic position on the Arabian Peninsula, they are exposed on their landward side only to vast desert tracts controlled by Saudi Arabia, with which they are linked by security treaties. Potential aggressors in the region, although heavily armed, lack the equipment or experience to project their forces over long distances. The only realistic possibility of overland attack seems to be in the north, where Kuwait has no natural line of defense and its oil facilities are near both Iran and Iraq. In early 1992, Kuwaiti officials disclosed plans to construct an electronic fence stretching more than 200 kilometers along the Kuwait-Iraq border. Although some obstacles might be emplaced to obstruct an Iraqi crossing, the main purpose of the fence is to prevent infiltration. Border guards of Kuwait's Ministry of Interior are to patrol the fence area.

In the south, reunited Yemen had inherited large stocks of military equipment from the Soviet Union's earlier support of the PDRY. Yemen's political support of Iraq in the Kuwaiti crisis caused the GCC states to regard it as a potentially hostile neighbor. Although offensive operations against Oman or Saudi Arabia, with which it shared long, undefined borders, seem unlikely, the encouragement of border infiltration by all three countries cannot be ruled out.

The Iranian Revolution of 1979 introduced a new threat to stability in the gulf. Shia form a majority of the population of Bahrain and an important part of the foreign labor force in Kuwait and are considered potential dissidents in any future hostilities. Numerous terrorist actions in Kuwait during the 1980s were attributed to domestic Shia instigated by Iran (see Kuwait: Internal Security, this ch.). Iran is one of the strongest military powers of the region and has historically sought to extend its influence to the Arab shore of the gulf. Nevertheless, fears of military confrontation subsided after the Iran-Iraq War ended. The influence of the more extremist elements within the Iranian government appears to have declined; Iran also had opposed Iraq's invasion of Kuwait.

In spite of Iraq's defeat in 1991, Kuwait remains the most vulnerable of the gulf states. Despite the crippling of Iraq's offensive military capabilities, it continues to be a formidable military power in the region. Its postwar manpower strength is estimated at 380,000, including at least three intact divisions of the elite Republican Guard, as well as large stocks of armor, artillery, and combat aircraft. Only with the assurance of outside support can the GCC states be confident that they can successfully resist renewed Iraqi aggression.

The gulf Arabs believe that a settlement of the Arab-Israeli conflict will enhance gulf security. Direct conflict with Israel was a remote contingency in early 1993, although Israel's doctrine of preemptive attack and its demonstrated ability to hit distant targets must be reckoned with in their strategic planning. Because the northwestern areas of Saudi Arabia are well within range of Israeli attack, air defense units that would otherwise be available to the GCC for gulf defense must be positioned there. Efforts of the Arab gulf states to upgrade their air defense systems have often been viewed by the United States Congress and by the public as hostile to Israeli interests.

In early 1993, two years after Saddam Husayn's defeat in the Persian Gulf War, the region's security appeared more stable than in many years. The fear of a communist encroachment or of a superpower confrontation has evaporated. Iran seems to be seeking greater accommodation with its gulf neighbors, although the Tehran government is continuing its military buildup and insists that it has a role in regional mutual security. Iraq, although still hostile, does not present an immediate military threat. The United States and other Western powers have indicated that they will act against any new instability in the gulf that endangers their interests.

Collective Security under the Gulf Cooperation Council

The six Persian Gulf states of the Arabian Peninsula—Bahrain, Kuwait, Oman, Qatar, Saudi Arabia, and the UAE—formed the GCC in May 1981 with the aim of "co-ordination, integration, and co-operation among the member-states in all fields." Although none of the committees initially established dealt with security, the final communiqué of the first meeting affirmed the will and the intention of the signatories to defend their security and independence and to keep the region free of international conflicts. Four months later, the chiefs of staff of the armed forces of the six member states met to discuss regional military cooperation. The immediate objective was to protect themselves from the dangers posed by the Iran-Iraq War and the political violence associated with revolutionary Islam. In a series of meetings over the years, the defense ministers and chiefs of staff devoted numerous sessions to the improvement of military cooperation and the creation of a

334

*Rulers of the member states of the Gulf Cooperation Council
pose for a photograph.
Courtesy Embassy of the Sultanate of Oman, Washington*

joint command and joint air defense mechanisms. Managing their common security challenges collectively has made progress in some areas, but little in others. Creation of a fully integrated air defense system was far from a reality as of early 1993. The GCC states have not realized plans to develop an arms production capacity, although they have launched a new effort to revive an earlier arrangement with Egypt to create a pan-Arab weapons industry.

Political differences among GCC members have been the main obstacles to placing gulf defense on a collective rather than on a bilateral basis, even in such matters as achieving interoperability of equipment and cooperating in training, logistics, and infrastructure. The GCC experienced delays in reaching agreement to cooperate in internal security matters because Kuwait, the chief target of terrorism, feared that its relatively liberal domestic security regime might be impaired. Until Kuwait accepted a GCC agreement in late 1987, Saudi Arabia and several other members of the GCC coordinated their efforts bilaterally, including the exchange of equipment, expertise, and training; the extradition of criminals; and the interception of border infiltrators. GCC members have adopted parallel policies on deportation and travel restrictions and share information on suspected terrorists and plots.

Ground and air units of the six member states have carried out small-scale combined training exercises. Military assistance, provided mainly by Saudi Arabia and Kuwait under GCC auspices, has enabled Bahrain to modernize its stock of combat aircraft and Oman to improve its air and sea defenses around the Strait of Hormuz. In 1984 GCC defense ministers agreed to create the Peninsula Shield force and base it at Hafar al Batin in Saudi Arabia, about sixty kilometers south of the Kuwaiti border. Under the command of a Saudi general, the unit consists of one Saudi brigade and a composite brigade with token personnel from the other states.

The limited reaction of the GCC to the August 2 Iraqi invasion of Kuwait exposed its weakness when faced with direct aggression against a member of the alliance by a much stronger power. The GCC immediately condemned the Iraqi action, but when GCC defense ministers met three weeks later, they could only agree on strengthening the Peninsula Shield force. During the Persian Gulf War, national contingents deployed separately as units of Arab task forces.

At the conclusion of the war on March 3, 1991, the six members of the GCC, along with Syria and Egypt, met in Damascus to agree on the establishment of a permanent security force to protect Kuwait against future aggression. Syria and Egypt were to contribute troop contingents on a reimbursable basis. The Damascus Declaration soon unraveled when differences emerged over the desirability of a long-term Egyptian and Syrian presence in the gulf. However, Egypt and Syria remain committed under the agreement to send military aid to Kuwait and the other gulf states if a threat arises.

Kuwait subsequently negotiated defense cooperation agreements with the United States, Britain, and France as an additional form of security if its borders were again threatened (see Kuwait: Background, this ch.). At a GCC meeting in late 1991, Oman proposed that the six GCC members develop a 100,000-strong joint security force under a unified military command. The Omani plan was set aside after other defense ministers questioned whether the manpower target was attainable and whether administrative and procedural problems could be overcome. The consensus of the ministers was that the Peninsula Shield force should be the nucleus of a unified army, the realization of which might be many years in the future.

Military Capabilities of the Persian Gulf States

During the decade after the outbreak of the Iran-Iraq War, all the gulf states set out to strengthen their armed forces by converting to the most modern weapons they could obtain and assimilate. By 1993 each state had at least a modest inventory of tanks and other armored equipment, air defense missiles, combat aircraft, armed helicopters, and missile-armed naval craft with which to deter an intruder. Kuwait is less prepared than the others, not having recovered from the losses it suffered in personnel and equipment during the Persian Gulf War. A fundamental constraint for all the gulf states has been the limited pool of qualified manpower and, in most countries, the problem of attracting recruits when better employment opportunities exist in the civilian sector. The emphasis on advanced weaponry is part of an effort to minimize the need for personnel. As stated by a senior Kuwaiti officer, the object is to obtain the best equipment technologically, "easy to maintain, understand, and operate . . . the greatest firepower for the smallest human effort." But integrating modern weapons into the gulf armies and ensuring their effective operation create other problems. Such problems include the necessity of continued reliance on foreign officers and foreign maintenance and training of staffs at a time when all gulf states are trying to achieve greater self-sufficiency. Dependence on foreign personnel, moreover, implies a degree of loyalty and trustworthiness that may not be forthcoming in times of crisis.

Although in every case the gulf armies are much larger than the air forces and navies, the ground forces have traditionally been oriented toward counterinsurgency actions and the protection of the ruling families. Most of the armies are organized into one or more combat brigades; actual fighting strengths are generally lower than the brigade structure implies. Except for the officers and men who were briefly exposed to modern military operations during the Persian Gulf War—and in the late 1960s and first half of the 1970s during Oman's war with Dhofari guerrillas and their supporters in the PDRY—most have not faced actual combat situations.

In recognition of the great strategic importance of their air and sea defenses, the gulf states have all introduced modern combat aircraft and air defense missile systems, such as the United States Hawk surface-to-air missile (SAM). Several of the states have in their inventories or on order attack helicopters to help protect their oil facilities and oil drilling platforms in the gulf. All the gulf states have communications, control, and warning systems for the effective use of their fighter aircraft and antiaircraft missiles. But each air force is small, and, unless integrated with others, the overall effectiveness of the GCC in air defense is marginal. In spite of the attention the problem has received, there is no common network linking all air defense squadrons and SAMs to the Saudi Arabian air defense system and to the Saudi airborne warning and control system (AWACS) aircraft. Technical difficulties, including the incompatibility of national communications systems and the reluctance to turn control of national air defense over to a unified command structure, account for this weakness.

Fast missile attack craft acquired by all of the gulf navies with small but well-trained crews could inflict damaging blows to heavier fleets and discourage hostile amphibious operations. The sixty-two-meter corvettes belonging to Bahrain and the UAE are the largest vessels among the gulf navies. As the Iran-Iraq War demonstrated, the navies lack minesweeping capability, and their shipboard defense weapons against air attack are also weak. Only Oman has available large amphibious transports to convey troops and vehicles for defending islands or remote coastal areas.

Defense expenditures of the gulf states are among the highest in the world relative to population. According to an analysis covering 1989, prepared by the United States Arms Control and Disarmament Agency, Qatar recorded the highest per capita military expenditures of any country in the world, followed by Israel and the United States. Oman ranked fourth and Kuwait sixth. The UAE was eleventh highest; Bahrain, listed in twenty-seventh place worldwide, had the lowest outlays relatively of the gulf states. Military spending as a percentage of central government expenditures also is high, amounting to more than 40 percent in Oman and the UAE, for example. In contrast, military spending in Bahrain is 13 percent of central government expenditure. Military expenditures as a percentage of the gross national product (GNP—see Glossary) are more moderate except for Oman, whose military outlays were more than 20 percent of GNP in 1989. Force ratios are also high in Oman and the UAE; both countries had about twenty men in uniform per 1,000 population in 1989. Their respective rankings were eleventh and twelfth highest in the world. Bahrain and Kuwait had manpower levels of about ten per 1,000 population, whereas the level for Qatar was fifteen per 1,000 in 1989.

In spite of the small personnel pools and the desire of all the gulf governments to train nationals to replace foreigners as quickly as possible, constraints found in traditional Islamic societies prevent the widespread recruitment of women to serve in the armed forces. Oman and Bahrain have allowed a few women to enlist. They receive combat-style training and learn how to operate small arms. In Bahrain, however, almost all the women have been assigned to hospital staffs. In 1990 the UAE introduced a five-month training course for female recruits with the assistance of a team of female soldiers from the United States. About 1,200 women applied; only seventy-four were accepted. Two top members of the first class were selected to continue with officer training at the Royal Military Academy at Sandhurst in Britain. The other graduates of the first class were assigned as bodyguards of female members of the ruling families and as specialists in such fields as military intelligence.

Before the Persian Gulf War, some women served in support departments of the Kuwaiti armed forces, including engineering, military establishments, moral guidance, and public relations. In July 1991, noting that a large number of women had volunteered for service in the postwar military, the minister of defense said that some would be accepted for a training period of three to six months but would initially be unsalaried. A role would then be found for them. The minister cautioned that acceptance by Kuwaiti society was essential for the government to move ahead with this plan.

Kuwait

Background

From 1899 until 1961, Kuwait remained, in effect, a British protectorate. A succession of amirs of the Al Sabah ruled the country, but the handling of its foreign affairs was a British prerogative, and Britain guaranteed the security of the amirate. Kuwaiti forces consisted of the amir's royal guard plus a small domestic police force or constabulary under the British administration. During the 1920s and 1930s, British protection became particularly important in deterring Saudi encroachment and later in blocking Iraqi territorial claims. By independence on June 19, 1961, the British had converted the 600-man constabulary into a combined arms brigade of 2,500 men trained by a British military mission. Small air and naval forces were also established in 1961 under British tutelage.

With its small size and enormous oil wealth, Kuwait occupies an uneasy position at the head of the gulf. One of its powerful neighbors, Iran, only forty kilometers away, had proclaimed its aim of exporting its Islamic revolution; another powerful neighbor, Iraq, had repeatedly challenged Kuwait's legitimacy (see Territorial Disputes, this ch.). Fearful of the radical leadership in Iran, Kuwait aided Iraq during the Iran-Iraq War by permitting the transshipment of goods across its territory and by loans of about US$6 billion. Kuwait responded to terrorist bombings and other violence inspired by Iran by intensifying its military cooperation with the GCC and by building up its own forces. Although formally neutral and reluctant to become involved with the great powers except as a last resort, Kuwait turned to the United States, the Soviet Union, and Britain for naval protection of its tanker fleet after twenty-one ships were attacked in the gulf in the six months preceding April 1987.

Iraq's surprise attack and occupation of Kuwait caused the virtual disintegration of the Kuwaiti armed forces. Large numbers of personnel were killed, captured, or dispersed, and most Kuwaiti equipment was destroyed or taken over by the Iraqi armed forces. The minister of defense said that 90 percent of military installations had suffered major damage. By early 1992, most army barracks were again usable, and the naval base was in operation but needed rebuilding. The air force flew temporarily from the civilian airport near the city of Kuwait while

Kuwaiti soldiers in formation during a dignitary's visit to their outpost in Operation Desert Shield
Kuwaiti M–84 main battle tank lays a smoke screen in an exercise during Operation Desert Shield.
Courtesy United States Air Force

the air bases were being reconstructed in 1992. Kuwait expected to spend about US$9 billion—six times the prewar defense budget—in 1992 to replace destroyed equipment and installations.

In a sharp departure from previous policy, Kuwait entered into a ten-year defense cooperation agreement with the United States in September 1991. The agreement included provisions for United States port access, military equipment storage, and joint training and exercises. The agreement did not provide for the stationing of United States military personnel in Kuwait; 1,500 personnel remaining after the gulf war were scheduled to leave within a few months. Similar but less extensive ten-year cooperation agreements were subsequently concluded with Britain and France.

Organization and Mission of the Forces

Under the constitution, the amir is the supreme commander of the armed forces. The minister of defense directs the armed forces through the chief of general staff. The National Guard has its own commander, who reports directly to the minister of defense. The public security forces are all under the minister of interior. The minister of defense in early 1993, Ali as Sabah as Salim Al Sabah, had been shifted from the Ministry of Interior as part of the military shakeup after the gulf war. The ruling family maintained a tight grip on the centers of power, including many senior posts in the security services.

Before the Iraqi invasion, the army's manpower strength was 16,000 officers and enlisted men. The principal combat formations were three armored brigades, one mechanized infantry brigade, and one artillery brigade with a regiment of self-propelled howitzers and a surface-to-surface missile (SSM) battalion. All the combat units were under strength; by one estimate, as of 1988 the army's entire fighting strength was the equivalent of only one Western brigade.

Kuwait's first-line main battle tanks are M–84s, Yugoslav versions of the Soviet T–72 tank. The army has various models of British armored cars and armored personnel carriers (APCs). Its artillery consists of 155mm self-propelled howitzers, mainly of French manufacture. Kuwait has a large inventory of antitank missile systems of British, French, and United States origin, including the improved TOW (tube-launched, optically sighted, wire-guided) missile from the United States. It has purchased the Soviet FROG–7, a mobile battlefield missile with a range of sixty kilometers. In 1984, after the United States rejected a Kuwaiti order for Stinger shoulder-fired SAMs, Kuwait turned to Moscow for air defense weapons, purchasing SA–7 and SA–8 SAMs and ZSU–23-4 antiaircraft guns.

An estimate of the postwar strength of the Kuwaiti army, published in *The Military Balance, 1992–1993*, revealed the devastating effect of the Persian Gulf War. The disparate ground forces, estimated to number about 8,000, were to be reconstituted into four understrength mechanized and armored brigades, a reserve brigade, and an artillery brigade. Little matériel survived the war: some tanks, APCs, and 155mm guns (see table 38, Appendix). Kuwait's postwar equipment orders include 200 M–84 tanks (from Serbia to offset previous Serb oil purchases) and eighteen self-propelled 155mm guns from France. Kuwait also has received United States, Russian, and Egyptian armored vehicles.

The air force complement in 1990 before the gulf war was estimated at 2,200, excluding foreign personnel. Its inventory included about eighty combat aircraft, mainly Mirage F1s from France and A–4 Skyhawks from the United States, and more than forty helicopters of French manufacture, some fitted for assault missions with antitank missiles. Ground-based air defense was structured around the United States improved Hawk (I–Hawk) missile system, tied into Saudi air defense to receive data transmitted by United States and Saudi AWACS aircraft that had been operating in the area since the start of the Iran-Iraq War.

The Military Balance estimated that the immediate postwar complement of the air force was 1,000, with thirty-four combat aircraft and twelve armed helicopters remaining. By early 1993, however, air force personnel numbered about 2,500, with seventy-four combat aircraft, including McDonnell Douglas A–4s and F–18s, and twenty armed helicopters. Its two air bases, at Ahmad al Jabir and Ali as Salim, badly damaged in the war, are being repaired. In addition to Iraq's capture of the four batteries of I–Hawk medium-range SAMs, most of the fleet of transport aircraft was lost to Iraq. Before the occupation of the amirate, the Kuwaiti air force had ordered forty United States F–18 fighter aircraft plus air-to-air missiles and cluster bombs. Deliveries under this order began in the first half of 1992. Kuwait will acquire the strongest air defense network in the Persian Gulf region under a proposal announced by the United States in March 1992 to transfer six Patriot antiballistic missile SAM firing units (each consisting of up to four quadruple launchers, radar, and a control station) and six batteries of

Hawk SAMs. The sale will include 450 Patriot missiles and 342 Hawk missiles.

The navy's strength had been estimated at 1,800 in 1990 before the Iraqi occupation. Previously a coastal defense force with police responsibilities, the navy's combat capabilities were significantly enhanced during 1984 with the delivery of eight fast-attack craft armed with Exocet antiship missiles from the West German Lürssen shipyard. The navy also operated a wide variety of smaller patrol craft. According to *The Military Balance,* the navy was reduced to about 500 personnel in 1992 as a result of the Persian Gulf War and the Kuwaiti policy of removing *bidun* ("without"—stateless persons without citizenship, many of whom had long-standing stays in Kuwait while others came in the 1960s and 1970s as oil field workers and construction workers) from the armed forces. By early 1993, however, naval personnel numbered about 1,200, including the coast guard. With the exception of two missile boats, the entire fleet was captured and sunk or badly damaged by coalition forces while being operated by the Iraqis. Some ships are believed to be salvageable. Five Republic of Korea (South Korea) twenty-four-meter patrol craft were among the vessels lost. However, delivery is expected on an additional four craft under an order pending when the war broke out.

Role of Kuwaiti Armed Forces in the Persian Gulf War

The Iraqi invasion in the early hours of August 2 was detected by a balloon-borne early warning radar, but the army had insufficient time to mount any organized resistance. Some contingents continued a small-unit defense, including those equipped with Chieftain tanks. About 7,000 soldiers escaped to Saudi Arabia; the remainder were killed or captured or participated in the internal resistance movement. Some Mirage and Skyhawk aircraft carried out attacks on the advancing Iraqi columns; when their air base in southern Kuwait was overrun, they flew to Saudi Arabian bases, as did some of the armed helicopters.

According to Norman Friedman, author of a study on the strategy and tactics of the Persian Gulf War, the Kuwaiti forces participating in Operation Desert Storm in February 1991 included the 35th Armored Brigade (renamed Martyr Brigade), the 15th Infantry Brigade, and the lightly equipped Liberation Brigade, which was armed with .50-caliber machine guns mounted on trucks. One source estimated that 7,000 Kuwaiti troops were involved. The Martyr Brigade was the first

of the units of Joint Forces Command East in the drive paralleling the coast northward when the allied operation began on
February 24, 1991. Along with Saudi, Qatari, and Bahraini
forces, supported by United States marines on their left flank,
their assignment of liberating the city of Kuwait incurred little
Iraqi resistance.

Of twenty-four Kuwaiti aircraft participating in strikes
against the Iraqi forces, one A–4 Skyhawk was lost to enemy
fire. The two surviving Kuwaiti missile craft, carrying small
marine contingents, were able to retake oil platforms and some
of the gulf islands. Kuwait suffered only one combat death,
according to an official British source.

Kuwait pledged contributions totaling more than US$16 bil-
lion to support the United States role in the Persian Gulf War.
An additional US$6 billion was promised to Egypt and other
member countries of the coalition to help offset the economic
effects of the war.

Personnel, Training, and Recruitment

Unlike other Persian Gulf states, Kuwait has a conscription
system that obligates young men to serve for two years beginning at the age of eighteen. Educational deferments are
granted, and university graduates serve for only one year. In
practice, exemptions are liberally granted, and most young
Kuwaitis are able to avoid military duty. Estimates are that only
20 to 30 percent of the prewar military ranks were filled by
Kuwaiti nationals. Military and security forces had been purged
of Shia personnel during the 1980s. At the outbreak of the gulf
war, Palestinians filled many technical positions, supported by
thousands of Pakistanis, Indians, and Filipinos in maintenance
and logistic functions. Officers on detail from Britain, Pakistan,
Egypt, and Jordan provided military expertise. Lower ranks in
the army and security forces were occupied predominantly by
bidun, who had taken reasonably well to military life but were
poorly prepared to absorb training in operating and servicing
modern equipment. In spite of reports that many *bidun* fought
well against the Iraqis, many were expelled from the army in
1991 for alleged collaboration. Because of their removal and
the removal of Palestinians and other non-Kuwaitis, the ranks
of the services became seriously depleted. Few Kuwaitis volun-
teer for military service, and conscription is not regarded as an
acceptable option. Under the circumstances, Kuwait will be
hard pressed to meet its goal of a postwar armed strength of
30,000. A relaxation of the policy toward *bidun* was hinted at by

the statement of the minister of defense that people of "unspecified nationality" may be retained after screening for loyalty and may even be given Kuwaiti citizenship. With respect to conscription, the minister of defense in July 1991 said that the system was being reviewed to make it more effective.

Most Kuwaiti officers are members of the ruling family or related tribal groups. Education standards are high—many are graduates of Sandhurst—and living conditions, pay, and benefits are excellent. The Kuwaiti Military College accepts secondary school graduates for eighteen months of cadet training in army, air force, and navy programs. The United States provides pilot training and assistance in developing a flight training facility within Kuwait. United States, British, and French military missions and civilian contractors provide training for more technologically advanced systems. A small Soviet advisory group provided training in the use of Soviet missile systems before the Persian Gulf War.

Traditionally, the officer corps—with its close links to the ruling family—was considered to be a loyal and trustworthy defender of the regime. In the aftermath of the Persian Gulf War, however, there were displays of discontent among officers arising from the inadequate response of the armed forces to the Iraqi invasion and the failure to launch postwar reforms. Many of the 6,000 officers and men taken prisoner by the Iraqis were prevented from rejoining the armed forces and were angered at their treatment by senior officers who fled to Saudi Arabia. In June 1991, some officers of the resistance group known as the Second of August Movement petitioned the amir to dismiss the former ministers of defense and interior from their cabinet posts and to investigate the reason the Kuwaiti army was not mobilized or on the alert when the Iraqis attacked. The petition also called for removal of the army chief of staff and his immediate staff and as many as twenty generals and seventy-five colonels.

In July fourteen senior officers were forced into retirement. The amir reportedly met with disaffected officers to tell them that their calls for reform would be considered. Officers threatened with dismissal for signing the petition were reinstated, and other reform-minded officers were reportedly promoted.

Internal Security

Many of the domestic strains in Kuwait arise from the disparities between the living standards of Kuwaiti nationals and the majority of Kuwait's foreign population. Palestinian workers presented problems for the Al Sabah rulers for several decades, but, during the 1980s, militants and terrorists advancing revolutionary Islam overshadowed the Palestinians as troublemakers. Kuwait's support for Iraq in the Iran-Iraq War accounted for much of the violence that disturbed internal stability during the 1980s. A series of terrorist bombings in 1983 aimed at Kuwaiti installations and the United States and French embassies were ascribed to events in Lebanon. A network of Hizballah terrorists was uncovered, and, in the spring of 1984, seventeen Shia were sentenced to long prison terms, and three were condemned to death. Airplane hijackings, explosions, car bombings, and an assassination attempt against the amir ensued. Kuwait steadfastly rejected demands for release of terrorists in its custody, most of whom were still in jail at the time of the Iraqi invasion and subsequently disappeared. A number of Kuwaiti Shia were sentenced for setting fires at oil installations in 1986 and 1987. The incidents declined after 1988.

Police and the Criminal Justice System

The Ministry of Interior has overall responsibility for public security and law and order. Under the ministry, the national police has primary responsibility for maintaining public order and preventing and investigating crimes. The National Guard, a semiautonomous body, has guard duties on the border and at oil fields, utilities, and other strategic locations. The guard acts as a reserve for the regular forces and reinforces the metropolitan police as needed.

Police selected for officer rank attend a three-year program at the Police Academy. National Guard officer candidates attend the Kuwaiti Military College, after which they receive specialized guard training. Women work in certain police departments, such as criminal investigation, inquiries, and airport security.

The principal police divisions are criminal investigation, traffic, emergency police, nationality and passports, immigration, prisons, civil defense, and trials and courts-martial. The criminal investigation division is responsible for ordinary criminal cases; Kuwait State Security investigates security-related offenses. Both are involved in investigations of terrorism and those suspected of collaboration with Iraq.

The Kuwaiti judicial system generally provides fair public trials and an adequate appeals mechanism, according to the United States Department of State's *Country Reports on Human*

Rights Practices for 1991. Under Kuwaiti law, no detainee can be held for more than four days without charge; after being charged by a prosecutor, detention for up to an additional twenty-one days is possible. Persons held under the State Security Law can be detained. Bail is commonly set in all cases. The lowest level courts, aside from traffic courts, are the misdemeanor courts that judge offenses subject to imprisonment not exceeding three years. Courts of first instance hear felony cases in which the punishment can exceed three years. All defendants in felony cases are required to be represented by attorneys, appointed by the court if necessary. Legal counsel is optional in misdemeanor cases, and the court is not obliged to provide an attorney.

Kuwaiti authorities contend that the rate of ordinary crime is low, and data available through 1986 tended to bear this out. Of more than 5,000 felonies committed in that year, only 5 percent were in the category of theft. The number of misdemeanors was roughly equal to the number of felonies, but only 10 percent were thefts. Offenses involving forgery, fraud, bribery, assaults and threats, and narcotics and alcohol violations were all more common than thefts.

Two separate State Security Court panels, each composed of three justices, hear crimes against state security or other cases referred to it by the Council of Ministers. Trials in the State Security Court, with few exceptions, are held in closed session. They do not, in the judgment of the Department of State, meet international standards for fair trials. Military courts, which ordinarily have jurisdiction only over members of the armed services or security forces, can try offenses charged against civilians under conditions of martial law. Martial law was imposed for the first time after the liberation of the country from Iraqi occupation. About 300 persons suspected of collaboration with Iraq were tried by military courts in May and June 1991, and 115 were convicted. Twenty-nine received sentences of death, later commuted to life imprisonment after international criticism of the trials. Human rights groups drew attention to the failure to provide adequate legal safeguards to defendants and an unwillingness to accept the defense that collaboration with Iraqi forces had been coerced. Many of the accused alleged that their confessions had been extracted under torture.

Human Rights Practices

Prior to the occupation of Kuwait in 1990, the principal

human rights concerns, aside from widespread restriction on the exercise of political expression, were instances of arbitrary arrest and mistreatment of prisoners and lack of due process in security trials. A number of Kuwaitis were arrested between late 1989 and mid-1990 for political reasons and for participating in unlicensed gatherings. Noncitizens could be arbitrarily expelled if deemed security risks and were also subject to deportation if they were unable to find work after being released from their initial employment. Some foreigners reportedly were held in deportation centers for up to five years because they were unable to provide for their own travel out of the country. According to the Department of State, there were plausible reports of occasional torture and violence in apprehending and interrogating criminal suspects.

The seven-month Iraqi occupation subjected Kuwaitis to a systematic terror campaign that included extrajudicial killings, torture and other inhuman treatment, kidnappings, and arbitrary arrest and detention. There were many credible accounts of killings, not only of members of the Kuwaiti resistance but also of their families, other civilians, and young children. Attacks on Iraqi soldiers resulted in reprisal actions in neighborhoods where attacks had taken place and included summary and random execution of innocent civilians. Many Kuwaiti citizens also disappeared at the hands of the Iraqi occupation authorities. Large-scale executions of young men by gunfire or by hanging were reported. About 850 Kuwaitis remained unaccounted for in early 1993, many of them presumably killed while in Iraqi detention. Iraq insisted that it had no Kuwaiti prisoners.

After the restoration of the amirate government in 1991, there were many reports of beatings and torture to extract confessions from suspected collaborators. The Department of State estimated that forty-five to fifty Palestinian and other foreigners were tortured to death by police or military personnel. As many as 5,800 persons, mostly non-Kuwaitis, were detained on suspicion of collaboration during the four months of martial law that followed the country's liberation. Many arrests were arbitrary, and some detainees were held for months without being charged. As of early 1993, about 900 persons were still in detention; these included persons convicted in the State Security Court or martial law courts and those under deportation order but with no place to go. Of the prewar population of about 400,000 Palestinians resident in Kuwait, only about 30,000 remained. Most of the departures occurred during the

Iraqi occupation; the remainder left because of less favorable living circumstances or because of Kuwaiti pressure.

Bahrain

After more than 100 years of British presence and protection, Bahrain gained full independence on August 15, 1971. The agreement granting independence contained no provision for British defense in an emergency, but it did provide for consultation. British authorities hoped that Bahrain, the most economically and socially advanced of the small gulf states, might take the lead in a federation similar to that of the UAE, but Bahrain opted instead for complete independence. Shaykh Isa ibn Salman Al Khalifa, leader of the Al Khalifa since the death of his father in 1961, became the newly independent country's first amir and continued as the hereditary ruler in 1993.

The constitution designates the amir supreme commander of the armed forces. In 1977 Isa ibn Salman chose his eldest son and heir apparent, Hamad ibn Isa Al Khalifa, to be minister of defense and commander in chief of the Bahrain Defense Force (BDF). In 1988 the former chief of staff, Major General Khalifa ibn Ahmad Al Khalifa, was named minister of defense, but Hamad ibn Isa retained the position of commander in chief in 1993. Other members of the Al Khalifa in prominent military positions include the new chief of staff, Brigadier General Abd Allah ibn Salman Al Khalifa, as well as the assistant chief of staff for operations, the chief of naval staff, and the commander of the air force. As in other Persian Gulf states, the ruling family keeps a tight hold on important positions in the national security structure.

The BDF is principally dedicated to the maintenance of internal security and the protection of the shores of the Bahrain archipelago. Nevertheless, with the rise of tensions in the Persian Gulf, the force has nearly tripled in size since 1984 and has added significantly to its inventory of modern armaments. Its total personnel strength in 1992 was about 6,150: army, 5,000; navy, 500; and air force, 650. The Bahraini army is organized into one brigade, consisting of two mechanized infantry battalions, one tank battalion, one special forces battalion, an armored car squadron, and two artillery and two mortar batteries. Its principal armored weapons are M–60A3 main battle tanks purchased from the United States in the late 1980s. Deliveries are awaited on an order for eighty United States M–113 APCs, supplementing a mixed accumulation of older armored

A–4KU Skyhawk aircraft of the Kuwaiti air force being serviced in Saudi Arabia in preparation for an Operation Desert Storm mission UH–1W Iroquois helicopter of the Bahrain Defense Force takes part in a training mission following Operation Desert Storm.
Courtesy United States Air Force

vehicles. The army's artillery pieces consist of a few towed 105mm and 155mm howitzers. Its principal antitank weapon is the BGM–71A–TOW wire-guided missile (see table 39, Appendix).

Until 1979, when its first fast-attack craft were ordered from the Federal Republic of Germany (West Germany), Bahrain's maritime force was a coast guard under the supervision of the minister of interior. As of 1992, the navy was equipped with two Lürssen sixty-two-meter corvettes. One Dauphin helicopter armed with an antiship missile has been delivered for use with the corvettes. The navy also has in its inventory four forty-five-meter Lürssen fast-attack craft and two thirty-eight-meter craft. The coast guard operates a variety of patrol craft, as well as three landing craft and a Hovercraft.

The Bahraini air force began operations in 1977 with a gradually expanding fleet of helicopters. Its first combat aircraft—United States F–5s—were acquired in 1986, followed in 1990 by more advanced F–16s. As of 1992, it had twelve F–5s and twelve F–16s. Eight Apache attack helicopters were ordered from the United States in 1991 to defend the archipelago and offshore oil platforms against incursions or terrorist action. I–Hawk SAMs are on order as the principal air defense weapon. After initially being denied shoulder-fired Stinger SAMs by congressional objections, Bahrain was allowed to purchase the weapons on a provisional basis and later to retain them permanently. The main air force base is adjacent to Bahrain International Airport on Al Muharraq. Another base developed for use in the Persian Gulf War is available near the southern tip of Bahrain; as of 1992, it was being used for servicing carrier-based United States aircraft.

Defense expenditures, which reached a peak of US$281 million in 1982, fell off sharply before gradually rising again to US$237 million in 1992. Because of its declining revenue from oil, the amirate has fewer resources available for defense than the more prosperous gulf states. The GCC had allotted Bahrain and Oman a special subsidy of US$1.8 billion between 1984 and 1994. Bahrain's share enabled it to purchase new fighter aircraft and to construct its new air base.

At the time of the British withdrawal in 1971, the United States leased port and docking facilities from the government of Bahrain for the United States Middle East Force. This was, in fact, an extension of a United States-British agreement, in effect since the late 1940s, enabling United States naval vessels to use facilities at Al Jufayr, a port section of the capital, Manama. The agreement was a sensitive one because none of the Arab states of the gulf wanted to appear to be submitting to any new form of colonialism or to be too closely associated with the United States, the main supporter of Israel. In 1977 the amir's government terminated the lease. The headquarters of the United States Middle East Force was compelled to move aboard one of the three ships that constituted the force. Otherwise, little changed as a result of the termination of the lease. United States ships—with the aid of a support unit staffed by about sixty-five United States naval personnel—were still permitted to use Bahraini port facilities for naval operations in the gulf to ensure the availability of fuel, communications, and supplies. During the Iran-Iraq War, when attacks on gulf shipping threatened Bahrain's oil refining and tanker servicing operations, United States personnel and military cargoes were permitted to transit the region via Bahrain International Airport. Large barges in Bahraini waters were used as bases for United States attack helicopters, radar, and air defense weapons. In October 1991, Bahrain signed a defense cooperation agreement with the United States similar to that previously concluded between the United States and Kuwait. The agreement provided for port access, equipment storage, and joint exercises.

Role in the Persian Gulf War

Bahrain played a limited but active role in the Persian Gulf War. Bahraini ground forces were among the 3,000 Peninsula Shield force of the GCC (exclusive of Saudi Arabian and Kuwaiti troops) that were assigned to a support role during Operation Desert Storm as part of Joint Forces Command East. Bahrain was the primary coalition naval base and was the point of origin for coalition air operations against Iraqi targets. Bahraini pilots joined other members of the coalition in flying strikes into Iraq. Three Scud missiles were aimed at Bahrain during the war. Only one landed in the country, and it did not hit a target area. There were no Bahraini combat deaths in the war.

Internal Security

The Bahraini national police force was believed by most sources to number about 2,000 in 1992. In addition to the usual police functions, the mission of the force is to prevent sectarian violence and terrorist actions. Bahrain has a high proportion of native Shia, possibly 65 to 70 percent of the population, who tend to resent their inferior status in the social and economic structure. The government sought to moderate the socioreligious cleavage by appointing Shia to a number of cabinet posts and senior civil service posts, although generally not in security-related positions. A failed coup d'état against the Al Khalifa in 1981 resulted in the expulsion or trial of many Shia dissidents. A number of persons were arrested in 1987. In 1989 twenty-two persons were sentenced to prison by the Supreme Court of Appeal, sitting as the Security Court, for plotting to overthrow the government.

Two clandestine political groups are active in Bahrain. The Islamic Front for the Liberation of Bahrain, which was responsible for the 1981 coup attempt, consists of militant Shia calling for violent revolution. The Islamic Call Party is more moderate, calling for social and economic reforms. Two secular leftist groups that espouse Arab nationalist ideologies are the Popular Front for the Liberation of Bahrain and the National Front for the Liberation of Bahrain. Their influence appeared to be on the decline as of early 1993. The agencies of the Ministry of Interior, the police force, and the Security and Intelligence Service (SIS) maintain strict control over political activity. It is thought that their operations are extensive and highly effective. Detention and arrest can result from actions construed as antiregime activity, such as membership in illegal organizations, antigovernment demonstrations, possession or circulation of antiregime writings, or preaching of sermons of a radical or extreme Islamist tone. The Department of State reported some loosening of controls in 1991 over actions previously regarded as subversive, reflecting the government's assessment that domestic and foreign threats to its security had receded.

Under the State Security Act of 1974, persons can be detained for up to three years, with a right of appeal after a period of three months and thereafter every six months. Arrested persons tried in ordinary criminal courts are provided the usual guarantees, such as public trials, the right to counsel (including legal aid if needed), and the right of appeal. Prisoners charged with security offenses are tried directly by the Supreme Court of Appeal, sitting as the Security Court. The procedural guarantees of the penal code do not apply: proceedings are in secret, and there is no right of judicial appeal, although cases can be referred to the amir for clemency.

According to Department of State human rights studies, there have been credible reports that the SIS engages in torture and mistreatment of detainees. Convictions in some cases have been based only on confessions that allegedly have been extracted by torture. There were, however, no confirmed cases of torture in 1991. The independent human rights group Amnesty International claimed that as of 1992, about seventy political prisoners, many with ties to banned Islamic groups, were serving sentences after unfair trials. Between 220 and 270 people were held in Bahraini jails in 1992. Of these, fewer than 100 were thought to be serving sentences for security offenses.

Qatar

In company with other gulf amirates, Qatar had long-standing ties with Britain but had remained under nominal Ottoman hegemony until 1916, when Qatar formally became a British protected state. During the next five decades, Britain also exercised considerable influence in the internal affairs of the amirate. When the announcement came that Britain would withdraw its military forces from the gulf by 1971, Qatari leaders were forced to consider how to survive without British protection. Unable to support a large military establishment, Qatar has placed its reliance on small but mobile forces that can deter border incursions. Nevertheless, the Iran-Iraq War brought attacks on shipping just beyond its territorial waters, underscoring Qatar's vulnerability to interference with oil shipments and vital imports. In addition to seeking collective security through the GCC, Qatar has turned to close ties with Saudi Arabia, entering into a bilateral defense agreement in 1982.

The ruler in 1992, Shaykh Khalifa ibn Hamad Al Thani, had taken control of the country twenty years earlier, when the leading members of the ruling family decided that Khalifa's cousin, Ahmad ibn Ali Al Thani, should be replaced because of his many shortcomings as amir. As supreme commander of the armed forces, Khalifa ibn Hamad issued a decree in 1977 appointing his son and heir apparent, Hamad ibn Khalifa Al Thani, to the post of commander in chief. The same decree created the Ministry of Defense and named Hamad ibn Khalifa as minister. Hamad ibn Khalifa was a graduate of Sandhurst and had attained the rank of major general.

At the time of independence on September 3, 1971, the armed forces consisted of little more than the Royal Guard Regiment and some scattered units equipped with a few armored cars and four aircraft. By 1992 it had grown to a force of 7,500, including an army of 6,000, a navy of 700, and an air force of 800. In addition to the Royal Guard Regiment, the army had expanded to include a tank battalion, three mechanized infantry battalions, a special forces company, a field artillery regiment, and a SAM battery. The combined combat strength of these units, however, is estimated to be no more than that of a reinforced regiment in a Western army.

Initially outfitted with British weaponry, Qatar shifted much of its procurement to France during the 1980s in response to French efforts to develop closer relations. The tank battalion is equipped with French-built AMX–30 main battle tanks. Other armored vehicles include French AMX–10P APCs and the French VAB, which has been adopted as the standard wheeled combat vehicle. The artillery unit has a few French 155mm self-propelled howitzers (see table 40, Appendix). The principal antitank weapons are French Milan and HOT wire-guided missiles. Qatar had also illicitly acquired a few Stinger shoulder-fired SAMs, possibly from Afghan rebel groups, at a time when the United States was trying to maintain tight controls on Stingers in the Middle East. When Qatar refused to turn over the missiles, the United States Senate in 1988 imposed a ban on the sale of all weapons to Qatar. The ban was repealed in late 1990 when Qatar satisfactorily accounted for its disposition of the Stingers.

Three French-built La Combattante III missile craft, which entered service in 1983, form the core of the navy. The missile craft supplement six older Vosper Thornycroft large patrol craft. A variety of smaller craft are operated by the marine police.

The air force is equipped with combat aircraft and armed helicopters. Its fighter aircraft include Alpha Jets with a fighter-ground attack capability and one air defense squadron of Mirage F1s, all purchased from France. All of the aircraft are based at Doha International Airport. The planned purchase of Hawk and Patriot missile systems from the United States will give Qatar a modern ground-based air defense. British pilots on detail remain on duty with the air force, and French specialists are employed in a maintenance capacity. Nevertheless, an increasing number of young Qataris have been trained as pilots and technicians.

The lack of sufficient indigenous personnel to staff the armed forces is a continuing problem. By one estimate, Qatari citizens constitute only 30 percent of the army, in which more than twenty nationalities are represented. Many of the officers are of the royal family or members of leading tribes. Enlisted personnel are recruited from beduin tribes that move between

Lieutenant General Charles Horner, commanding general, United States Central Air Force, congratulates Major Hamad ibn Abd Allah Al Khalifa, commander of Bahrain's Shaykh Isa Squadron, after awarding him the Legion of Merit for his support during Operation Desert Storm. A Qatari air force pilot performs a preflight check on his Mirage F1 aircraft before a mission during Operation Desert Storm.
Courtesy United States Air Force

Qatar and Saudi Arabia and from other Arab groups. Many Pakistanis serve in combat units. In 1992 there were still a number of British officers, as well as British, French, Jordanian, and Pakistani advisers and technicians. More young Qataris are being recruited, and the number of trained and competent Qatari officers is steadily increasing.

Although official data on military expenditures are not published, the defense budget estimate of US$500 million for 1989 was 8 percent of the gross domestic product (GDP—see Glossary). The estimate of US$934 million for 1991, an increase of 80 percent over 1989, was presumably attributable to the costs of the Persian Gulf War.

During the hostilities, the Qatari tank battalion was deployed to the Saudi-Iraqi border as part of Joint Forces Command East. Beginning on January 22, 1991, Qatari aircraft joined other countries in carrying out strikes against Iraqi forces. United States, Canadian, and French fighter squadrons flew daily missions from Doha during the gulf war. Saudi and Qatari forces that had dug in to defend the road leading south from the border town of Ras al Khafji were forced to withdraw when the Iraqis made their only incursion into Saudi territory on January 29, 1991. The three Saudi battalions and the one tank battalion from Qatar maintained contact with the Iraqi forces and participated in the coalition counterattack two days later that drove the Iraqis out of the town with considerable losses. The Qatari contingent, composed mostly of Pakistani recruits, acquitted itself well. The Qatari battalion also formed part of the Arab forces that advanced across Iraqi positions toward the city of Kuwait during the general coalition offensive on February 24, 1991. One Qatari tank was lost in the engagement, and a number of Arab soldiers were killed or wounded. No Qatari combat deaths were reported during the war.

Although the amirate has experienced little internal unrest, the large number of foreigners—forming 80 percent of the work force—is regarded as a possible source of instability. Qatar is determined to maintain control over their activities and limit their influence. A significant number of resident Palestinians, some of whom included prominent businessmen and civil servants, were expelled after the Iraqi invasion of Kuwait. Iranian Shia have not been the source of problems but are nevertheless looked on as potential subversives. Foreigners are liable to face arbitrary police action and harassment and often complain of mistreatment after their arrest.

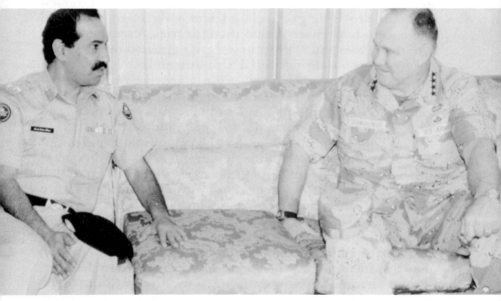

General H. Norman Schwarzkopf, commander in chief, United States Central Command, with Brigadier General Muhammad ibn Abd Allah al Attiyah of Qatar, whom he presented with the Legion of Merit for his role in Operation Desert Storm

General H. Norman Schwarzkopf speaks with Lieutenant General Khamis ibn Humaid ibn Salim al Kilbani, chief of staff, Royal Oman Land Forces, while touring As Sib Air Base during Operation Desert Storm.

Courtesy United States Air Force

The Ministry of Interior has controlled the police force of about 2,500 members since 1990. The local police enforces laws and arrests violators. The General Administration of Public Security, which in 1991 replaced the Criminal Investigation Department, is a separate unit of the ministry charged with investigation of crimes. The Mubahathat (secret police office), a nearly independent branch of the Ministry of Interior, deals with sedition and espionage. The army's mission does not include internal security, although the army can be called on in the event of serious civil disturbances. Nevertheless, a separate agency, the Mukhabarat (intelligence service), is under armed forces jurisdiction. Its function is to intercept and arrest terrorists and to keep surveillance over political dissidents.

Qatar has both civil and sharia courts, but only sharia courts have jurisdiction in criminal matters. Lacking permanent security courts, security cases are tried by specially established military courts, but such cases have been rare. In sharia criminal cases, the proceedings are closed, and lawyers play no formal role except to prepare the accused for trial. After the parties state their cases and after witnesses are examined by the judge, the verdict is usually delivered with little delay. No bail is set, but in minor cases, charged persons may be released to a Qatari sponsor. Most of the floggings prescribed by sharia law are administered, but physical mutilation is not allowed, and no executions have occurred since the 1980s.

The police routinely monitor the communications of suspects and security risks. Although warrants are usually required for searches, this does not apply in cases involving national security. The security forces reportedly have applied severe force and torture in investigating political and security-related cases. Suspects can be incarcerated without charge, although this is infrequent. The United States Department of State noted that standards of police conduct have improved in spite of a 1991 incident in which a group of Qataris were detained without charge for two months in connection with the unauthorized publication of tracts and letters critical of the government; at least one member of the group, which included several members of the ruling family, is said to have been beaten.

United Arab Emirates

Background

The numerous treaties that Britain concluded with the sev-

eral gulf amirates in the nineteenth century provided, inter
alia, that the British were responsible for foreign relations and
protection from attack by sea. Until the early 1950s, the principal military presence in the Trucial Coast states (sometimes
referred to as Trucial Oman) consisted of British-led Arab
security forces and the personal bodyguard units of the ruling
shaykhs. In 1951 the British formed the Trucial Oman Levies
(later called the Trucial Oman Scouts) under a British commander who reported to the British political agent of the gulf.
Arabs from the Trucial Coast made up only about 40 percent of
the strength; Omanis, Iranians, Pakistanis, and Indians made
up the remainder. Organized as light armored cavalry, the
scouts used British weapons, trucks, and armored cars in carrying out police functions and in keeping peace among the tribes
of the various amirates. During its approximately two decades
of existence, the unit was respected for its impartial role in
maintaining public order on the coast.

By the time the United Arab Emirates (UAE) became independent on December 2, 1971, the scouts had become a
mobile force of about 1,600 men, trained and led by about
thirty British officers assisted by Jordanian noncommissioned
officers (NCOs). At the time of independence and federation,
the Trucial Oman Scouts became the nucleus of the Union
Defense Force (UDF), responsible to the federal minister of
defense, the Supreme Council of the Union, and—ultimately—to the president of the federation, Shaykh Zayid ibn
Sultan Al Nuhayyan, ruler of Abu Dhabi, who continued to fill
this office in 1993. Separate amirate forces are also authorized
by the provisional constitution, and the separate entities of the
union—especially Abu Dhabi—have made clear that they
intend to maintain their own forces. Drawing on tremendous
oil wealth accumulated in the early 1960s, the amir of Abu
Dhabi gave high priority to the development of the Abu Dhabi
Defense Force (ADDF) when the British withdrawal from the
gulf was announced. The ADDF—with 15,000 men and primarily British and Jordanian officers—consisted of three army battalions, an artillery battery, twelve Hawker Hunter fighter-
bombers, and a sea defense wing of four fast patrol boats.
Dubayy had a much smaller force of 2,000, Ras al Khaymah had
900, and Sharjah had even fewer.

Personnel for the UDF and separate amirate forces were
recruited from several countries of the region, but soon after
independence enlistments from the Dhofar region in Oman
and from the People's Democratic Republic of Yemen (PDRY,

also seen as South Yemen) were curtailed out of fear that personnel from these areas might spread dangerous revolutionary doctrines. As the largest in territory, the most populous, and by far the richest of the amirates, Abu Dhabi has borne the brunt of funding the federation's military establishment. A major step toward unification of forces occurred in 1976 when Abu Dhabi, Dubayy, and Ras al Khaymah announced the merger of their separate armed forces with the UDF. Sharjah had previously merged its police and small military units into the UDF.

Despite the promises and pledges of 1976, true integration and unification of the UAE armed forces has not occurred. The UDF is seen by some, particularly the amir of Dubayy, as merely an extension of Abu Dhabi power. Individual amirs view their forces as symbols of sovereignty no matter the size or combat readiness of the units. The separate forces therefore continue as they had earlier, but they are called regional commands, only nominally part of the UDF. Shaykh Zayid ibn Sultan's attempt to install his eighteen-year-old son as commander in chief in 1978 shook the fragile unity of the UDF. Although the appointment was rescinded, Dubayy strengthened its resolve to maintain the autonomy of the Central Military Command, its own regional military command.

As of 1992, the commander in chief of the UDF was Zayid ibn Sultan. The crown prince, Lieutenant General Khalifa ibn Zayid Al Nuhayyan, held immediate command as deputy commander in chief. The chief of staff with operational responsibilities was Major General Muhammad Said al Badi, a UAE national who replaced a Jordanian general in the post in the early 1980s. His headquarters was in Abu Dhabi. The minister of defense was Shaykh Muhammad ibn Rashid Al Maktum, son of the ruler of Dubayy. The ministry, located in Dubayy, concerned itself primarily with administrative, personnel, and logistic matters and apparently had little influence on operational aspects of the UDF.

In data published by the Department of State in mid-1991, the total strength of the UDF with responsibility for defense of six of the seven amirates was estimated at 60,000. Dubayy forces of the Central Military Command with responsibility for the defense of Dubayy were given as 12,000. The Department of State estimated that there were 1,800 in the UDF air force and 1,000 in the navy. Estimates of ground forces given in *The Military Balance, 1992–1993* were significantly lower.

The Military Balance stated that perhaps 30 percent of the armed services consist of foreigners, although other sources

General H. Norman Schwarzkopf presents the Legion of Merit to Major General Muhammad Said al Badi, chief of staff, United Arab Emirates Union Defense Force, for his contribution to the coalition during Operation Desert Storm.
Courtesy United States Air Force

claim that the forces have a much higher proportion of non-UAE nationals. Omanis predominate in the enlisted ranks, but there are also many Pakistanis among the more than twenty nationalities represented. Well into the 1980s, many mid-level officers were Britons under contract, as well as Pakistanis and Omanis. By 1991 the officer corps was composed almost exclusively of amirate nationals, according to the Department of State. The UAE lacks a conscription system and is unlikely to adopt one. It was announced in 1990 that all university students would undergo military training as a requirement for graduation. Although adopted as a reaction to the Iraqi invasion of Kuwait, the UAE authorities reportedly are considering continuation of the requirement as a possible prelude to reservist training.

Organization and Equipment

The principal units of the UDF in 1993 were one mechanized infantry brigade, one armored brigade, two infantry brigades, one artillery brigade, and the Royal Guard, organized along brigade lines. The Central Military Command of Dubayy

363

supplies one infantry brigade. Major weapons include French AMX–30 main battle tanks, of which an additional twenty-five tanks are on order. The Central Military Command separately purchased Italian OF–40 Mk 2 Lion tanks. French armor predominates throughout the army; it includes reconnaissance vehicles, infantry fighting vehicles, APCs, and 155mm self-propelled howitzers (see table 41, Appendix). Negotiations were reportedly under way in 1992 for the purchase of 337 M1A1 tanks from the United States. The UAE also has a variety of older British armored vehicles, many of them in storage, as well as Brazilian APCs. The army's antitank guided wire missiles include twenty-five TOWs from the United States, some of them mounted on Urutu chassis, as well as French Milan and HOT and the older British Vigilant systems. Because of difficulties of coordination between air- and ground-based defenses, the operation of air defense missiles was shifted to the air force in 1988. The army's tactical air defense is limited to 20mm and 30mm guns.

The most powerful units of the UDF navy are two Lürssen corvettes delivered by Germany in 1991, similar to those of the Bahraini navy. The corvettes are supplemented by fast-attack craft and large patrol boats.

The air force is organized into two fighter-ground attack squadrons, one air defense squadron, and one counterinsurgency squadron. The fighter-ground attack squadrons are equipped with Mirage IIIs and British Hawks, the latter with a combined attack and training role. The fighter squadron is composed of Mirage 5s and Mirage 2000s. The counterinsurgency squadron is equipped with the Italian Aermacchi. In addition, the air force has four early warning aircraft. A number of French helicopters are armed with Exocet, HOT, and other air-to-ground missiles. In 1991 the United States agreed to the sale of twenty Apache attack helicopters after the administration overcame objections in Congress by pointing out that the helicopters were needed to defend the UAE's oil platforms in the gulf and to enable the UAE to contribute more effectively to the deterrence of aggression by Iraq.

The existing air defense system is based on one air defense brigade organized into thirteen batteries armed with Rapier, Crotale, and RBS–70 SAMs. Five batteries of improved Hawk missiles were being formed in 1992, with training provided by the United States.

The Role of the United Arab Emirates in the Iran-Iraq War and the Persian Gulf War

The attitude of the UAE during attacks on international shipping in the Iran-Iraq War was ambivalent. The amirates were profiting from a brisk reexport trade with Iran; furthermore, they felt vulnerable because their offshore oil facilities were exposed to the danger of Iranian attack. Dubayy and Ras al Khaymah in particular, with a substantial number of Iranians and native Shia, leaned toward Iran and were reluctant to abandon their neutrality. Abu Dhabi, however, as the richest oil state, adopted a pro-Arab stance in the war favoring Iraq. An offshore oil platform belonging to Abu Dhabi was hit by Iranian missiles in 1987; although denying responsibility, Iran paid an indemnity. The Department of State credited the UAE with supporting the United States Navy during its convoy operations despite Iranian threats of retaliation.

Reversing its earlier policy of avoiding collaboration with foreign military powers, the UAE, according to the Department of State, was the first Persian Gulf state to propose combined military action to deter Iraq when it threatened war against Kuwait. An air refueling exercise between United States and UAE aircraft one week before the invasion of Kuwait was intended as a warning signal to Iraq. During the Persian Gulf War, UAE troops, reportedly numbering several hundred, participated in the conflict as part of the GCC Peninsula Shield force that advanced into the city of Kuwait. United States aircraft bombed Iraqi positions from the UAE, and United States ships, including aircraft carriers, operated out of UAE ports. The UAE air force also carried out strikes against Iraqi forces. A total of six UAE combat deaths were reported as a result of the fighting.

The UAE defense budget remained fairly stable at about US$1.6 billion between 1988 and 1991. However, an additional US$3.3 billion represented UAE contributions and pledges in 1991 to other countries in connection with the war. Total UAE support to other countries participating in the Persian Gulf War was reported to have reached US$6 billion by mid-1991; payments of nearly US$3.8 billion had been made to the United States, US$500 million to Britain, and US$1.4 billion to Egypt, Jordan, Turkey, and seven other nations, combined, to offset their economic losses from the war. Oil prices and UAE oil production rose significantly after the outbreak of the gulf crisis; exports rose from US$15.5 billion in 1989 to US$21.0 billion in 1990. However, the balance of payments was negative for the first time as a result of UAE contributions to other countries affected by the crisis and large capital transfers out of the country during the period.

Internal Security Problems

In the past, internal dynastic rivalries within individual amirates were often sources of tension and even bloodshed. In part, this resulted from the absence of clearly established rules of succession. More recently, however, heirs apparent have usually been designated, most often the eldest son of the amir. Intra-UAE rivalries no longer take a violent form, but the continued existence of independent military forces and competition in acquiring arms bring with them a costly proliferation of weapons that complicates training and logistics.

The threat of subversion from resident Iranians and native Shia seems to be less acute in the UAE than in other gulf states in spite of the large Shia population in Dubayy. Dubayy and Sharjah have traditionally maintained good relations with Iran and enjoyed profits from maritime trade, particularly the transshipment of items officially banned in Iran to conserve foreign exchange.

The provisional constitution authorizes federal police and security guard forces, which are subordinate to the Ministry of Interior. The strength of the police force has not been reported but is estimated as relatively large and vigilant in exercising control over political activities. Individual shaykhs had their own police forces before independence and maintained those forces after unification. Both the federal government and the amirate of Dubayy retain independent internal security organizations. The police forces of the other amirates are also involved in antinarcotic and antiterrorist activities.

Criminal cases are tried either by sharia courts administered by each amirate or by civil courts of the federal system that exist in several amirates. Rights of due process are accorded under both systems. Defendants are entitled to legal counsel. No formal public defender system exists, but the judge has responsibility for looking after the interests of persons not represented by counsel. Under the Criminal Procedures Code adopted in 1992, the accused has the right to defense counsel, provided by the government, if necessary, in cases involving possible sentence of death or life imprisonment. There are no jury trials, but trials are open except in cases involving national security or morals offenses. No separate security courts exist, and military courts try only military personnel in a system based on Western

Lieutenant General Charles Horner presents Muhammad an Nahyan, a United Arab Emirates Union Defense Force air force officer, with a pistol in recognition of his performance during Operation Desert Storm.
Courtesy United States Air Force

military judicial principles. According to Department of State human rights reports, the criminal court system is generally regarded as fair. Despite the lack of a formal bail system, there are instances of release on deposit of money or passport.

Detentions must be reported to the attorney general within forty-eight hours; the attorney general must decide within twenty-four hours whether to charge, release, or allow further limited detention. Most persons receive expeditious trials, although Iraqis and Palestinians had been held incommunicado in detention for one or two months in 1991. Others were being held in jail because they were unwilling or unable to return to their countries of origin.

Oman

Background

As a regional commercial power in the nineteenth century, Oman held territories on the island of Zanzibar off the coast of East Africa, in Mombasa along the coast of East Africa, and until 1958 in Gwadar (in present-day Pakistan) on the coast of the Arabian Sea. When its East African possessions were lost,

Oman withdrew into isolationism in the southeast corner of the Arabian Peninsula. Another of the Persian Gulf states with long-standing ties to the British, Oman became important in the British-French rivalry in the nineteenth century when France challenged the British Empire for control of the trade routes to the East. Although nominally an independent sultanate, Oman enjoyed the protection of the empire without being, de jure, in the category of a colony. With its external defenses guaranteed and its overseas territories lost, the sultanate had no need for armed forces other than mercenaries to safeguard the personal position of the sultan.

In 1952 a small Saudi constabulary force occupied the Al Buraymi Oasis, where tribes from Oman and Abu Dhabi had traditionally resided. When arbitration failed, the British sent a force of Trucial Oman Scouts to expel the Saudis in 1955. Later in the same decade, the sultan called on British troops to aid in putting down a rebellion led by the former imam (see Glossary) of Oman, who attempted to establish a separate state free of rule from Muscat. British ground and air forces dispatched to aid the Muscat and Oman Field Force succeeded in overcoming the rebels in early 1959. Nevertheless, instead of a minor intertribal affair in Oman's hinterland, the rebellion became an international incident, attracting wide sympathy and support among members of the League of Arab States (Arab League) and the UN.

An agreement between Sultan Said ibn Taimur Al Said and the British government in 1958 led to the creation of the Sultan's Armed Forces (SAF) and the promise of British assistance in military development. The agreement included the detailing of British officers and confirmed the existing rights of Britain's Royal Air Force to use facilities at Salalah in the Dhofar region and on Masirah, an island off the Omani coast in the Arabian Sea.

Sultan Said ibn Taimur was ultraconservative and opposed to change of any kind. Kindled by Arab nationalism, a rebellion broke out in 1964 in Dhofar, the least developed area of Oman. Although begun as a tribal separatist movement against a reactionary ruler, the rebellion was backed by leftist elements in the PDRY. Its original aim was the overthrow of Said ibn Taimur, but, by 1967, under the name of the Popular Front for the Liberation of the Occupied Arabian Gulf, which in 1974 was changed to the Popular Front for the Liberation of Oman (PFLO), it adopted much wider goals. Supported by the Soviet Union through the PDRY, the rebellion hoped to spread revolution throughout the conservative regimes of the Arabian Peninsula.

Said ibn Taimur's reprisals against the Dhofari people tended to drive them into the rebel camp. In 1970, as the Dhofari guerrilla attacks expanded, Said ibn Taimur's son, Qabus ibn Said Al Said, replaced his father in a coup carried out with the assistance of British officers. Qabus ibn Said, a Sandhurst graduate and veteran of British army service, began a program to modernize the country and to develop the armed forces. In addition to British troops and advisers, the new sultan was assisted by troops sent by the shah of Iran. Aid also came from India, Jordan, Pakistan, Saudi Arabia, and the UAE, all interested in ensuring that Oman did not become a "people's republic." An Iranian brigade, along with artillery and helicopters, arrived in Dhofar in 1973. After the arrival of the Iranians, the combined forces consolidated their positions on the coastal plain and moved against the guerrillas' mountain stronghold. By stages, the Omanis and Iranians gradually subdued the guerrilla forces, pressing their remnants closer and closer to the PDRY border. In December 1975, having driven the PFLO from Omani territory, the sultan declared that the war had been won. Total Omani, British, and Iranian casualties during the final two and one-half years of the conflict were about 500.

Mission of the Armed Forces

After 1970 the Sultan's Armed Forces (SAF; later renamed the Royal Armed Forces) became one of the more modern and better trained fighting forces among the Arab gulf states. Recognizing its strategic importance guarding the Strait of Hormuz (through which nearly one-fifth of the world's oil transited) and the Gulf of Oman, the sultanate has struggled to maintain a high degree of military preparedness in spite of its limited financial means. Its defense budget in 1992 was estimated at US$1.7 billion, exclusive of the GCC subsidy shared with Bahrain. It has periodically tested the capabilities of its armed forces by engaging in joint exercises with Western powers, particularly in regular exercises with British forces. Oman has taken the initiative in efforts to strengthen regional collective security through the GCC. At the conclusion of the Persian Gulf War, it proposed the development of a GCC regional security force of 100,000 personnel.

For many years after the defeat of the Dhofari insurgents, Oman regarded its southern border with the PDRY as the most likely source of future conflict. The PDRY provided the Dhofari rebels with supplies, training camps, and refuge from attacks. Omani ground and air strength was concentrated at Salalah, Thamarit, and other towns near the PDRY border. The threat of PFLO dissident activity supported by the PDRY or border operations against Oman declined after reconciliation with the PDRY, marked by the exchange of ambassadors in 1987.

Apart from its military role, the SAF carried out a variety of civic-action projects that, particularly in Dhofar, were an important means of gaining the allegiance of the people. Military engineers assisted road construction in mountain areas. The air force carried out supply operations and provided medical service to remote areas. The navy performed similar duties along Oman's long coastline. The navy also patrolled the sultanate's territorial waters and the 370-kilometer Exclusive Economic Zone to deter smuggling and illegal fishing.

Organization and Equipment of the Armed Forces

Sultan Qabus ibn Said retained for himself the positions of prime minister and minister of defense. The sultan's uncle, Fahar ibn Taimur Al Said, served as deputy prime minister for security and defense. Between 1970 and 1987, the armed forces commander, as well as the heads of the air force and navy, were British generals and admirals on loan. As of early 1993, the chief of staff and the three service commanders were Omanis. As of 1992, personnel strength of the Royal Armed Forces (as they were renamed—RAF) had reached about 35,700, including 6,000 Royal Household troops (a 4,500 Royal Guard of Oman (RGO) brigade, two Special Forces regiments totaling 700, the Royal Yacht Squadron of 150, and 650 other personnel) and foreign personnel, believed to number about 3,700. The army, known as the Royal Oman Land Forces (ROLF), is the largest of the service branches with a strength of 20,000. The ROLF is organized into regiments, although each regiment is of no more than battalion size. It includes two armored regiments composed of three tank squadrons; one armored reconnaissance regiment composed of three armored car squadrons; eight infantry regiments, three of which are staffed by Baluchis; four artillery regiments; one air defense regiment of two batteries; one infantry reconnaissance regiment composed of three reconnaissance companies; two independent reconnaissance companies; one airborne regiment; and one field engineering regiment of three squadrons. A small tribal militia of rifle company strength on the Musandam Peninsula is known as the Musandam Security Force.

One divisional headquarters and two brigade headquarters are maintained, within which the independent regiments can be combined into larger fighting units. The separate Royal Household troops consist of the RGO, the Special Forces elements (trained by British commandos), and personnel to staff the royal yacht and a number of transport aircraft and helicopters. The RGO, an elite corps with the primary function of protecting the sultan and performing ceremonial duties, has a separate identity within the ROLF but is trained to operate in the field alongside other army formations.

The two tank squadrons are equipped with United States M–60A1 and M–60A3 tanks and with British Chieftains. The armored car squadrons are outfitted with British Scorpion light tanks and French VBC–90s. The ROLF lacks armored equipment for troop movement, depending on Austrian Steyr cross-country vehicles. In July 1991, Oman ordered US$150 million worth of armored vehicles from the United States. The ROLF has a variety of towed artillery pieces; its principal antitank weapons are TOW and Milan guided missiles. Air defense is provided by a variety of guns and shoulder-fired SAMs (see table 42, Appendix).

Initially, nearly all the army officers and men were Baluchis from Pakistan, except for senior commanders, who were British. As of early 1993, most of the officers were Omanis, although British involvement continued, especially in the armored regiment. The training battalion of the RAF conducts recruit training for all services at the RAF training center near Muscat. Officer candidates—who must serve at least one year in the enlisted ranks—attend the Sultan Qabus Military College and the Officers' Training School. In 1988 the first class of twenty officers graduated from the Sultan's Armed Forces Command and Staff College near Muscat. This is a tri-service school to prepare mid-ranking officers for senior command and staff appointments. Officers of other government security services and some civilian officials also attend.

The Royal Oman Navy (RON), with a strength of 3,000 in 1992, has its headquarters at As Sib, thirty-six kilometers west of Muscat. The principal naval establishment is the Said ibn Sultan Naval Base, completed in 1987, at Wudham Alwa near As Sib. One of the largest engineering projects ever undertaken in Oman, it provides a home port for the RON fleet, training facilities, and workshops for carrying out all maintenance and repair activities. The Naval Training Center, located at the base, offers entry-level courses for officers and enlisted personnel, as well as specialized branch training. Initially, the navy was staffed almost entirely by British officers and Pakistani NCOs. By the late 1980s, most ship commanders were Omanis, although many Pakistani and British technical personnel remained.

The navy's main combat vessels are four Province-class missile craft built by Vosper Thornycroft. Armed with Exocet antiship missiles and 76mm guns, the last ship was delivered in 1989. The navy also operates four Brook Marine fast-attack craft with 76mm guns and four inshore patrol craft. The navy is well equipped for amphibious operations and has one 2,500-ton landing ship capable of transporting sixty-ton tanks and three landing craft, mechanized. Oman has ordered two corvettes with eight Exocet missiles, scheduled for delivery from Britain in 1995–96, and hopes to remedy its lack of minesweepers.

The Royal Oman Air Force (ROAF) had a strength of about 3,500 in 1992. Its forty-four combat aircraft of British manufacture consist of two fighter-ground attack squadrons of modern Jaguars, a ground attack and reconnaissance squadron of older Hunters, and a squadron of Strikemasters and Defenders for counterinsurgency, maritime reconnaissance, and training purposes. The air force is fairly well equipped with three transport squadrons and two squadrons of helicopters for troop transport and medical transport. Rapier SAMs are linked to an integrated air control and early warning network based on a Martello radar system. Skyvan aircraft fitted with radar and special navigational gear conduct maritime reconnaissance and antipollution patrols. The principal air bases are at Thamarit in the south and on Masirah. Others are co-located with the international airport at As Sib, at Al Khasab on the Musandam Peninsula, at Nazwah, and at Salalah. Officer and pilot training takes place at the Sultan Qabus Air Academy on Masirah. Pilots of fighter aircraft receive advanced training in Britain.

Omani Role in the Persian Gulf War, 1991

Oman's perceptions of the strategic problems in the gulf diverge somewhat from those of the other Arab gulf states. Geographically, it faces outward to the Gulf of Oman and the Arabian Sea, and only a few kilometers of its territory—the western coast of the Musandam Peninsula—border the Persian Gulf. Nevertheless, sharing the guardianship of the Strait of Hormuz with Iran, Oman's position makes it of key importance to the security of the entire Persian Gulf. In its willingness to

Gunboat of the Royal Oman Navy prepares to transfer a crew member injured while patrolling the Strait of Hormuz.
Courtesy Aramco World

Weapons training for women of the Royal Oman Police Courtesy Embassy of the Sultanate of Oman, Washington

enter into strategic cooperation with the United States and Britain, Oman has always stood somewhat apart from the other gulf states. In 1980 Muscat and Washington concluded a ten-year "facilities access" agreement granting the United States limited access to the air bases on Masirah and at Thamarit and As Sib and to the naval bases at Muscat, Salalah, and Al Khasab. The agreement was renewed for a further ten-year period in December 1990. Although some Arab governments initially expressed their disapproval for granting the United States basing privileges, the agreement permitted use of these bases only on advance notice and for specified purposes. During the Iran-Iraq War, the United States flew maritime patrols from Omani airfields and based tanker aircraft to refuel United States carrier aircraft. The United States Army Corps of Engineers carried out considerable construction at the Masirah and As Sib air bases, making it possible to pre-position supplies, vehicles, and ammunition. Hardened aircraft shelters were built at As Sib and Thamarit for use by the ROAF.

Oman's traditionally good relations with Iran were strained by Iran's attacks on tanker movements in the Persian Gulf and Iran's emplacement of Chinese Silkworm antiship missile launchers near the Strait of Hormuz. The sultanate reinforced its military position on the Musandam Peninsula, which is only about sixty kilometers from Iranian territory.

After the Iraqi invasion of Kuwait, Oman declared its support for the multinational coalition ranged against Iraq. The facilities on Masirah became an important staging area for the movement of coalition forces to the area of conflict. Oman also contributed troops to Operation Desert Storm as part of the Arab contingent of Joint Forces Command East. A reinforced Omani brigade, along with Saudi, UAE, Kuwaiti, and other forces, participated in the ground assault paralleling the gulf coast that converged on the city of Kuwait. No Omani combat deaths were reported.

Internal Security

Oman has not been exposed to a significant internal threat since the defeat of the Dhofari insurgents in 1975. Tribal dissension, a factor in the past, is considered unlikely to recur because most tribal chiefs and leading families share the advantages of rising oil income. The foreign labor force is large—estimated at 60 percent of the working population—and most foreign workers are Indians and Pakistanis who are not politically active. A few observers foresee an internal power struggle over the succession because Sultan Qabus ibn Said has no designated successor, but others believe that the country is stable enough to avoid strife over the selection of a new ruler.

The sultanate has not been the target of terrorist acts; it faces few problems from the narcotics trade and considers the level of general crime to be remarkably low. The security services are described as large and efficient but not overly intrusive.

The Royal Oman Police (ROP), commanded by the inspector general of police and customs, is under the supervision of the Ministry of Interior. The size of the force was estimated in 1992 at 7,000, but this number is believed to include customs, immigration, civil defense, firefighters, coast guard, and prison service. The principal crime fighting unit is the Directorate General of Criminal Investigation. An oil installation division has responsibility for security of the oil industry and patrols pipelines, oil rigs, and oil terminals. The mounted division patrols border areas on horseback and camel and also provides security control at airports and border points. The coast guard contingent numbers 400; it is equipped with fifteen AT–105 APCs and eighteen inshore patrol craft.

The home guard (*firqat*) units had been raised and trained for irregular counterinsurgency operations by troops of the British army's Special Air Services. Armed with small arms, *firqat* units serve as tribal police and defense forces for the mountain people engaged in herding cattle in areas infiltrated by the Dhofari insurgents during the rebellion. After the insurgency, they remained as paramilitary tribal police, numbering about 3,500 in 1992.

Oman's criminal court system provides for fair trials within the framework of Islamic judicial practice. The defendant in criminal trials is presumed innocent and cannot be detained for longer than twenty-four hours without review of the case by a magistrate, who may then allow the police to hold a suspect up to fourteen days—extended if necessary up to seventy days—to carry out further investigation. Some suits have been filed against police officers for illegal arrest.

The accused can be represented by an attorney, but the government does not pay for a public defender. There are no jury trials and no right to a public trial. The judge can release the accused on payment of bail. Only the judge questions witnesses at the trial. The verdict and sentencing are frequently pronounced within a day. Sentences of more than two months and more than US$1,300 in fines are subject to appeal. No executions have been carried out since 1975 and are, in any event, subject to the sultan's ratification. A rarely used security court system handles internal security cases. The government can search private residences and monitor telephones and private correspondence without a warrant but generally confines such actions to investigations of potential security threats and individuals suspected of criminal activity.

According to the Department of State's *Country Reports on Human Rights Practices for 1991*, torture, mistreatment, and cruel punishment are not systematically practiced, nor are they countenanced by Omani authorities. The traditional punishments authorized by Islamic law, such as amputation and stoning, are not imposed. The Department of State reported that some prisoners had complained of beatings by police in 1991, and other physical abuse had been reported in earlier years. Prison conditions are described as harsh, with extreme temperatures in cells without proper ventilation. However, a practice of punitive hard labor under grueling desert conditions was discontinued in 1991.

*   *   *

Much of the foregoing data concerning the size and equipment of the armed forces of the Persian Gulf states is based on *The Military Balance* and on *Jane's Fighting Ships*. Some of the discussion of internal security practices and judicial systems is drawn from *Country Reports on Human Rights Practices for 1991*, prepared by the United States Department of State.

Two general works, *The Making of the Modern Gulf States* by Rosemarie Said Zahlan and *The Turbulent Gulf* by Liesl Graz, provide background on security perceptions and problems facing the smaller states of the gulf. Anthony H. Cordesman's *The Gulf and the West* contributes details on the individual armed forces, the military strengths and shortcomings of each state, and each state's involvement in the naval confrontation in the gulf in the 1980s. *The Middle East*, published by the Congressional Quarterly, treats numerous topics dealing with Persian Gulf security, including local disputes, United States military sales, and the events leading up to the 1990–91 gulf crisis.

Studies of the military strategy employed in Operation Desert Storm in *Desert Victory* by Norman Friedman and *Thunder in the Desert* by James Blackwell give limited mention to the role played by the Persian Gulf states. Several analyses of the geostrategic environment in the region, although dating from the mid-1980s, still have relevance. They include *Arms and Oil* by Thomas L. McNaugher and *Saudi Arabia: The West and the Security of the Gulf* by Mazher A. Hameed. (For further information and complete citations, see Bibliography.)

Appendix

Table 1. Metric Conversion Coefficients and Factors

When you know	Multiply by	To find
Millimeters	0.04	inches
Centimeters...........................	0.39	inches
Meters	3.3	feet
Kilometers	0.62	miles
Hectares (10,000 m²)	2.47	acres
Square kilometers	0.39	square miles
Cubic meters	35.3	cubic feet
Liters	0.26	gallons
Kilograms	2.2	pounds
Metric tons...........................	0.98	long tons
....	1.1	short tons
....	2,204.0	pounds
Degrees Celsius	1.8	degrees
(Centigrade)	and add 32	Fahrenheit

Table 2. *Kuwait: Population by Nationality, Selected Years, 1957–89*

Census Year and Nationality	Population	Percentage
1957		
Kuwaiti	113,622	55.0
Non-Kuwaiti	92,851	45.0
Total	206,473	100.0
1961		
Kuwaiti	161,909	50.3
Non-Kuwaiti	159,712	49.7
Total	321,621	100.0
1965		
Kuwaiti	220,059	47.1
Non-Kuwaiti	247,280	52.9
Total	467,339	100.0
1970		
Kuwaiti	347,396	47.0
Non-Kuwaiti	391,266	53.0
Total	738,662	100.0
1975		
Kuwaiti	472,088	47.5
Non-Kuwaiti	522,749	52.5
Total	994,837	100.0
1980		
Kuwaiti	565,613	41.7
Non-Kuwaiti	792,339	58.3
Total	1,357,952	100.0
1985		
Kuwaiti	681,288	40.1
Non-Kuwaiti	1,016,013	59.9
Total	1,697,301	100.0
1989[1]		
Kuwaiti	826,586	38.6
Non-Kuwaiti	1,316,014	61.4
Total	2,142,600	100.0

[1] Estimated.

Source: Based on information from Kuwait, Ministry of Planning, Central Statistical
Office, *Annual Statistical Abstact, 1989*, Kuwait, 1990, Tables 11 and 12, 27.

Table 3. Kuwait: Enrollment in Government Schools by Education Level, Nationality, and Gender, Academic Year 1989–90 (ten years of age and older)

Education Level	Kuwaiti	Non-Kuwaiti
Primary		
Males	35,042	24,592
Females	34,619	24,525
Total primary	69,661	49,117
Intermediate		
Males	31,601	30,325
Females	30,575	27,799
Total intermediate	62,176	58,124
Secondary		
Males	21,072	28,498
Females	23,033	25,314
Total secondary	44,105	53,812

Source: Based on information from Kuwait, Ministry of Planning, Central Statistical Office, *Annual Statistical Abstract, 1990–91*, Kuwait, 1992, Table 269, 324.

Table 4. Kuwait: Number of Teachers, Students, and Schools, Selected Academic Years, 1962–63 to 1988–89

	1962–63	1967–68	1972–73	1977–78	1982–83	1988–89
Teachers						
Males	1,551	3,342	5,734	9,673	12,052	12,286
Females	1,390	3,053	5,771	10,101	13,085	16,145
Total teachers	2,941	6,395	11,505	19,774	25,137	28,431
Students						
Males	35,674	64,366	88,897	136,714	176,368	190,624
Females	23,877	47,655	71,334	116,498	158,574	182,063
Total students	59,551	112,021	160,231	253,212	334,942	372,687
Schools	140	195	273	394	519	642

Source: Based on information from Kuwait, Ministry of Planning, Central Statistical Office, *Annual Statistical Abstract, 1989*, Kuwait, 1990, Table 305, 355.

383

Table 5. Kuwait: Government Medical Facilities and Personnel,
Selected Years, 1979–88

	1979	1982	1984	1986	1988
Hospitals and sanitoriums	9	15	17	16	16
Clinics	49	54	62	62	65
Dental clinics	78	114	140	169	193
Maternal care centers	15	18	21	22	23
Child care centers	24	28	32	38	42
Preventive health centers........	16	23	25	28	29
School clinics	420	494	540	626	688
Physicians	1,555	2,254	2,442	2,548	2,641
Dentists	167	223	259	294	320
Nurses and assistant nurses	5,322	7,866	9,000[1]	8,069	8,500[1]
Pharmacists and assistant pharmacists	578	687	719	769	805

[1] Estimated.

Source: Based on information from Kuwait, Ministry of Planning, Central Statistical
Office, *Annual Statistical Abstract, 1989,* Kuwait, 1990, Table 339, 397.

Table 6. Kuwait: Production of Crude Oil, Selected Years, 1946–92
(in thousands of barrels)

Year	Production	Year	Production
1946	5,900	1970	1,090,600
1950	125,700	1975	760,700
1955	402,700	1980	607,268
1960	619,100	1985	387,363
1965	861,500	1992	41,061

Source: Based on information from M.W. Khouja and P.G. Sadler, *The Economy of*
Kuwait, London, 1979, 26; Kuwait, Ministry of Planning, Central Statistical
Office, *Annual Statistical Abstract, 1989,* Kuwait, 1990, Table 200, 210; and
Organization of the Petroleum Exporting Countries, *Annual Statistical Bulletin,*
1993, Vienna, 1993, 23.

Table 7. Kuwait: Government Revenues, Fiscal Years 1985 and 1989
(in thousands of Kuwaiti dinars) [1]

	1985	1989
Oil revenues	2,094,675	1,941,969
Taxes		
Customs duties and fees	59,481	65,877
Taxes on net income and profits of nonoil companies	11,634	13,000
Taxes on real estate property transfers	1,348	2,250
Taxes and fees on goods and services and entry and registration fees	477	538
Total taxes	72,940	81,665
Service charges		
Transportation and communications	67,014	89,425
Electricity and water	50,311	60,078
Housing and public utilities	10,645	10,038
Security and justice	9,091	7,733
Financial stamps revenue	6,410	14,800
Education	4,538	5,606
Health	581	720
Other	974	670
Total service charges	149,564	189,070
Miscellaneous revenues and fees	20,718	17,546
Sales of land and real estate	7,196	250
TOTAL	2,345,093	2,230,500

[1] For value of the Kuwaiti dinar—see Glossary.

Source: Based on information from Kuwait, Ministry of Planning, Central Statistical Office, *Annual Statistical Abstract, 1989*, Kuwait, 1990, Table 257, 286.

Table 8. *Kuwait: Principal Exports, 1983, 1984, and 1985[1]*
(in Kuwaiti dinars)[2]

Commodity	1983	1984	1985
Food and live animals	30,905	36,152	28,290
Mineral fuels and lubricants			
Crude petroleum	1,578,171	1,920,958	n.a.[3]
Refined petroleum products	1,259,269	1,258,690	n.a.
Gas (natural and manufactured)	100,752	77,287	77,486
Other	15	0	0
Total mineral fuels and lubricants	2,938,207	3,256,935	2,845,178
Chemicals			
Manufactured fertilizers	18,352	33,237	22,258
Other	32,033	35,172	30,961
Total chemicals	50,385	68,409	53,219
Basic manufactures			
Nonmetallic mineral manufactures	36,255	18,848	10,094
Other	85,881	67,909	65,942
Total basic manufactures	122,136	86,757	76,036
Machinery and transportation equipment			
Transportation equipment	95,580	80,108	78,024
Other	48,967	45,379	52,871
Total machinery and transportation equipment	144,547	125,487	130,895
Miscellaneous manufactured articles	50,157	44,301	40,234
Other	27,420	13,429	11,216
TOTAL	3,363,757	3,631,470	3,185,068

[1] Free on board. Total exports were KD2,105 million in 1986; KD2,304.4 million in 1987, of which KD666.8 million consisted of crude petroleum out of a total of KD1,925.4 million for petroleum and petroleum products; KD2,166.2 million in 1988, of which KD524.6 million consisted of crude petroleum out of a total of KD1,783.2 million for petroleum and petroleum products; and KD3,378.0 million in 1989. Further breakdown not available.
[2] For value of the Kuwaiti dinar—see Glossary.
[3] n.a.—not available.

Source: Based on information from *The Middle East and North Africa, 1993*, London, 1992, 606.

Table 9. Kuwait: Principal Imports, 1986, 1987, and 1988[1]
(in thousands of Kuwaiti dinars)[2]

Commodity	1986	1987	1988
Food and live animals			
Live animals	46,350	37,684	42,713
Grains and grain products	34,459	33,731	32,537
Fruits and vegetables	79,139	81,659	82,181
Other	106,498	115,440	121,899
Total food and live animals	266,446	268,514	279,330
Chemicals	98,872	110,489	132,027
Basic manufactures			
Paper, cardboard, and manufactures........	24,382	29,904	37,051
Textile yarn and fabrics	75,150	80,642	92,126
Nonmetallic mineral manufactures.........	47,822	48,588	58,751
Iron and steel	87,807	52,321	81,086
Other	85,229	81,034	103,625
Total basic manufactures	320,390	292,489	372,639
Machinery and transportation equipment			
Nonelectric machinery	147,844	131,750	107,714
Electrical machinery and apparatus	285,230	213,108	152,873
Transportation equipment...............	213,408	171,036	234,140
Total machinery and transportation equipment.........................	646,482	515,894	494,727
Miscellaneous manufactured articles			
Clothing (excluding footwear)	81,257	85,308	107,289
Scientific instruments and watches	43,307	40,573	43,023
Other	141,736	125,502	148,093
Total miscellaneous manufactured articles	266,300	251,383	298,405
Other	62,741	91,942	137,028
TOTAL	1,661,231	1,530,711	1,714,156

[1] Cost, insurance, and freight. Total imports in 1989 were KD1,849.4 million; breakdown not available.
[2] For value of the Kuwaiti dinar—see Glossary.

Source: Based on information from *The Middle East and North Africa, 1993*, London, 1992, 605.

Table 10. *Kuwait: Major Trading Partners, 1990 and 1991*
(in percentages)

Country	1990[1]	1991[2]
Exports		
Japan	20.6	12.3
Netherlands	13.0	n.a.[3]
United States	7.5	7.9
Singapore	5.5	n.a.
Pakistan	5.3	7.6
India	3.4	n.a.
France	n.a.	16.1
Italy	n.a.	14.9
Britain	n.a.	11.1
Egypt	n.a.	10.0
Spain	n.a.	5.0
Imports		
Japan	11.6	12.4
United States	11.1	34.8
Germany	9.1[4]	7.8
Britain	8.5	8.8
Italy	6.2	n.a.
Saudi Arabia	4.1	n.a.
Canada	n.a.	8.7
South Korea	n.a	3.5
France	n.a.	3.1

[1] Figures based on partners' trade data to August 2, 1990, invasion.
[2] Figures based on partners' trade data after February 1991 liberation.
[3] n.a.—not available.
[4] West Germany.

Source: Based on information from Economist Intelligence Unit, *Country Report: Kuwait* [London], No. 1, 1992, 3; and Economist Intelligence Unit, *Country Report: Kuwait* [London], No. 1, 1993, 3.

Table 11. *Kuwait: Balance of Payments, 1987, 1988, and 1989[1]*
(in millions of United States dollars)

	1987	1988	1989
Merchandise exports, f.o.b.[2]	8,221	7,709	11,383
Merchandise imports, f.o.b.	– 4,945	– 6,064	– 5,746
Trade balance	3,276	1,645	5,637
Exports of services	1,030	1,158	1,328
Imports of services	– 4,073	– 4,204	– 4,228
Other income received	5,867	7,626	8,840
Other income paid	– 470	– 487	– 756
Private unrequited transfers, net	– 1,102	– 1,179	– 1,287
Official unrequited transfers, net	– 158	– 140	– 211
Current account balance	4,371	4,419	9,323
Direct investment, net	– 115	– 254	– 507
Portfolio investment, net	219	– 487	– 330
Other capital, net	– 4,913	– 6,028	– 6,859
Capital account balance	– 4,809	– 6,769	– 7,696
Errors and omissions, net	– 1,409	355	– 372
Overall balance	– 1,847	– 1,996	1,255

[1] Figures may not compute to balances because of rounding.
[2] f.o.b.—free on board.

Source: Based on information from *The Middle East and North Africa, 1993*, London, 1992, 605.

Table 12. *Kuwait: Government Budget, Fiscal Years 1990 and 1991*
(in millions of Kuwaiti dinars)[1]

	1990	1991
Revenues		
Oil	2,109	700
Non-oil	296	170
Total revenues	2,405	870
Expenditures		
Education	491	456
Electricity and water	486	245
Defense	450	2,641
Social security	410	816
Health	245	187
Security and justice	237	196
Public utilities	233	217
Administrative services	202	237
Land purchase	150	100
Housing	104	68
Communications	90	54
Foreign obligations	83	108
Information	69	57
Financial services	68	71
Fisheries	64	45
Transportation	24	17
Religious affairs	21	15
Mining and exploration	16	24
Trade and industry	9	8
Unspecified	182	525
Total expenditures	3,634	6,087
Reserve Fund for Future Generations	240	87
TOTAL	− 1,469	− 5,304

[1] For value of the Kuwaiti dinar—see Glossary.

Source: Based on information from *Middle East Economic Digest* [London], 36, No. 3, January 17, 1992, 15.

Appendix

Table 13. *Bahrain: Enrollment by Education Level and Gender,*
Selected Academic Years, 1977–78 to 1991–92[1]

Education Level	1977–78	1980–81	1984–85	1986–87	1991–92[2]
Primary[3]					
Males	24,185	23,849	25,000	26,268	29,009
Females	19,042	20,305	25,180	25,953	28,165
Total primary	43,227	44,154	50,180	52,221	57,174
Intermediate					
Males	5,260	9,068	10,099	10,816	12,283
Females	4,513	7,394	8,777	9,740	11,804
Total intermediate	9,773	16,462	18,876	20,556	24,087
Secondary, secular and vocational					
Males	4,885	4,561	7,614	7,824	8,518
Females	4,767	3,926	6,815	7,551	9,528
Total secondary, secular and vocational	9,652	8,487	14,429	15,375	18,046
Secondary, religious[4]	31	20	126	20	41
Higher education					
Males	485	1,255	1,381	1,898	1,837
Females	206	1,093	1,347	2,248	2,543
Total higher education	691	2,348[5]	2,728	4,146	4,380[6]

[1] Until 1986–87 included only students in government schools; thereafter, included students in both government and religious schools.
[2] 1991–92 figures for government schools only.
[3] Until 1986–87 included students in both government and religious schools.
[4] Males only.
[5] Figures for 1981–82
[6] 1988–89 figures for University of Bahrain only.

Source: Based on information from Germany, Statistisches Bundesamt, *Länderbericht Bahrain, 1991*, Wiesbaden, 1992, 38; and America-Mideast Educational and Training Services, *Education in the Arab World*, 1, Washingtron, n.d.

Table 14. Bahrain: Government Budget, 1987–92
(in millions of Bahraini dinars)[1]

	1987	1988	1989	1990[2]	1991[2]	1992[2]
Revenues						
Oil sector	247	210	n.a.[3]	250	292	314
Other	180	191	n.a.	190	180	184
Total revenues	427	401	438	440	472	498
Expenditures						
Current	356	377	392	415	445	478
Development	111	105	104	125	145	145
Total expenditures[4]	466	482	496	540	590	623
TOTAL	−39	−81	−58	−100	−118	−125

[1] For value of the Bahraini dinar—see Glossary.
[2] Projected.
[3] n.a.—not available.
[4] Figures may not add to totals because of rounding.

Source: Based on information from Economist Intelligence Unit, *Country Profile: Bahrain, Qatar, 1991–92*, London, 1991, 16.

Table 15. Bahrain: Summary of Oil and Gas Statistics, Selected Years, 1984–89

	1984	1986	1988	1989
Crude oil production (in barrels per day)	39,835.0	39,578.0	39,595.0	39,033.0
Natural gas production (in millions of cubic meters per day)	15.2	19.9	19.9	20.5
Petroleum products exports (in millions of United States dollars)	2,712.0	1,970.0	1,774.0	2,129.0
Refinery capacities (in thousands of barrels per day)	250.0	250.0	250.0	250.0

Source: Based on information from Economist Intelligence Unit, *Country Profile: Bahrain, Qatar, 1991–92*, London, 1991, 11.

Table 16. Bahrain: Gross Domestic Product (GDP) by Sector, Selected Years, 1982–90
(in millions of Bahraini dinars at constant 1985 prices)[1]

Sector	1982	1984	1985	1986	1990
Agriculture and fishing	22.2	20.3	19.9	20.0	14.3
Mining and quarrying	309.2	364.1	390.5	355.7	323.9
Manufacturing	154.6	153.1	140.7	205.9	252.7
Electricity, gas, and water	17.9	24.4	25.8	23.3	28.7
Construction	123.0	166.5	133.7	115.3	94.1
Wholeasale and retail trade, restaurants, and hotels	202.5	136.2	119.2	111.6	147.9
Transportation and communications	142.0	174.3	167.1	143.0	140.2
Financial institutions and insurance	283.0	240.4	227.8	289.6	} 192.5
Real estate and business services	83.3	91.2	81.5	80.7	
Other services	41.6	48.9	53.4	51.3	78.9
Government services	203.0	228.2	243.3	243.8	314.3
GDP at factor cost	1,582.3	1,647.6	1,602.9	1,640.2	1,587.5[2]

[1] For value of the Bahraini dinar—see Glossary.
[2] GOP at current prices, 1990.

Source: Based on information from Economist Intelligence Unit, *Country Profile: Bahrain, Qatar, 1991–92*, London, 1991, 8; and "Bahrain: Statistical Survey," in *The Middle East and North Africa, 1994*, London, 1993, 294.

Table 17. Bahrain: Balance of Payments, Selected Years, 1984–89[1]
(in millions of United States dollars)

	1984	1986	1988	1989
Merchandise exports, f.o.b.[2]	3,204.0	2,199.5	2,411.4	2,831.1
Merchandise imports, c.i.f.[3]	–3,131.6	–2,164.6	–2,334.0	–2,820.2
Trade balance	72.3	34.8	77.4	10.9
Exports of services	813.8	764.4	899.5	872.9
Imports of services	– 555.1	– 327.1	– 529.3	– 559.8
Inflows of IPD[4]	335.6	277.9	263.0	494.1
Outflows of IPD	– 447.3	– 675.0	– 694.1	– 743.6
Private transfers, net	– 125.5	– 264.6	– 193.1	– 195.7
Official transfers, net	124.5	120.7	366.5	102.1
Current account balance	218.4	– 68.9	189.9	– 19.1
Direct investment	140.7	– 31.9	222.1	180.9
Other capital	– 176.3	– 41.8	– 448.9	– 362.5
Capital account balance	– 35.6	– 73.7	– 226.8	– 181.6
Errors and omissions	– 192.8	– 36.9	136.7	12.3
Overall balance (– indicates inflow)	10.1	179.4	– 99.7	188.5
Change in reserves (– indicates increase)	123.9	170.3	– 103.2	201.7

[1] Figures may not compute to balances because of rounding.
[2] f.o.b.—free on board.
[3] c.i.f.—cost, insurance, and freight.
[4] IPD— interest, profits, and dividends.

Source: Based on information from Economist Intelligence Unit, *Country Profile: Bahrain, Qatar, 1991–92*, London, 1991, 20.

Table 18. Bahrain: Major Trading Partners, 1987, 1988, and 1989[1]
(in percentages)

Country	1987	1988	1989
Exports			
Saudi Arabia	16.4	19.7	18.2
United States	15.3	11.4	7.3
Japan	13.4	12.7	5.9
Kuwait	7.6	5.2	4.3
India	6.4	4.0	4.5
South Korea	3.2	4.7	4.0
United Arab Emirates	2.8	12.1	6.9
Imports			
United States	19.2	11.6	12.4
Britain	18.3	19.6	16.3
Japan	10.5	10.2	10.5
Australia	5.6	6.0	6.9
West Germany	5.3	6.2	6.9
Italy	3.9	4.0	4.7
Saudi Arabia	2.6	4.4	4.7

[1] Excludes oil sector.

Source: Based on information from Economist Intelligence Unit, *Country Profile: Bahrain, Qatar, 1991–92,* London, 1991, 19.

Table 19. *Qatar: Enrollment in Government Schools by Education Level and Gender, Selected Academic Years, 1975–76 to 1988–89*

Education Level	1975–76	1979–80	1983–84	1984–85	1985–86	1988–89
Primary						
Males	11,150	12,452	15,285	16,014	16,573	n.a.[1]
Females	10,252	11,796	13,941	14,501	15,271	n.a.
Total primary	21,402	24,248	29,226	30,515	31,844	48,097
Intermediate						
Males	2,737	4,328	5,331	5,659	6,028	n.a.
Females	2,480	4,032	5,369	5,687	6,003	n.a.
Total intermediate...	5,217	8,360	10,700	11,346	12,031	13,875
Secondary						
Males	1,544	2,195	3,201	3,139	3,224	n.a.
Females	1,086	2,401	3,588	3,776	4,251	n.a.
Total secondary.....	2,630	4,596	6,789	6,915	7,475	8,303[2]
Vocational, secular[3]						
Males	224	105	n.a.	n.a.	n.a.	n.a.
Females	269	55	n.a.	n.a.	n.a.	n.a.
Total vocational, secular	493	160	220	204	294	924[4]
Vocational, religious						
Males	200	287	350	377	406	n.a.
Females	0	0	0	0	0	n.a.
Total vocational, religious......	200	287	350	377	406	
University of Qatar						
Males	355	722	1,582	1,799	1,875	n.a.
Females	428	1,303	2,483	2,822	3,182	n.a.
Total University of Qatar......	783	2,025	4,065	4,621	5,057	5,692[5]

[1] n.a.—not available.
[2] Includes intermediate and secondary schools.
[3] Females are only admitted to the teacher training schools.
[4] Includes secular and religious vocational schools.
[5] 1987–88.

Source: Based on information from Federal Republic of Germany, Statistisches Bundes-amt, *Länderbericht Katar, 1988*, Wiesbaden, 1988, 29; and "Qatar," in *The Middle East and North Africa, 1993*, London, 1992, 762.

Table 20. Qatar: Summary of Oil and Gas Statistics, Selected Years, 1985–89

	1985	1987	1988	1989
Crude oil production (in thousands of barrels per day)	290.0	291.0	319.0	395.0
Natural gas production, marketed (in billions of cubic meters per day)	5.5	5.6	5.7	6.1
Crude oil exports (in thousands of barrels per day)	280.0	254.0	305.0	320.0
Oil export revenues (in billions of United States dollars)	3.1	1.8[1]	1.7[1]	2.0[1]

[1] Estimated.

Source: Based on information from Economist Intelligence Unit, *Country Profile: Bahrain, Qatar, 1991–92*, London, 1991, 28.

Table 21. Qatar: Gross Domestic Product by Sector, 1984 and 1989 (in millions of Qatari riyals at current prices)[1]

Sector	1984	1989
Agriculture and fishing	206	238
Oil and natural gas	11,330	7,117
Manufacturing industries	1,829	3,144
Electricity and water	165	368
Building and construction	1,411	1,152
Trade, restaurants, and hotels	1,506	1,457
Transportation and communications	480	667
Finance, insurance, and real estate services	1,919	2,350
Other services	6,162	7,715
TOTAL	25,008	24,208

[1] For value of the Qatari riyal—see Glossary.

Source: Based on information from Economist Intelligence Unit, *Country Profile: Bahrain, Qatar, 1991–92*, London, 1991, 26.

Table 22. Qatar: Government Budget, Selected Fiscal Years, 1986–91[1]
(in millions of Qatari riyals)[2]

	1986	1988	1989	1990[2]	1991[3]
Revenues	5,884	7,688	9,057	7,786	8,438
Expenditures					
Current	8,949	12,694	9,358	9,920	9,911
Capital	1,484	1,689	1,013	1,789	1,795
Total expenditures	10,433	14,383	10,371	11,709	11,706
TOTAL	− 4,549	− 6,695	− 1,314	− 3,923	− 3,268

[1] Fiscal year followed Islamic calendar until 1989, when fiscal year changed to April 1–March 31 in Gregorian calendar.
[2] For value of the Qatari riyal—see Glossary.
[3] Projected.

Source: Based on information from Economist Intelligence Unit, *Country Profile: Bahrain, Qatar, 1991–92*, London, 1991, 33.

Table 23. Qatar: Balance of Payments, 1984–89
(in millions of Qatari riyals)[1]

	1984	1985	1986	1987	1988	1989[2]
Exports, f.o.b.[3]	12,245	11,277	6,730	7,435	8,045	9,658
Imports, c.i.f.[4]	− 4,230	− 4,147	− 4,000	− 4,128	− 4,613	− 4,827
Trade balance	8,015	7,130	2,730	3,307	3,432	4,831
Services and private transfers, net	− 4,995	− 5,132	− 3,417	− 3,923	− 4,382	− 4,977
Current account balance	3,020	1,998	− 687	− 616	− 950	− 146
Capital account balance	− 2,005	− 2,360	− 1,085	− 1,031	− 1,286	− 92
Change in reserves (− indicates increase)	− 1,015	362	1,772	1,647	2,236	238

[1] For value of the Qatari riyal—see Glossary.
[2] Provisional.
[3] f.o.b.—free on board.
[4] c.i.f.—cost, insurance, and freight.

Source: Based on information from Economist Intelligence Unit, *Country Profile: Bahrain, Qatar, 1991–92*, London, 1991, 36.

Table 24. Qatar: Major Trading Partners, 1987, 1988, and 1989
(in percentages)

	1987	1988	1989
Exports			
Japan	39.6	50.0	54.4
Singapore	13.5	10.0	4.0
South Korea	3.1	2.1	3.6
India	2.9	3.3	2.8
Saudi Arabia	2.6	2.8	2.5
United Arab Emirates	2.2	2.1	3.4
Thailand	2.2	4.3	5.0
Imports			
Japan	16.3	17.6	18.8
Britain	16.0	13.8	11.6
United States	11.9	9.3	8.8
West Germany	7.1	7.9	7.3
Italy	4.9	4.3	7.8
France	4.3	4.0	4.7
United Arab Emirates	3.0	3.1	4.4

Source: Based on information from Economist Intelligence Unit, *Country Profile: Bahrain, Qatar, 1991–92*, London, 1991, 35.

Table 25. United Arab Emirates: Official Estimated Population and Population Distribution by Amirate, 1991

Amirate	Population	Percentage of Total Population	Area[1]	Density[2]
Abu Dhabi	798,000	41.8	67,340	11.9
Ajman	76,000	4.0	259	293.4
Al Fujayrah	63,000	3.3	1,166	54.0
Dubayy	501,000	26.2	3,885	129.0
Ras al Khaymah	130,000	6.8	1,683	77.2
Sharjah	314,000	16.4	2,590	121.2
Umm al Qaywayn	27,000	1.4	777	34.7
UNITED ARAB EMIRATES[3]	1,909,000	100.0	77,700	24.6

[1] In square kilometers. Excludes islands; approximate only because boundary with Saudi Arabia is undemarcated.
[2] Inhabitants per square kilometer. Excludes islands.
[3] Figures may not add to totals because of rounding.

Source: Based on information from "The United Arab Emirates," in *The Middle East and North Africa, 1993*, London, 1992, 933.

Table 26. United Arab Emirates: Enrollment by Education Level and Gender, Selected Academic Years, 1980–81 to 1986–87

Education Level	1980–81	1983–84	1984–85	1985–86	1986–87
Primary					
Males	46,300	65,900	71,600	78,800	85,300
Females	42,300	60,800	66,100	73,300	80,200
Total primary	88,600	126,700	137,700	152,100	165,500
Secondary					
Males	17,400	27,200	29,100	31,600	34,300
Females	14,500	24,100	27,000	29,900	33,300
Total secondary	31,900	51,300	56,100	61,500	67,600
Teacher training institutions	422	615	607	604	638
Quran schools	1,770	1,930[1]	n.a.[2]	n.a.	n.a.
Higher education, university					
Males	1,393	2,854	2,851	3,152	3,295
Females	1,126	2,761	3,475	3,988	4,559
Total higher education, university	2,519	5,615	6,326	7,140	7,854
Higher education, other					
Males	35	14	30	50	n.a.
Females	180	238	500	450	n.a.
Total higher education, other	215	252	530	500	n.a.

[1] Figures for 1982–83.
[2] n.a.—not available.

Source: Based on information from Germany, Statistisches Bundesamt, *Länderbericht Vereinigte Arabische Emiraten, 1990*, Wiesbaden, 1990, 31.

Table 27. *United Arab Emirates: Summary of Oil and Gas Statistics,*
Selected Years, 1985-91

	1985	1987	1989	1990	1991
Crude oil Production[1]					
Abu Dhabi	788.0	1,058.0	1,470.0	1,650.0	1,946.0
Dubayy	351.0	365 .0	431.0	435.0	434.0
Ras al Khaymah	9.0	10.0	10.0	10.0	0.8
Sharjah	64.0	45 .0	35.0	37.0	25.0
Total production	1,212.0	1,495.0	1,946.0	2,132.0	2,405.0
Exports[1]	978.0	1,250.0	1,650.0	1,865.0	2,195.0
Export revenues[2]	11.8	8.7	11.5	15.0	n.a.[3]
Natural gas Production[4]					
Marketed	13.2	18.9	22.4	22.1	25.9
Nonmarketed	9.2	8.2	7.4	7.7	n.a.
Total production	22.4	27.1	29.8	29.8	n.a.
Exports[4]	3.0	2.9	3.1	3.2	3.5

[1] In thousands of barrels per day.
[2] In billions of United States dollars.
[3] n.a.—not available.
[4] In billions of cubic meters.

Source: Based on information from Economist Intelligence Unit, *Country Profile: United*
Arab Emirates, 1991–92, London, 1991, 16; and Organization of the Petroleum
Exporting Countries, *Annual Statistical Bulletin, 1991,* Vienna, 1991, 6, 14, 16.

Table 28. United Arab Emirates: Gross Domestic Product
(GDP) by Sector, Selected Years, 1982–87
(in billions of UAE dirhams at current prices)[1]

	1982	1983	1985	1986	1987
Agriculture and fishing	1,144	1,198	1,440	1,540	1,596
Oil and gas	55,982	46,145	44,707	26,171	32,423
Mining	298	309	309	282	48
Manufacturing	9,436	9,584	9,255	7,172	8,151
Electricity and water	1,851	1,746	2,143	2,132	2,063
Construction	10,168	10,520	8,882	8,945	8,400
Transportation, storage, and communications	5,465	4,780	4,224	4,582	4,746
Commerce and hotels	10,913	9,701	8,715	9,385	9,625
Finance and insurance	4,741	5,520	5,154	5,447	5,404
Real estate	6,634	6,587	5,176	4,525	4,672
Government services	9,632	9,847	11,001	10,542	10,972
Other	1,633	1,854	2,009	2,138	4,038
Less imputed bank service charges	− 2,243	− 2,287	− 1,025	− 1,029	− 1,324
GDP at factor cost	115,654	105,504	101,990	81,832	89,218

[1] For value of the UAE dirham—see Glossary.

Source: Based on information from Economist Intelligence Unit, *Country Profile: United Arab Emirates, 1991–92,* London, 1991, 12.

Table 29. *United Arab Emirates: Federal Government Budget,*
1987, 1988, and 1989[1]
(in millions of UAE dirhams)[2]

	1987	1988	1989[3]
Revenues			
Taxes	473	479	573
Grant support from amirates[4]	9,865	10,950	11,298
Other	2,296	1,442	775
Total revenues........................	12,634	12,871	12,646
Expenditures			
Defense	5,827	5,827	5,827
Education	1,773	1,882	1,985
Internal security	1,713	1,697	1,789
Health	912	919	916
Economy	670	582	572
Social security	423	420	420
Energy	401	324	329
Agriculture	106	105	96
Other	1,433	1,429	1,330
Total expenditures	13,258	13,185	13,264
TOTAL[5]	−624	−314	−618

[1] As of December 31.
[2] For value of the UAE dirham—see Glossary.
[3] Provisional.
[4] Belived to be exclusively from Abu Dhabi and Dubayy.
[5] Financed exclusively from domestic sources.

Source: Based on information from Economist Intelligence Unit, *Country Profile: United*
Arab Emirates, 1991–92, London, 1991, 26.

Table 30. *United Arab Emirates: Balance of Payments, Selected Years, 1985–90[1]*
(in billions of UAE dirhams)[2]

	1985	1987	1988	1989	1990
Exports, f.o.b.[3]	54.2	45.0	44.7	57.2	75.2
Imports, c.i.f.[4]	– 23.5	– 26.0	– 31.3	– 36.7	– 41.1
Trade balance	30.7	19.0	13.4	20.4	34.1
Services, private transfers, and official grants	– 4.7	– 4.8	– 4.8	– 5.0[5]	n.a.[6]
Current account balance	26.0	14.2	8.7	14.8[5]	n.a.
Capital account balance	– 23.4	– 8.0	– 6.4	– 9.3	n.a.
Overall balance	2.6	6.2	2.3	5.5	n.a.

[1] Figures may not compute to balances because of rounding.
[2] For value of the UAE dirham—see Glossary.
[3] f.o.b.—free on board.
[4] c.i.f.—cost, insurance, and freight.
[5] Unrevised Central Bank figures, which do not agree with revised trade figures.
[6] n.a.—not available.

Source: Based on information from Economist Intelligence Unit, *Country Profile: United Arab Emirates, 1991–92*, London, 1991, 31–32.

Table 31. United Arab Emirates: Major Trading Partners, 1986, 1988, and 1990
(in percentages)

Country	1986	1988	1990
Exports			
Japan	34.8	30.7	35.1
United States	4.0	3.5	3.7
India	2.3	3.4	2.6
Singapore	0.6	3.6	5.8
South Korea	0.1	3.7	3.5
Oman	0.1	2.7	2.0
Imports			
Japan	18.3	16.4	14.2
Britain	11.2	9.7	9.6
United States	9.7	9.5	9.5
West Germany.................................	8.6	7.1	9.2[1]
France	5.3	3.4	5.2
Italy	4.6	4.5	5.0

[1] Includes East Germany, beginning in July.

Source: Based on information from Economist Intelligence Unit, *Country Profile: United Arab Emirates, 1991–92*, London, 1991, 30.

Table 32. Oman: Enrollment in Government Schools by Education Level and Gender, Selected Academic Years, 1975–76 to 1989–90

Education Level	1975–76	1981–82	1985–86	1988–89	1989–90
Primary					
Males	39,700	65,400	98,000	122,400	129,300
Females	14,800	36,200	77,500	106,300	113,700
Total primary	54,500	101,600	175,500	228,700	243,000
Secondary, lower and upper					
Males	900	12,200	21,600	31,000	35,900
Females	200	4,400	11,100	20,300	25,300
Total secondary, lower and upper	1,100	16,600	32,700	51,300	61,200
Higher education					
Males	143	1,788	6,971	7,490	9,572
Females	57	696	3,763	7,700	9,689
Total higher education...	200	2,484	10,734	15,190	19,261

Source: Based on information from Germany, Statistiches Bundesamt, *Länderbericht Oman, 1991,* Wiesbaden, 1991, 34.

Table 33. Oman: Government Budget, 1987–92[1]
(in millions of Omani riyals)[2]

	1987	1988	1989	1990	1991	1992[3]
Revenues						
Oil and gas	1,182	995	1,130	1,588	1,290	1,344
Other	245	203	220	270	281	283
Total revenues ...	1,428	1,198	1,349	1,859	1,570	1,628
Expenditures						
Current						
Defense and national security	584	589	601	742	643	665
Civilian	500	535	600	660	674	625
Interest	73	84	95	92	69	100
Other	67	63	66	75	76	83
Total current	1,223	1,271	1,361	1,570	1,463	1,472
Capital						
Non-oil	240	204	177	163	241	252
Oil	99	76	94	123	151	157
Lending and equities, net	16	9	13	14	– 1	– 6
Total capital	354	289	284	300	390	404
Total expenditures ...	1,576	1,560	1,645	1,870	1,853	1,876
TOTAL	– 149	– 362	– 296	– 11	– 283	– 248

[1] Figures may not add to totals because of rounding.
[2] For value of the Omani riyal—see Glossary.
[3] Provisional.

Source: Based on information from Central Bank of Oman, *Annual Report, 1991*, Muscat, 1992, 41.

Table 34. Oman: Balance of Payments, 1987, 1988, and 1990
(in millions of United States dollars)

	1987	1988	1990
Merchandise exports, f.o.b[1]	3,805	3,342	5,508
Merchandise imports, f.o.b.	− 1,769	− 2,107	− 2,519
Trade balance	2,036	1,235	2,989
Services	− 558	− 824	− 949
Transfers	− 694	− 720	− 874
Current account balance	784	− 309	1,166
Direct investment in Oman	35	92	141
Other long-term capital of resident official sector	− 135	181	− 403
Other short-term capital of deposit money banks	− 72	− 86	− 96
Other short-term capital of other sectors	− 18	34	− 211
Reserves	− 108	467	− 109
Capital account balance	− 298	688	− 678
Errors and omissions, net	− 486	− 379	− 488

[1] f.o.b—free on board.

Source: Based on information from International Monetary Fund, *Balance of Payments Statistics Yearbook, 1992*, Washington, 1993, 520–21.

Table 35. *Oman: Major Trading Partners, 1987, 1989, and 1990*
(in millions of United States dollars)

Country or Region	1987	1989	1990
Exports			
Middle East	1,862	3,049	2,984
Asia	454	571	542
Britain	204	158	275
Japan	122	46	96
United States	99	150	168
Africa	61	45	193
West Germany	61	25	31
France	22	26	62
Imports			
Middle East	433	632	729
Japan	277	354	455
Britain	268	263	308
Asia	186	219	268
West Germany	146	124	130
United States	122	191	251
France	66	76	115
Africa	2	3	10

Source: Based on information from International Monetary Fund, *Direction of Trade Statistics, 1992 Annual*, Washington, 1992, 309–10.

Table 36. *Oman: Summary of Oil and Gas Statistics, 1988–91*

	1988	1989	1990	1991
Crude oil production (in thousands of barrels per day)	621.0	641.0	685.0	708.0
Crude oil exports (in thousands of barrels per day)	580.0	592 .0	628.0	644.0
Natural gas production, gross (in billions of cubic meters)	4.9	5.2	5.2	5.3
Natural gas production, marketed (in billions of cubic meters)	2.1	2.3	2.8	3.1

Source: Based on information from Central Bank of Oman, *Annual Report, 1991*, Muscat, 1992, 31–32; and *Le gaz naturel dans le monde*, Paris, 1988–91.

Table 37. Oman: Gross Domestic Product (GDP) by Sector,
Selected Years, 1987–91
(in millions of Omani riyals at constant 1978 prices)[1]

Sector	1987	1989	1990	1991
Agriculture	63	75	78	83
Fishing	21	19	19	18
Crude oil	906	1,001	1,071	1,101
Oil refining	5	7	7	8
Natural gas	20	21	22	23
Mining and quarrying	10	10	8	9
Manufacturing	79	81	93	93
Construction	145	111	115	144
Utilities	95	131	157	160
Transportation and communications	80	90	103	113
Trade, restaurants, and hotels	192	228	257	304
Financial and business services and real estate	226	243	281	271
Government and other services.............	296	321	332	372
Import duties	16	17	18	22
Less imputed bank service charges	− 58	− 67	− 100	− 75
GDP at factor cost[2]	2,096	2,289	2,461	2,646

[1] For value of the Omani riyal—see Glossary.
[2] Figures may not add to totals because of rounding.

Source: Based on information from Central Bank of Oman, *Annual Report, 1991*, Muscat, 1992, 146.

Table 38. Kuwait: Major Military Equipment, 1992

Type and Description	Country of Origin	In Inventory
Army		
Main battle tanks		
M–84	Yugoslavia	200
Other armored vehicles		
Ferret reconnaissance..................	Britain	n.a.[1]
BMP–2 infantry fighting vehicle	Yugoslavia	39
M–113 personnel carrier	United States	37
Fahd personnel carrier..................	Egypt	44
Artillery		
M–101 105mm howitzer	United States	8
M–109A2 155mm self-propelled howitzer ...	-do-	3
GCT 155mm self-propelled howitzer.......	France	18
Antitank guided missiles.................		
TOW/improved TOW, some self-propelled	United States	n.a.
Navy		
Missile craft		
Lürssen 57-meter, each with 4 Exocet missiles	Germany	1
Lürssen 45-meter, each with 4 Exocet missiles	-do-	1
Air force		
Fighter-ground attack		
A–4TA Skyhawk	United States	22
F/A18	-do-	8
Fighters		
Mirage F1	France	15
Counterinsurgency and training		
Hawk 64............................	Britain	12
Shorts	-do-	16
Helicopters		
AS–332 Super Puma and SA–330 Puma.....	France	13
SA–342 Gazelle with HOT	-do-	16

[1] n.a.—not available.

Source: Based on information from *The Military Balance, 1992–1993*, London, 1992, 113–14; and *Jane's Fighting Ships, 1992–93*, Alexandria, Virginia, 1992, 391.

Table 39. Bahrain: Major Military Equipment, 1992

Type and Description	Country of Origin	In Inventory
Army		
Main battle tanks		
M–60A3	United States	81
Other armored vehicles		
AML–90 reconnaissance	France	22
AT–105 Saxon	Britain	10
Panhard M–3	France	110
Artillery		
105mm light	Britain	8
155mm M–198	United States	14
Antitank guided missiles		
BGM–71A–TOW	-do-	15
Navy		
Corvettes		
Lürssen 62-meter, each with 4 Exocet missiles	Germany	2
Missile craft		
Lürssen 45-meter, each with 4 Exocet missiles	-do-	4
Patrol craft		
Lürssen 38-meter	-do-	2
Air force		
Fighter-ground attack		
F–5E/F	United States	12
Fighters		
F–16C/D	-do-	12
Helicopters		
AB–212 Agusta-Bell (8 armed)	Italy and United States	12
Bo-105 (armed)	Germany	4

Source: Based on information from *The Military Balance, 1992–1993*, London, 1992, 105–6; and *Jane's Fighting Ships, 1992–93*, Alexandria, Virginia, 1992, 37.

Table 40. *Qatar: Major Military Equipment, 1992*

Type and Description	Country of Origin	In Inventory
Army		
Main battle tanks		
AMX–30	France	24
Other armored vehicles		
AMX–10P infantry fighting vehicle	-do-	30
VAB, wheeled armored personnel carrier	-do-	160
Artillery		
G5 155mm howitzer	South Africa	12
AMX Mk F–3 155mm, self-propelled	France	6
Antitank guided missiles		
Milan	-do-	100
HOT (mounted on VAB)	-do-	24
Navy		
Missile craft		
La Combattante III, 56-meter, each with 8 Exocet missiles	France	3
Patrol craft		
Inshore, Vosper Thornycroft 33-meter	Britain	6
Air force		
Fighter-ground attack and training		
Alpha Jet	France and Germany	6
Fighters		
Mirage F1	France	12
Attack helicopters		
SA–342L Gazelle with HOT	-do-	12
Commando MK3 with Exocet missile	Britain	8

Source: Based on information from *The Military Balance, 1992–1993*, London, 1992, 119–20; and *Jane's Fighting Ships, 1992-93*, Alexandria, Virginia, 1992, 508.

Table 41. United Arab Emirates: Major Military Equipment, 1992

Type and Description	Country of Origin	In Inventory
Army		
Tanks		
AMX–30	France	95
OF–40 Mk 2 Lion	Italy	36
Scorpion, light	Britain	76
Reconnaissance vehicles		
AML–90	France	90
Armored personnel carriers and fighting vehicles		
AMX–10P	-do-	15
VCR...	-do-	50
Panhard M–3	-do-	240
EE–11 Urutu	Brazil	100
Artillery and rocket launchers		
105mm	Various	77
130mm	-do-	20
155mm Mk F–3 self-propelled howitzers	France	20
G–6 155mm howitzers	South Africa	40
FIROS 25 122mm multiple rocket launchers	Italy	40
Antitank guided missiles		
Milan	France	230
HOT, self-propelled	-do-	20
Vigilant	Britain	n.a.[1]
TOW	United States	25
Navy		
Corvettes		
Lürssen 62-meter, each with 4 Exocet missiles, Crotale SAM, 76mm gun, and SA–316 Alouette helicopter	Germany	2
Missile craft		
Lürssen 50-meter, each with 4 Exocet missiles	-do-	2
Lürssen 45-meter, each with 4 Exocet missiles	-do-	6
Inshore patrol		
Vosper Thornycroft 33-meter	Britain	6
Air force		
Fighter-ground attack		
Mirage III	France	14
Hawk Mk 63	Britain	18
Fighters		
Mirage 5 AD	France	12
Mirage 2000 EA	-do-	22

Table 41. United Arab Emirates: Major Military Equipment, 1992

Type and Description	Country of Origin	In Inventory
Counterinsurgency		
Aermacchi MB–326, MB–339A	Italy	11
Reconnaissance		
Mirage 2000	France	8
Mirage 5–R	-do-	3
Early warning		
Casa C212 Aviocar	Spain	4
Helicopters		
AS–332F Super Puma with Exocet missile.............	France	2
SA–342K Gazelle with HOT	-do-	10
SA–316/319 Alouette III	-do-	7
Air defense missiles		
Improved Hawk	United States	5 batteries[2]
Rapier	Britain	12
Crotale.......................................	France	8
RBS–70	Sweden	13

[1] n.a.—not available.
[2] Being formed.

Source: Based on information from *The Military Balance, 1992–1993*, London, 1992, 125; and *Jane's Fighting Ships, 1992-93*, Alexandria, Virginia, 1992, 714.

Table 42. *Oman: Major Military Equipment, 1992*

Type and Description	Country of Origin	In Inventory
Army	·	
Tanks		
M–60A1/A3	United States	49
Chieftain	Britain	29
Scorpion (light)	-do-	37
VBC–90 (light)	France	6
Armored personnel carriers		
VAB PC and VAB VCI	-do-	8
Artillery		
105mm and 130mm guns, towed	Various	66
Antitank guided missiles		
TOW	United States	18
Milan	France	32
Navy		
Fast attack craft		
Province-class 56-meter, one with 6 and three with 8 Exocet missiles	Britain	4
Brook Marine 37-meter, each with 76mm gun	-do-	4
Inshore patrol craft		
Vosper Thornycroft 25-meter.....................	-do-	4
Air force		
Fighter-ground attack		
Jaguar Mk 1	-do-	15
Hunter FGA–73	-do-	10
Counterinsurgency and training		
BAC–167 Strikemaster	-do-	12
BN–2 Defender	-do-	7
Helicopters		
Agusta-Bell 205, 206, 212, and 214 (transport)	Italy and United States	36
Air defense missiles		
Rapier	Britain	28

Source: Based on information from *The Military Balance, 1992–1993*, London, 1992, 118–19; and *Jane's Fighting Ships, 1992–93*, Alexandria, Virginia, 1992, 456.

Bibliography

Chapter 1

Abu Saud, Abeer. *Qatari Women, Past and Present.* London: Longman, 1984.

Adams, Michael. *The Middle East.* New York: Facts on File, 1987.

Agwani, M.S. (ed.). *The Gulf in Transition.* New Delhi: South Asian, 1987.

Allen, Calvin. *Oman: The Modernization of the Sultanate.* Boulder, Colorado: Westview Press, 1987.

Anani, Ahmad, and Ken Whittingham. *The Early History of the Gulf Arabs.* London: Longman, 1986.

Asimov, Isaac. *The Near East.* Boston: Houghton Mifflin, 1968.

Bennet, Norman R. *Arab Versus European: Diplomacy and War in Nineteenth-Century East Central Africa.* New York: Africana, 1986.

Clements, Frank. *Kuwait.* Oxford: Clio Press, 1985.

Cole, Donald. *Nomads of the Nomads: The Al Murrah Bedouin of the Empty Quarter.* Chicago: Aldine, 1975.

Cordesman, Anthony H. *The Gulf and the West: Strategic Relations and Military Realities.* Boulder, Colorado: Westview Press, 1988.

Cottrell, Alvin (ed.). *The Persian Gulf States: A General Survey.* Baltimore: Johns Hopkins University Press, 1980.

Coulson, Noel. *A History of Islamic Law.* Lahore: Lahore Law Times, 1979.

Crystal, Jill. *Kuwait: The Transformation of an Oil State.* Boulder, Colorado: Westview Press, 1992.

————. *Oil and Politics in the Gulf: Rulers and Merchants in Kuwait and Qatar.* New York: Cambridge University Press, 1990.

Daftary, Farhad. *Isma'ilis: Their History and Doctrines.* New York: Cambridge University Press, 1990.

Eickelman, Christine. *Women and Community in Oman.* New York: New York University Press, 1984.

Esposito, John. *Islam: The Straight Path.* Oxford: Oxford University Press, 1988.

The Evolving Culture of Kuwait. Edinburgh: Royal Scottish Museum, 1985.

Fakhro, Munira A. *Women at Work in the Gulf: A Case Study of Bahrain.* London: Kegan Paul International, 1990.

Farah Talal, Toufic. *Protection and Politics in Bahrain, 1899–1915.* Beirut: American University Press, 1985.

Fisher, Sidney N. *The Middle East.* New York: McGraw-Hill, 1990.

Graz, Liesl. *The Turbulent Gulf.* New York: St. Martin's Press, 1990.

Great Power Interests in the Persian Gulf. New York: Council on Foreign Relations, 1989.

Hawley, Donald. *The Trucial States.* London: Allen and Unwin, 1970.

Haykal, Muhammad H. *The Life of Muhhammad.* Indianapolis: American Trust, 1976.

Helms, Christine. *The Cohesion of Saudi Arabia.* Baltimore: Johns Hopkins University Press, 1981.

Hodgson, Marshall. *The Venture of Islam.* (3 vols.) Chicago: University of Chicago Press, 1974.

Holt, P.M., Ann K.S. Lambton, and Bernard Lewis (eds.). *Cambridge History of Islam, 1: The Central Islamic Lands.* New York: Cambridge University Press, 1970.

————. *Cambridge History of Islam, 2: The Further Islamic Lands, Islamic Society, and Civilization.* New York: Cambridge University Press, 1970.

The Holy Qur'an. (Trans., 'Abdallah Yusuf 'Ali.) Brentwood, Maryland: Amana, 1989.

Hopfe, Lewis. *Religions of the World.* Encino, California: Glencoe, 1976.

Hopwood, Derek (ed.). *The Arabian Peninsula: Society and Politics.* Totowa, New Jersey: Rowman and Littlefield, 1972.

Innes, Neil McLeod. *Minister in Oman: A Personal Narrative.* New York: Oleander, 1987.

Izkiwi, Sarhan ibn Sa'id. *Annals of Oman to 1728.* New York: Oleander, 1984.

Janzen, Jorg. *Nomads in the Sultanate of Oman: Tradition and Development in Dhofar.* Boulder, Colorado: Westview Press, 1986.

Jenner, Michael. *Bahrain: Gulf Heritage in Transition.* London: Longman, 1984.

Kalus, Ludvik. *Inscriptions Arabes des Îles de Bahrain.* Paris: Guethner, 1990.

Khuri, Fuad. *Tribe and State in Bahrain: The Transformation of Social and Political Authority in an Arab State.* Chicago: University of Chicago Press, 1980.

Kupchan, Charles. *The Persian Gulf and the West: The Dilemmas of Security.* Boston: Allen and Unwin, 1987.

Lawson, Fred H. *Bahrain: The Modernization of Autocracy.* Boulder, Colorado: Westview Press, 1989.

Lewis, Bernard. *Origins of Isma'ilism: A Study of the Historical Background of the Fatimid Caliphate.* Cambridge, United Kingdom: Heffer, 1940.

Maamiry, Ahmed Hamoud. *Oman and Ibadhism.* New Delhi: Lancers Books, 1989.

———. *Omani Sultans in Zanzibar: 1832–1964.* New Delhi: Lancers Books, 1988.

The Middle East and North Africa, 1991. London: Europa, 1990.

Miles, S.B. *The Countries and Tribes of the Persian Gulf.* London: Frank Cass, 1966.

Mossa, Abdulrasool al-. *Immigrant Labor in Kuwait.* London: Croom Helm, 1985.

Narula, Subhash. *India's Gulf Exports: Features, Trends, and Prospects.* New Delhi: Anupama, 1988.

Nugent, Jeffrey B., and Theodore Thomas. *Bahrain and the Gulf: Past Perspectives and Alternative Futures.* New York: St. Martin's Press, 1985.

Peck, Malcolm C. *The United Arab Emirates: A Venture in Unity.* Boulder, Colorado: Westview Press, 1986.

Peterson, John E. *The Arab Gulf States: Steps Toward Political Participation.* New York: Praeger, 1988.

Phillips, Wendell. *Oman: A History.* London: Longman, 1967.

Pridham, B.R. *Oman: Economic, Social, and Strategic Developments.* London: Croom Helm, 1987.

Pridham, B.R. (ed.). *The Arab Gulf and the Arab World.* London: Croom Helm, 1988.

Qasimi, Muhammad al-. *The Myth of Arab Piracy in the Gulf.* London: Croom Helm, 1986.

Risso, Patricia. *Oman and Muscat: An Early Modern History.* New York: St. Martin's Press, 1986.

Rush, Alan. *Al-Sabah: Genealogy and History of Kuwait's Ruling Family, 1752–1986.* Atlantic Highlands, New Jersey: Ithaca Press, 1987.

Sen Gupta, Bhabani (ed.). *The Persian Gulf and South Asia: Prospects and Problems of Inter-Regional Cooperation.* New Delhi: South Asian, 1987.

Sindelar, H. Richard, III, and John E. Peterson (eds.). *Crosscurrents in the Gulf: Arab Regional and Global Interests.* London: Routledge, 1988.

Skeet, Ian. *Oman Before 1970: The End of an Era.* London: Faber and Faber, 1985.

Soffan, Lina U. *The Women of the United Arab Emirates.* London: Croom Helm, 1980.

Stivers, William. *America's Confrontation with Revolutionary Change in the Middle East, 1948–83.* New York: St. Martin's Press, 1986.

Survey of the Shores and Islands of the Persian Gulf, 1820–1829. Farnham, United Kingdom: Archive Editions, 1990.

Wikan, Unni. *Behind the Veil in Arabia: Women in Oman.* Baltimore: Johns Hopkins University Press, 1982.

Wilkinson, John C. *The Imamate Tradition of Oman.* Cambridge: Cambridge University Press, 1987.

Wright, Robin. *Sacred Rage: The Wrath of Militant Islam.* New York: Touchstone, 1986.

Chapter 2

Abu-Hakima, Ahmad. *Modern History of Kuwait.* London: Luzac, 1983.

Alessa, Shamlan. *The Manpower Problem in Kuwait.* London: Kegan Paul, 1981.

Assiri, Abdul-Reda. "Kuwait's Dinar Diplomacy: The Role of Donor-Mediator," *Journal of South Asian and Middle Eastern Studies,* 14, Spring 1991, 24–32.

———. *Kuwait's Foreign Policy: City-State in World Politics.* Boulder, Colorado: Westview Press, 1990.

Assiri, Abdul-Reda, and Kamal al-Monoufi. "Kuwait's Political Elite: The Cabinet," *Middle East Journal,* 42, Winter 1988, 48–58.

Crystal, Jill. *Kuwait: The Transformation of an Oil State.* Boulder, Colorado: Westview Press, 1992.

———. *Oil and Politics in the Gulf: Rulers and Merchants in Kuwait and Qatar.* New York: Cambridge University Press, 1990.

Darwiche, Fida. *The Gulf Stock Exchange Crash: The Rise and Fall of the Souq al-Manakh.* London: Croom Helm, 1986.

Economist Intelligence Unit. *Country Report: Kuwait* [London], No. 1, 1992.

———. *Country Report: Kuwait* [London], No. 1, 1993.

The Europa World Yearbook, 1991, 2. London: Europa, 1991.

Field, Michael. *The Merchants: The Big Business Families of Saudi Arabia and the Gulf States.* Woodstock, New York: Overlook Press, 1985.

Ibrahim, Hassan. *Kuwait: A Political Study.* Kuwait: Kuwait University, 1975.

Ismael, Jacqueline. *Kuwait: Social Change in Historical Perspective.* Syracuse: Syracuse University Press, 1982.

Khouja, M.W., and P.G. Sadler. *The Economy of Kuwait: Development and Role in International Finance.* London: Macmillan, 1979.

Kuwait. Ministry of Information. *Kuwait: Facts and Figures, 1992.* Kuwait: 1992.

———. Ministry of Information. *Kuwait on the March.* Kuwait: 1989.

———. Ministry of Planning. Central Statistical Office. *Annual Statistical Abstract, 1989.* Kuwait: 1990.

———. Ministry of Planning. Central Statistical Office. *Annual Statistical Abstract, 1990–91.* Kuwait: 1992.

Mallakh, Ragaei El, and Jacob Atta. *The Absorptive Capacity of Kuwait.* London: Croom Helm, 1986.

The Middle East and North Africa, 1993. London: Europa, 1992.

The Military Balance, 1993–1994. London: International Institute for Strategic Studies, 1993.

Organization of the Petroleum Exporting Countries. *Annual Statistical Bulletin, 1993.* Vienna: 1993.

Peterson, John E. *The Arab Gulf States: Steps Toward Political Participation.* New York: Praeger, 1988.

Rush, Alan. *Al-Sabah: Genealogy and History of Kuwait's Ruling Family, 1752–1986.* Atlantic Highlands, New Jersey: Ithaca Press, 1987.

Sabah, Suad al-. *Development Planning in an Oil Economy and the Role of the Woman: The Case of Kuwait.* London: Eastlords, 1983.

————. *Kuwait: Anatomy of a Crisis Economy.* London: Eastlords, 1984.

Sabah, Y.S.F. al-. *The Oil Economy of Kuwait.* London: Kegan Paul, 1980.

United Nations Development Programme. *Human Development Report, 1990.* New York: Oxford University Press, 1991.

United States. Central Intelligence Agency. *Chiefs of State and Cabinet Ministers of Foreign Governments.* Washington: 1992.

(Various issues of the following publications were also used in the preparation of this chapter: *Arab News* [Jiddah]; *Economist* [London]; *Financial Times* [London]; Foreign Broadcast Information Service, *Daily Report: Near East and South Asia; Middle East Economic Digest* [London]; *Middle East International* [London]; *Middle East Journal; Middle East Report; New York Times;* and *Wall Street Journal.*)

Chapter 3

America-Mideast Educational and Training Services. *Education in the Arab World,* 1. Washington: n.d.

Anthony, John Duke. *Arab States of the Lower Gulf: People, Politics, Petroleum.* Washington: Middle East Institute, 1975.

"Bahrain: Statistical Survey." In *The Middle East and North Africa, 1994.* London: Europa, 1993.

Chubin, Shahram, Robert Litwak, and Avi Plascov. *Security in the Gulf: Domestic Political Factors.* Aldershot, United Kingdom: Gower for International Institute of Strategic Studies, 1982.

Clarke, Angela. *Bahrain: Oil and Development, 1929–1989.* London: Immel, 1991.

Cottrell, Alvin (ed.). *The Persian Gulf States: A General Survey.* Baltimore: Johns Hopkins University Press, 1980.

Economist Intelligence Unit. *Country Profile: Bahrain, Qatar, 1991–92.* London: 1991.

Field, Michael. *The Merchants: The Big Business Families of Saudi Arabia and the Gulf States.* Woodstock, New York: Overlook Press, 1985.

Germany. Statistisches Bundesamt. *Länderbericht Bahrain, 1991.* Wiesbaden: Metzler/Poeschel for Federal Statistical Office, 1992.

Halliday, Fred. *Arabia Without Sultans.* Baltimore: Penguin, 1974.

Held, Colbert C. *Middle East Patterns: Places, Peoples, and Politics.* Boulder, Colorado: Westview Press, 1989.

Hopwood, Derek (ed.). *The Arabian Peninsula: Society and Politics.* Totowa, New Jersey: Rowman and Littlefield, 1972.

Khuri, Fuad I. *Tribe and State in Bahrain: The Transformation of Social and Political Authority in an Arab State.* Chicago: University of Chicago Press, 1980.

Larsen, Curtis E. *Life and Land Use on the Bahrain Islands.* Chicago: University of Chicago Press, 1983.

Lawson, Fred H. *Bahrain: The Modernization of Autocracy.* Boulder, Colorado: Westview Press, 1989.

The Middle East and North Africa, 1991. London: Europa, 1990.

Nakleh, Emile A. *Bahrain: Political Development in a Modernizing Society.* Lexington, Massachusetts: Lexington Books, 1976.

Niblock, Tim. *Social and Economic Development in the Arab Gulf.* London: Croom Helm, 1980.

Peterson, Erik. *The Gulf Cooperation Council: Search for Unity in a Dynamic Region.* Boulder, Colorado: Westview Press, 1988.

Rumaihi, Ghanim al-. *Bahrain: A Study on Social and Political Changes since the First World War.* Kuwait: Kuwait University Press, 1975.

Sadik, Muhammad, and William Snavely. *Bahrain, Qatar, and the United Arab Emirates: Colonial Past, Present Problems, and Future Prospects.* Lexington, Massachusetts: Lexington Books, 1972.

Sampson, Anthony. *The Seven Sisters: The Great Oil Companies and the World They Made.* New York: Viking Press, 1975.

World Almanac and Book of Facts, 1991. (Ed., Mark S. Hoffman.) New York: Pharos Books, 1990.

(Various issues of the following publications were also used in the preparation of this chapter: Foreign Broadcast Information Service, *Daily Report: Near East and South Asia; Middle East* [London]; *Middle East International* [London]; *Middle East Journal; Middle East Report; New York Times;* and *Washington Post.*)

Chapter 4

Abu Saud, Abeer. *Qatari Women, Past and Present.* London: Longman, 1984.

Amin, S.H. *Political and Strategic Issues in the Persian-Arabian Gulf.* Glasgow: Royston, 1984.

Anani, Ahmad, and Ken Whittingham. *The Early History of the Gulf Arabs.* London: Longman, 1986.

Anthony, John Duke. *Arab States of the Lower Gulf: People, Politics, Petroleum.* Washington: Middle East Institute, 1975.

Azhary, M.S. El (ed.). *The Impact of Oil Revenues on Arab Gulf Development.* London: Croom Helm, 1984.

Bulloch, John. *The Persian Gulf Unveiled.* New York: Congdon and West, 1984.

Burrows, Bernard. *Footnotes in the Sand: The Gulf in Transition, 1953–1958.* Salisbury, United Kingdom: Michael Russell, 1990.

Crystal, Jill. *Oil and Politics in the Gulf: Rulers and Merchants in Kuwait and Qatar.* New York: Cambridge University Press, 1990.

Economist Intelligence Unit. *Country Profile: Bahrain, Qatar, 1991–92.* London: 1991.

Federal Republic of Germany. Statistisches Bundesamt. *Länderbericht Katar, 1988.* Wiesbaden: Federal Statistical Office, 1988.

Izzard, Molly. *The Gulf: Arabia's Western Approaches.* London: John Murray, 1979.

Kubursi, Atif A. *Oil, Industrialization, and Development in the Arab Gulf States.* London: Croom Helm, 1984.

Lawless, R.I. (ed.). *The Gulf in the Early 20th Century: Foreign Institutions and Local Responses.* Durham, United Kingdom: University of Durham Centre for Middle Eastern and Islamic Studies, 1986.

Mallakh, Ragaei El. *Qatar: Energy and Development.* London: Croom Helm, 1985.

Middle East Contemporary Survey, 1982–83. (Eds., Colin Legum, Haim Shaked, and Daniel Dishon.) New York: Holmes and Meier for Shiloah Center for Middle Eastern and African Studies, Tel Aviv University, 1985.

Middle East Contemporary Survey, 1983–84. (Eds., Haim Shaked and Daniel Dishon.) Tel Aviv: Dayan Center for Middle Eastern and African Studies, Tel Aviv University, 1986.

Middle East Contemporary Survey, 1984–85. (Eds., Itamar Rabinovich and Haim Shaked.) Tel Aviv: Dayan Center for Middle Eastern and African Studies, Tel Aviv University, 1987.

Middle East Contemporary Survey, 1986. (Eds., Itamar Rabinovich and Haim Shaked.) Boulder, Colorado: Westview Press for Dayan Center for Middle Eastern and African Studies, Tel Aviv University, 1988.

Middle East Contemporary Survey, 1987. (Eds., Itamar Rabinovich and Haim Shaked.) Boulder, Colorado: Westview Press for Dayan Center for Middle Eastern and African Studies, Tel Aviv University, 1989.

Middle East Contemporary Survey, 1988. (Eds., Ami Ayalon and Haim Shaked.) Boulder, Colorado: Westview Press for Dayan Center for Middle Eastern and African Studies, Tel Aviv University, 1990.

Misnad, Sheikha al-. *The Development of Modern Education in the Gulf.* London: Ithaca Press, 1985.

Nafi, Zuhair Ahmed. *Economic and Social Development in Qatar.* London: Francis Pinter, 1983.

Netton, Ian Richard (ed.). *Arabia and the Gulf: From Traditional Society to Modern States.* London: Croom Helm, 1986.

Niblock, Tim (ed.). *Social and Economic Development in the Arab Gulf.* London: Croom Helm, 1980.

Othman, Naser al-. *With Their Bare Hands: The Story of the Oil Industry in Qatar.* London: Longman, 1984.

Potts, Daniel T. *The Arabian Gulf in Antiquity.* Oxford: Clarendon Press, 1990.

Pridham, B.R. (ed.). *The Arab Gulf and the West.* New York: St. Martin's Press, 1985.

"Qatar." Page 685 in *Britannica Book of the Year, 1991.* Chicago: Encyclopaedia Britannica, 1991.

"Qatar." Pages 751–62 in *The Middle East and North Africa, 1993.* London: Europa, 1992.

Ramazani, R.K. *The Gulf Cooperation Council: Politics, Problems, and Prospects.* New York: Praeger, 1986.

————. *The Gulf Cooperation Council: Record and Analysis.* Charlottesville: University Press of Virginia, 1988.

Robins, Philip. *The Future of the Gulf: Politics and Oil in the 1990s.* Brookfield, Vermont: Dartmouth University Press, 1989.

Twinam, Joseph Wright. "Reflections on Gulf Cooperation, with Focus on Bahrain, Qatar, and Oman." Pages 21–45 in John A. Sandwick (ed.), *The Gulf Cooperation Council: Moderation and Stability in an Interdependent World.* Boulder, Colorado: Westview Press, 1987.

United Nations Development Programme. *Human Development Report, 1990.* New York: Oxford University Press, 1991.

United States. Central Intelligence Agency. *Chiefs of State and Cabinet Members of Foreign Governments.* Washington: 1992.

Unwin, P.T.H. (comp.). *Qatar,* 36. (World Bibliographical Series.) Oxford: Clio Press, 1982.

Zahlan, Rosemarie Said. *The Creation of Qatar.* London: Croom Helm, 1979.

(Various issues of the following publications were also used in the preparation of this chapter: Foreign Broadcast Information Service, *Daily Report: Near East and South Asia; Middle East Economic Digest* [London]; *Middle East International* [London]; *New York Times;* and *Washington Post.*)

Chapter 5

Abdullah, Muhammad Morsy. *The United Arab Emirates: A Modern History.* London: Croom Helm, 1978.

Alkim, Hassan Hamdan al-. *The Foreign Policy of the United Arab Emirates.* London: Saqi, 1989.

Anthony, John Duke. *Arab States of the Lower Gulf: People, Politics, Petroleum.* Washington: Middle East Institute, 1975.

Chubin, Shahram, Robert Litwak, and Avi Plascov. *Security in the Gulf: Domestic Political Factors.* Aldershot, United Kingdom: Gower for International Institute of Strategic Studies, 1982.

Cottrell, Alvin (ed.). *The Persian Gulf States: A General Survey.* Baltimore: Johns Hopkins University, 1980.

Economist Intelligence Unit. *Arabian Peninsula: Economic Structures and Analysis.* London: 1988.

————. *Country Profile: United Arab Emirates, 1991–92.* London: 1991.

Fenelon, K.G. *The United Arab Emirates: An Economic and Social Survey.* London: Longman, 1976.

Field, Michael. *The Merchants: The Big Business Families of Saudi Arabia and the Gulf States.* Woodstock, New York: Overlook Press, 1985.

Gabriel, Erhard (ed.). *The Dubai Handbook.* Institute for Applied Economic Geography, 1987.

Germany. Statistisches Bundesamt. *Länderbericht Vereinigte Arabische Emiraten, 1990.* Wiesbaden: Metzler/Poeschel for Federal Statistical Office, 1990.

Halliday, Fred. *Arabia Without Sultans.* Baltimore: Penguin, 1974.

Hawley, Donald. *The Trucial States.* London: Allen and Unwin, 1970.

Heard-Bey, Frauke. *From Trucial States to United Arab Emirates.* London: Croom Helm, 1982.

Held, Colbert C. *Middle East Patterns: Places, Peoples, and Politics.* Boulder, Colorado: Westview Press, 1989.

International Monetary Fund. *Balance of Payments Statistics Yearbook, 1992.* Washington: 1993.

_____. *Direction of Trade Statistics, 1992 Annual.* Washington: 1992.

Khalifa, Ali Mohammad. *The United Arab Emirates: Unity in Fragmentation.* Boulder, Colorado: Westview Press, 1979.

Khoury, Enver. *The United Arab Emirates: Its Political System and Politics.* Hyattsville, Maryland: Institute of Middle Eastern and North African Affairs, 1980.

Maddison, Katya. "United Arab Emirates." Pages 160–67 in *The Middle East Review, 1992.* Saffron Walden, United Kingdom: World of Information, 1992.

Mallakh, Ragaei El-. *The Economic Development of the United Arab Emirates.* London: Croom Helm, 1981.

Organization of the Petroleum Exporting Countries. *Annual Statistical Bulletin, 1991.* Vienna: 1991.

Peck, Malcolm C. *The United Arab Emirates: A Venture in Unity.* Boulder, Colorado: Westview Press, 1986.

Peterson, Erik. *The Gulf Cooperation Council: Search for Unity in a Dynamic Region.* Boulder, Colorado: Westview Press, 1988.

Peterson, John E. *The Arab Gulf States: Steps Toward Political Participation.* New York: Praeger, 1988.

427

Qasimi, Muhammad al-. *The Myth of Arab Piracy in the Gulf.* London: Croom Helm, 1986.

Taryam, A.O. *The Establishment of the United Arab Emirates, 1950– 85.* London: Croom Helm, 1987.

"United Arab Emirates." Page 722 in *Britannica Book of the Year, 1991.* Chicago: Encyclopaedia Britannica, 1991.

"United Arab Emirates." Pages 587–88 in *The International Year Book and Statesmen's Who's Who, 1992.* East Grinstead, United Kingdom: Reed Information Services, 1991.

"United Arab Emirates." Pages 2017–31 in George Thomas Kurian (ed.), *Encyclopedia of the Third World.* (4th ed.) New York: Facts on File, 1992.

"The United Arab Emirates." Pages 920–46 in *The Middle East and North Africa, 1993.* London: Europa, 1992.

Vine, Peter, and Paula Casey. *United Arab Emirates: Heritage and Modern Development.* London: Immel, 1992.

Yearbook of the United Nations, 1988–89. New York: United Nations, Department of Public Information, 1989.

Zahlan, Rosemarie Said. *The Origins of the United Arab Emirates.* New York: St. Martin's Press, 1978.

(Various issues of the following publications were also used in the preparation of this chapter: Foreign Broadcast Information Service, *Daily Report: Near East and South Asia*; *Middle East Economic Digest* [London]; *Middle East International* [London]; *New York Times*; and *Washington Post.*)

Chapter 6

Allen, Calvin H. *Oman: The Modernization of the Sultanate.* Boulder, Colorado: Westview Press, 1987.

Azzam, Henry T. *The Gulf Economies in Transition.* London: Macmillan, 1988.

Central Bank of Oman. *Annual Report, 1991.* Muscat: 1992.

———. *Quarterly Report, March 1992.* Muscat: 1992.

Commercial Fisheries in Oman (Final Report). Washington: Arthur Young, 1988.

Economist Intelligence Unit. *Country Profile: Oman, Yemen, 1991–92.* London: 1991.

———. *Country Profile: Oman, Yemen, 1992–93.* London: 1992.

Eickelman, Christine. *Women and Community in Oman.* New York: New York University Press, 1984.

Eickelman, Dale F. "Kings and People: Oman's State Consultative Council," *Middle East Journal*, 38, Winter 1984, 51–71.

Le gaz naturel dans le monde (1988–1991 editions). Paris: Centre
international d'information sur le gaz naturel et tous hydro-
carbures gazeux, 1988–91.

Germany. Statistisches Bundesamt. *Länderbericht Oman, 1991*.
Wiesbaden: Metzler/Poeschel for Federal Statistical Office,
1991.

Graz, Liesl. *The Omanis: Sentinels of the Gulf.* London: Longman,
1982.

International Monetary Fund. *Balance of Payments Statistics Yearbook, 1992*. Washington: 1993.

———. *Direction of Trade Statistics, 1992 Annual.* Washington:
1993.

Kechichian, Joseph A. "Oman and the World," *American-Arab
Affairs*, No. 35, Winter 1990–91, 135–50.

Landen, R.G. *Oman since 1856.* Princeton: Princeton University
Press, 1967.

"Legitimacy and Political Change in Yemen and Oman," *Orbis*,
27, Winter 1984, 971–98.

Looney, Robert E. "Reducing Dependence Through Investment in Human Capital: An Assessment of Oman's Development Strategy," *Socio-Economic Planning Sciences*, 24, No. 1,
1990, 65–75.

McNaugher, Thomas L. "Arms and Allies on the Arabian Peninsula," *Orbis*, 28, Fall 1984, 489–526.

Oman. Ministry of Development. National Statistical Department. *Statistical Yearbook, 1990.* Muscat: 1991.

———. Ministry of Finance and Economy. *Annual Budget.* (Fiscal years 1986 through 1993.) Muscat: 1985–92.

*Oman Fisheries Development and Management Project: First Annual
Work Plan, November 1991–April 1993*, Washington: Chemon-
ics, 1991.

Peterson, John E. "American Policy in the Gulf and the Sultanate of Oman," *American-Arab Affairs*, 8, Spring 1984, 117–30.

———. *Oman in the Twentieth Century: Political Foundations of an
Emerging State.* London: Croom Helm, 1978.

Phillips, Wendell. *Oman: A History.* London: Longman, 1967.

Sandwick, John A. (ed.). *The Gulf Cooperation Council.* Boulder,
Colorado: Westview Press, 1987.

Sindelar, H. Richard, III, and John E. Peterson (eds.). *Crosscurrents in the Gulf: Arab Regional and Global Interests.* London: Routledge, 1988.

Skeet, Ian. *Oman Before 1970: The End of an Era.* London: Faber and Faber, 1985.

Social and Institutional Aspects of Oman: Review of Literature. N. pl.: Institute for Development Anthropology, 1982.

Socio-economic Aspects of the Fisheries of Oman. Kingston: International Center for Marine Resource Development, University of Rhode Island, June 1984.

Townsend, John. *Oman: The Making of a Modern State.* London: Croom Helm, 1977.

United Nations. Department of International Economic and Social Affairs. *World Population Policies: Oman to Zimbabwe.* New York: 1990.

Wikan, Unni. *Behind the Veil in Arabia: Women in Oman.* Baltimore: Johns Hopkins University Press, 1982.

Wilkinson, John C. *The Imamate Tradition of Oman.* Cambridge: Cambridge University Press, 1987.

Zimmerman, Wolfgang. "Transformation of Rural Employment Structures: The Example of the Sultanate of Oman, South-east Arabia," *Applied Geography and Development,* 33, 1989, 7–26.

(Various issues of the following publications were also used in the preparation of this chapter: *Financial Times* [London]; Foreign Broadcast Information Service, *Daily Report: Near East and South Asia; Middle East* [London]; *Middle East Economic Digest* [London]; *Middle East Economic Survey* [Nicosia, Cyprus]; *Oil and Gas Journal; Petroleum Economist* [London]; and *Petroleum Intelligence Weekly.*)

Chapter 7

Amnesty International. *The 1993 Report on Human Rights Around the World.* Alameda, California: Hunter House, 1993.

Bishku, Michael B. "Iraq's Claim to Kuwait: A Historic Overview," *American-Arab Affairs,* 37, Summer 1991, 77–88.

Blackwell, James. *Thunder in the Desert: The Strategy and Tactics of the Persian Gulf War.* New York: Bantam, 1991.

Braun, Ursula. "The Gulf Cooperation Council's Security Role." Pages 252–67 in B.R. Pridham (ed.), *The Arab Gulf and the Arab World*. London: Croom Helm, 1988.

Capps, Alan P. "Gullivers and Lilliputians in the Mideast," *Defense and Diplomacy*, 9, Nos. 9–10, August–September 1991, 47–50.

Cordesman, Anthony H. *The Gulf and the West: Strategic Relations and Military Realities*. Boulder, Colorado: Westview Press, 1988.

Defense and Foreign Affairs Handbook, 1990–91. (Ed., Gerald R. Copley.) Alexandria, Virginia: International Media, 1990.

Dickey, Christopher. *Expats: Travels in Arabia, from Tripoli to Tehran*. New York: Atlantic Monthly, 1990.

Diller, Daniel C. (ed.). *The Middle East*. (7th ed.) Washington: Congressional Quarterly, 1991.

DMS Market Intelligence Reports: Foreign Military Markets: Middle East and Africa. Alexandria, Virginia: Jane's Information Group, 1989.

Economist Intelligence Unit. *Country Profile: Bahrain, Qatar, 1991–92*. London: 1991.

———. *Country Profile: Kuwait, 1991–92*. London: 1991.

———. *Country Profile: Oman, Yemen, 1991–92*. London: 1991.

———. *Country Profile: United Arab Emirates, 1991–92*. London: 1991.

Friedman, Norman. *Desert Victory: The War for Kuwait*. Annapolis: Naval Institute Press, 1991.

Fulghum, David A. "Allied Air Power, Forward Controllers Back Arabs to Make Their Drive Succeed," *Aviation Week and Space Technology*, 134, No. 16, April 22, 1991, 71–73.

Gazir, Schlomo, and Zeev Eytan. *The Middle East Military Balance, 1988–1989*. Boulder, Colorado: Westview Press, 1989.

Graz, Liesl. *The Turbulent Gulf*. New York: St. Martin's Press, 1990.

Hameed, Mazher A. *Saudi Arabia: The West and the Security of the Gulf*. London: Croom Helm, 1986.

Jane's Fighting Ships, 1992–93. (Ed., Richard Sharpe.) Alexandria, Virginia: Jane's Information Group, 1992.

Kechichian, Joseph A. "Oman and the World," *American-Arab Affairs*, No. 35, Winter 1990–91, 135–50.

Keegan, John (ed.). *World Armies*. Detroit: Gale Research, 1983.

Kuwait. Ministry of Information. *Kuwait: Facts and Figures, 1992.* Kuwait: 1992.

McNaugher, Thomas L. *Arms and Oil: Military Strategy and the Persian Gulf.* Washington: Brookings Institution, 1985.

Meacham, Jim. "A New Middle East Security Equation," *Defense and Diplomacy*, 9, Nos. 11–12, November 1991, 43–46.

The Middle East. (7th ed.) Washington: Congressional Quarterly, 1991.

The Military Balance, 1992–1993. London: International Institute for Strategic Studies, 1992.

Oman. Ministry of Information. *Oman, 1989.* Muscat: 1989.

Peterson, Erik R. *The Gulf Cooperation Council: Search for Unity in a Dynamic Region.* Boulder, Colorado: Westview Press, 1988.

Peterson, John E. *Defending Arabia.* New York: St. Martin's Press, 1986.

Peterson, John E. (ed.). *Saudi Arabia and the Gulf States: Workshop Papers.* Washington: Defense Academic Research Support Program and Middle East Institute, 1988.

Ramazani, R.K. *The Gulf Cooperation Council: Record and Analysis.* Charlottesville: University Press of Virginia, 1988.

Sciolino, Elaine. *The Outlaw State: Saddam Hussein's Quest for Power and the Gulf Crisis.* New York: Wiley, 1991.

Tétreault, Mary Ann. "Kuwait: The Morning After," *Current History*, 91, No. 561, January 1992, 6–10.

Tusa, Francis. "Defense No Longer 'Business as Usual' in UAE," *Armed Forces Journal International*, 128, No. 6, January 1991, 18–19.

United States. Arms Control and Disarmament Agency. *World Military Expenditures and Arms Transfers, 1990.* Washington: GPO, 1991.

————. Department of Defense. *Congressional Presentation for Security Assistance Programs, FY 1992.* Washington: 1991.

————. Department of State. *Country Reports on Human Rights Practices for 1991.* (Report submitted to United States Congress, 102d, 2d Session, House of Representatives, Committee on Foreign Affairs, and Senate, Committee on Foreign Relations.) Washington: GPO, 1992.

————. Department of State. *Patterns of Global Terrorism, 1990.* Washington: 1991.

Zahlan, Rosemarie Said. *The Making of the Modern Gulf States.*
London: Unwin Hyman, 1989.

(Various issues of the following publications were also used
in the preparation of this chapter: *Congressional Quarterly; Econo-
mist* [London]; *Facts on File;* Foreign Broadcast Information
Service, *Daily Report: Near East, South Asia;* Joint Publications
Research Service, *Near East/South Asia Report; Keesing's Record of
World Events* [London]; *Middle East International* [London];
Middle East Journal; New York Times; United States Department
of State, *Dispatch;* and *Washington Post.*)

Glossary

Al—Uppercased, it connotes family of, or belonging to, as in Al Sabah, Al Khalifa, Al Thani, Al Nuhayyan, Al Maktum, Al Qasimi, and Al Said. Lowercased, it represents the definite article *the*, as in Ras al Khaymah.

amir—Literally, commander. In many of the Arab states of the Persian Gulf, amir often means ruler or prince.

amirate—Political entity under the rule of an amir. Analogous to a shaykhdom and, if an independent state, to a kingdom.

Bahraini dinar (BD)—Consists of 1,000 fils. Bahrain has maintained a fixed exchange rate according to which in 1993 US$1 equaled BD0.376.

barrels per day (bpd)—Production of crude oil and petroleum products is frequently measured in barrels per day. A barrel is a volume measure of forty-two United States gallons. Conversion of barrels to tons depends on the density of the specific product. About 7.3 barrels of average crude oil weigh one ton. Heavy crude is about seven barrels per ton. Light products, such as gasoline and kerosene, average close to eight barrels per ton.

downstream—The oil industry views the production, processing, transportation, and sale of petroleum products as a flow process starting at the wellhead. Downstream includes any stage between the point of reference and the sale of products to the consumer. Upstream (*q.v.*) is the converse.

gross domestic product (GDP)—A value measure of the flow of domestic goods and services produced by an economy over a period of time, such as one year. Only output values of goods for final consumption and investment are included because the values of primary and intermediate production are assumed to be included in final prices. GDP is sometimes aggregated and shown at market prices, meaning that indirect taxes and subsidies are included; when these have been eliminated, the result is GDP at factor cost. The word *gross* indicates that deductions for depreciation of physical assets have not been made. *See also*

435

gross national product (GNP).

gross national product (GNP)—The gross domestic product (*q.v.*) plus the net income or loss stemming from transactions with foreign countries. GNP is the broadest measurement of the output of goods and services by an economy. It can be calculated at market prices, which include indirect taxes and subsidies. Because indirect taxes and subsidies are only transfer payments, GNP is often calculated at factor cost by removing indirect taxes and subsidies.

hadith—Tradition based on the precedent of Muhammad's words and deeds that serves as one of the sources of Islamic law (sharia).

hijra—Literally, to migrate, to sever relations, to leave one's tribe. Throughout the Muslim world, hijra refers to the migration of the Prophet Muhammad and his followers to Medina. In this sense, the word has come into European languages as hegira. The year of Muhammad's hijra constitutes the beginning of the Islamic calendar.

ibn—Literally, son of; *bint* means daughter of; and *bani* is literally sons of, hence clan or tribe.

imam—Word used in several senses. In general use, it means the leader of congregational prayers; as such it implies no ordination or special spiritual powers beyond sufficient education to carry out this function. It is also used figuratively by many Sunni (*q.v.*) Muslims to mean the leader of the Islamic community. Among Shia (*q.v.*) the word takes on many complex meanings; in general, however, and particularly when uppercased, it indicates that particular descendant of the Party of Ali who is believed to be God's designated repository of the spiritual authority inherent in that line. The identity of this individual and the means of ascertaining his identity have been major issues causing divisions among Shia. Among the Ibadis of Oman, the imam was elected to office and was regarded by all as the spiritual leader of the community and by some as the temporal ruler as well. Claims of various Omani imams to secular power led to open rebellions as late as the 1950s.

import-substitution industrialization—An economic development strategy that emphasizes the growth of domestic industries, often by import protection using tariff and non-tariff measures. Proponents favor the export of industrial goods over primary products.

International Monetary Fund (IMF)—Established along with the World Bank (*q.v.*) in 1945, the IMF is a specialized agency affiliated with the United Nations and is responsible for stabilizing international exchange rates and payments. The main business of the IMF is the provision of loans to its members (including industrialized and developing countries) when they experience balance of payments difficulties. These loans frequently carry conditions that require substantial internal economic adjustments by the recipients, most of which are developing countries.

jihad—The struggle to establish the law of God on earth, often interpreted to mean holy war.

Kuwaiti dinar (KD)—The national currency, consisting of 1,000 fils. The exchange rate of the Kuwaiti dinar to the United States dollar has fluctuated somewhat; in May 1993 the exchange rate was US$1 = KD0.30.

majlis—Tribal council; in some countries the legislative assembly. Also refers to an audience with an amir (*q.v.*) or shaykh (*q.v.*) open to all citizens.

Omani rial (RO)—Monetary unit of Oman, divided into 1,000 baizas. Oman has maintained a fixed exchange rate according to which in 1993 US$1 equaled RO0.3845.

Qatari riyal (QR)—The national currency consisting of 100 dirhams. Qatar has maintained a fixed exchanged rate according to which in 1993 US$1 equaled QR3.64.

shaykh—Leader or chief. Applied either to a political leader of a tribe or town or to a learned religious leader. Also used as an honorific.

Shia (from Shiat Ali, or Party of Ali)—A member of the smaller of the two great divisions of Islam. The Shia supported the claims of Ali and his line to presumptive right to the caliphate and leadership of the world Muslim community, and on this issue they divided from the Sunnis (*q.v.*) in the major schism within Islam. Later schisms have produced further divisions among the Shia over the identity and number of imams (*q.v.*). Most Shia revere twelve Imams, the last of whom is believed to be in hiding. *See also* Twelve Imam Shia.

special drawing rights (SDR)—An International Monetary Fund (IMF—*q.v.*) unit of account made up of a basket of major international currencies consisting of the United States dollar, the German deutsche mark, the Japanese yen, the British pound sterling, and the French franc.

Sunni—The larger of the two great divisions of Islam. The Sunnis, who rejected the claims of Ali's line, believe that they are the true followers of the sunna, the guide to proper behavior composed of the Quran and the hadith (*q.v.*).

Twelve Imam Shia—The majority group among Shia (*q.v.*), who believe that the Imamate began with Ali, the fourth caliph, or successor ruler, in Islam. The line continued through his sons until the Twelfth Imam, who is believed to have ascended to a supernatural state to return to earth on Judgment Day.

UAE dirham (Dh)—National currency of the United Arab Emirates (UAE), consisting of 100 fils. The UAE has maintained a fixed exchange rate according to which in 1993 US$1 equaled Dh3.671.

ulama—Collective term for Muslim religious scholars.

upstream—The converse of downstream (*q.v.*), it includes the exploration and drilling of wells in the petroleum production process.

Wahhabi—Name used outside Saudi Arabia to designate adherents to Wahhabism (*q.v.*).

Wahhabism—Name used outside Saudi Arabia to designate official interpretation of Islam in Saudi Arabia. The faith is a puritanical concept of unitarianism (the oneness of God) that was preached by Muhammad ibn Abd al Wahhab, whence his Muslim opponents derived the name. The royal family of Qatar and most indigenous Qataris are Wahhabis (*q.v.*).

World Bank—Informal name used to designate a group of four affiliated international institutions that provide advice and assistance on long-term finance and policy issues to developing countries: the International Bank for Reconstruction and Development (IBRD), the International Development Association (IDA), the International Finance Corporation (IFC), and the Multilateral Investment Guarantee Agency (MIGA). The IBRD, established in 1945, has as its primary purpose the provision of loans at market-related rates of interest to developing countries at more advanced stages of development. The IDA, a legally separate loan fund but administered by the staff of the IBRD, was set up in 1960 to furnish credits to the poorest developing countries on much easier terms than those of conventional IBRD loans. The IFC, founded in 1956, supplements the activities of the IBRD through loans and assistance specifically designed to encourage the growth of productive private enterprises in the less developed countries. The president and certain officers of the IBRD hold the same positions in the IFC. The MIGA, which began operating in 1988, insures private foreign investment in developing countries against various noncommercial risks. The four institutions are owned by the governments of the countries that subscribe their capital. To participate in the World Bank group, member states must first belong to the International Monetary Fund (IMF—*q.v.*).

Index

Contributors

Jill Crystal, Assistant Professor of Political Science at the University of Michigan, has published several works on Kuwait and the Persian Gulf.

Eric Hooglund currently serves as Editor of the *Middle East Journal*; he has taught courses on the Middle East at several universities.

Helen Chapin Metz is Supervisor, Middle East/Africa/Latin America Unit, Federal Research Division, Library of Congress.

Fareed Mohamedi is Senior Economist, Petroleum Finance Company, and author of articles on the Middle East and international oil affairs.

William Smyth is an independent author who writes on the Middle East; he served as Visiting Assistant Professor at Emory University from 1989 through 1991.

Jean R. Tartter is a retired Foreign Service Officer who has written extensively on the Middle East and Africa for the Country Studies series.

Anthony Toth, who has lived in Qatar and the United Arab Emirates, has written widely on the Middle East for a number of publications.

Published Country Studies

(Area Handbook Series)

550–65	Afghanistan		550–28	Ethiopia
550–98	Albania		550–167	Finland
550–44	Algeria		550–155	Germany, East
550–59	Angola		550–173	Germany, Fed. Rep. of
550–73	Argentina		550–153	Ghana
550–169	Australia		550–87	Greece
550–176	Austria		550–78	Guatemala
550–175	Bangladesh		550–174	Guinea
550–170	Belgium		550–82	Guyana and Belize
550–66	Bolivia		550–151	Honduras
550–20	Brazil		550–165	Hungary
550–168	Bulgaria		550–21	India
550–61	Burma		550–154	Indian Ocean
550–50	Cambodia		550–39	Indonesia
550–166	Cameroon		550–68	Iran
550–159	Chad		550–31	Iraq
550–77	Chile		550–25	Israel
550–60	China		550–182	Italy
550–26	Colombia		550–30	Japan
550–33	Commonwealth Caribbean, Islands of the		550–34	Jordan
550–91	Congo		550–56	Kenya
550–90	Costa Rica		550–81	Korea, North
550–69	Côte d'Ivoire (Ivory Coast)		550–41	Korea, South
550–152	Cuba		550–58	Laos
550–22	Cyprus		550–24	Lebanon
550–158	Czechoslovakia		550–38	Liberia
550–36	Dominican Republic and Haiti		550–85	Libya
550–52	Ecuador		550–172	Malawi
550–43	Egypt		550–45	Malaysia
550–150	El Salvador		550–161	Mauritania

550–79	Mexico	550–179	Spain
550–76	Mongolia	550–96	Sri Lanka
550–49	Morocco	550–27	Sudan
550–64	Mozambique	550–47	Syria
550–35	Nepal and Bhutan	550–62	Tanzania
550–88	Nicaragua	550–53	Thailand
550–157	Nigeria	550–89	Tunisia
550–94	Oceania	550–80	Turkey
550–48	Pakistan	550–74	Uganda
550–46	Panama	550–97	Uruguay
550–156	Paraguay	550–71	Venezuela
550–185	Persian Gulf States	550–32	Vietnam
550–42	Peru	550–183	Yemens, The
550–72	Philippines	550–99	Yugoslavia
550–162	Poland	550–67	Zaire
550–181	Portugal	550–75	Zambia
550–160	Romania	550–171	Zimbabwe
550–37	Rwanda and Burundi		
550–51	Saudi Arabia		
550–70	Senegal		
550–180	Sierra Leone		
550–184	Singapore		
550–86	Somalia		
550–93	South Africa		
550–95	Soviet Union